Mania for Freedom

Mania for Freedom
American Literatures of Enthusiasm from the Revolution to the Civil War

John Mac Kilgore

The University of North Carolina Press CHAPEL HILL

This book was published with the assistance of the College of Arts and Sciences at Florida State University.

© 2016 The University of North Carolina Press
All rights reserved
Manufactured in the United States of America
Set in Espinosa Nova by Westchester Publishing Services

The University of North Carolina Press has been a member of the
Green Press Initiative since 2003.

Cover illustration: *"Raising the Liberty Pole," 1776* (ca. 1875); painted by F. A. Chapman; engraved by John C. McRae; courtesy of the Library of Congress, LC-DIG-pga-02159.

Library of Congress Cataloging-in-Publication Data
Names: Kilgore, John Mac, author.
Title: Mania for freedom : American literatures of enthusiasm from the
   Revolution to the Civil War / John Mac Kilgore.
Description: Chapel Hill : University of North Carolina Press, [2016] |
   Includes bibliographical references and index.
Identifiers: LCCN 2016008741| ISBN 9781469629711 (cloth : alk. paper) |
   ISBN 9781469629728 (pbk : alk. paper) | ISBN 9781469629735 (ebook)
Subjects: LCSH: Enthusiasm in literature. | Protest literature, American—
   History and criticism. | American literature—Revolutionary period,
   1775–1783—History and criticism. | American literature—1783–1850—
   History and criticism. | American literature—19th century—
   History and criticism.
Classification: LCC PS195.E57 K55 2016 | DDC 810.9/003—dc23
   LC record available at https://lccn.loc.gov/2016008741

Chapter 2 was previously published as "The Rise of Dissent: Literatures of Enthusiasm and the American Revolution," *Early American Literature* 48 (2013), 367–98. Chapter 5 was previously published as "The Free State of Whitman," *ESQ: A Journal of the American Renaissance* 58 (© 2015 by the Board of Regents of Washington State University), 529–64. Both are reprinted in revised form with permission.

There is no coming at a thorow-pac'd enthusiast. He is proof against every method of dealing with him.
—CHARLES CHAUNCY

Awakenings and Revivals are not peculiar to Religion. Philosophy and Policy at times are capable of taking the Infection.
—JOHN ADAMS

The best we get from history is that it rouses our enthusiasm.
—GOETHE

Contents

Acknowledgments xi

Introduction 1
Enthusiasm, Event, Literature

CHAPTER ONE
An Answer to the Question 31
"What Is Enthusiasm?"

CHAPTER TWO
Rites of Dissent 65
Literatures of Enthusiasm and the American Revolution

CHAPTER THREE
Shaking Hands with the Prophet 98
The War of 1812 and Native American Enthusiasms

CHAPTER FOUR
The Revival of Revolt 130
Conjure, Slave Insurrection, and the Novel of Enthusiasm

CHAPTER FIVE
The Free State of Whitman 165
John Brown, the Civil War, and the Dis-memberment of Enthusiasm in the 1860 Leaves of Grass

Epilogue 199
The Tramp and Strike Question: Terminal Enthusiasms

Notes 213
Bibliography 243
Index 269

Figures

1. Object 17 of William Blake's *America a Prophecy* 10
2. *Enthusiasm display'd: or, the Moor Fields congregation* 89
3. Adalbert John Volck's "Worship of the North" 176

Acknowledgments

First and foremost, I want to thank the Department of English at UC-Davis and the Council on Research and Creativity at Florida State University for the fellowship and grant funding that supported this project.

I am infinitely grateful to David Simpson, Elizabeth Freeman, and Hsuan Hsu for their brilliant feedback and bracing criticism, to say nothing of their spirited encouragement, in the early drafting and development of this manuscript. You are each the Apollo to this study's Dionysus. My thanks to Michael Ziser, Nathan Brown, and Kari Lokke for the energizing conversations which convinced me that enthusiasm was a worthwhile topic to pursue. As this study moved toward publication, many other kind friends and colleagues offered helpful advice and assistance on this or that issue, including Barry Faulk, Robin Goodman, Christian Weber, and Anick Boyd. One individual shared and affirmed my commitment to this book's ideas to such a degree that I can no longer separate her from them: Andrea Actis.

I wish to profusely thank Mark Simpson-Vos at the University of North Carolina Press for first taking interest in this project, my incredible editor at the Press, Lucas Church, for smoothly guiding my manuscript to publication, and my anonymous readers through the Press for their patient, careful reading of this book and invaluable suggestions for revision.

Shorter, less mature versions of chapter 2 and chapter 5 first appeared in *Early American Literature* 48.2 (2013) and *ESQ: A Journal of the American Renaissance* 58.4 (2012), respectively, and are reprinted here with permission. One paragraph in chapter 1 (where I introduce dictionary definitions of enthusiasm) was previously published in *PMLA* 130.5 (2015). I owe a great debt to the editors (and affiliated readers) of those journals for helping me to sharpen my ideas on enthusiasm. On that point, Sandra Gustafson deserves special thanks.

Finally, much love to my parents, Johnny and Pat; my sister, Lee Beth; and my comrade, John Harkey: your moral support has kept me afloat all these years.

Mania for Freedom

Introduction
Enthusiasm, Event, Literature

> Nothing but insubordination, eleutheromania, confused unlimited opposition in their heads.
> —THOMAS CARLYLE, 1837

I

Mania for Freedom is a study of "political enthusiasm" in American literature and culture from the Revolution to the Civil War. That "enthusiasm" now generically denotes strong excitement, passionate engagement, or all-absorbing interest obscures its long historical usage, from the seventeenth to the mid-nineteenth century, as a term linked variously to the revolutionary or utopian passions, divine or artistic inspiration, and a wildly ecstatic or delusional state of mind. I tell a story, though, about the formation and development of the early U.S. national period that highlights cultures of enthusiasm and their close association with a politics of emancipation. At this historical moment, the concept of enthusiasm was often deployed to describe—positively or negatively—a strong democratic fervor, what Thomas Carlyle called *eleutheromania* (a "mad zeal" or "mania" "for freedom");[1] and it was most often attached to persons—commoners, slaves, Native Americans, women, abolitionists—who activated dissent against institutional tyranny and forged transnational, counternational, or antinationalistic political affiliations in the process. In privileging such affiliations, I depict the early U.S. nation-state as an embattled terrain that defined itself through and against the experimental, often illegal, actions for political justice enacted by enthusiasts. Accordingly, I argue that, opposite a political and literary culture of sentimental nationalism, a distinct but overlooked tradition and category of American literature (literatures of enthusiasm) flourished from the American Revolution through the Civil War era. As a discursive form of enthusiastic publicity, literatures of enthusiasm are those texts that transform writing into a species or inciter of democratic revival and revolt.

Despite the fact that the politics of enthusiasm played a key role in the evolution of the United States, as an academic subject it has by and large remained a curiosity and minor topic in studies of Protestant religious culture and British literary history up through the eighteenth century. Only a small body of critical literature exists on the topic,[2] but this makes some sense given that enthusiasm was so often a shifting, slippery, capacious label, not a fixed object. It has a confusing genealogy to boot. It would probably be fairer to say, then, that enthusiasm has not been considered a substantial and sticky enough phenomenon to merit its own sustained investigation as an ideological tradition analogous to, say, neoclassicism or sentimentalism. Even the existing literature on enthusiasm tends to be mired in theologically or philosophically informed responses *to* the "enthusiast" as a smear word or bogeyman, and, thus, it has underappreciated enthusiasm's most significant historical referent—popular revolt. Moreover, studies of enthusiasm have most often focused on its European history and etymology even though, as this study will show, the term remained important in the United States at least through the Civil War when Abraham Lincoln could still call John Brown an "enthusiast" who "broods over the oppression of a people till he fancies himself commissioned by Heaven to liberate them,"[3] and Walt Whitman could ejaculate without irony, "Enthusiasts! Antecedents!"[4]

I wish to unravel the mystery behind the intellectual and historical elision of U.S. political enthusiasm. Toward that end, the legacy of both the English Civil War and the French Revolution as exemplary specimens of political enthusiasm ought to clue us in to what sort of cultural associations were tethered to the term, what kind of debates define its terrain, and why many critics would find it so problematic. I will have occasion to demonstrate, however, the importance of both the English and French Revolutions (as well as many other political events) to liberation movements in the United States, movements which have, like the French Revolution, been "at once acknowledged and disavowed," "registered and elided," in "a perpetual syncopation between originary inscription and subsequent transcription, translation, or re-edition."[5] Clement Hawes argues a similar point about the English Civil War: "later cultural memory has designated manic enthusiasm as the very sign of that ill-digested revolutionary trauma,"[6] a sentiment that equally applies to the United States' own troubled relationship to its revolutionary histories.

Consider, for example, that in an October 2011 television appearance on the Fox Business Network's *Follow the Money with Eric Bolling*, conservative pundit Ann Coulter compared the slogans of the Occupy Wall Street protests to "mob" ideas in the French Revolution, the Russian Revolution, and even Nazi Germany. "It [the protest rhetoric] all comes from the French Revolution," said Coulter, and thus it represents the "molecular opposite of the beginning of this country, with the American Revolution."[7] All bald ideology aside, Coulter testifies to the endurance of a familiar historical narrative that juxtaposes the conservative, prudent ideology of the American Revolution and the radical, excessive ideology of the French Revolution. Philosophers and historians, cultural critics and literary scholars, across a wide intellectual spectrum—from Hannah Arendt to Gordon Wood, Sacvan Bercovitch to Antonio Negri—have tended to agree with Coulter on at least this point: the American Revolution certainly was not a movement of "mob" protest or manic enthusiasm, introducing a "wild and dangerous politics,"[8] to quote Edmund Burke in his foundational critique of 1790s (French) radicalism.[9]

And yet, even Burke did not or could not successfully divorce the American and French Revolution. In his *Letter... to a Noble Lord* (1795, 1796), he recalls the "portentous crisis from 1780 to 1782" in England, spawned by the Gordon Riots against the Crown's war to subdue America: "Had the portentous comet of the rights of man ... crossed upon us in that internal state of England, nothing human could have prevented our being irresistibly hurried, out of the highway of heaven, into all the vices, crimes, horrours, and miseries of the French revolution."[10] This comment blatantly refuses to name the said comet but instead thanks the heavenly highways that France was not at that time "jacobinized."[11] Whereas the American colonies, despite the Revolutionary crisis, presented no threat to England's domestic safety, their English supporters, standing for "Wilkes and Liberty" and taking over the streets of London and Bristol, most certainly did. But notice how Burke folds the unnamed Atlantic Revolution into the French Revolution and the "crisis from 1780 to 1782" through a kind of paratactical displacement: "Her [France's] hostility was at a good distance. We had a limb cut off; but we preserved the body: We lost our Colonies; but we kept our Constitution. There was, indeed, much intestine heat; there was a dreadful fermentation. Wild and savage insurrection quitted the woods, and prowled about our streets in the name of reform. Such was the distemper of the publick mind, that there was no madman, in his maddest ideas, and maddest projects, who might not count upon numbers to support his principles and execute his designs."[12] If these madmen, who expressed solidarity with the "Liberty

Boys" of Boston and Philadelphia,[13] had been successful, then "not France, but England, would have had the honour of leading up the death-dance of Democratick Revolution."[14] It appears that Burke's circumscription of American radicalism has to do with its "good distance" from the mainland, for otherwise it would be unnecessary for him to slide from France to the loss of the colonial limb as if France was responsible for the impairment (of course, as Revolutionary America's ally it partly was).

But like conservative commentators today, Edmund Burke does not so much attack the French Revolution as he does hyperbolically marshal a political Francophobia in order to champion national institutions. The French Revolution was merely the symptom of a disease that might as well have convulsed England in the 1780s; this would have been "French" politics *avant la lettre*, a political illness that has a historical antecedent and appellation—enthusiasm. We know this from Burke's *Reflections on the Revolution in France* (1790), in which the Revolution serves as the most extreme example of a modern historical tendency. Once again, Burke responds to an English problem, specifically the pro-French sentiments promulgated in a popular sermon by Richard Price, a British preacher by trade in the dissenting tradition but also the "first and original Left-Wing Intellectual" in British history.[15] Burke labels Price a resurrected Hugh Peter of the English Civil War, and he uses *Reflections* as a wholesale denunciation of what he considers fanatical Protestantism, past and present. As J. G. A. Pocock puts it, Burke's French Revolution stands for a "kind of secular enthusiasm and a continuation of Puritanism in politics."[16]

I will have more to say about Burke's theory of enthusiasm in chapter 1, but for the moment I wish to demarcate a historical territory outlined by Burke, a territory that is a point of departure for *Mania for Freedom*. When he proceeds to give his reader a remarkable tableau of enthusiastic historical heresies, Burke first invokes the "Anabaptists of Munster, in the sixteenth century," whose "system of levelling and their wild opinions concerning property" led to an "epidemical fanaticism," "the spirit of atheistical fanaticism," which has returned on the streets of Paris.[17] Second, the French Revolution will have been, not the Glorious Revolution of the true patriotic Englishman, but the English Civil War—"the rapture of 1648."[18] Third, the Revolutionaries do dishonor to themselves by acting like a "gang of Maroon slaves, suddenly broke loose from the house of bondage" and "a procession of American savages, entering into Onondaga."[19] Fourth, he points to ferocious "women lost to shame, who, according to their insolent fancies, direct, control, applaud, explode [with]" the French "mob" and "sometimes mix and take their seats amongst them" as irrefutable proof that the French Revolution has "inverted order in all things."[20] Finally, the Enlightenment's "philosophical fanatics," also dubbed "enthusiasts," spread the plague of liberty like bigoted divines with their "violent and malignant zeal" for uncompromising ideals of justice, coupled with a trite sympathy "for the poor."[21] Here Burke manages to assemble and weave together virtually every cultural association with enthusiasm up through the Civil War: it travels from the Protestant rebellions of Münster and the English Civil War to renegade slaves and indigenous peoples in the Americas to politicized women and radical Enlighteners. Cutting across Europe, the black Atlantic, Native America, and the United States, enthusiasm represents the fervor for "fanatical" democracy and the spirit of rebellion underwriting the political history of modernity. *Mania for Freedom* will show that Burke was not alone in narrating modern history in this way—indeed, a study of the U.S. period from the Revolution to the Civil War tends to demonstrate that Americans understood themselves to be living in a veritable Age of Enthusiasm two centuries old.

Furthermore, Burke's polemic against the French Revolution borrows the same language of enthusiasm that had circulated in the American colonies ever since the Antinomian Crisis of 1636–38, a language which continued to have rhetorical purchase during the Anglo-American crisis of the 1770s and 1780s. After all, America was a dumping ground for nonconformists. From the Familists, Anabaptists, and Quakers of religious antinomianism to the motley crew of sailors, commoners, slaves, and Paineites of the American Revolution, the "enthusiast" described any person who preached a democratic authority invested in the people or the individual rather than in the institutional mediations of government or church, and who claimed the right (by Heaven or by natural law) to throw off or resist governments and laws when they fail to affirm said authority. In colonial America up through the Great Awakening of the 1740s, Puritan orthodoxy consistently banished enthusiasts as immoral radicals. On both sides of the Atlantic, enthusiasts, by stressing spiritual freedom over institutional form, tended (in the orthodox estimate) toward promiscuity, social leveling, anarchy, the convulsion of the state, and even folk communism. To partisans of the existing order a few decades later, "revolutionary radicals" during the American Revolution were also "political enthusiasts, that is, fanatics, unhinged from political convention, even civilised [sic] conduct, and who, like their religious counter-parts, were subversive and conspiratorial and a menace to government and society and the accepted order of things."[22]

This brings me to a crucial point. That the American Revolution has been registered and elided as a prudent and conservative revolution, even an antirevolution, attests to the fact that, "for much of the revolutionary generation," "during the postwar decade, the elite founding fathers had waged—and won—a counter-revolution against popular democratic ideals."[23] Once Federalist America reasserted its fidelity to a strong state apparatus of constitutional form, patriotic histories began to downplay or remove all enthusiasm in the narrative of colonial rebellion and assign it to slaves and mobs and Native Americans. This was a necessary expedient: political elites knew that the French Revolution was threatening to unleash a *reedition* of the American Revolution in 1793 "when ten thousand People in the Streets of Philadelphia, day after day, threatened to drag Washington out of his House, and effect a Revolution in the Government, or compel it to declare War in favour of the French Revolution, and against England," as John Adams recalled to Thomas Jefferson in 1813.[24] As I'll emphasize time and again in this study, the precipitating problem was that the principles of 1776 kept inspiring further acts of political resistance *against* the United States through the Civil War, and no doubt for this reason, such political enthusiasm has been made to virtually disappear in the Revolutionary and post-Revolutionary era at the moment of its highest cultural ferment.

My suspicion, then, is that the absence of U.S. enthusiasm speaks to the victory of a historical narrative taking it for granted that no serious political or ideological alternatives were posed against the triumphant path, the manifest destiny, of presidential, capitalist democracy in the United States, so that any enthusiast in history will have been caught up despite herself in America's mission to be an Empire of Liberty, Thomas Jefferson's phrase that we now read as openly ironic. Enthusiasm then becomes flattened as a harmless, precocious, or complicit specter of the pre–nation-state era when critics do not confuse it with religious fundamentalism or dreamy Romanticism. In many respects, our often anachronistic historical approaches to early modern and Anglo-American dissent were prepared by our ancestors, and if enthusiasm has become a vacuous word, this will say more about what has been done *with* it and *to* it in the unfolding of the West; unconsciously or not, it is no coincidence that the term's once troubling significations have been evacuated as part of a determined amnesia about the shaping of our histories.

But if "the discourse on enthusiasm"²⁵ has been undervalued in the United States, then so has the literary culture that emerged around or in response to it. This strikes me as curious indeed. Why? Because, from the "generous enthusiasm which kindles into rapture the coldest hearts" when women "espouse the cause of the oppressed or unfortunate" in Gilbert Imlay's *The Emigrants* (1793) to that "Enthusiast to Duty," Pierre, and his unhinged "enthusiastic heart," in Herman Melville's *Pierre* (1852), from the "enthusiastic temper" of the young William Fletcher and Magawisca's "enthusiasm of devotion" in Catharine Maria Sedgwick's *Hope Leslie* (1827) to the "kneeling enthusiasts" of the New Faith inaugurated by the mad doctor and sorcerer Ravoni (with his "absorbing enthusiasm") in George Lippard's *The Quaker City* (1845), enthusiasm is a constantly recurring, nearly obsessive, theme in American literature before the Civil War.²⁶ For scholars of British literature, especially of the Romantic era, engagements with enthusiasm have not been neglected to the same degree. To be sure, William Blake—for whom "Meer Enthusiasm is the All in All!"²⁷—has become the poster boy of enthusiasm in the arts, but tellingly, the American Revolution played a monumental role in shaping the young Blake's swerve toward prophetic radicalism. To Blake, America's "civil war" with Albion was anything but antienthusiastic.²⁸ He not only supported the French Revolution as an outgrowth of the American Revolution but also, by his own account, participated in the Gordon Riots that so outraged Burke and wrote them into the first of his continental prophecies, *America a Prophecy* (1793), a work that also serves as a concise introduction to literary appropriations of enthusiasm.

One will recall the basic premise of *America*: "red Orc" breaks free from despotic reason's (Urizen's) chains, impregnates the depressed and nameless "shadowy daughter" of earthbound imagination (Urthona), whose consequent "first-born smile" ignites the American Revolution.²⁹ Orc's chains are doubled by America's in plate 3.³⁰ But when the daughter first sees Orc, she notices in him "the image of God who dwells in darkness of Africa" before glancing at the revolts on the North American plains, only to recognize Orc's "lightnings" and the birth pangs of revolution (in various totemic forms) on the horizon of Canada, Mexico, Peru, and the South Seas—that is, the horizon of the Americas generally, not merely the North American colonies.³¹ As one event in Orc's universal struggle, the American Revolution has no priority in the global scale of concatenating emancipation. It would even appear that liberty for Africa is Orc's revolutionary prerequisite.

Plate 4 then introduces Blake's most consistent image of Atlantic revolution as a volcanic conflagration from below—"Swelling, belching from its [the Atlantic's] deeps red clouds & raging Fires!"—that propels itself toward the sky:

> And in the red clouds rose a Wonder o'er the Atlantic sea;
> Intense! naked! a Human fire fierce glowing, as the wedge
> Of iron heated in the furnace; his terrible limbs were fire[32]

As Susie Tucker details, disease and plague, intoxication and madness, heat and fire (including volcanic eruption), lightning and storms—all figures of excess and disorder—were the most common metaphors for enthusiasm in its long historical signification,[33] and one sees this imagery used by both critics and apologists such as Burke and Blake. In the latter's poetic universe, Orc is the embodiment of political enthusiasm in and for itself, and the above passages lead to Blake's own Declaration of Independence:[34]

> Reviving shake, inspiring move, breathing! awakening!
> Spring like redeemed captives when their bonds & bars are burst;
> Let the slave grinding at the mill, run out into the field:
> Let him look up into the heavens & laugh in the bright air;
> Let the inchained soul shut up in darkness and in sighing,
> Whose face has never seen a smile in thirty weary years;
> Rise and look out, his chains are loose, his dungeon doors are open.
> And let his wife and children return from the opressors [*sic*] scourge;
> They look behind at every step & believe it is a dream.
> Singing. The Sun has left his blackness, & has found a fresher morning
> And the fair Moon rejoices in the clear & cloudless night;
> For Empire is no more, and now the Lion & Wolf shall cease.[35]

This scene crystallizes a theme of this book: the *revival of revolt* is also the *revolt of a revival,* with enthusiasm acting as both an anterior condition for staging acts of freedom and a posterior response to events of emancipation, embodied collectively by "a naked multitude."[36] Enthusiasm materializes in an open and borderless space that becomes quickly vertiginous; and it defines itself through a language of convulsive states performatively announcing and encouraging their content along a positive and negative axis: the shaking and singing and laughing of the redeemed captives on the one hand, and the "convuls'd" body of Albion's Angel on the other.[37] The redeemed captives passage is at once a singular event of enthusiasm—the American Revolution—and a virtual registration or archetypal prophecy of all further events of enthusiasm. At the end of the work, we learn that "France reciev'd"[38] [sic] the same spirit of enthusiasm, but it doesn't end with France: the revival of revolt is like an eternal return and anthem of every event that participates in liberation until the continental prophecies have come true.

The text and art of plate 15 (figure 1, listed as object 17 in the William Blake Archive in accordance with the Bentley plate numbering system) arguably presents Blake's self-referential literary vision of the enthusiast. Here the "Priests" hide "from the Fires of Orc, / That play around the golden roofs in wreaths of fierce desire, / Leaving the females naked and glowing with the lusts of youth."[39] Then Blake says this about these females: "They feel the nerves of youth renew . . . / Over their pale limbs as a vine when the tender grape appears"; the enjambed last line continues on plate 16: "Over the hills, the vales, the cities, rage the red flames fierce."[40] The fires of Orc and the wreaths of fierce desire are incarnations of each other, two expressions of the same substance, both material and passional, in an affective field of pregnant transformation. Although Blake certainly imagines desire as all-consuming like a wreath or vine (surrounding or wreathing the world), the art of figure 1 speaks to a different vision of wreathing consistent with his conflagration imagery.

The flames of Orc emerge from the bottom of the plate as two women, like darting flames themselves, bend and fly upward on the left margin. To the right of them, at the bottom of the plate, four other women (three clustered together) cower at the flames in fear, but they represent "the female spirits of the dead pining in bonds of religion" prior to their liberation.[41] This is an action sequence moving from right to left that shows the trajectory of the women's release from slavery. That grapes—leaf, vine, and cluster—grow in the furnace reinforces this reading: Blake asks us to see the flames not only as a destructive force but as a life-giving spirit of renewal, as Dionysian delight. But if the vines that move vertically up the plate, emerging out of the flames just as the woman in the middle left margin morphs into vines or tree limbs herself, are the "wreaths of fierce desire," then one also has to notice that the eruption of the fire, from the bottom up, produces and illuminates Blake's words—his poem takes form out of the wreathed smoke-cum-vegetation. Blake has added vines in between or growing out of his writing so that the textual inscription, in its cursive lyricism,

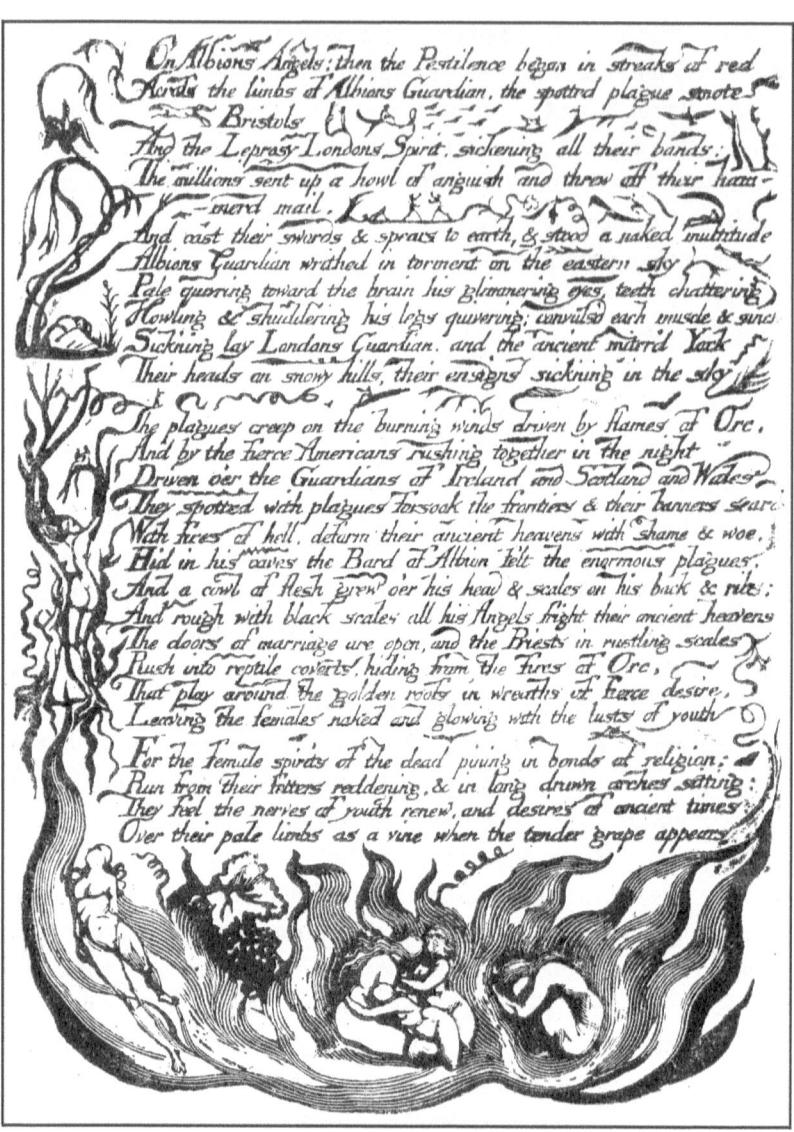

FIGURE 1 Object 17 (Bentley 17, Erdman 15, Keynes 15) of *America a Prophecy*, copy E. Lessing J. Rosenwald Collection, Library of Congress. Copyright © 2015 William Blake Archive. Used with permission.

becomes an incarnate (not metaphorical) desire-wreath itself, operating on the same plane as the content of the poem. This attempt to represent enthusiastic communication as part and parcel of the selfsame movement of revolutionary enthusiasm suspended in political air—the open space of crisis and creativity—will be a signature feature of literatures of enthusiasm. For literatures of enthusiasm are, each in their own way, self-proclaimed wreaths of fierce desire—a literary mania for freedom.

II

But why enthusiasm now, it may be asked? What are the conditions that make it available or interesting to us? At least four reasons present themselves. The first one I have already gestured toward—the global horizon of enthusiastic politics through the Civil War. As Jordana Rosenberg states in her analysis of seventeenth- and eighteenth-century British enthusiasms, "The spreading of literary, historical, and intellectual study beyond the confines of the nation-state has been an energizing and indispensable movement forward for humanistic research. Enthusiasm is primed for such an energization, since this discourse has long been a transatlantic concept."[42] In taking up a study of American enthusiasms, I echo Paul Giles's argument in *The Global Remapping of American Literature* (2011): "My general hypothesis, then, is that the nationalist phase of American literature and culture extended from 1865 until about 1981 and that the current transnational phase actually has more in common with writing from the periods on either side of the War of Independence, when national boundaries were much more inchoate and unsettled."[43] While he roots the nationalist phase of American literature and culture in the politics of the Cold War, Donald Pease agrees with Giles when he states that American exceptionalism represents a national fantasy anachronistically used to describe U.S. origins, but he also contends that one motive for this (crucial for enthusiasm) was the need of American studies scholars, policymakers, and the press to see the "national past as lacking the history of class antagonism that they posited as the precondition for world communism."[44] Without a doubt, antagonisms arising not only out of class conflict but also out of anti-imperial and antiracist efforts among and on behalf of minorities—a "minor transnationalism"—must be foregrounded in the "global remapping" of American enthusiasm; and, while admittedly my analysis doesn't present a global picture of the late eighteenth and nineteenth centuries, I do illustrate how traditionally major and minor authors of American literary history, like Thomas Paine and Phillis Wheatley or Harriet Beecher Stowe and Martin Delany, shared certain enthusiastic ideals, creating a "productive relationship" between "major" and "minor cultural articulations" of enthusiasm in their respective attempts to establish "national and transnational" political affiliations.[45] By emphasizing the universal love of liberty over/against the injustices of the nation-state, American enthusiasts (and their critics) understood their commitments in the context of transnational political cultures and histories. Their viewpoint conduces a very different narrative of some of the most enduringly national events: for example, the American Revolution becomes a return of the Cromwellian English Revolution; the War of 1812 becomes a Native American Revolution linking American Indian nations to both the American Revolution and Canada's resistance to U.S. imperialism; U.S. slave insurrection becomes an extension of the French and Haitian Revolution, Caribbean emancipation, and European liberation movements from Hungary to Greece; and the Civil War becomes a condensation and crystallization of many of these events. In sum, enthusiasm names the way that U.S. emancipatory projects participated in what Susan Buck-Morss calls "universal history," a freedom narrative in common, a narrative which belongs to all humanity.[46]

Moreover, from a nonnational view, I offer a different way to read a period in American studies and literature that has primarily been framed in terms of the matrix of sentimentalism. While critics of sentimental literature have called attention to its capacity to voice political suffering, promote equality, criticize power, and challenge accepted forms of social exchange, they have underemphasized the ways that the discourse of sympathy equally spilled over into a public politics of active dissent against the nation. I locate enthusiasm here. My thesis on this point is as follows: whereas sentimentality expresses civic feeling bound to *national reform* or "domestic empire"[47] (uniting people around the shared fantasy of a national home in which all are equal), enthusiasm expresses a more subversive variant of civic feeling bound to *international or antinational revolt* (uniting people around a shared fantasy of a global home in which all are equal). As such, I do not agree that the sentimental novel was "the most radical popular form available to middle-class culture."[48] At the same time, I do not mean to cleanly bifurcate sentimentality and enthusiasm as opposed cultural logics either. On the contrary, as I'll touch upon in chapter 1, the two exist on a shared continuum—enthusiasm represents sentimentality's point of excess. When the critique of power, the recognition of suffering among marginalized communities, and the passionate ideals of democratic possibility—the hallmarks of progressive sentimentality—translate into an apology for direct resistance to national forms of oppression, then one has a politics of enthusiasm. Insofar as this politics finds public expression, enthusiasm constitutes a kind of "counterpublic" in Michael Warner's terms, since, against "the background of the public sphere," "its exchanges remain distinct from authority and can have a critical relation to power; its extent is in principle indefinite, because it is not based on a precise demography but mediated by print, theater, diffuse networks of talk, commerce, and the like."[49] At least one American literary critic has duly noted this: Caleb Smith, in his study of early national legal discourse and justice-making claims, ties the legacy of enthusiasm to what he characterizes as a literature of "the *curse*," a "kind of utterance" "spoken from the other side of legal authority," in a "style of protest more dangerous than critique or sentimentality."[50]

But my analysis of enthusiasm also builds on the influential work of pioneering critics (Nancy Ruttenburg, Jay Fliegelman, Sandra Gustafson) who have emphasized the pivotal, even primary, contributions of impassioned oratory, public assembly, and embodied voice, including enthusiastic speech, to both the ethos of the American public sphere and American literature. In more recent studies of early American religion, literature, and culture, critics such as Joanna Brooks and John Lardas Modern have further stressed the irreducible role that the evangelical tradition—in essence, religious instantiations of enthusiasm—played in the development of American literature and popular thought before the Civil War.[51] I shift the emphasis of this scholarly legacy by calling attention not only to the preacher and the pundit but also to the protester who contested, contributed to, and invigorated both the form and content of early national American literature.

That enthusiasm, as a politics of incendiary protest, was so often understood as anti-American activity—a threat to national institutions and domestic safety—operating both within and in excess to the nation already begins to answer the question of its invisibility in traditionally nationalistic accounts of American literature and culture. For the same reason, it only makes sense that political theory's academic interest in enthusiasm, from Jason Frank's *Constituent Moments* (2010) to Alberto Toscano's *Fanaticism* (2010), has emerged alongside scholarly efforts to disambiguate legitimate movements of democratic political struggle from

Introduction 13

the problem of "terrorism" in a contemporary political climate of resurgent activism and popular dissent. This fact grounds the second reason that a study of enthusiasm seems timely. We should not forget that enthusiasts—American Revolutionary insurgents who opposed the Crown, Native Americans who challenged U.S. expansionism, black individuals who resisted slavery, and abolitionists who tried to emancipate slaves at the expense of the nation—were often dismissed as agents of "terror" in a cavalier fashion. On this point, my analysis echoes Toscano, who gives a wide-ranging intellectual history of the way that "advocates of radical equality" around the globe have been historically maligned as "dangerous fanatics," and he includes "enthusiasm" as part of a conceptual family for attacking all "radical politics of emancipation and egalitarianism."[52] But since enthusiasm, to Toscano, plays the "nobler cousin"[53] to fanaticism, it merits examination in only one chapter and ends up as a more polite synonym for the latter.

Yet one of the most helpful, if unstable, semantic distinctions among eighteenth-century critics was the isolation of enthusiasm as an affective-physiological disposition linked to a fervor for freedom—sometimes noble, sometimes not—and a corresponding reservation of the word "fanaticism" for a specifically religious phenomenon that today we might call "fundamentalism" or "religious extremism." The thorny problem here is that enthusiasm was, for most of its historical life, also defined as an essentially religious concept that did often get conflated with fanaticism (Burke does precisely this), and, as my chapters will show, religious cultures were never extraneous to the politics of enthusiasm either. This fact should be of interest to scholars working in new secular or postsecular studies. While it is not a primary goal of *Mania for Freedom* to explicitly address secularization in the early national period or to entangle myself in complicated problems of enthusiasm's "religious" and "secular" status, these issues are nevertheless vital to my study, if only as a background that throws into relief the freedom movements that I aim to foreground. I do want it to be clear, though, that I am in critical agreement with postsecular scholars who begin with the premise that there is nothing *essentially* "religious" or "secular,"[54] and the story that I will tell attests to the impossibility—or simply the irrelevance—of trying to demarcate the sacred and the secular with respect to enthusiastic politics. On the other hand, it's important to emphasize that, just as postsecularism, as a mode of meta-critique, examines the ways that discursive fields and institutional powers historically produce the binary of the religious and the secular for particular ends, as "changes in concepts articulate changes in practices"[55] in the "religious-secular continuum,"[56] the historical critique of enthusiasm is intimately bound to the emergence of Enlightenment philosophy and republican political theory, as well as the birth of religion as an academic—and putatively secular—object of philosophical and scientific inquiry.[57] If I have any stance on this point, it's that Frederick Beiser's diagnosis of the early seventeenth-century English Enlightenment's allergy to enthusiasm continues to hold true in the post-Revolutionary United States, if we exchange the "champions of secularism" for the "champions of reason" in the following quotation: "We expect the champions of reason to defend such liberal causes as freedom of thought and equality of opportunity, and we assume that they will criticize such evils as social privilege and political oppression. . . . But . . . [i]t was the enthusiasts who defended liberty of conscience and social equality, and it was the rationalists who defended social privilege and religious authority and conformity. The spirit, not reason, was the sanction for the more liberal and progressive values."[58] Only, in the U.S. context of the early national period, what passes for secularization really amounts to a hegemonic form of religious-secular ideology, what Tracy Fessenden calls a "nonspecific Protestantism," or "post-Protestant secularism," that is, a liberalized and diffuse Protestantism that naturalizes itself through a secular (civic) ethos and consequently becomes an "unmarked category."[59]

As one might imagine, enthusiasm plays a curious, often contradictory, role vis-à-vis the progress of mainstream Protestantism and liberal-secular thought. On the one hand, as a social force of dissensus, enthusiasm was a heavily marked category that, adjacent to working-class, indigenous, and black cultures (among others), continually threatened to upset the status quo; but on the other hand, the status quo also worked very hard to coopt and domesticate—to produce and regulate, in Jon Mee's terms—the "mania for freedom," to channel enthusiasm into more socially acceptable, moderate forms, even while the labor to do so required drawing boundaries that inevitably alienated other culturally different and politically unorthodox religious-secular formations. What results is a semantic pluralization—and conceptual metamorphosis—of enthusiasm itself whereby its signification depends on a differential typology of cultural forms and expressions such as "poetic enthusiasm," the "enthusiasm of love," "patriotic enthusiasm," and obviously "religious enthusiasm" (itself subject to internal stratification and complex atomization), all of which

Introduction 15

become genres of discourse that on closer scrutiny cross-pollinate to such a degree that the categorical clarity desired is highly polluted.

By the mid-eighteenth century, enthusiasm had, generally speaking, coalesced into a diagnosis of psycho-physiological excess, an evaluative term for various forms of extreme or ecstatic self-dispositions. Samuel Johnson's 1755 dictionary lists three definitions: "1. A vain belief of private revelation; a vain confidence of divine favour or communication"; "2. Heat of imagination; violence of passion; confidence of opinion"; and "3. Elevation of fancy; exaltation of ideas."[60] Johnson's definitions track, in order, the continuum between enthusiasm's negative valence (an illegitimate claim to divine authority, or religious enthusiasm), neutral or generic valence (a physiological-affective state linked to confidence), and positive valence (the modality of mental uplift characteristic of the poetic or philosophical sublime). It's worth noting, too, that Noah Webster's first edition of the *American Dictionary of the English Language* (1828) reproduces, amplifies, and copiously clarifies Johnson's definitions of enthusiasm, albeit by crunching the second and third senses into one signification. Johnson's first definition remains basically the same in Webster: "1. A belief or conceit of private revelation; the vain confidence or opinion of a person, that he has special divine communications from the Supreme Being, or familiar intercourse with him." Then Webster gives us this verbose, essayistic explanation of enthusiasm: "2. Heat of imagination; violent passion or excitement of the mind, in pursuit of some object, inspiring extravagant hope and confidence of success. Hence the same heat of imagination, chastised by reason or experience, becomes a noble passion, an elevated fancy, a warm imagination, an ardent zeal, that forms sublime ideas, and prompts to the ardent pursuit of laudable objects. Such is the *enthusiasm* of the poet, the orator, the painter and the sculptor. Such is the *enthusiasm* of the patriot, the hero and the christian."[61] Not only are the categorical differences among vain belief, violence of passion, and ardent zeal tenuous and slippery, but also a historical genealogy of enthusiasm reveals that the above dictionary entries obscure the political context in which these definitions were strategically and invidiously exploited—namely, as a language for claiming one set of superlative moral/cultural values (the enthusiasm of the American patriot and so on) in contradistinction to another (but inextricably linked) set of inadmissible moral/cultural values (the enthusiasm, for example, of "savage" African or Native religions, interpreted according to the first definition). Above all else, enthusiasm was leveraged on a case-by-case basis to alienate any unwonted manifestation of political dissent, which Webster himself obliquely acknowledges when, as the sole example of his latter definition, he rather awkwardly quotes Fisher Ames as saying, "Faction and *enthusiasm* are the instruments by which popular governments are destroyed,"[62] one assumes in reference to that "heat of imagination" unchastised by "reason or experience."

Out of the dense conceptual web of assorted enthusiasms, my goal is to emphasize the relationship between enthusiastic ideals and specific political events. With regard to religion and politics, it is the distinction between "enthusiasm" and "fanaticism" that interests me the most in the criticism of the period, and I will go so far as to defend the position—no doubt my most controversial one—that enthusiasm should be rigorously viewed, with David Hume, as a passion for and *"friend to... civil liberty,"* however misguided. By political, I mean simply that the goal of said enthusiasm has an explicit *civic or legal objective,* without assuming such objectives are a priori "secular." Contrariwise, what we normally call fanaticism—or superstition, for Hume—is a passion that expresses itself politically as *"an enemy to civil liberty."*[63] Germaine de Staël will analogously, if more flamboyantly, call enthusiasm a liberating feeling for "the interest and the beauty of all things," "connected with the harmony of the universe; it is the love of the beautiful, elevation of soul, enjoyment of devotion, all united in one single feeling which combines grandeur and repose," as opposed to fanaticism, which is the bigot's "exclusive passion" for a "single idea, or a single object."[64] The likely rebuttal to this distinction is that it surely overlooks a wide variety of conservative enthusiasms in the antebellum era and beyond, but to the letter, "conservative enthusiasm," by Hume's definition, would be a contradiction in terms and properly belong to the category of fanaticism; not only that but through a critique of enthusiasm's conceptual history, I will make the case that political rhetoric nearly always linked enthusiasm to emancipatory ideals, however extreme, contradictory, or flawed the manifestations of those ideals may have been. In other words, I do not count every project of popular political dissent as an instance of enthusiasm, and I preempt the flattening out of the term accordingly. More concretely, the fact is that, on the whole, rebellious slaves were charged with enthusiasm, not lynch mobs or anti-Catholic vigilantes; Native Americans, not settler colonials; abolitionists, not Southern secessionists. And while it would be terribly false to claim that every time the word "enthusiasm" was used, it necessarily had a "radical" subtext, my point is that, for the politics of revolution and dissent, enthusiasm definitely did conjure the historical specter of rebellion in political criticism. My archive is delimited to such cases and does not—it could not—aim to cover the entire field of enthusiasm's semantic usage. As a related point of clarification, another potential problem with the language of enthusiasm has to do with critical slippage between the opprobrious tag—a label applied to persons by critics—and the active embrace of enthusiasm as a politics or ideal. My argument here is that, while conservatives and moderates lampooned sundry dissidents as enthusiasts in order to mar their reputation, some of them *were* enthusiasts, claimed and defended their own variant of enthusiasm, and experimented with a mode of literature that formalized political rites of dissent. I analyze both sides. This is what I find most compelling about the topic—there are *competing claims* for a definition of enthusiasm in the era, and political enthusiasm speaks to *the terms of a debate* about the right to resist tyranny and under what conditions.

In addition to its transnational scope and its centrality for American histories of political protest, an analysis of enthusiasm contributes, thirdly, to studies of affect in literature, understood not only as a cultural politics of the emotions, but also as a form of inquiry rooted in "what it means to feel and to be historical at a particular moment."[65] Enthusiasm's relevance can hardly be underestimated in this light. In fact, it is arguably something like a term for the flow of affect—"the aleatory, open nature" of social forces[66]—in an earlier historical period that tried to check the excessive, contingent, creative, or counterrational exchanges of feeling which it associated with the dangers of radical democracy and nonnormative sociability. Elizabeth Freeman goes so far as to suggest that enthusiasm is a "hieroglyph for the problem of affect itself" and "a figure for the very excess that affect both is and produces."[67] If so, perhaps only now can we see that enthusiasm was our historical ancestor who may have a lot to teach us. Steven Goldsmith argues a similar point. He believes that the academic resurrection of William Blake's "dangerous enthusiasm"[68] stems from the fact that "Blake's enthusiasm, despite its premodern roots, is already a substantially modern phenomenon and that the current academic enthusiasm for emotion belongs to a continuum that includes Blake as an early practitioner."[69] The "desire to historicize enthusiasm, and thus to identify its difference from our own modernity, is indistinguishable from a desire to activate that difference anew," "enabling the future" and "placing charged affect at the vanguard of critique, creativity, and change."⁷⁰ In short, I follow through on Goldsmith's claim in the U.S. context where it has not yet been fully explored.

But why *hasn't* enthusiasm been a central topic in scholarship on political affect? Perhaps a partial answer to this question has to do with our long-impoverished capacity to appreciate affective states as opposed to subjective emotions. Following Deleuze and Guattari, Brian Massumi influentially explains that emotion relates to private ownership, subjective content, the personal quality of experience and the processing of that experience ("It is intensity owned and recognized"),⁷¹ while affect relates to exteriorized, intercorporeal, and pre-personal intensity or contact that has to do with relations exceeding but including the self, escaping "confinement in the particular body whose vitality, or potential for interaction, it is."⁷² Or, as Deleuze and Guattari write in *A Thousand Plateaus* (1980, 1987 in English), "For the affect is not a personal feeling, nor is it a characteristic; it is the effectuation of a power of the pack that throws the self into upheaval and makes it reel" ("Affects are becomings").⁷³ Most basically, emotion interprets and translates an affective field that is responsible for uniting the self to others and its environment. In *The Transmission of Affect* (2004), Teresa Brennan points out that an affective atmosphere, although "social in origin," "literally gets into the individual" and has a "physiological impact" on him or her."⁷⁴ She calls this "the intelligence of the flesh,"⁷⁵ that is, the way communication and judgments occur at a physical level, transmitted across bodies through interactions below the radar of my individual consciousness and its presumption of self-containment. When Brennan uses the word "affect," she refers to the physiological stimuli of experience. We feel affects but we feel *with* emotions. As Melissa Gregg and Gregory Seigworth remark, "With affect, a body is as much outside itself as in itself—webbed in its relations—until ultimately such firm distinctions cease to matter."⁷⁶

But if affect helps us to explain, for instance, "why it is that people in groups, crowds, and gatherings can often be 'of one mind,'"⁷⁷ "the breaches in the borders between self and other evidenced by the contagiousness of 'collective' affects,"⁷⁸ then it also helps us to explain enthusiasm, which was often used interchangeably with the "crowd psychology" of collective swarming or "the vulgar culture of the crowd" and its "bodily ecstasies,"⁷⁹ especially in a political context. Just maybe we are now better equipped to delineate and assess enthusiasm's nonpersonalizing associations with transformative collective energies, with Blake's "Reviving shake, inspiring move, breathing! awakening!" Invocations of the "affective event"[80] and "processual creativity"[81] certainly belong to the enthusiastic tradition as I will discuss it, and the enthusiast will have also been trying to tell us that "affect seems to demand that we not dwell so much on questions of being, but rather on matters of belonging."[82]

However, in ways that incorporate the global, political, and affective concerns of today's intellectual landscape, we still need a more precise heuristic for enthusiasm that encompasses the lived experience, rituals, and expressions of political bodies in their effort to transform—and belong in excess of—the status quo, and that links these experiences, rituals, and expressions to historical events. Toward this end (and as my fourth and final point on enthusiasm's relevance), we can learn a lot from contemporary philosophies of "the event" that have themselves revitalized the concept of enthusiasm, most often in readings of Immanuel Kant's 1798 response to the French Revolution in *The Contest of Faculties*, specifically the section "A Renewed Attempt to Answer the Question: 'Is the Human Race Continually Improving?'" To name only a few examples[83] about which much could be said, Jean-François Lyotard understands "enthusiasm . . . as a pure aesthetic feeling," delivered in response to a liberating event, in order to register the judgment "*There is progress*";[84] and Fredric Jameson reads "enthusiasm" as an "approach to History," "the awakening of immense possibilities and the sense that *tout est possible*" corresponding to the "end of [historical] encagement" and the "jubilee" that it produces.[85] And while he doesn't directly cite Kant, Alain Badiou similarly defines "enthusiasm" as "the immediate and immanent experience that one is participating . . . in the becoming of a truth," sutured to political events of liberty and giving us a "local sign" of a "new maxim of equality."[86] From the above perspectives, enthusiasm is a form of critical judgment and an affective supplement linked to an event of historical progress.

Let me now establish a working definition of the event that will prove fruitful for the analysis to come. In Badiou's sense, an event, at the most rudimentary level (I cannot do justice here to the complexity and rigor of his philosophy to say nothing of that philosophy's mathematical articulation), denotes a paradigmatic rupture of a novel truth, a "universal singularity" that is of "the order of a sudden emergence"[87]—"the 'beyond-the-law' of situations."[88] This novelty, at the "evental site," crystallizes into—presents itself as—a localized historical point: "The event is attached, in its very definition, to the place, to the point, in which the historicity of the situation is concentrated."[89] But because an event, to be registered as such, must be reflexively named and elaborated, it becomes a "truth" only insofar as its bound articulation presents an unforeseen possibility previously inexistent or voided within a paradigm of love, politics, science, or art. Attendantly, a "faithful procedure" begins: that is, one works to show what "existing multiples are or are not connected to the event" and one unfolds its consequences for the world.[90] This is what Badiou calls a "truth procedure." It is necessarily procedural because an event "can only be *revealed* in the retroaction of an interventional practice which is itself entirely thought through."[91] In other words, the event is only as good as the decisive interventions made on its behalf. Badiou calls the fidelity to a past "outline or statement, in the world, of the disappeared event," a "resurrection"—the process by which a truth becomes reactivated and claimed by others (the past as condition) but in another logic of its appearance (the present as agent): "Therefore we will say that every faithful subject can also reincorporate into the eventual present the fragment of truth whose bygone present had sunk under the bar of occultation. It is this reincorporation that we call resurrection."[92]

In *Metapolitics* (1998, 2005 in English), Badiou argues that an eventual politics—which is to say, a truth procedure specific to politics—must meet the following three conditions: (1) the event is "ontologically collective"—"a virtual summoning of all," intrinsically universal or generic, inclusive of everyone;[93] (2) the event invokes an open-ended, infinite "egalitarian principle"—"the situation is open, never closed, and the possible affects its immanent subjective infinity"[94] (Put in ethical terms, this means that the event can never be the "absolutization of the power of a truth,"[95] exhausting or positively realizing that truth. It is always possible to expand, build upon, and revise an eventual truth); and (3) the event, bearing along an "egalitarian maxim," "summons the state of the situation," configures and measures, "put[s] at a distance," "the power of the State,"[96] introducing an excluded, unrepresented part of that situation relative to a localized structure of injustice. That is the way the political event shows up and defines itself, but it is lived and evinced in practice by the subject of "enthusiasm."

This outline of the event is crucial to my argument if only because it's another way that I reinforce the claim that enthusiasm—as affect's name for the event—must have an egalitarian, collective destination even while it may have many ideological voids or limits as the enthusiast works out a political truth procedure in response to specific historical issues.

Furthermore, the event unites the global aspirations and affective particularities of enthusiastic dissent. In chapter 1, I will also develop the position that the event is another way of talking about the political theory of *constituent power*—the "power of a people to make, and therefore also to break, the constituted authority of the state,"[97] or, the power of a people to make events happen. I turn to Kant's critique of enthusiasm in order to establish this point, first because he gives us a robust model for understanding constituent power and enthusiasm together, and second, because he is part of an intellectual history and conversation contemporaneous with my case studies. What surfaces, finally, is the following argument: the enthusiast names any agent of "constituent power" who breaks, or advocates for breaking and remaking, the constituted power of the state under formally articulated conditions of oppression.

Taken all together, the strains of thought introduced above point to the fact that the conceptual orbit of enthusiasm beggars easy description, and an exhaustive investigation of its historical import extends well beyond the scope of my perforce delimited study. I would like my reader to see *Mania for Freedom*, then, as an initial foray into an expansive field of inquiry by which I mean to encourage further critical pursuit and analysis of enthusiasm in American literary studies if not beyond.

III

I now need to address the real question of consequence for my study: how does American literature specifically figure in the politics of enthusiasm? Let me illustrate with the example of Frederick Douglass. In his August 1, 1880, commemoration speech on West India Emancipation, Douglass celebrates 1834 as the "great event" (the "birth-day of negro emancipation") that galvanized the eventual abolition of slavery in the United States, but that's not why an American should eulogize the event: "Human liberty excludes all idea of home and abroad. It is universal and spurns localization."[98] Thus, black emancipation has a universal, cosmopolitan destination, inclusive of everyone. At the same time, the event, while it "spurns localization" with regard to its importance for humanity, nevertheless only answered a local and contextual problem of black freedom: Caribbean slavery. Fifteen years after the adoption of the Thirteenth Amendment, all Americans, but especially African Americans, need to remember the event as a postbellum index that the black population may be de jure emancipated but not de facto so. The antiracist egalitarian principle of the 1834 event is, therefore, open-ended and still unfolding; consequently, it requires actors who are faithful to its historicity and will resurrect it in the present. Because the "old master class is to-day triumphant, and the newly-enfranchised class in a condition but little above that in which they were found before the rebellion,"[99] the push for new political mornings continues, says Douglass. The event should serve as an inspiration for the present. It highlights an "enduring enthusiasm" both for making history and history made, including the ebullient way that the slave population responded: "I have been told by eye-witnesses of the scene, that, in the first moment of it, the emancipated hesitated to accept it for what it was. They did not know whether to receive it as a reality, a dream, or a vision of the fancy."[100] When the event of emancipation turns out to be a historical fact, an enthusiasm breaks loose that speaks to liberation not only as a political abstraction but as something lived and experienced by a community of affected persons and bodies: "When fully assured ... that their limbs were no longer chained, but subject to their own will, the manifestations of their joy and gratitude knew no bounds, and sought expression in the loudest and wildest possible forms. They ran about, they danced, they sang, they gazed into the blue sky, bounded into the air, kneeled, prayed, shouted, rolled upon the ground and embraced each other. They laughed and wept for joy. Those who witnessed the scene say that they never before saw anything like it."[101] This is a historical incarnation of Blake's redeemed captives. But Douglass narrates these scenes to show both the (racial) progress made and the regressive forces at work in the ongoing "battle against popular prejudice,"[102] a battle that will demand reviving the selfsame spirit of 1834.

By the time he publishes his novella *The Heroic Slave* in 1853, Frederick Douglass was already writing a black counterhistory of American freedom that ramified black liberation events in the Atlantic. In this story, the event is the 1841 *Creole* slave rebellion. Most obviously, Douglass uses this historical episode as an occasion to defend slave revolt's participation in an age of Enlightenment revolution; the heroic slave, Madison Washington, not only participates in an evental history of black freedom but he also resurrects the American Revolution through a spirit possession of his namesakes: "It seemed as if the souls of both the great dead (whose names he bore) had entered him."[103] Washington's successful revolt results in "the wildest shouts of exultation,"[104] a jubilee enthusiasm of the event, just as West India Emancipation did in 1834. However, without a faithful statement of the event, through the act of writing, the

Introduction 23

event itself would fall under the bar of occultation, threatened by historical loss, whereas it needs to inspire further acts of revolutionary struggle on the part of slaves. Literature for Douglass is not merely a representation of black enthusiasm but an enthusiastic act itself, the operator of fidelity for further emancipatory events. Douglass's repeated return to "the principles of 1776"[105] must also be seen as his attempt to establish a universal measure recognized by the American public at large, to include all Americans in eventual black history and vice versa. Likewise, since the American Revolution did not yet effect the abolition of slavery in the United States, its egalitarian principle was still unfolding, and Douglass's own public declaration—his narrative of enthusiasm—attempts to resurrect the truth of the American Revolutionary event in a new logic of its appearance (slave emancipation). An example such as Frederick Douglass shows us how a transnational, affective, and eventual politics of enthusiasm work together in order to define a literary project.

More precisely, I claim that enthusiasm, as played out in historical instances, forces a response that results in a unique kind of script, not in an absolute way that one might call a genre, but rather in a way that makes *enthusiastic use* of any given genre, metamorphosing it. I do not mean, then, that this body of literature adheres to a formally generic template in the way that one might talk about the ballad, tragic drama, or the romance, but I do mean to suggest that such literatures have a shared ethos that manifests itself in distinct rhetorical properties, properties capable of modifying any given genre from within. I'll demonstrate this through readings of dramas, lyric poems, novels, sermons, stories, speeches, and pamphlets. Just as Silvan Tomkins argues that affects inhere in narrative plots, "a magnified set of scenes" and social scripts (*"sets of ordering rules* for the interpretation, evaluation, prediction, production, or control of scenes"),[106] in other words, that a given affect (such as shame or joy) is always embedded in a story, a script, a narrative that gives it structure and significance, my own approach to enthusiasm will be, in a certain sense, a rather traditional one of script analysis—the historicization and close reading of texts with an attention to how "the national [and transnational] is lived simultaneously in diffused and specific places as well as in bodies that are working out the terms of what it means to feel and to be historical at a particular moment."[107]

Since there is no political event without a constituent activation and response, I read literatures of enthusiasm as a *narrative of the event*, the event's supplemental being. But this is a claim that will have to be borne out in the chapters to come. Here I wish to define the triadic orientation of literatures of enthusiasm organized around a political sensibility of convulsive crisis. First, literatures of enthusiasm relate directly to a *convulsive context*, an immediate crisis of the text, an urgent and dour situation of injustice that demands a rupture with a given political state of being. This context corresponds to an essential historical presupposition of enthusiastic politics—a contrariety to or abrogation of constituted but tyrannical authority and order, "the primary enemy as the Antichrist of civil oppression."[108] This can be thought of as the political *logos* of enthusiasm: it structures the field of politics in a specific location and configures the state of the situation. Second, in response to the convulsive context, literatures of enthusiasm incite the reader to action or internalize writing as a form of direct contact with its audience; I name this the *convulsive address* that calls for a collective (popular) conversion of the immediate context, which presupposes the constituent power of subjects to alter their reality without recourse to any authority other than a democratic imperative. This address is convulsive in the strong sense of affecting the reader—shocking, gripping, pushing, goading the reader to stop reading. The convulsive address corresponds to an essential historical presupposition of enthusiastic relationship—"the separation of the thinker [or writer] from the mass, the theoretical articulation from the act, has not yet transpired."[109] This can be thought of as the political *ethos* of enthusiasm. And third, literatures of enthusiasm not only address readers but also represent them (and, reflexively, acts of literature) as part and parcel of collective events, forces of transformation, and democracy-in-action. I call this *convulsive affect*. Enthusiastic affect corresponds to the essential historical presupposition of enthusiastic society—"immanence of spirit"[110] among a revival public, an enthusiastic collectivity seized by a "mania for freedom." Here I am referring to the embodied "convulsions" of a people antecedent and/or posterior to a political action. This can be thought of as the political *pathos* of enthusiasm.

In chapter 1, I establish a broader conceptual, historical, and literary framework for the rest of the book, fleshing out the long history and philosophy of enthusiasm from early America through the end of the eighteenth century. From Immanuel Kant to Thomas Paine, Anne Hutchinson to Nathaniel Hawthorne, I argue that enthusiasm and the event, as stated earlier, are terms that should be historically understood in relationship to "constituent power." Subsequently, this chapter shows how, in early American debates about religious antinomianism (especially women's access to political or social power), the language of enthusiasm was a theological vision of "constituent power" that became increasingly politicized (which is not to say secularized) in the Revolutionary era. Finally, via Charles Brockden Brown's *Ormond* (1799) and Sarah Pogson's *The Female Enthusiast* (1807), I demonstrate that certain literatures of the early Republic positively understand the politics of enthusiasm—as women's dissent and constituent power, acknowledging no home or abroad—to exceed the limits of "proper" sentiment and sensibility.

Chapters 2 through 5 examine events attached to enthusiastic traditions from the American Revolution to the Civil War, and my primary objective is to reveal the historical continuity—and unfolding literary history—of enthusiasm, cutting across the most important issues of the era, from the Revolution and the formation of the republic to settler colonialism and Native American dispossession, from slavery and abolitionism to the sectional crisis and the Civil War. The chapters are plotted out sequentially. In chapter 2, the event is the American Revolution. I introduce the Loyalist view that colonial resistance in the years leading up to and during the American Revolution was a species of *English* enthusiasm. Through selected works by Mercy Otis Warren, Phillis Wheatley, and Thomas Paine, I argue that literatures of enthusiasm, as a composition of the American Revolutionary event, invent an insurgent American print culture that transforms aesthetic labor into a project of dissent—a "theatre of action" that goads the reader to participate in a living historical drama. Not only in rebellion against the British Empire, these texts also shake off the institutionalized or prescriptive uses of literary genres and press them into the service of social protest.

In chapter 3, the event is the War of 1812 filtered through the lens of Native America, or to be more precise, the movement for a united American Indian confederacy. This chapter shows how the cultural politics of enthusiasm was used to discount Native American nation building, especially the right to resist U.S. imperialism, and yet how indigenous cultures of prophetic enthusiasm did indeed inspire anticolonial revolt. First, I read accounts of Tenskwatawa (the Shawnee Prophet) and his brother Tecumseh's mobilization of indigenous dissent as a performance of enthusiasm. Subsequently, I analyze three obscure War of 1812 novels—Samuel Woodworth's *The Champions of Freedom* (1816), "Don Pedro Casender"'s *The Lost Virgin of the South* (1832), and James Strange French's *Elkswatawa* (1836)—in order to prove the point that pro-American ideology of the War of 1812 betrays a disavowed understanding that the

American Indian confederacy—and its "patriotic enthusiasm"—now occupies the position of the American colonists in their revolt against British tyranny. Finally, I look to William Apess—in particular, his response to the War of 1812—as the first author to significantly argue for indigenous resistance as political enthusiasm.

In chapter 4, the event (or series of events) is black slave revolt in the Americas. I first discuss the historical role that African and Afro-Protestant revival and conjure religion played in fomenting various slave rebellions. After pointing to the influence this enthusiasm had on antebellum antislavery novels in the wake of the sectional crisis, I then argue that Harriet Beecher Stowe's *Dred* (1856) and Martin Delany's *Blake* (1859–62) deserve to be read as novels of enthusiasm that place black resistance in a transatlantic context among insurgent and enthusiastic maroons. Furthermore, Stowe and Delany turn novel writing itself into an enthusiastic contact zone (of call and response) with the reader, soliciting us to speed up the political crisis of slavery through direct intervention.

In chapter 5, the event is John Brown's raid on Harper's Ferry as a prelude to the Civil War. I focus on Walt Whitman's poetics of enthusiasm in relationship to this event, specifically the 1860 *Leaves of Grass* and six poems Whitman later clustered as "Songs of Insurrection." I make a case for Whitman, not as the national bard of American Unionism and integralism who speaks for all and heals the nation's fragmentation, but as the bard of American civil war and international sectarianism who speaks only for the enthusiast in a global context and calls for political dismemberment of the Union. Finally, Whitman offers us a new model of enthusiasm as a dis-membered community of the affections, which is to say, queerly, openly, heterogeneously membered.

If Walt Whitman concludes my study, it is because he best sums up the preceding century of American literary enthusiasms that I examine; inversely, in order to understand the possibility of an über-canonical author such as Whitman, one must first grasp the enthusiastic legacy—a major and minor transnational tradition—that he inherits and tallies. With regard to the Civil War, Whitman would later say in *Memoranda during the War* (1875–76): "As I have look'd over the proof-sheets of the preceding pages, I have once or twice fear'd that my diary would prove, at best, but a batch of convulsively written reminiscences. Well, be it so. They are but parts of the actual distraction, heat, smoke and excitement of those times. The war itself, with *the temper of society preceding it*, can indeed be best described by that very word convulsiveness."[111] Likewise, the temper of the enthusiastic literature preceding Walt Whitman can be best described by the very word convulsiveness, but this is a convulsiveness that the enthusiast claims as a *sine qua non* of both democratic politics and art.

Take an exemplary case of Whitman's own literary enthusiasm such as the 1860 poem "Calamus 5," a poem eventually dismembered and incorporated into both "Over the Carnage Rose Prophetic a Voice" and "For You O Democracy." Therein, Whitman writes about the convulsive context of the sectional crisis and an impending civil war. As I'll show in chapter 5, the problem of the crisis concerns two or three bad possibilities: a Confederate empire of slavery, a divided Union held together by sheer force of law, and a Union saved through compromises with slavery. Whitman's convulsive address to the States posits the crisis as follows:

> 1. STATES!
> Were you looking to be held together by the lawyers?
> By an agreement on a paper? Or by arms?[112]

In every possible scenario, Whitman rejects a Unionism based on juridical compact or constitutional form, reinforced by force of law or force of arms. We know this because the next stanza responds to these questions with an emphatic "Away!" Whitman comes to teach us about a compact "beyond all the forces of courts and arms." He then apostrophizes democracy as the "mother" for whom we must intervene: "Behold, there shall from me be much done for you." This motivates Whitman's convulsive address, which does not separate Whitman from his audience or the act: "The old breath of life, ever new, / Here! I pass it by contact to you, America." A new maxim of equality will define the compact of the States, and this maxim will follow from a Whitmanian affect theory of popular love: "Affection shall solve every one of the problems of freedom, / Those who love each other shall be invincible."[113] And later: "The dependence of Liberty shall be lovers, / The continuance of Equality shall be comrades."[114] But the poem does not merely announce this future: it also performs it in the present.

Furthermore, if one wanted to confine Whitman's affectionate Unionism to a nationalist project, it would be necessary to explain why the circulating friendship of "countless linked hands" and the affection given "in all directions" draws its sustenance from a "perfume" "wafted" to "the Mannahatta from Cuba or Mexico."[115] This is a poem posted toward the "dauntless and rude" anywhere, whose "innovations" shall organize a "new power" errant with respect to the given constitutional and national order: Whitman internalizes his immediate audience as America, not the United States alone, and democracy will come *from* Cuba or Mexico; it will establish a horizontal ensemble of companions.[116] In the latter part of the poem, Whitman gives himself completely over to a convulsive affect of enthusiasm: "These shall tie and band stronger than hoops of iron, / I, extatic [sic], O partners! O lands! henceforth with the love of lovers tie you"; "I will make the continent indissoluble, [...] I will make divine magnetic lands." The poetic enthusiast forges a chain like a magnet that attracts iron rings, binding the lands together in a wreath of fierce desire, while the performative "I" of the poem emphasizes the present agency of the self "to serve you," "O Democracy": "For you! for you, I am trilling these songs."[117] Whitman is a conduit of democratic life. He passes that life on and transmits it through the song. He addresses the reader with a future imperative but also fashions the present (crisis) as an open space for democratic mutation and becoming—the present as metamorphosis. That future can be claimed through participation in the affective, affectionate throng of democratic love. Elsewhere, Whitman calls such participation "the struggle and the daring, rage divine for liberty, / Of aspirations toward the far ideal, enthusiast's dreams of brotherhood."[118]

Said enthusiast's dreams, though, also inform Whitman's larger understanding of U.S. history from the American Revolution to the Civil War, the scope of *Mania for Freedom*. In "The Centenarian's Story" from *Drum-Taps* (1865), Whitman recalls the American Revolution and links it to the Civil War: "The two, the past and present, have interchanged, / I myself as connector, as chansonnier of a great future, am now speaking."[119] The word "interchanged" has many conceptual valences that work all at once here. Crudely, it denotes changing places. The past event (the American Revolution) has become the present one (the Civil War) as its extension and resurrection; and the present event has become the past one, which implies a future anteriority such that the American Revolution claimed in advance a "great future" that Whitman sings. Moreover, the Civil War is *already* a past that claims, like the American Revolution before it, all future liberation events as part of itself. But this is only true insofar as the "I" of the poem, and the poem itself, effects the interchange, publishing the enthusiasm of the past in order to route the event through a new logic of its appearance and to project future acts of freedom. Thus, "interchange" also denotes a gift economy of mutual exchange. The two events, like intimate friends or lovers, affect each other; they transform one another's purpose and destiny. In this sense, "interchange" implies, moreover, a terminal or junction where vehicles can change routes or persons can change vehicles en route; while the two events may enter a process of exchange and continuity, it's also a divergence or transposition in a new direction, equally convulsive with respect to an existing state of affairs. The new event must also work through the limits and problems with the previous one: to inherit the event is also to dissent *from* it in the name of a problem that it left unsolved (slavery, for sure, but there are many others). Whitman himself acts as the junction or terminal that connects the past to the present and the present to the future: this present is a caesura, an interstice, a site of interchange between a past and future emancipation, and it is the time of crisis that requires political intervention.

Since literature allows for historical interchange, Whitman must be ecstatic in the root sense of *ex-stasis*, against stasis; caught and posited and divided in an open-ended, Janus-faced present of historical becoming. In one of his notebooks, Whitman has an entry on "Dithyrambus. Dithyramb," which he defines as follows:

> In ancient poetry a hymn or song in honor of Bacchus, full of transport and poetical rage....
> A song of Bacchus in which the wildness of intoxication is infused.
> Any poem in which ecstasy and wildness are expressed in kind.
> Caesura. Caesural pause (from Caesum, the cutting thing). A pause in verse so introduced as to aid the recital and make melody—divides a line into equal or unequal parts."[120]

This note refers us back to "I, extatic, O partners!" and the "rage divine for liberty"—the "eleutheromania" of the enthusiast. The poet's song of ecstasy is a historical caesura for aiding the recital of past events and making a new melody: it marks the terminal juncture of the realized past and virtual future. In one gesture, Whitman replays the past and relays it toward a democracy to come. The enthusiast is the connector, the chansonnier, the terminal of democracy. But anybody who situates herself inside the time of the event, whether she be a chansonnier or critic, occupies the position of Whitman. To publish enthusiasm is to be a terminal for enthusiasm, changing its meaning in the process. In that sense, I myself, as connector, am now speaking.

CHAPTER ONE

An Answer to the Question
"What Is Enthusiasm?"

> Perhaps there is not another word, which has been received into the English language, that is so frequently used, and so little understood, as the word *Enthusiasm*.
> —*Methodism Vindicated*, 1795

If the motto of Enlightenment is *Sapere Aude!* (dare to know), then the motto of enthusiasm is *Agere Aude!* (dare to act). Or *acti agimus*: "acted upon, we act." To riff on Immanuel Kant's 1784 essay "An Answer to the Question: 'What is Enlightenment?,'" my answer to the question "What is enthusiasm?" can be stated as follows: *enthusiasm is humankind's awakening from its self-incurred political impassivity.* **Impassivity** here means the inability to be affected, aroused, moved—especially to action—by a convulsive context of injustice. My task in this chapter is to flesh out a theory and genealogy of enthusiasm, first, that will provide a sound critical foundation to the above "answer," and second, that will prove fruitful for an analysis of American literature and culture broadly.

Let me begin with a canonical example of the American enthusiast, Ralph Waldo Emerson, and his well-known aphorism, "Nothing great was ever achieved without enthusiasm." That this claim reads like an innocuous truism today perhaps best illustrates our amnesia about the conceptual history of enthusiasm. Where this line appears in the last paragraph of "Circles" (1841), Emerson uses enthusiasm to refer to a "way of life . . . by abandonment," to an "insatiable desire . . . to forget ourselves, to be surprised out of our propriety, to lose our sempiternal memory and to do something without knowing how or why; in short to draw a new circle";[1] but more surprising, Emerson appeals to the infamous Protector of the British Commonwealth, Oliver Cromwell, as a supporting arm for said enthusiasm, as one who illustrates "the facilities of performance through the strength of ideas" behind all "great moments of history"—the "works of genius and religion."[2] Elsewhere, in "Politics" (1844), the essay where "enthusiasm" is said "to fill the heart of youth" "with the broad design of renovating the State on the principle of right and love," even if that means denying "the authority of the laws, on the simple ground of his own moral nature," Emerson enlists Cromwell again as a "man of strong will" who reminds us that "society is fluid" and all state institutions "alterable," without "roots and centres."[3] Thus, if Emerson promotes ecstatic action beyond all utilitarian ends and daring innovation without precedent as the essence of enthusiasm, the term necessarily includes a lawless breach with constituted authority, associated here with the controversial icon of civil war Puritanism.

As it turns out, Emerson did not coin the famous aphorism on enthusiasm; he plagiarized it—copied it down—from his reading of Samuel Taylor Coleridge's published sermon *The Statesman's Manual* (1816),[4] wherein Coleridge criticizes the modern historian's penchant for slandering "heroic spirits"—specifically, "the founders and martyrs of our church and constitution, of our civil and religious liberty"—as so many "fanatics and bewildered enthusiasts." He then makes the following argument about authentic history: "[It confirms] by irrefragable evidence the aphorism of ancient wisdom, that nothing great was ever atchieved [sic] without enthusiasm. For what is enthusiasm but the oblivion and swallowing-up of self in an object dearer than self, or in an idea more vivid? . . . [I]n the genuine enthusiasm of morals, religion, and patriotism, this enlargement and elevation of the soul above its mere self attest the presence, and accompany the intuition of ultimate PRINCIPLES alone."[5] However, Coleridge was not the first modern critic to make the statement on enthusiasm either; in fact, the appeal to enthusiasm's intuition of ultimate principles reflects his reading of Immanuel Kant, who states in "Essay on the Maladies of the Head" (1764) that the excitation of one's fantasy—a mental exaltation and rapturous feeling—by "moral sensations that are in themselves good is *enthusiasm*, and nothing great has ever been accomplished without it."[6] I will have much more to say about Kantian enthusiasm below, but to continue with our constellation of source materials, it also seems likely that Emerson would have been familiar with a statement made by the eighteenth-century New England divine, Jonathan Edwards, who wrote in *Some Thoughts Concerning the Present Revival of Religion in New-England* (1742), "Most of the great things that have been done in the world of mankind, the great revolutions that have been accomplished in the kingdoms and empires of the earth, have been chiefly owing to these things"—"zeal and resolution," and Edwards lists among his examples none other than Oliver Cromwell, but also the most famous evangelical field preacher and archreligious enthusiast of the eighteenth century, George Whitefield.[7] Taken all together, the above examples show that enthusiasm has a remarkably consistent discursive formation—valorized positively—as the passionate absorption and the loss of the self in or for a moral principle, generative of great historical actions, an idea that weaves together various representatives of Anglo-American Protestantism, Continental Enlightenment, British Romanticism, and American Transcendentalism.

Furthermore, Emerson shares both Coleridge and Edwards's belief in a complementary relationship—a coidentity, even—between revival enthusiasms and political revolution, civil liberty and religious liberty. When, in "Nature" (1836), he celebrates "the action of man upon nature with his entire force," via an "instantaneous in-streaming causing power," Emerson highlights the exemplary and parallel cases of political and religious transformation, "the achievements of a principle, as in religious and political revolutions, and in the abolition of the slave-trade; [and] the miracles of enthusiasm, as those reported of Swedenborg, Hohenlohe, and the Shakers," a perspective which lies at the root of his exhortation: "Build therefore your own world. As fast as you conform your life to the pure idea in your mind, that will unfold its great proportions. A correspondent revolution in things will attend the influx of the spirit."[8] Here the religiously enthused and the politically enthused participate in the same revolution of the world from the inside out, through the strength of ideas and their uncompromising application. Let us note, moreover, that the Emersonian poet likewise abandons himself to his enthusiastic intellect: "The poet knows that he speaks adequately then only when he speaks somewhat wildly, or 'with the flower of the mind'; not with the intellect used as an organ, but with the intellect released from all service and suffered to take its direction from its celestial life."[9] The politico, the prophet, and the poet: for Emerson, all three are modalities of an enthusiasm that releases selfhood and thought from their functional, instrumental deployment while conflating the values of progressive thought and original revelation, revolutionary activity and creative or divine ecstasy.

Emerson's thinking on enthusiasm is, finally, more a radical summation of antebellum cultural logics than a defiance of them; it reflects a distinct swerve toward inspired selfhood that became popular in the 1830s as an outgrowth of the Second Great Awakening.[10] No matter where one lay on the political spectrum and cultural-regional map, Americans in Emerson's day by and large ascribed to "the two major systems of belief in early nineteenth-century America—Protestant evangelical Christianity and natural rights philosophy,"[11] although Emerson's Transcendentalism certainly represented one of the most extreme and subversive variants of the enthusiastic mode to his contemporaries. Regarding the citation of Cromwell, for instance, the Anglo-American Puritan heritage invoked by Emerson had been largely flattened or revamped in the antebellum era to describe what it (Puritanism) never actually tolerated: "a lawflouting individualism that appeared variously in militant Abolitionism, Transcendentalist self-reliance, and the 'individual sovereignty' championed by anarchists and free-love activists."[12] One proslavery satire of Emerson sheds light on the way that critics recognized the dangerous political implications of enthusiasm: "Emerson, holds that he is God; that God is every thing; therefore he is every thing.... Do you wonder, therefore, that since he makes the Negro a part of himself, he holds him to be his equal?"[13] This critique recalls the most consistent definition of the religious enthusiast between the years 1650 and 1850—one who pretends to be in immediate contact with God. To be sure, the satire of Emerson taps into a legacy of antienthusiasm that goes back to the historical site of civil war Puritanism itself, and it invokes the same logic behind Enlightenment critiques of enthusiasm from the seventeenth and eighteenth century.[14]

Take Henry More's foundational 1656 disquisition against the Protectorate and enthusiastic sectaries during the Interregnum, *Enthusiasmus Triumphatus*, which argues that enthusiasm should be treated as an inflammation and disorder of the passions, a "*naturall inebriation*" or "*heated* Melancholy"[15] that expresses itself variously depending on how dry or wet, hot or cold, it happens to be in a given enthusiast. When he levels his criticism against natural philosophy (the Theosophists and Chemists) and "political *Enthusiasm*" respectively, More contends that the former type of enthusiasm blasphemes by professing that "Nature is the Body of God, nay God the Father, who is also the World, and whatsoever is any way sensible or perceptible"; as a result, "a mans self is God," since "all is Gods self,"[16] a critique that is identical to the charge against Emerson. In a complementary fashion, political enthusiasts play God when, having "a strong sense of Civil rights, *Melancholy* heating them makes them sometimes fancy themselves great Princes (at least by divine assignment) and Deliverers of the people sent from God."[17] Looking forward to Edmund Burke's historical genealogy of enthusiastic heresies as mentioned in my introduction, More makes sure to mention that the German Anabaptists only pretended to have a politics, when a perverse desire to take many wives was their true motivation, just as the Quakers (who were persecuted at this time) confuse their epileptic paroxysms with divine inspiration.[18]

It will be helpful to note here that the modern European usage of the word "enthusiasm" did first describe religious sects associated with radical Protestantism, especially in the German Peasants' War of 1524–25 and the Münster Rebellion of 1534–35. As J. G. A. Pocock explains, the modern currency of enthusiasm referred to "the fury of the millennial sects, expressed by those who had figured in the Peasants War in Germany and the Anabaptist rebellion at Münster, in whom the Spirit seemed to have come to overturn the Law and to have inspired an antinomian determination to destroy the ruling structures of church, state, and land, together with conventional morality."[19] According to Susie Tucker, the earliest definitions of enthusiasm or the enthusiast in the seventeenth century—namely, "one pretending to divine revelation and inspiration"—derive from the historical context of the Anabaptists.[20] The baton is then passed from the Anabaptist rebellion to the English Civil War with Oliver Cromwell fitted to the play the role of Thomas Müntzer; in English culture, the term "enthusiasm" came into circulation as part of the "polemics against the radical sects emerging around time of the [English] Civil War."[21]

Given that the emergent Enlightenment had "acute anxieties about the continuing public threat posed to the state by Enthusiastic sectaries, as evidenced in the excesses of the Interregnum,"[22] perhaps it comes as no surprise that Henry More's brand of antienthusiasm would find new historical avatars in eighteenth-century Europe and the "culture of reform"[23] linked to the cultivation of sentiment and sensibility. As Jon Mee states in *Romanticism, Enthusiasm, and Regulation* (2003), the discursive formation of enthusiasm "across the long eighteenth century" was meant "to identify something that was taken to transgress the boundaries of the emergent bourgeois public sphere" and that "swept away domesticity and work discipline into the inchoate passions of the crowd, or, at the other extreme, tempted the prophet into an unsociable and unworldly isolation":[24] "in general the discourse of sensibility deserves to be understood as a process for regulating enthusiasm."[25] However, this process of regulation eventually brought enthusiasm itself "inside the conversation of culture,"[26] effectively transforming and complicating the term, namely, through its "gradual aestheticization" as a core element of exceptional poetic practice.[27]

One finds an exemplary and illuminating case of this regulation at work in Voltaire's *Philosophical Dictionary* (1764) and *Questions on the Encyclopedia* (1770–74).[28] In the entries on "Enthousiasme" and "Fanatisme" included in both works (albeit much expanded in *Questions*), the great polemicist's first instinct is to introduce a comparative distinction between the two terms, the latter of which is a specifically religious error, whereas enthusiasm is a normative but nevertheless dangerous affective quality of the imagination. Fanaticism refers to frenzied religious zealots who kill in the name of God and willfully contest the critical use of reason. Here we have the true enemy of Enlightenment. Enthusiasm, on the other hand, refers more generically to a physiological condition, specifically a mode of the affections that he curiously defines from the Greek as the "*disturbance of the entrails, internal agitation.*" Voltaire then asks a series of philological questions about the term but has no definitive answer; among other things, he wonders if the term originally describes "the precipitate rush of the fiery spirits that mount from the entrails to the brain when one is deeply moved," or if it was "first given to the contractions of that Pythia who, on the tripod at Delphi, received the spirit of Apollo through a part which seems made only to receive bodies,"[29] a wry allusion to accounts that the spirits entered the Oracle of Delphi through her vaginal canal.

Voltaire finally has recourse to an example that will best explain enthusiasm. We are in attendance at a tragic play. A geometrician politely judges its aesthetic qualities, a young man next to him experiences the pure pleasure of the spectacle, a woman cries in response, but "another young man is so carried away ["transporté," enraptured] that, unhappily for him, he also decides to write a tragedy: he has caught the disease of enthusiasm"[30] ["la maladie de l'enthousiasme"].[31] This comic scene captures the contagious and mimetic associations of enthusiasm in the eighteenth century but turns it into a symptom of the artist complex, and from there, Voltaire can then extract a more or less contemporary definition of enthusiasm as a drunkenness specific to "devoted and possessed partisans"[32] of any beloved object: "Enthusiasm is precisely like wine: it can excite so much tumult in the blood vessels, and such violent vibrations in the nerves, that the reason is entirely destroyed."[33] Therefore, as he puts it in *Questions*, enthusiasm still has a qualitative relationship to the irrationalism of fanaticism: "enthusiasm then is at it highest point, fanaticism; and fanaticism has become madness"[34] ["l'enthousiasme alors est parvenu à son dernier degré qui est le fanatisme; et ce fanatisme est devenu rage"].[35] If an enthusiast reaches the summit of drunken fury, she crosses the threshold of sensibility into a new category that has its own entry in the dictionary; in sum, enthusiasm becomes a religious passion synonymous with madness, no matter the object, when it reaches a certain temperature.

But based on his definition, Voltaire also has to admit that enthusiasm is a constitutive affect of the body such that it is not a matter of opposing but tempering it. In proper combination with reason, which "consists of always seeing things as they are," enthusiasm is a healthy tonic without which no great oratory and art exists. As Voltaire's analogy goes, one can drink a little wine without getting drunk so as to "cause only slight jolts, which merely produce a little more activity in the brain. This is what happens in great outbursts of eloquence, and above all in sublime poetry. Rational enthusiasm ["L'enthousiasme raissonable"][36] is the attribute of great poets." Subsequently, Voltaire says that reason is to enthusiasm as the design or structure of an artwork is to its animation and imagination. Reason holds the brush, but enthusiasm "takes over" as the painter endows characters "with passions,"[37] an image that is consistent with Voltaire's definition of the fanatic as a lawless individual who acknowledges no design or order in politics or religion. One assumes that our young tragedian, although no fanatic proper, tends toward aesthetic fanaticism on a continuum between reason and madness, between sublime art and frenzied religion. It's an attempt, then, on Voltaire's part to divide aesthetic and religious inspiration around the categories of enthusiasm and fanaticism. Fanatics obey, comprehend, or listen to no other law *than* their enthusiasm: "their enthusiasm is the only law to which they need attend"[38] ["leur enthousiasme est la seule loi qu'ils doivent entendre"].[39] Once again, it is not enthusiasm itself that causes the error but enthusiasm unhinged and lawless. Enthusiasm is the mediating term for the affections distributed between the order of rational Enlightenment (philosophy) and the disorder of irrational Fanaticism (religion).

But why, finally, does the dividing line between enthusiasm and fanaticism matter? Ultimately, because they lead to different political consequences. In *Questions*, Voltaire cites Oliver Cromwell as the representative fanatic who confuses his politics with religion, or to be more precise, marshals his religion for politically despotic ends; on the other hand, his early supporter but eventual critic Edmund Ludlow was "an enthusiast for liberty," not "a fanatic in religion" like Cromwell. As for the New Model Army, "Mahomet himself was never better served by soldiers."[40] That Cromwell might or might not be an enthusiast for liberty, depending on the shifting scale of historical judgment, speaks to both the incompatible intellectual worlds of Voltaire and Emerson but also the instability—perhaps impossibility—of drawing a clear boundary between religious and secular, reasonable and unreasonable, embodiments of enthusiasm; and in a wonderful irony, only a few decades after publishing his dictionary, Voltaire himself will be sullied as a philosophical fanatic, interchangeable with an unhinged enthusiast, in Edmund Burke's diatribe against Enlightenment reformers. Notice though that, while Voltaire's critique demarcates and defines enthusiasm according to genres and disciplines (art, politics, and religion), Emerson, writing in the 1830s United States, no longer has any use for such clear-cut distinctions, it would seem because art, religion, and politics exist for him less as distinct institutions or cultures and more as conduits or domains through which the univocal "energizing spirit" of enthusiasm passes. Over/against the critical standards of the seventeenth and eighteenth century that forged the conceptual terrain of antienthusiasm, Emerson's ability to unapologetically condone enthusiasm reflects a shift in sensibility that Charles Taylor influentially describes as the "nova effect"—a historical understanding of "secularity" defined, not as the decline of discrete religious commitment or the liberal separation of secular and sacred institutions, but rather as the pluralization, fragmentation, and ambiguous collusion or piecemeal adoption of religious and secular ideas, including an "ever-widening variety of moral/spiritual options" that emerges out of the Enlightenment but comes to fruition in the nineteenth century.[41] With Emerson and other Transcendentalists, we see the cultural ascent of that enthusiasm denounced in the eighteenth century: "The Enthusiast whether religious or poetic," who "stands for freedom, individual personality, non-conformity, imagination—in a phrase, for the heart rather than the head."[42] As Amos Bronson Alcott wrote in *The Dial* in 1840, "Believe, youth, that your heart is an oracle; trust her instinctive auguries, obey her divine leadings; nor listen too fondly to the uncertain echoes of your head. The heart is the prophet of your soul, and ever fulfills her prophecies.... Great is the heart: cherish her; she is big with the future, she forebodes renovations. Let the flame of enthusiasm fire alway [sic] your bosom. Enthusiasm is the glory and hope of the world."[43]

Still, this affirmative shift in the concept of enthusiasm deserves further explanation on at least two fronts: working backward, by attending, first, to the transformative effects of the Revolutionary era on the political meaning of enthusiasm and, second, to the history of enthusiasm in the American colonies leading up to the Revolution. In the context of the French Revolutionary debates, I turn primarily to Immanuel Kant in order to develop a strong theory of enthusiasm as the constituent power of the people's right to dissent, a theory that Kant both explains and dismisses by claiming a constitutional notion of moral enthusiasm compatible with the ideals of deliberative reform. Contrariwise, Thomas Paine adopts precisely that form of enthusiasm rejected by Kant. The Kantian-Paineite problematic of enthusiasm will show up time and again throughout this study; it indicates the competing claims for enthusiasm in the era and its process of regulation at work. By way of illustrating enthusiasm's influence on the literary imagination, I also take up the fiction of Nathaniel Hawthorne, not in order to make the case that he is an enthusiast, but to demonstrate that a recognized antebellum author such as Hawthorne belongs to the same intellectual tradition of Kant and Paine and continues to work through—and interpret—the long history of enthusiasm in narrative form. After my discussion of the French Revolutionary debates, I show how the theory of enthusiasm in the American colonies already looks forward to Paine and the modern political theory of constituent power, and I argue that, from the Antinomian Crisis to the First Great Awakening, the back history of religious enthusiasm in colonial America should be read as an expression of constituent power against the Biblical constitutionalism of the Puritan ruling class. Finally, in the last section, I turn back to the Revolutionary context and emphasize how the politics of enthusiasm discussed in the previous sections influences the development of early U.S. literature and forces us to distinguish it from the culture and literature of sentiment. My two examples—Charles Brockden Brown's *Ormond* (1799) and Sarah Pogson's *The Female Enthusiast* (1807)—make it clear, first, that literature intervened on the debates surrounding enthusiasm in philosophy, politics, and religion, and second, that Brown and Pogson in particular defend the enthusiast—specifically the constituent power of women—against the status quo of sentimental selfhood and domestic rationalism.

Tremulous Enthusiasm: Constituent Power and the Paradox of Constitutionalism

In a series of unpublished essays and lecture transcripts on Immanuel Kant dating from 1978–1984 and compiled as *The Politics of Truth* (1997, 2007), Michel Foucault argues that the critical project of modernity that Kant reflected in philosophy transformed the task of thinking from high metaphysics to an engagement with the historical present as both a singular event and ongoing process of human emancipation from its self-incurred bondage. Kant taught us that the present—"our own actuality, what is happening around us"[44]—should be both the object and the condition of thought, and this took the form of two questions that Foucault believes still have not been answered: "What is Enlightenment?" and "What is Revolution?" The eponymous 1784 essay devoted to the first question is well known; Kant took up the latter question most explicitly in the lesser-known book *The Contest of Faculties* (1798), specifically the section "A Renewed Attempt to Answer the Question: 'Is the Human Race Continually Improving?'," which Foucault sees as a follow-up to "An Answer to the Question: 'What is Enlightenment?'"

In "Renewed Attempt," Kant explains that, for moral philosophy, the function of history is not to record or account for the deeds and fortunes of humans or to archive the past but to measure human progress strictly against the ideal of "popular enlightenment" as constituted by civil law. Kant's belief, however, that we live in "age of *enlightenment*," not a fulfilled "*enlightened age*,"[45] would remain purely theoretical without the "search for an event," a "rough indication or *historical sign*," that can prove to the world that "man has the quality or power of being the *cause* and ... the *author* of his own improvement."[46] Once published to the world, this event would deliver a knowledge of political freedom that will never allow humanity to submit to political retrogression, but instead will inspire further acts of political self-authorship. Even if it ultimately fails to accomplish the aim, the French Revolution's "moral cause" was such an event, evoking sympathy in "the onlookers as it reveals itself *in public* while the drama of great political changes is taking place."[47] That these onlookers live far from the scene of that drama, have nothing to gain from it personally, and may even be subject to punishment for sympathizing with it proves the disinterested nature of the moral judgment connected to enthusiasm for the cause: "All this [the foundation of republican government], along with the *passion* or *enthusiasm* with which men embrace the cause of goodness (although the former cannot be entirely applauded, since all passion as such is blameworthy), gives historical support for the following assertion, which is of considerable anthropological significance: true enthusiasm is always directed exclusively toward the *ideal*, particularly toward that which is purely moral (such as the concept of right), and it cannot be coupled with selfish interests."[48] For Kant, enthusiasm is properly an affect oriented toward the political future: it manifests itself in the present as a collective feeling about an event measured against an ideal right that does not currently exist. Nevertheless, humankind can progress through a commitment to the ideal.

As Foucault is quick to emphasize, the "historical sign" of enlightenment does not lie in the Revolution itself or depend upon the actual success or failure of the Revolution but rather in the *"enthusiasm* for the Revolution which is something other than the revolutionary enterprise itself."[49] Foucault's interest in this text has to do with Kant's decoupling of the ongoing will for revolutionary enlightenment and the failure of the revolutionary events to live up to their own possibilities or the ideals of right; and yet, at the same time, the French Revolution can still be a historical index (a memory that will not be forgotten, according to Kant) that humanity wanted, wants, and will want revolution and enlightenment—"to rise up and make renewed attempts of the same kind as before,"[50] says Kant. If we take Kant (and Foucault) at his word, then the question "What is Revolution?" is more exactly the question "What is Enthusiasm?" The French Revolution is dead and gone but the enthusiasm for an event of self-authored freedom lives on. Enthusiasm is both our affective response to and expectation of further moral progress.

However, three ideas need to be highlighted in Kant's account of enthusiasm: first, it is a posterior condition of responsive spectatorship; second, Kant curiously goes on to add that the people may not "pursue their rights by revolution, which is at all times unjust"; and last, the "historical sign" of enthusiasm actually indexes not the Revolution or the moral ideal as such, but "the *evolution* of a constitution governed by *natural right*."[51] Each of these points derives from one and the same idea: true enthusiasm does not accord with revolutionary participation. The question becomes: how can Kant deny the right to revolution and yet enthuse over its outcomes, its constitutional effects, its moral idea? The first part of the question has a clear answer; the latter not so much. In "Renewed Attempt," he explains: "These [civil] rights, however, always remain an idea which can be fulfilled only on condition that the *means* employed to do so are compatible with morality. This limiting condition must not be overstepped by the people, who may not therefore pursue their rights by revolution, which is at all times unjust."[52] In other words, constitutional means must be employed to reform government since constitutional ends are the goal of politics. It is a contradiction to act unconstitutionally in the name of constitutionalism. By the same logic, in "On the Common Saying: 'This May Be True in Theory, but It Does Not Apply in Practice'" (1793), Kant argues that the state's authority is absolute: "The reason for this is that the people, under an existing civil constitution, has [sic] no longer any right to judge how the constitution should be administered."[53] This idea goes to the core of what some constitutional theorists call "the paradox of constitutionalism": republican constitutions, to the letter, derive their power and authority from the consent of the people, but at the same time, propping up the apparatus of the state, constitutions exercise authority and power over—they constitute—the people, who no longer have any right to abolish, alter, or reform forms of government even though those rights were presupposed in the founding act of the constitution itself. Kant supports constitutional form, not "constituent power," that is, the "power of a people to make, and therefore also to break, the constituted authority of the state"[54] when the former's "real" sovereignty has been compromised by the powers claiming to speak on the people's behalf.[55]

In *Insurgencies: Constituent Power and the Modern State* (1992, 1999 in English), Antonio Negri argues that Kant's critique of political judgment is powerful insofar as it posits that the "revolution can never end: it is the soul of ethics," but this nevertheless turns out to be a Kantian sophism that negates constituent power: "Constituent power is entrusted to ethics and therefore taken away from politics."[56] This leads to Negri's own definition and defense of constituent power: "the paradigm of constituent power is that of a force that bursts apart, breaks, interrupts, unhinges any preexisting equilibrium and any possible continuity. Constituent power is tied to the notion of democracy as absolute power," and thus it "clashes with constitutionalism."[57] According to Negri, constituent power is the "revolutionary extension of the human capacity to construct history, as a fundamental act of innovation, and therefore as an absolute procedure" of democracy. In the American context, we tend to think of constituent power less in terms of revolutionary and more in terms of governing power, that is, as a principle of constituted authority rooted in a strong doctrine of popular sovereignty, for example, in the creation of the early state constitutions from which the term "constituent power" derives.[58] But of course, such a governing power, as many of the early state constitutions recognized, is unthinkable apart from the revolutionary conditions articulated by the Declaration of Independence, a document that formalizes the "expression of the rights preceding any constitution" as the "permanent expression of constituent power."[59] Although Americans often extol the Constitutional Convention of 1787 as the exemplary case of the people's constituting action,[60] legal historian Christian Fritz has demonstrated that a vibrant, contentious debate over competing constitutional visions of popular sovereignty continued through the Civil War: against a "constrained" conception of government-sanctioned constitutional reform, some Americans took an "expansive" view of constituent power that guaranteed the right of a majority to revise constitutions without limit, "even independent of government."[61] A strong theory of constituent power posits that progressive, ever-evolving democratic rights, sometimes blocked by constitutional limits, give "rationality and substance to the law,"[62] not the other way around. Just as there is no political event, in Kant's sense, without its posterior response, there is also no event, no democratic progress, no constitutional revolution, without antecedent action, without the constituent power unleashed by the subjects of a politics. From the posterior angle, isolated historical events of constituent power do produce political memories, but these become springboards for further events, "a product of constituent power in action; it is not continuity but innovation" pushing off from a past memory: "It makes of each event a testimonial and of each testimonial an act of militancy."[63]

In "The Gray Champion" (1835, 1837), Nathaniel Hawthorne illustrates the idea of revolutionary constituent power in the American context and, tellingly, conjures the specter of Oliver Cromwell as its historical incarnation. The historical plot of this story revolves around the 1689 Boston revolt against the authoritarian rule of Sir Edmund Andros, governor of the Dominion of New England, and James II's revocation of the New England colonial charters. Outraged by the renunciation of their privileges, the town multitudes gather as the royal administration and British troops parade through the streets; the regal pomp and power of the latter illustrates a "moral," says the narrator: it shows "the deformity of any government that does grow out of the nature of things and the character of the people."[64] And yet, the old colonial patriarch and former governor of Massachusetts Bay, Simon Bradstreet, enjoins the crowd to submit to the authorities, pray to God, and otherwise wait patiently for deliverance: in other words, he admonishes them to be good Kantians. The people's rights cannot be claimed through extralegal means. But as the crowd cries out for a champion of the people, a shadowy, ancient figure arrives whom nobody recognizes. He remains nameless, a "venerable stranger,"[65] but he wears the dress of an old Puritan. He stops the Crown's parade. Then the narration reads, "A tremulous enthusiasm seized upon the multitude. That stately form, combining the leader and the saint, so gray, so dimly seen, in such an ancient garb, could only belong to some old champion of the righteous cause, whom the oppressor's drum had summoned from his grave. They raised a shout of awe and exultation, and looked for the deliverance of New-England."[66] This enthusiastic seizure, so fraught with anxiety and anticipation, represents the opposite of eventual posteriority—the Gray Champion stands for the extralegal confrontation with constituted power. As the Gray Champion speaks, "his voice stirred their [the people's] souls. They confronted the soldiers, not wholly without arms, and ready to convert the very stones of the street into deadly weapons."[67] Now they burn with a "lurid wrath," compelling the British soldiers to retreat. The Gray Champion's message further reveals himself to be the allegorical embodiment of constituent power: "I am here . . . because the cry of an oppressed people hath disturbed me in my secret place" for the "good old cause."[68] After their victory, "the people were thronging tumultuously"[69] but the Champion disappears; he himself *does* nothing, but his words inspire the people to convert themselves into a public of tremulous enthusiasm.

Moreover, Hawthorne writes the "Gray Champion" as a constituent memory of the American Revolution. The ending makes the allegory clear: the Gray Champion appears in King Street at the Boston Massacre, "on the green" at Lexington, and finally at Bunker Hill. Then: "Long, long may it be, ere he comes again! His hour is one of darkness, and adversity, and peril. But should domestic tyranny oppress us, or the invader's step pollute our soil, still may the Gray Champion come."[70] The revival of the Gray Champion's revolt breaks out in any political crisis of tyranny, past, present, or future. He is a sign that Americans wanted, want, and will want to defend democracy, and, at least according to one of the royal governor's men, he gives his "proclamation in Old Noll's name!"[71]—a nickname for Cromwell. Always a great reader of history, Hawthorne probably knew that Cromwell was invoked as an inspiration for the American Revolution, a subject I will return to in the next chapter, but here I wish only to repeat that Cromwell, for both Emerson and Voltaire, is the archetypal figure of the enthusiast, understood by Hawthorne like his fellow American as a symbol for revolutionary constituent power.

Kant also cites Cromwell in "Renewed Attempt," albeit as an example of unconstitutional political activity. If one were to warrant the appearance of the Gray Champion, then, as Kant puts it in *The Metaphysics of Morals* (1797), "the supreme legislation would have to contain a provision to the effect that it is not supreme, so that in one and the same judgement, the people as subjects would be made sovereign over the individual to whom they are subject."[72] Along the same line of reasoning, Kant resorts to this tortured logic in a footnote from "Perpetual Peace: A Philosophical Sketch" (1795): in the case of "a violent *revolution* resulting from a previous bad constitution, it would then no longer be permissible to lead the people back to the original one, even although everyone who had interfered with the old constitution by violence or conspiracy would rightly have been subject to the penalties of rebellion during the revolution itself."[73] Thus, if the illegal act of revolution produces a better constitution, it is also illegal to restore the old constitution that it was illegal to violate. This is, in fact, the very logic that implicitly informs and explains Kant's stance on the French Revolution. Although I am well aware that it is possible to claim a formal consistency to Kant's argument (a logical separation between his affirmation of legitimate moral ends and his critique of the illegitimate violent means for achieving them),[74] the *historical* contradiction remains that each and every constitution that Kant commends (that of Switzerland, the United Netherlands, and Great Britain) was, as he himself admits, brought into existence by revolution, but he nevertheless maintains that political transformation must occur "by the sovereign himself through *reform*."[75] We are left with this impasse of a thesis: revolutionary constituent power is never right or constitutional, but only it produces right or republican constitutions.

Kant's recuperative concept of enthusiasm, then, turns out to be the antithesis of enthusiasm as I have introduced it, and Kant usually reserved the language of "Schwärmerei," or fanaticism, for such cases. In "Renewed Attempt," this enthusiasm is alluded to in a footnote where Kant says that philosophers have every right to "think up political constitutions which meet the requirements of reason (particularly in matters of right)," but "it is *foolhardy* to put them forward seriously, and *punishable* to incite the people to do away with the existing constitution." The "pleasant dream" of realizing such ideas is, in H. B. Nisbet's translation, the result of "the fantasies of an overheated mind,"[76] translated by Mary J. Gregor as "the dreaming of a distraught mind."[77] The German reads "Träumerei eines überspannten Kopfs,"[78] more literally, the dreaming or raving of an overstretched/overextended mind. This dreaming thinker expects too much from humanity, and only Oliver Cromwell, with his "abortive attempt to establish a despotic republic," was crazy enough to follow through on his utopian fantasies, to try out "in practice" his ideas.[79] Clearly, the enthusiast is the Gray Champion who runs roughshod over existing laws or constitutions—*he or she is the agent of constituent power*.

In order to better understand Kant's ideas on the overextended brain of enthusiasm, one has to return to an early text, *Observations on the Feeling of the Beautiful and Sublime* (1764). Therein, Kant defines enthusiasm as the point of immoral excess in the sublime personality: "In the degenerate form of this character, seriousness inclines to dejection, piety to zealotry ["Schwärmerei," fanaticism], the fervor for freedom to enthusiasm ["Enthusiasmus"]."[80] Like Voltaire, Kant goes on to distinguish fanaticism and enthusiasm as the difference between a strictly religious and an affective-ethical error: "Fanaticism ["Der Fanaticism"] must always be distinguished from **enthusiasm** ["Enthusiasmus"]. The former believes itself to feel an immediate and extraordinary communion with a higher nature, the latter signifies the state of the mind which is inflamed ["erhitzt," heated] beyond the appropriate degree by some principle, whether it be by the maxim of patriotic virtue, or of friendship, or of religion, without involving the illusion of a supernatural community."[81] The key term here is "inflammation," akin to Cromwell's distraught, overheated, or overextended state of mind, but most important of all, fanaticism has now taken over the older negative definition of enthusiasm as a pretense of divine communication or identity, thus allowing Kant to tether enthusiasm to positive ideas—the "fervor for freedom," an ethical "principle" or virtuous maxim.

By the time he writes *Critique of the Power of Judgment* (1790), Kant betrays a new ambivalence about said enthusiasm. On the one hand, it still occurs when the "idea of the good" has been corrupted by "blind" "affect," which results in a "movement of the mind" overwhelming our "free consideration of principles" under the court of pure reason, but on the other hand: "Nevertheless, enthusiasm is aesthetically sublime, because it is a stretching of the powers through ideas," although the proper, or superior, sublime necessitates a disinterested "affectlessness."[82] Enthusiasm, as a species of the sublime aesthetic judgment, happens when the body gets too excited and inflamed about an otherwise unimpeachable ethical principle or idea such as the concept of right. In the contemplation of the "**idea of freedom**" beyond any "positive presentation" or "determining ground outside it [the moral law]," if one gives in to "tumultuous and unpremeditated" affections comparable to a "**delusion of sense**"—"Wahnsinn,"[83] madness or mania—then a threshold or border has been crossed, and this is enthusiasm: "a passing accident, which occasionally affects the most healthy understanding" when it reflects upon the sublime object under consideration.[84]

Now we can finally understand why the onlooker's sympathy for the French Revolution "borders almost on enthusiasm"[85] ("die nahe an Enthusiasm grenzt"):[86] it nearly reached the point of excess where the response was *interested* and corrupted by a strong affection that would threaten to make one a mad partisan. Furthermore, I can now fully accent why Kant speaks of a "true enthusiasm," implicitly, *as opposed to a false enthusiasm*. This true enthusiasm points to Kant's regulation of the term on par with Voltaire's "rational enthusiasm": it faces only the sublime ideal of freedom and not any sensible or manifest "phenomenon" of that freedom—the French Revolution. So we have two enthusiasms in play. While true enthusiasm supports the "moral cause" of republican constitutionalism, false enthusiasm crosses the border into France and becomes inflamed by revolution or conjures up the Gray Champion to convert the stones into weapons. The confusion and intersection of these two enthusiasms is the confusion and intersection of constituent power and constitutional power—the paradox of constitutionalism. And yet, as one imagines Governor Bradstreet doing, Kant still allows us to sit on the border of France and perhaps even indulge in a "transitory accident" of a not entirely defensible affected enthusiasm, so long as this moral response does not definitively cross that border.

While Kant's desire to preempt his French Revolution and have it too obscures the pivotal role that "false enthusiasm" plays in the people's constituent power, this role is easier to discern and appreciate in the French Revolutionary debates between Edmund Burke and Thomas Paine. In *Reflections on the Revolution in France* (1790), Burke represents Kant's view of enthusiasm without the paradox of constitutionalism: if constituent power is wrong, then so is anything that this power effects, constitutional or otherwise, which is why he emphasizes that the members of the French national assembly who seized power "do not hold the authority they exercise under any constitutional law of the state."[87] Accordingly, the main thrust of Burke's argument, part and parcel of the secularizing discourse of antienthusiasm, reduces to what he views as a confusion of clear institutional categories—religion and politics. Since the pulpit and politics, the passions for divine and civil equality, should never mix, a radical preacher such as Richard Price refutes himself by delivering a "political sermon" with a "political gospel"—while his "enthusiasm kindles"—in support of the French Revolution.[88] Enlightenment intellectuals and men of letters are all enthusiasts insofar as they, after Rousseau, promote a "species of the marvelous" "in life, in manners, in characters, and in extraordinary situations, giving rise to new and unlooked-for strokes in politics and morals."[89] The French Revolution itself—in particular, the mob violence against the Crown—resembles "Theban and Thracian Orgies" kindling a "prophetic enthusiasm" of "unguarded transport."[90] Burke's allusion to orgiastic and prophetic cultures of ancient Greece shows his due and rigorous attention to philology: enthusiasm, literally derived from the Greek *enthousiasmos* for an "in-pouring or in-breathing of the divine,"[91] denoted possession by the god or gods and "came into use to describe the ecstasy of the Dionysian rites. The Dionysian reveler was an 'enthusiast' because he became inspired by drinking the wine in which Dionysus literally dwelled. The aesthetic meaning given to 'enthusiasm' was thus an extension of its religious meaning, stemming from the Greek belief in the religious inspiration of poetry."[92] However, it is often not understood (especially for those of us most familiar with Nietzsche's philosophical appropriation of Dionysus) that Dionysus "was essentially a god of the people, offering freedom and joy to all, including slaves as well as freemen excluded from the old lineage cults."[93] Even in ancient Rome, the Senate took strong actions to control and suppress the Bacchanalia, and Dionysian publics more or less posed the same kind of threat for Livy as the French Revolutionaries do for Burke.

One of the key enthusiasts to oppose Burke's thinking was, of course, Thomas Paine. And, in *Rights of Man* (1791), Paine's vision of democracy can be read as a strong apology for a positive theory of constituent power. That's why, in his critique of Burke, Paine states that the "error of those who reason by precedents drawn from antiquity, respecting the rights of man, is, that they do not go far enough into antiquity"[94] to the constituent foundation of tradition or authority. When one does this, it becomes clear that governments, at their root, "must have arisen, either *out* of the people, or *over* the people," through constituent forms of governance from below by right of compact or through despotic forms of governance from above by right of conquest.[95] As Paine's constitutional logic goes, "A constitution is a thing *antecedent* to a government, and a government is only the creature of a constitution. The constitution of a country is not the act of its government, but of the people constituting a government."[96] Both Kant and Burke, by synthesizing the constitution and the government, make the constitution *of* governments, prior to their own authorization, formally impossible to think from within their own categories, since any constituting power, at its foundational moment, will necessarily have broken all the moral laws that they deem absolute. Put simply, governments and constitutions can be established only by revolutionary democracy or revolutionary tyranny. Paine removes the paradox of constitutionalism from the opposite angle: all constitutions dynamically remain the people's creation. It is no coincidence that Kant's enlightened absolutism, founded on a defense of constituent tyranny, has never produced any constitution that meets his standards: that is why the paradox exists. For sure, the paradox of constitutionalism means that a government has already robbed the people of their constituent power by law—the nation-state has "suffocated" and "absorbed" it.[97]

For Paine, the constituent principle of revolution should, contrariwise, never be curbed until every monarchical regime has been overthrown. The "revolutions of America and France have thrown a beam of light over the world," and the "more it is struck, the more sparks it will emit; and the fear is, it will not be struck enough";[98] at the same time, Paine incorporates Kant's core idea that an enthusiasm for democracy and self-authored political progress is delivered over to the world through the political event. He says of French Revolutionary enthusiasm, "That the Bastille was attacked with an enthusiasm of heroism, such only as the highest animation of liberty could inspire, and carried in the space of a few hours, is an event which the world is fully possessed of," and once possessed of that event, history cannot regress: "Those who talk of a counter revolution in France, shew how little they understand of man. There does not exist in the compass of language, an arrangement of words to express so much as the means of affecting a counter revolution. The means must be an obliteration of knowlege [*sic*]; and it has never yet been discovered, how to make man *unknow* his knowledge, or *unthink* his thoughts."[99] As a writer, Paine takes up his pen to disseminate the knowledge of this event, to give evental posterity to enthusiasm, just as one can read Hawthorne's "Gray Champion" as an act of constituent memory posted to the future. And yet Paine's enthusiasm, like the enthusiasm of the Gray Champion, does not so much live among the spectators as among the actors who attacked the Bastille and among the partisans of the "good old cause" whose "animation of liberty" will always move people to storm the Bastille wherever it exists. Paine's "enthusiasm of heroism," finally, translates into his own ethical maxim of public right and constituent power: "Lay then the axe to the root, and teach governments humanity."[100]

Error in the Wilderness: The Enthusiastic Origins of the American Self

When he presses Matthew 3:10 ("And now also the axe is laid unto the root of the trees: therefore every tree which bringeth not forth good fruit is hewn down, and cast into the fire") into the service of revolutionary demands, Thomas Paine invokes a political-theological tradition of American enthusiasm. To name only one example, during the Antinomian Controversy of 1636–38 in the Massachusetts Bay Colony, dissenting preacher John Wheelwright used the same verse in his "Fast-Day Sermon" (1637) in order to argue that Christ came "to send fire upon the earth" and purge those false Christians—the Puritan rulers—who live under "a covenant of works."[101] Consequently, Wheelwright was banished from the colony as an enthusiast.

If orthodox Puritanism in the Massachusetts Bay was defined by the "duty of suppressing heresy, of subduing or somehow getting rid of dissenters—of being, in short, deliberately, vigorously, and consistently intolerant,"[102] then it is necessary to either decouple the Puritan self from the enthusiast or train ourselves to see Puritanism as a polyvalent and heterogeneous phenomenon. Official Puritanism, opposite enthusiasm, adhered to a Biblical polity and constitutional order that articulated a covenant theology strengthening the "legalistic character of the government."[103] Anybody challenging that relationship was by definition an enthusiast, often exiled to Rhode Island, or the "*Iland* [sic] *of errors*,"[104] the most notable example of which is Anne Hutchinson, sister-in-law of John Wheelwright, who "countermanded the New England Way."[105] In the 1636–38 controversy over antinomianism, a word literally meaning "against or opposed to the law," if one reads law as Biblical constitutionalism, then the crux of the debate is about theological constituent power, concretely considered, the right of Hutchinson and her followers to organize their own meetings and advocate for radical reform of church leadership and covenant theology. Take John Wheelwright's aforementioned "Fast-Day Sermon." Wheelwright's thesis against ritual fasting strongly emphasizes what John Cotton phrased as the *"Proxima Potentia"* or "immediate power"[106] of Christ in believers. The antinomian debate was, for him, between two visions of salvation: the justification of believers through a "spiritt [sic] that quickens"—a covenant of grace—versus the sanctification of believers "under a covenant of works" and a sinful state of debt to God.[107] Sanctification organized the Puritan ethic of labor and submission to law as obedience to God's sublime penal authority; to preach justification, however, freed people from coercive, state-mediated institutions—Christ, who is after all the constituent power, the authorizing agent, of the Church, joins himself to the saints. He creates "a mystical community of the elect," exempt from Law, not a contractual relationship "to fulfill God's work in the New World" as the chosen people.[108] The political stakes of this "opinion of Enthusianisme"[109] preoccupied the Puritan elite. John Wheelwright, for instance, proposed to dispense with a clerical order and the biblical errand to conquer sin and convert the faithless: his teaching would, as a result, "cause a combustion in the Church and comon [sic] wealth."[110] John Winthrop said that Wheelwright would have "all things... turned upside down among us";[111] or, as he opines in "The Examination of Mrs. Ann Hutchinson at the court at Newtown," any time religion "runs to enthusiasm," "it overthrows all."[112] Accordingly, the enthusiast's heresy can, to my mind, be reduced to two basic errors out of Winthrop's staggering list of eighty-two: first, "Presume not above that which is written,"[113] or, presume not to innovate upon the colony's constitutional law; and second, "To take delight in the holy service of God, is to go a whoring from God,"[114] or, to relate to God affectively, as a direct and immanent experience, leads to a breach with lawful order, for these *"soule-ravishing expressions and affections"* of the antinomian tempt individuals to *"dance after this pipe"* of enthusiastic heresy.[115]

My sense is that we should take the Assembly of Churches seriously when it claimed that the opinion of enthusiasm was not a mere theological dispute but a civil crisis—*"to raise sedition amongst us, to the indangering of the Common-wealth,"*[116] or in truth, to challenge the Puritan establishment's authority over the people's religious and civic activities. That a woman spreads this heresy, without proper jurisdiction, speaks for itself, but a woman's politics has another threat as well: Hutchinson's influence will certainly be popular among the lower orders. If enthusiasm is synonymous with "*Dux foemina facti*"—"the woman the leader in the act"[117]—then what act? The answer is clear: "that filthie Sinne of the Comunitie of Woemen and all promiscuus and filthie cominge togeather of men and Woemen without Distinction or Relation of Marriage, will necessarily follow"; a woman's enthusiasm leads to "Epicurisme and Libertinisme,"[118] but presumably also a polyamorous communism of the passions. The legalistic opposition to a "desperate enthusiasm" becomes even clearer when Anne Hutchinson, at her trial, gives lucid defenses of her religious positions (countermanding constitutional form) and the court disputes her claims with the correction of tradition. John Cotton betrays the real issue at hand: the "revelations" of the "Enthusiasts and Anabaptists" "broach new matters of faith and doctrine."[119] Ergo, they must be false revelations in a society where the Spirit of God and the Biblical polity are united: "we see not that any should have authority to set up any other exercises besides what authority hath already set up."[120] The debate, then, is over the constituent power of people to break and innovate upon codified understandings of the Bible, and as John Winthrop reminds his audience one hundred and fifty years before Edmund Burke, the Münster tragedy—the "warres in *Germany*"—began as a mere theological dispute over the "sword of the Spirit, yet it was soone changed into a sword of steele."[121]

In his effort both to wrestle with the early woman's (literary) movement in antebellum America[122] and to extract stories out of the American historical archive, Nathaniel Hawthorne once again gives us a critical portrait of enthusiasm's legacy, this time with reference to Anne Hutchinson, in *The Scarlet Letter* (1850). If, as Sacvan Bercovitch famously argues, the political allegory of Hester Prynne teaches the rites of progressive American liberalism, the means by which the nation produces sociopolitical "assent"—moral tolerance, pluralism—through the value-ideal of the separate individual, the "stranger or prophet, rebel or revolutionary, lawbreaker or truth-seeker," "who rejoins the community by compromising for principle,"[123] this allegory could not be more wrong with respect to the historical specter of Anne Hutchinson in the novel, a specter which returns not through Hester but through her daughter Pearl. There are two references to Hutchinson. The first connects her to the "rosebush" that grows outside the town prison where she, like Hester, was held: "it had sprung up under the footsteps of the sainted Ann Hutchinson, as she entered the prison-door."[124] Later Pearl tells Reverend Wilson that "she had not been made at all, but had been plucked by her mother off the bush of wild roses that grew by the prison-door,"[125] that is, she is a flower of Hutchinson's bush. Hold this thought and then look at the second and last Hutchinson reference: "Yet, had little Pearl never come to her [Hester] from the spiritual world, it [her conformity "to the external regulations of society"] might have been far otherwise. Then, she might have come down to us in history, hand in hand with Ann Hutchinson, as the foundress of a religious sect. She might, in one of her phases, have been a prophetess. She might, and not improbably would, have suffered death from the stern tribunals of the period, for attempting to undermine the foundations of the Puritan establishment. But, in the education of her child, *the mother's enthusiasm of thought had something to wreak itself upon.* Providence, in the person of this little girl, had assigned to Hester's charge the germ and blossom of womanhood."[126] First, out of a sense of responsibility to Pearl, Hester does *not* take the way of Anne Hutchinson, who cannot perform Puritan rites of assent. Hester's "enthusiasm of thought," which otherwise would have meant sectarianism and then the political guillotine, directs its energies toward Pearl's education. But where does Hester's "enthusiasm of thought" come from? In the previous paragraph, Hawthorne defines it as the "freedom of speculation, then common enough on the other side of the Atlantic, but which our forefathers, had they known it, would have held to be a deadlier crime than that stigmatized by the scarlet letter."[127] Hawthorne refers to the English Civil War—a watershed moment for radical female prophets[128]—contemporaneous with the novel's events. Hester has absorbed but regulated the spirit of enthusiastic sectaries, a far worse affair than adultery, and this is attached to Anne Hutchinson's antiestablishment ideas.

Pearl, on the other hand, is the unhinged reembodiment of Hutchinson's enthusiasm. In Hawthorne's heretical typology, Hester Prynne, as the anti–Virgin Mary, resembles "by contrast" the "sacred image of sinless motherhood, whose infant was to redeem the world."[129] This turns Pearl into the anti–Christ figure, "worthy to have been brought forth in Eden"[130]—she knows no sin. Here Hawthorne represents antinomianism as post-Calvinist sanctification: "The child could not be made amenable to rules."[131] But outside of the rules, Pearl discovers the enfranchisement of the unbridled wilderness and becomes something like a figure for constituent power understood in affective, vitalistic terms: her "wild flow of spirits," her "wild energy," her "ever creative spirit," and her "perverse merriment" make her a "little jet of flame" that "seemed to remove her entirely out of the sphere of sympathy or human contact."[132] Since she has "nothing in common with a bygone and buried generation, nor owed herself akin to it,"[133] Pearl can roam freely outside the Puritan establishment. And even though they stand on the border of the wilderness, as Kantian onlookers, "breathing the wild, free atmosphere of an unredeemed, unchristianized, lawless region,"[134] neither Hester nor Dimmesdale—chained, ultimately, to a constitutional sense of moral right—can become enthusiastic participants.

One hundred years later in the First Great Awakening of the 1730s and 1740s, the debate over enthusiasm—as religious constituent power—has not significantly changed. If anything, it has intensified. Enthusiasts begin to aggressively, corporately countermand, if only in practice, the unity of church and state in the Congregational establishment. Historians of the Awakening have been strongly divided on a proper interpretation of their importance,[135] but I wish to stress only that the revivalists "promoted a more pluralistic, egalitarian, and voluntaristic social order by defending the free flow of itinerant preachers and their converts across community and denominational lines. The revivalists also imagined an enlarged society: an intercolonial and transatlantic network of congregations."[136] Catering to the masses (women, slaves, "savages") and encouraging them with the language of freedom and equality, religious revivals, to the chagrin of orthodox church establishments, began to spread like wildfire as increased emigration also introduced unprecedented religious pluralism to the colonies. Meanwhile, at the height of the revivals, Britain was at war with Catholic Spain and indirectly France for control of the West Indies. Not only that but the Spanish were accused of inciting America's staple commodity to desertion, and rumors of impending war with Spain may have encouraged slaves to rebel in the largest revolt of British North America: the 1739 Stono Rebellion in South Carolina. The transatlantic traffic of goods and persons brought on by the eighteenth-century consumer revolution did more than deal in dangerous slaves from the West Indies; it also produced a stratified social economy of urban poor and social elites, and an influx of European immigrants, English felons predominant among them. Enthusiasm is a symptom of this unstable and paranoid, fluid and dynamic, climate in colonial North America.[137]

In February 1741, an anonymous and outraged author, writing under the pseudonym of "Theophilus Misodaemon," provides a beautiful figure of speech for the Great Awakening—the "Wonderful Wandering Spirit," which has "haunted our Borders" but also penetrated and confused the polity from within.[138] Some clear characteristics of the Wonderful Wandering Spirit include the following: "[it] deals much by Feelings and Impulses, in violent bodily Convulsions; and pretends to uncommon Discernments. When it possesses the Mob, which it delights to torture, they swell and shake like *Virgil*'s enthusiastick Sybil, or those possess'd with the Devil in the Gospel."[139] The horror of enthusiasm lies in its resistance to borders or discrete form, thwarting any attempt to discover and comprehend its essence: "from the Mobs and Disorders that attend it," some call it Belial "taking a Tour in Disguise;" others hold that "it must be the [lewd] Spirit that inspired the *Bachanals*," still others that it belongs to "the fierce and savage Temper," the fanaticism, of Muhammad; and it was also alive in the spirit that "possess'd the Enthusiasts of *Munster*: The Ranters in *America*, &c. But all that read the History of the Roman Pontifs, think that it was ador'd in dark Times by Pope *Gregory* or *Hildebrand*, and some others of these Holy Necromancers."[140] The paranoia and xenophobia surrounding enthusiasm, then, has by now transcended its roots in Protestant heresy to describe any theological-political culture deemed a threat to the colonial establishment, including the shadowy presence of Catholic Spain.

Thus, once again, the charge of enthusiasm—the very term "enthusiasm" itself—speaks to a political crisis, articulated explicitly as a threat to the civil structure of society and not as a matter of separate church doctrine or theological vision. As Old Light pastor Isaac Stiles said in 1743, the enthusiast is *"given to Change with reference to Civil Affairs."*[141] Enthusiasm begins as an embodied experience of ecstatic disorder that perforce leads to political revolution: "In consequence of this *Vertigo*, or dizziness in the Head, this instability, fickleness & variation in Opinion and Judgment, they are ever & anon for change of Government, and thence are raising a Dust, making a Bustle, and endeavouring to Overset the Government; to turn things *topsy turvy* and bring all into Confusion."[142] The class-consciousness of this sentiment is anything but subtle: the "giddy Multitude of unthinking Mortals"[143] willingly adopt and praise the errors of the enthusiast. Anglican minister Charles Brockwell wrote in 1742, "It is impossible to relate the convulsions into which the whole Country is thrown by a set of Enthusiasts that strole about harangueing the admiring Vulgar in *extempore* nonsense, nor is it confined to these only, for Men, Women, Children, Servants, & Nigros are now become (as they phrase it) Exhorters."[144]

Echoing Stiles and Brockwell, Boston clergyman Charles Chauncy launched the most sustained attack on enthusiasm, and he elaborates on the concrete threats that it posed. On a gendered axis, enthusiasm spreads due to "*one* or *two weak Women*" whose religious "Shrieks catch from one to another, till a great Part of the Congregation is affected."[145] In *Seasonable Thoughts on the State of Religion in New-England* (1743), Chauncy further militates against "*Passion* or *Affection*" as a guide in religion, adding: "Who can boast of greater Transports of Affection, than the wildest Enthusiasts?";[146] and, a year earlier, in *Enthusiasm Described and Caution'd Against* (1742), he defined said enthusiasm much like contemporaneous Enlightenment critics as a delusional inspiration born of "an over-heated imagination," a "bad temperament of the blood and spirits; 'tis properly a disease, a sort of madness."[147] On this point, he proves himself to be well read in past literature on enthusiasm, citing the Münster case as one must always do, but also the more recent convulsions of the French Prophets and Convulsionnaires of Saint-Médard. This shows the degree to which Old Light orthodoxy could speak the language of the Enlightenment in the manner of More and Voltaire, and therefore the degree to which American and European histories of enthusiasm overlap profoundly. Chauncy provides these historical examples, like John Winthrop before him, in order to prove how the "Progress of Error" implicitly desires to take up "*Arms* against the lawful *Authority*,"[148] how it has "made strong attempts to destroy all property, to make all things common, *wives* as well as *goods*."[149] This is the exact same language used against Anne Hutchinson one hundred years earlier and the French Revolution fifty years later.

If we continue reading Hawthorne's fiction as a chronicle of colonial enthusiasm, then his narrative vision of the Great Awakening is surely "My Kinsman, Major Molineux" (1832), a story that takes place in 1730s New England. Here, the spirit of Pearl has taken over colonial society, as the urban mob parades through the street, taking up arms against lawful authority, and I think not coincidently a lady in a "scarlet petticoat" adds to the laughter of the "applauding spectators," "with their shrill voices of mirth or terror."[150] But like "The Gray Champion," this story is ultimately about constituent power. The narrator frames the events as follows: "The people looked with most jealous scrutiny to the exercise of power, which did not emanate from themselves," and this is the context for an "inflammation of the popular mind" and a series of popular disputes with colonial governors "till the [American] Revolution,"[151] the selfsame language Kant uses to describe enthusiastic excess.

While Hawthorne makes no explicit reference to enthusiasm in "My Kinsman, Major Molineux," the story nevertheless captures, through Robin's eyes, the Wonderful Wandering Spirit in its vigorous opposition to arbitrary authority. As the mob with its "frenzied merriment" leads Major Molineux through the streets, "several women ran along the sidewalks, piercing the confusion of heavier sounds, with their shrill voices of mirth and terror."[152] Furthermore, we also encounter another figure like the Gray Champion, who comes "clad in a military dress" and "appeared like war personified.... In his train, were wild figures in the Indian dress . . . giving the whole march a visionary air, as if a dream had broken forth from some feverish brain":[153] once again, the feverish and dreaming brain of Kant's critique has made the mistake of applying its ideas beyond the boundaries of reason and moral right. This Wonderful Wandering Spirit of enthusiasm moves through the streets of eighteenth-century America "till the Revolution," that is, for Hawthorne, as a prelude to the American Revolution.

The Winds of Will: Enthusiasm, Sentimentality, and Women's Constituent Power

That enthusiasm has a privileged relationship to the history of "disorderly women,"[154] revolutionary female prophets, and their political constituent power from the English Civil War through at least the Romantic movement[155] makes it all the more curious that our dominant cultural—and literary—histories have tended to pigeonhole women's politics of the eighteenth and nineteenth centuries in terms of the culture of sentiment. As I mentioned earlier, the theory of sensibility across the long eighteenth century defined itself over/against the transgressive sociability of mobbish enthusiasm; however, just as Kant establishes a continuum, even troubled intimacy, between proper sympathy (disinterested judgment, "true enthusiasm") and improper enthusiasm (interested affect, excessive fervor), one must view the relationship between enthusiasm and sentimentality,[156] not as one of thesis and antithesis, but rather as one of variable "degrees" of "heat and ferment by co-acervation," to quote Samuel Taylor Coleridge on the distinction between enthusiasm and fanaticism.[157]

With regard to the literature of the early Republic—and I'm thinking of canonical favorites such as *Charlotte Temple* (1791) and *The Coquette* (1797)—my position is that we should understand it as a battleground for defining the border between proper sentiment and illegitimate enthusiasm, or, depending on the writer, proper and improper forms of enthusiasm; and in that sense, it is part of the same conversation, worked out in literary narrative, that preoccupies Voltaire and Kant. The border in early national literature very often has to do with the limits of women's constituent power in politics or society to newly make or break constituted domestic authority, but for the same reason, it also means that this literature could occasionally embrace a literary posture of enthusiasm beyond the bounds of sentimentality, although our current literary taxonomies make no room for enthusiasm as a distinct mode or sensibility of literature. This thesis follows from Cathy Davidson's explanation that early novels and popular literature of the Republic "provided an alternate public forum on democracy" for those—especially women—who had no voice in the privileged domain of representative government. This has dangerous implications. If "the early novel embraced a new relationship between art and audience, writer and reader, a relationship that replaced the authority of the sermon or Bible with the enthusiasms of sentiment, horror, or adventure, all of which relocate authority in the individual response of the reading self," then the reader might easily put down her book and, with this newly relocated authority in the constituent power of the feeling self, take up the actual sentiments, horrors, or adventures of the enthusiast—"novel reading today, licentious riot and senseless revolution tomorrow."[158]

It has long been a truism that American sentimentalism conflates or confuses the personal and the political, the private and the public, such that, in its most traditional form, "*family* stands as the model for social and political affiliation," and female chastity as a "symbol of republican virtue and innocence."[159] No one will be surprised to learn, then, that the problem of enthusiasm for women most often is framed in terms of an antidomestic disorder of the passions occasioned by an excessive interest in wildfire liberty. Foregrounding politics rather than romance, this is the thesis, for example, of Sarah Pogson's historical drama *The Female Enthusiast: A Tragedy in Five Acts* (1807),[160] based on Charlotte Corday, the Girondin sympathizer and assassin of Jean-Paul Marat, and a drama which works to recuperate, to a degree, "enthusiasm" as a model of women's constituent power. Outraged by the Jacobin purges but inspired by the claims of romantic revolution, Corday, in response to this convulsive context, decides to be the political agent of Marat's death in the name of republican virtue but ceases to be a "sensible" woman—or a "woman" as such—in the process:

> [. . .] The monster's name
> Steals every thought, and female weakness flies.
> With strength I'm armed, and mighty energy
> To crush the murderer and defy the scaffold.
> Let but the deed be done. For it, *I'll die*.
> For it, I sacrifice—I quit—myself
> And all the softness of a woman's name,[161]

While other characters tag Corday an enthusiast in a pejorative sense—her brother calls her a deluded "Enthusiastic girl," whose "sentiments / Are worthy of a Roman, yet are vain," and François Chabot labels her a "mad enthusiast"—Pogson means to partially apologize for Corday and thus to redeem enthusiasm itself. Corday exclaims positively, "Enthusiastic fervor bears me on, / And gentler passions fly before its power!"[162] In other words, enthusiastic affect is the agent of a woman's constituent political power to remedy tyranny, and it is not defined here solely by those who oppose it.

However, the tragic commitment of Corday, in Pogson's view, ultimately upholds the same ambivalent understanding of the enthusiast's error as in Kant: while one can forgive Corday for acting out in the name of a moral cause, against the oppressive administration of the Jacobins, she nevertheless becomes inflamed beyond the appropriate degree by a maxim of patriotic virtue. Yet, unlike Kant, *The Female Enthusiast* does not oppose revolutionary activity in and of itself, only its more radicalized phase leading to the Terror; like the majority of Americans at the time, the drama sympathizes with the overthrow of the monarchy, and this likewise explains why Pogson takes a strikingly positive stance on Charlotte Corday as a political, if misguided, patriot and martyr. The second storyline in the drama serves to equally delegitimize the Ancien Régime, in the form of the overbearing father, Duval, who forbids his daughter, Estelle, to marry for love and outside her class to a soldier, the brother of Charlotte, Henry Corday. Estelle's defiance of her father represents, according to him, the domestic and affective analogue to French Revolutionary ideals:

> But this hated, monstrous revolution
> Seems to extend its baleful influence
> Even to the hearts of individuals,
> Making our children as disobedient
> To the natural government of parents
> As to the good old regime of France.[163]

Notice, first, that domestic politics of home and nation collapse in the figure of the "natural government of parents" and the "good old regime of France," then that the revolution produces a culture of disobedience—of disobedient women—against that regime. Furthermore, in the play's denouement, since, as Henry says to Estelle, "France and thy father frown" on their desire for democracy in marriage, the lovers decide to emigrate to none other than the United States in order to live among "the sons of true-born liberty."[164] In the last analysis, Pogson's drama offers a schema in which the far revolutionary left, represented by Marat, stands for political fanaticism, the Royalist right, represented by Duval, stands for political conservatism, and the happy, democratic, republican middle ground, represented by the United States (and the American Revolution), stands for a reasonable model of enthusiasm. Charlotte Corday, however, represents any individual who, in defense of that moral ground, allows herself to put on the costume of the revolutionary, to overstep the domestic romance and deliberative politics preached by her female better, Estelle, yet with a sympathetic outcome—the overthrow of tyranny. And that is what one calls "the female enthusiast."

We see an analogous understanding of women's enthusiasm in Charles Brockden Brown's *Ormond; or The Secret Witness* (1799), a novel "the whole performance of which," according to a reviewer of the anti-Jacobin press, represents "the effusions of a pragmatic enthusiast! a mad-headed metaphysician!"[165] Depicting, if not manifesting, a jungle of mad-headed enthusiasms specific to 1790s Philadelphia, the novel works hard to demarcate good and bad forms of social engagement, contributing to the contemporaneous political diagnostics of Enlightenment criticism. Here too enthusiasm plays out, as in Pogson's drama, around women's role in the revolutionary Enlightenment. As the novel's heroine, Constantia Dudley represents Brown's ideal social type of the independent and progressive woman,[166] well educated and rational, responsible and resourceful, resolute in the face of adversity and animated by a "mild and steadfast enthusiasm"; not only that but she rejects marriage as legalized slavery for women and advocates for a model of community and (erotic) intimacy defined by mutual aid and "social pleasure."[167] Via the struggles of Constantia, Brown voices a scathing critique of liberal individualism and the capitalist ethic as symptoms of cultural barbarism—the United States is a theater of manipulation and deception based on a ruthless indifference to others and a dysfunctional infrastructure.

Critics have duly noted the limits of sentimentality in *Ormond*'s treatment of Constantia and other women in the novel.[168] Defending *Ormond* as arguably the most radical work of fiction before *Moby-Dick*, Philip Barnard and Stephen Shapiro write that Brown eschews "the ways in which sentimental texts participate in the objectification of women by presenting them primarily as bearers of emotional distress whose crises illustrate but do little to suggest ways of resisting or altering existing states of domination."[169] I would like to suggest, therefore, that the novel ought to be viewed through the lens of enthusiasm, only Brown speaks to a wide range of discrepant positions among his enthusiasts.[170] The most interesting character here is the mysterious cosmopolitan and Girondin revolutionary Martinette de Beauvais, a French-speaking émigré of eastern Mediterranean origins who flees to the United States from the Jacobin purges under Marat. Martinette, herself a former would-be assassin of the Duke of Brunswick, is another Charlotte Corday—a female enthusiast. Through her tales of grand passion and grand revolution, Martinette serves an important educational function in Constantia's life; she opens the young Philadelphian's eyes to the infinite possibilities, varieties, and powers of female action on the world's stage. In response, Constantia feels her world to be circumscribed and impoverished. More to the point, a political enthusiasm overwhelmingly defines Martinette's purpose in life. This is the term that she uses to describe her former English lover, Wentworth, "a political enthusiast, who esteemed nothing more graceful or glorious than to die for the liberties of mankind."[171] Wentworth's classical education in ancient political heroics develops into a passion for liberty that—in a Kantian turn of phrase—becomes "an enthusiasm that bordered upon phrenzy,"[172] leading him to betray his own country and, along with Martinette, to join the rebels in the American Revolution. Martinette then shares her reflections on becoming a soldier with Constantia: "I delighted to assume the male dress, to acquire skill at the sword, and dexterity in every boisterous exercise. The timidity that commonly attends women, gradually vanished. I felt as if embued by a soul that was a stranger to the sexual distinction."[173] Added to this loss of timidity and sexual distinction is a rejection of sentimental responses to war and suffering. When Martinette enthuses over her participation in the violence of the French Revolution, it appalls Constantia; she asks in puzzlement, "But a woman—how can the heart of women be inured to the shedding of blood?," to which Martinette answers, "Have women, I beseech thee, no capacity to reason and infer? ... My hand never faultered [sic] when liberty demanded the victim," a comment that connects back to her avowed preference for "danger": "I am an adorer of liberty, and liberty without peril can never exist.... Am I not a lover of liberty, and must I not exult in the fall of tyrants, and regret only that my hand had no share in their destruction?" Brown's "woman warrior"[174] goes on to explain to Constantia that hundreds of women fought in the Revolution with different motives, a code for different manifestations of enthusiasm: "Some were impelled by the enthusiasm of love, and some by a mere passion for war; some by the contagion of example; and some, with whom I myself must be ranked, by a generous devotion to liberty."[175] By emphasizing the plurality of energies and interests that compel women to participate in projects of emancipation, Martinette sloughs off the sentimental domestication of women's politics as a world of spectatorship, passivism, emotional vulnerability, and polite, labor-based reform. Furthermore, like Pogson and Thomas Paine, Brown keeps the Girondin phase of the French Revolution conjoined to the American cause of liberty.

Remarkably, Brown does not check or challenge Martinette's perspectives, at least not unambiguously; if anything, the conversation helps to revolutionize Constantia's mind. She becomes enthused herself by the prospect of journeying to Italy and having her own adventures, and this sets up one of the most significant passages in the novel: "This burst of new ideas and new hopes on the mind of Constance took place in the course of a single hour. No change in her external situation had been wrought, and yet her mind had undergone the most signal revolution. The novelty as well as greatness of the prospect kept her in a state of elevation and awe, more ravishing than any she had ever experienced. Anticipations of intercourse with nature in her most august forms, with men in diversified states of society, with the posterity of Greeks and Romans, and with the actors that were now upon the stage, and above all with the being whom absence and the want of other attachments, had, in some sort, contributed to deify, made this night pass away upon the wings of transport."[176] Constantia's revolution of the mind, the "ferment of her thoughts," attended by multiple active and convulsive qualifiers (bursting, ravishing, intercoursing, transporting), suggests a new female subjectification of constituent power and a corresponding, if soft, state of "political enthusiasm." The latter "being" in this quote refers to the narrator, Sophia Westwyn Courtland, with whom Constantia has an undefined but nevertheless unmistakable erotic relationship;[177] yet even the sexual energy between them has been prepared by Constantia's infatuation for the radiant, cross-dressing Martinette, as if queer womanhood and enthusiastic politics are mutually constitutive. But like the novel's suggestion of lesbian exchange, Constantia's new political enthusiasm never takes concrete form, and Brown leaves the direction toward which it tends open-ended for the reader.

I do not mean to suggest, then, that Charles Brockden Brown gives us a quintessential view of enthusiasm. Quite the contrary. Anglo-Jacobin in his sympathies, Brown himself believed more in cultural than political revolution, and he and his fellow members of the Friendly Club (an elite circle of New York intellectuals and professionals) "aimed to launch a revolution of manners among men and women in the republic of intellect." Still, Brown's background as a Quaker and his devotion to the cosmopolitan ideals of universal Enlightenment certainly align him with a variant of enthusiasm for his time.[178] *Ormond* should be read as Brown's attempt to clear out a path for "true enthusiasm" in contrast to the most available political ideologies in the early Republic: Federalism, Jeffersonianism, (French) Jacobinism, or everyday mercantilism.

But just as Brown removes Martinette to the margins of the novel, so has "political enthusiasm" been removed to the margins of American literary history, especially for women, although enthusiasm has no interest in preserving "sexual distinction." As Susan Howe suggests, from Anne Hutchinson to Emily Dickinson, the antinomian, experimental energies in American women's literature have by and large remained a kind of expurgated marginalia; and she says of Dickinson, as Hutchinson's poetic avatar, "Wayward Puritan. Charged with enthusiasm. Enthusiasm is antinomian."[179] It is this marginal sense of enthusiasm that, in the chapters to come, I bind into a textual tradition—a tradition that might be said to follow from Dickinson's own sense of constituent power as "the Winds of Will" that stir the life of revolution to test if liberty be dead:

> Revolution is the Pod
> Systems rattle from
> When the Winds of Will are stirred
> Excellent is Bloom
>
> . . . .
>
> Left inactive on the Stalk
> All it's Purple fled
> Revolution shakes it ["Liberty"] for
> Test if it be dead –[180]

CHAPTER TWO

Rites of Dissent
Literatures of Enthusiasm and the American Revolution

> The American war is over: but this is far from being the case with the American revolution. On the contrary, nothing but the first act of the great drama is closed.
>
> —BENJAMIN RUSH, 1787

While chapter 1 sketched, in broad outline, the enthusiastic roots of the Revolutionary era and the theory of constituent power in foundational American writings related to enthusiasm, this chapter will color in and detail that picture by focusing on the literature and culture of the American Revolution. However one understands its shaping, the American Revolution certainly did not tend toward political enthusiasm, according to most commentators.[1] Two arguments for a conservative/moderate American Revolution (and its aftermath) that have been influential on American literary scholarship are the Puritan thesis and the Anglicization thesis. Representative of the former, Sacvan Bercovitch recently republished his classic 1975 text, *The Puritan Origins of the American Self*, in which he continues to assert that the American Revolution was, for its ideologues, the political consummation of a sacred mission rooted in longstanding Puritan theories of America's divinely appointed "federal identity."[2] As Bercovitch concisely puts it in *Rites of Assent* (1993), "The sacred origin was the Puritan migration; the telos was the Revolution."[3] The false parity between the strict logic of Puritanism and Revolutionary bourgeois society is irrelevant: what matters are "the forms and strategies of cultural continuity" that unify all American political—and literary—projects around the central myth of a "sacred teleology" embodied by the American self.[4] From Jonathan Edwards to Ralph Waldo Emerson, Thomas Paine to Nathaniel Hawthorne, the narrative of a special, cosmic American identity survives through various historical and literary mutations, transforming all political dissent into new strains of cultural consensus about the American mission. When pressed as to the deeper point of this mission, Bercovitch tends to accent the conservative, capitalistic economic values of American liberalism: nationalist exceptionalism translates into "middle-class hegemony" in the making, and multidenominationalism, "clothed in the brightest rhetoric of the millennium," translates into the "spiritual version of free enterprise."[5]

Recent eighteenth-century scholarship, however, tells a very different story than Bercovitch does, but arguably one no less consensus-based in its understanding of the American Revolution. This is known as the "Anglicization" thesis of American independence,[6] which states that, in the cultural, political, and economic development of the American colonies, part and parcel of the "integration or centralization" of the Empire, an intensifying identification with Englishness, in "economics, politics, ideology," led to an eventual crisis: the colonies came to see themselves as central, rather than peripheral, actors in the Empire, deserving of the same political rights and guarantees, certainly, but also ultimately warring in defense of true Englishness so as to supplant the compromised or corrupted Crown while also asserting their own economic and material interests.[7] In this view, the Revolutionary War was fought over the constitution of empire, not a desire for discrete and special American nationhood; a move away from the Puritan migration back across the Atlantic so to speak, in a *cultural continuity of Englishness*, resulted paradoxically in a political collision that led to Anglo-American civil war. As Leonard Tennenhouse underscores in *The Importance of Feeling English* (2007), Americans, especially in their literature from 1750 to 1850, saw Americanness as a distinctive culture of Englishness transplanted in North America, part and parcel of a British diaspora in which English-derived cultures forged their own unique version of the English heritage. This narrative arguably replaces American rites of assent with English ones: Americans organize dissent in order to forge unique consensual models of a separate English identity.

In this chapter, I question not the legacies of Puritanism or Anglophilia but the logic of triumphant consensus that underwrites the above narratives of the American Revolution. Echoing historians and critics such as Peter Linebaugh and Marcus Rediker, Terry Bouton, Gary Nash, and Jason Frank, who stress the heterogeneous, internally combative political constituency of American Revolutionary society, I argue for a version of the American Revolution and its literature in which enthusiastic "rites of dissent" play a constitutive role for supporters and critics alike.[8] This is where the transatlantic study of Anglo-American civil war proves crucial: I take seriously the claim, framed from the Loyalist perspective and situated in historical context, that colonial revolt was, relative to British standards, a "War of Plunder, of general levelling and taking away the Distinction of rich and poor."⁹ On this point, I am in sympathy with scholarship that approaches early American dissent "in less anachronistic and less deterministic ways. With an eye on the shaping of history rather than the unfolding of it," it is imperative to "point towards time-bound but alternative radicalisms, the 'agency' of the popular movements"; "for there was no single ideological tradition or social component, nor was there only one route Anglo-American radicalism might have taken."¹⁰ By stressing rites of dissent, I do not challenge the Anglicization thesis or, with some essential revisions, the Bercovitch thesis on the Puritan origins of the American self. On the contrary, I aim to show that the legacy of enthusiasm, as I have discussed it so far, was available to Revolutionary critics, who traced American rites of dissent back to their English *and* Puritan origins, and this legacy, in both politics and literature, has been mostly obfuscated by traditional narratives of the American Revolution up to our own time.

Literatures of enthusiasm in the Revolutionary era exemplify what Sandra Gustafson describes as the fraught interaction between prophetic-biblical rhetoric and classical-deliberative rhetoric in the early Republic.¹¹ In the context of the Anglo-American crisis, I see these literatures as a hybrid form that refashions sermonic oratory and the ideals of revival democracy into a literary mode of protest that exceeds—rather than opposes—deliberative norms through urgent pleas for direct, collective action against the Crown. Certain historians of the Revolutionary era have disabused us of the conventional secularization narrative of American Independence, pointing instead to a deep structural, if complex and diversified, relationship between dissenting enthusiastic religion and dissenting political ideology.¹² In this sense, I mean to amplify John Stauffer's comment in his foreword to Zoe Trodd's anthology of American protest literature: "A revivalist is essentially a protest artist, creating protest literature with words, images, and oratory to effect conversion"; conversely, "protest literature, much like revivals, can lead to permanent social change when the protest occurs during an awakening."¹³ While I do aim to emphasize, like Jason Frank, how insurgent political actions molded the public sphere of both print and oratory, what Frank has elsewhere dubbed "enthusiastic politics,"¹⁴ my main goal is to highlight how certain print literatures adopt an explicit heritage of political enthusiasm as I have defined it (convulsive context, address, and affect), thereby inventing an insurgent American print culture, a type of "American protest literature," that transforms aesthetic labor into enthusiastic dissent.

In the next section, I take up the first part of my argument, which is to establish more fully the historical and literary viewpoint on the American Revolution as a species of enthusiasm. Here I elaborate on the conservative associations of enthusiasm with a fanatical or terroristic love of liberty. This sets up the ensuing three sections in which I read examples of enthusiasm in literature: I demonstrate, on a synchronic axis, the distinct features and expressions of literatures of enthusiasm as exhibited by various authors during the Anglo-American crisis, and on a diachronic axis, the political relationship and critical differences between these authors in their respective rites of literary dissent. I begin with a work in the Whig Revolutionary tradition, Mercy Otis Warren's pamphlet-drama *The Adulateur* (1773), and I argue that Warren imports the republican and Puritan idea of a "great theatre of action" for her interventionist politics of literary enthusiasm. Next, I look at the *Pennsylvania Magazine* (1775–76), a Revolutionary periodical edited and contributed to by Thomas Paine. I make the case that, in Paine's vision, the magazine becomes an operative way to democratize enthusiastic literary participation, as against the republican gentry model of Warren. Then I turn to the poetry of Phillis Wheatley, especially her "Elegiac Poem" for the Great Awakening revivalist, George Whitefield, and "To His Excellency General Washington," the latter situated in the context of its publication in the *Pennsylvania Magazine*; and I contend that Wheatley opens political enthusiasm up to a black, enslaved audience, attaching African peoples to the throng of democratic dissent. Finally, in a short concluding section, I explain that, as a result of the post-Revolutionary suppression of political enthusiasm, what Gordon Wood says of Thomas Paine—he "seems destined to remain a misfit, an outsider"[15]—is also true for Warren and Wheatley. By virtue of their task to adapt aesthetic labor for the purposes of active dissent, these authors did not take part in an autonomous culture of literature and letters, and yet, I aim to recuperate enthusiasm as a way of approaching literature—it is an elective affinity that allies Warren, Paine, and Wheatley. Read together, they offer us a theater of literary action about what the unfolding and foundational event of the American Revolution—and concomitantly, an "American Literature"—meant or *came to mean* for enthusiasts by the end of the eighteenth century, which saw not only the death of George Washington in 1799, but with him, "the end of an era in American Revolutionary tradition."[16]

By the Rule of Topsy-Turvies:
Acts of Civil War Enthusiasm

In order to establish more fully the historical (and literary) viewpoint on the American Revolution as an event of enthusiasm, it is necessary to pay to attention to the language of Loyalists and British apologists for parliamentary sovereignty. Loyalist verse, for example, clearly sees popular resistance to Britain as anything but rational, moderate, republican; take Joseph Stansbury's critique of one American chaplain's sermon to a Philadelphia militia: "Yet what can we look for but Faction and Treason / From a flaming Enthusiast, fann'd by the Devil!"[17] Even George Washington, the icon of the American Revolution, was, in his time, not exempt from the charge of political enthusiasm. Other Loyalist poems refer to George Washington as a kind of resurrected Oliver Cromwell—a "Patron of villainy, of villains chief"—as well as an ally of the traitorous Continental Congress, that "hydra-headed form" and "its lords the mob."[18] Or, as Captain J. F. D. Smyth puts it in his 1777 "Verses Written in Captivity":

> These Colonies, of British freedom tir'd,
> Are by the phrensy of distraction fir'd;
> ....
> Surrounding Nations, in amazement, view
> The strange infatuations they pursue.
> Virtue in tears deplores their fate in vain,
> And Satan smiles to see disorder reign:
> The days of Cromwell, Puritanic rage,
> Return'd to curse our more unhappy age.[19]

Such vituperative language against Puritan enthusiasm as political infatuation also shows up in the first pro-independence plays to feature George Washington as a man of action, John Leacock's *The Fall of British Tyranny* and Hugh Henry Brackenridge's *The Battle of Bunkers-Hill*, both published in 1776. In the former drama, a Tory ("Judas") excoriates the Washington-led army for its "enthusiastic zeal" in lieu of courage, and, in the latter, British General Howe does the same for its war cause: "wild-fire liberty."[20] In the popular satirical poem, John Trumbull's *M'Fingal* (1775–82), the titular Tory tags the colonists in revolt as "madbrain'd rebel[s]," "dirtbed patriots," "dregs" and "skum," who have "call'd up anarchy from chaos" and "by the rule of topsyturvys" raised "this Maypole of sedition!"[21] Elsewhere, Edmund Burke wrote to a friend in 1775 about George Washington and his aide-de-camp Thomas Mifflin, "What think you of that political Enthusiasm, which is able to overpower so much religious Fanaticism?"[22] And Loyalist Peter Oliver had this to say about the role of military chaplains in the Continental Army: "Mr. *Washington* was provided with a Chaplain, who, with a Stentorian Voice & an Enthusiastick Mania, could incite his Army to greater Ardor than all the Drums of his Regiments."[23]

However polemically charged these Loyalist sentiments may be, they nevertheless conjure the historical fact that, in Henry May's terms, the Revolutionary Enlightenment, unlike the earlier Moderate and Skeptical Enlightenment, was not "ranged in sharp opposition to popular enthusiasm and especially popular religion. The Revolutionary Enlightenment was itself enthusiastic and religious in spirit."[24] As Ruth Bloch observes, "On the level of popular culture, especially, religion deeply informed political ideology."[25] In his March 22, 1775, "Speech . . . For Conciliation with the Colonies," the incisive Burke explains the enthusiastic lifeblood in American rebellion, its "free spirit," by defining its religion as, at core, "a principle of energy":[26] the problem is that the American colonies have this spirit to an excessive degree. Burke remarks, "But the religion in our Northern Colonies is a refinement on the principle of resistance; it is the dissidence of dissent; and the protestantism of the protestant religion. This religion, under a variety of denominations, agreeing in nothing but in the communion of the spirit of liberty, is predominant in most of the Northern provinces."[27] The dissenting spirit of a hyper-Protestantism—a popular enthusiasm raised to the second power—allies the interests of the colonies, otherwise fragmented by heterogeneous backgrounds. Six years earlier, in a 1769 sermon titled "On Schisms and Sects," Anglican clergyman and Loyalist Jonathan Boucher looks forward to Burke, but he explicitly uses the language of enthusiasm as synonymous with vulgar sectarianism in both religion and politics: "Composed as these sectaries of our western world in general are of a confused heterogeneous mass of infidels and enthusiasts, oddly blended and united, (most of them ignorant, and all of them shamefully illiterate,) it is not easy, in a serious discourse, to speak of them with becoming gravity."[28] These sectaries, who criticize church and state, serve "the causes of deism and revolution," says Boucher, and this is because religious and political revolts are mutually constitutive phenomena: "By a sort of mutual action and reaction they produce one another; both, in their turns, becoming causes and effects."²⁹ And again: "A sect is, in fact, a revolt against the authority of the Church, just as a faction is against the authority of the State; or, in other words, a sect is a faction in the Church, as a faction is a sect in the State: and the spirit which refuses obedience to the one, is equally ready to resist the other."³⁰ This sectarian tendency in the present hour, Boucher argues, reenacts the "grand rebellion" of the seventeenth century—the English Civil War.³¹ Its main attribute is an antinomian disregard for authority and law, and it has come to take the most debased form imaginable among the "meager, dejected, and squalid people crowding to hear field preachers."³² Thus there is a chain of dissent—a constituent power unleashed against the lawful authorities of the state and church—from contemporary field preaching to revolution, from the English Civil War to American rebellion.

Given the polite republican ethos of the Revolutionary gentry, it may seem strange to label George Washington a political enthusiast, but in the practical repertoires of colonial resistance and riots from the 1760s through the Revolution, Whig elites and common people closely interacted together. Even though they were divided by conflicting class interests and ideology, they also exerted influence upon each other in a common struggle against British authorities.³³ Relative to Great Britain, class distinctions in Revolutionary-era America, where the yeomanry controlled 70 percent of the land, were much less pronounced and much more porous, and the wealth of the colonial aristocracy was nothing compared to that of the English ruling class.³⁴ This is partly why the English satirized Americans as rude, clownish Yankee Doodles, and George Washington, in the satirical drama *The Blockade of Boston* (performed in 1776), could be "represented as an uncouth countryman, dressed shabbily, with large wig and long rusty sword."³⁵ Moreover, the Revolutionary gentry, like the emergent bourgeoisie, often encouraged and participated in popular actions against the Crown.³⁶ In Philadelphia, circa 1775 and 1776, "they [the lower classes] broke out of this 'subaltern' position and began to assert themselves and gain political power through a coalition with 'middling' radicals. The 'lower sort' began to affect, and even shape, provincial and continental events."³⁷ One cannot uphold, then, a sharp and neat division between the popular enthusiasms of the masses and the popular republican ideology of the elites. If the revolt against "parliamentary sovereignty" was the "most profound breach ever to have occurred in anglophone political practice," then it is necessary, in my estimate, to read even a figure such as George Washington, in the *shaping* of Anglo-American civil war, as an English enthusiast, not anachronistically as an American hero.[38]

Likewise, we should take more seriously the above criticisms of the Revolution as a second English Civil War. It is hardly shocking that General George Washington resonates for English critics as the resurrected leader of a New Model Army; yet, in the Whig republican tradition to which Washington adhered, Cromwell was also viewed as a tyrant and fanatic associated with the terrors unleashed by popular democracy. Contrariwise, according to Alfred Young, in the "folk traditions and enthusiastic religion" of colonial and Revolutionary America (especially in the aftermath of the Great Awakening), the English revolutionary tradition was embraced to inspire popular revolt against governmental tyranny: the spirit of Cromwell returned "to right the wrongs suffered by the common people."[39] In a Connecticut Stamp Act protest of 1765, for instance, participants comically prayed to Cromwell rather than the Lord: "We beseech thee, O Cromwell, to hear (our prayers) us," and "O Cromwell, deliver us!"[40] Ten years later, John Leacock published a bizarre, uproarious, irreverent mock-Biblical pamphlet, *The First Book of the American Chronicles of the Times* (1774–75), in which the patriots, via the prophet and witch Mother Carey (perhaps an allusion to the Fifth Monarchist prophet Mary Cary),[41] raise Oliver Cromwell from the dead as Lord Protector of Massachusetts Bay and chief of their dissenting actions: all the people celebrate "the new birth of Oliver."[42] This is an example of how Americans embraced contrary versions of Englishness, and there was no more a consensus on what it meant *to be* English and revolutionary than on what it meant *to be* American and revolutionary.

But if the protest crowds were a mixed-class group, then it is not only that the "mob" began "to think and to reason," as Gouverneur Morris said in 1774;[43] it is also that, in a manner of speaking, the gentry began to feel and act. Rhys Isaac highlights this with regard to Revolutionary Virginia: "By 1775, the passionate involvement of gentlemen and their followers in the patriot movement had reached the pitch where it could be aptly designated by a critical participant as 'political enthusiasm,' and there were indeed certain common features between the movements. Most notable was the use in both cases of popular assemblies for communication, emotional sharing, and the intensification of the involvement of common people."[44] In other words, "political enthusiasm" was a term for the people's self-authorizing political actions (their constituent power) against English tyranny. Cultures of enthusiasm were linked to a vision of performative democracy as a "space beyond formal observance": "By 1769, the transformation into 'political enthusiasm' of religious enthusiasm and its various manifestations, including what those in authority regarded as outbursts of illegitimate popular speech, was definitively recognized."[45] However, the space beyond formal observance is not only the space of illegitimate popular speech but also the space of illegitimate political action—the space of constituent power inextricably linked to it. Correspondingly, as I'll argue below, literary production before and during the cause for American independence did not occur on the sidelines; as an extension of the resistance effort, literature played an important role as an agent in consolidating and emboldening a Revolutionary public, or, to borrow from John Adams's comment on John Dickinson's 1768 "Liberty Song," written in the wake of the Townshend Acts and sung by the Sons of Liberty in many of their subsequent demonstrations, "This [literature] is cultivating the Sensations of Freedom."[46] In the terms that I established in chapter 1, the space beyond formal observance here refers to the space of constituent power not only beyond constitutional boundaries but also beyond a public sphere predicated on disinterested exchange: whereas literatures of enthusiasm shake off institutionalized or prescriptive observances of *literary form* by encouraging readers to become interested actors in the performance of dissent.

The Great Theatre of Action: The Performance of Enthusiasm in Mercy Otis Warren

Mercy Otis Warren has a unique relationship to the Boston resistance movement of the 1760s and 1770s: her brother James Otis Jr. and husband, James Warren, along with their close ally Samuel Adams Jr. were among its most vocal public figures. James and Mercy Otis Warren hosted meetings of the Sons of Liberty, "the earliest intercolonial organization to coordinate anti-imperial resistance,"[47] and an organization feared by Loyalists as a "trained mob."[48] Otis and Adams were arguably the most radical of the Boston leaders insofar as they spoke out in support of lower-class "mob" actions; according to Gary Nash, they "espoused a vision of politics that gave credence to laboring-class views and regarded as entirely legitimate the participation of artisans and even laborers in the political process."[49] After the 1768 Massachusetts Assembly passed a vote of 92 to 17 in favor of a united front against "taxation without representation," the Sons of Liberty appeared to run Boston, but fear was mounting over the arrival of British troops: "To keep up popular enthusiasm for the cause, Otis and [Samuel] Adams kept the presses screaming."[50]

Not incidentally, then, Otis and Adams (outfitted as the Romans Brutus and Cassius) play lead roles in Mercy Otis Warren's first dramatic sketch, *The Adulateur. A Tragedy, As It Is Now Acted in Upper Servia*, parts of which were first published anonymously in two 1772 installments of the radical newspaper the *Massachusetts Spy*. Responding both to the hated colonial governor Thomas Hutchinson (named Rapatio in the drama) and the 1770 Boston Massacre, the 1773 version of the play, published as a pamphlet, speaks more to literatures of enthusiasm as I have defined them,[51] especially since, as Jason Shaffer notes, it "engages more fully not only with the events of the [Boston] massacre but also with the torrent of political passion it unleashed."[52] Participating in the radical orality closely associated with the likes of Samuel Adams and James Otis, *The Adulateur* incorporates popular enthusiasm for a "theatre of human action," as Warren once put it,[53] in response to the Boston Massacre. *The Adulateur* is best read as a convulsive oratorical address to and for the patriotic masses. Warren's dramatic sketch for *historical* actors undergoes a conceptual metamorphosis, namely, in its intent to admonish the reader not to read or attend a play—*The Adulateur* was never performed—but to enter the stage of the political crisis and confront the convulsive context.

The full title of *The Adulateur* itself elides the difference between a drama, marked generically as a tragedy, and a contemporary historical spectacle, "now acted" in Boston under the fictional name of "Upper Servia." The present progressive tense identifies the text, not as a *re-presentation* of past events, read or observed by patrons of the arts, but as a *present-ation* of a continuing and unfinished drama, participated in by patriots of the arts. If *The Adulateur* is "more weapon than work of art,"[54] this follows from an act of literature that directly intervenes in a political situation. Warren prefaces her deictic action writing with a telling epigraph from Joseph Addison's 1713 play *Cato, A Tragedy*:

Then let us rise my friends, and strive to fill
This little interval, this pause of life,
(While yet our liberty and fates are doubtful)

With resolution, friendship, Roman bravery,
And all the virtues we can crowd into it,
That Heav'n may say it ought to be prolong'd.[55]

As a Revolutionary reframing of this epigraph, *The Adulateur* exhorts the reader to claim a phatic temporality, the time of an event in a monumental present tense, undetermined and open-ended, but absolute and pivotal; the play is concerned with a political interstice, an opening ready to be filled—crowded, saturated, occupied—with meanings endowed with eternal significance (or so says Heaven). But the time of the event is also the time of crisis. The fate of liberty hangs in the balance. In the context of that crisis, Warren's citation of a popular English play about republican virtue and governmental tyranny situates the colonial resistance movement as the republican tradition's new vanguard but also as a new dispensation or living literature of republican drama. Warren doubles this idea within the play by bending the plot, not only into a contemporary *Julius Caesar*, but also into a contemporary *Hamlet* in which the ancestral ghosts of Puritan independence, outraged and baffled by the late events, return to announce the necessity of defying the despotic Crown.

In order to grasp the ethos of political enthusiasm that informs Warren's synthesis of drama and political rebellion, one must first understand that eighteenth-century audiences would not have heard Warren's "theatre of human action" as merely figurative speech. On the contrary, this theater reflects a prevailing belief that singular historical action was already substantively endowed with sacred literary power, part and parcel of a *theatrum mundi*. As Jeffrey Richards has abundantly clarified, one of the most distinctive features of American dissent was its conception as a "ritualized theater of the masses in the streets" participating in "the exalted theater of God's Providence."[56] This holds true for republican invocations of the theater—such as Warren's use of *Cato*—as well. Take George Washington, whose role model was Cato the Younger, famous for his efforts in the civil war against the tyrannical Julius Caesar, but popularized for eighteenth-century audiences in Addison's *Cato*. This drama was one of Washington's favorites, so much so that the Continental Army performed it for him in the camp of Valley Forge. Washington's war theater, like Mercy Otis Warren's rites of dissent in *The Adulateur*, invokes the oft-deployed "'Catonic' image" of patriotic sacrifice that was central to the Whig tradition of republicanism.[57] And yet, as Jeffrey

Richards explains, the American appropriation of *Cato* was highly unorthodox: "in England ... *Cato* may inspire political debate, but its ideological message can never fully escape its medium of presentation, that of a commercial stage production. In America, however, without a theatrical tradition to hold them, the issues raised by *Cato* are played out on a political stage that includes the streets and fields and waterfronts of the colonial landscape."[58] It was presumptuous, and no less enthusiastic, for the colonists to assume and embody the lived position of Cato, and they did so out of a "nonconformist conception of life" rooted in Puritan millennialism.[59] Thus, when General George Washington, in his 1783 resignation speech before Congress, said, "Having now finished the work assigned me, I retire from the great theatre of action,"[60] he invoked precisely this legacy of enthusiastic performance.

As informed by the nonconformist conception of life, *The Adulateur* represents an innovative formal experiment in adapting the dramatic tradition to a new convulsive context. The play begins *in medias res*, in the caesura or interval of political events. Brutus, chief of the patriots, looks upon a street drama drenched in blood as a historical regression, "the sweet retreat of freedom" "dearly purchas'd" by his ancestors. With this tragedy—the loss of lives and liberty—a ghost enters: "the sullen ghost of bondage, / Stalks full in view—already with her pinions, / She shades the affrighted land."[61] The time is out of joint: an undead and atavistic tyranny opens the curtain on the present drama, but the apparition's dark presence—historically announcing "the dread name of slaves"—has also summoned the memory of those goodly ghosts, our "noble ancestors," who, in life, died to be rid of this name. If they rose from the grave and were in our position: "That good old spirit, / Which warm'd them once, would rouse to noble actions." There is a symmetry, a coidentity even, between the arousal to noble actions and the arousal of enthusiasm, what Brutus calls the inspiration of "a noble passion[.] / It glows within me, and every pulse I feel, / Beats high for glory."[62] In the name of this passion, Brutus says to his fellow patriots, "I conjure you," which Warren intends in a double sense, most obviously to incite the people to action, to fill up the present hour, but also to conjure the "good old spirit" of liberty that lies dormant in them.[63]

But while, in Act I, it is only a matter of remembering the ancestral spirit of independence, in Act II, Scene I, the ghost of Cassius's father, restless over sullied freedom, actually appears to Cassius and addresses him directly, commanding him to defend the "fair possession" for which he died. Importantly, only when Cassius occupies the "pause of life" and sits "musing, / On evils past, and trembling at the future" does the ghost "burst" on his "startled fancy."[64] The reader now understands that the epigraph was meant for the likes of Cassius, seized and paralyzed by an unjust condition that threatens to disarm his ability to act with the "noble spirit"[65] of his ancestors. In Scene III, after future terrors have now indeed happened (i.e., the Boston Massacre), Brutus too receives a visit from a ghost: "What do I see?—or is it merely fancy? / Methinks yon rising ghost stares full in view, / Points to its wounds and cries aloud— REVENGE." The two conjurations of the ghost serve the same purpose: "'Twould rouze you into action."[66] Accordingly, one more ghost appears in Act III, Scene I, *exposing his wounds*," in order to "push us on."[67] But the specters of independence—now including the recent corpses on the streets of Boston—do not only reappear to the patriots; the "ghost of freedom" also haunts the "midnight hours" of Rapatio, who vows to exorcize the "dear remains of virtue," "tho' dreary spectres / Scare all his soul and haunt his midnight slumber."[68]

By invoking the patriotic dead as haunting figures for the unfulfilled restitution of political liberties, *The Adulateur* borrows from expressive conventions in Boston Massacre commemoration orations. Take Joseph Warren's rousing March 5, 1772, oration wherein he admonishes his fellow patriots to "feel the true fire of patriotism" that burned in the breasts of the original colonists: "The voice of your Fathers blood cries to you from the ground; MY SONS, SCORN TO BE SLAVES! . . . We bled in vain, if you, our offspring want valour to repel the assaults of her invaders!"[69] As Sandra Gustafson explains, Boston Massacre orations "adapted the sacred technologies of the pulpit to patriotic political needs," as part of a general trend, popularized by Patrick Henry, in which republican orators incorporated plain-speaking homiletic methods as a "semisecularized variant of the evangelical sermon."[70] One can see this, for instance, in the heavy-handed, motivational religious rhetoric of John Hancock's March 5, 1774 Oration on the Boston Massacre, or as the title theatrically refers to the event, the "Bloody Tragedy." Tellingly, the oration drenches its defense of American resistance to the Crown in the pulpit language of sin and deliverance; to name only one example, Hancock describes the Massacre as an event whereby "Satan with his chosen band open'd the sluices of New-England's blood, and sacrilegiously polluted our land with the dead bodies of her guiltless sons."[71] Loyalists considered hyperbolic language like this to encourage a conspiratorial inflammation of the antinomian passions—or enthusiasm. After all, toward the end of the oration, Hancock asks his audience—"my friends," as he calls them—to heed the example of Boston leaders, specifically Samuel and John Adams, in the following terms: "from them let us catch the divine enthusiasm; and feel, each for himself, the God-like pleasure of diffusing happiness on all around us; of delivering the oppressed from the iron grasp of tyranny; of changing the hoarse complaints and bitter moans of wretched slaves, into those cheerful songs, which freedom and contentment must inspire."[72] Anyone who catches the divine enthusiasm will, in a curious phrase, "play the man for our God,"[73] which is to say, take part in a sacred theater of political redemption. But in order to inspire the people to enter the political stage, Hancock, like Mercy Otis Warren, rhetorically asks the English Rapatios, "Tell me, ye bloody butchers ... do you not sometimes feel the gnawings of that worm which never dies? Do not the injured shades of Maverick, Gray, Caldwell, Attucks and Carr, attend you in your solitary walks, arrest you even in the midst of your debaucheries, and fill even your dreams with terror?"[74] In Warren's drama, the tyrants, with their "hateful passions," do indeed live in fear of the "scoundrell mob"[75] that shadows their every action.

Both internal to the play and also external to it in its simultaneous address to the patriotic reader, *The Adulateur* demands that one *imagine* historical tragedy, not only in the sense of to summon or conceive an image of its horrors but in the sense of "to devise, plot, plan," to conceive "a thing to be performed" (OED), so that every scene of the "Bloody Tragedy" necessarily compels us to *reenact* the plot of dissent. This is how Warren gives us a cue—not as onlookers or readers but as actors—to plot a future and then enter the "great theatre of action." Hence Warren's obsession with showing us "human gore" on the streets: she intends to address the reader's "cold inactive spirit / That *slumbers* in its chains."[76] Anyone who *saw* the "promiscuous slaughter" or *heard* "the groans of innocence" in what we call the Boston Massacre would be in revolt, and with that Massacre, the convulsive context has reached its climax: "Now is the crisis; if we lose this moment, / All's gone forever," says Brutus, echoing Cassius's lines two scenes prior: "Oh! Brutus, what a scene! the hour is come—/ Our fates are at a crisis—Servia shakes."[77]

Embroiled in a popular debate about the prescriptive limits to resistance, Warren also argues, like Enlightenment critics, for responsible rites of dissent regulating the enthusiastic passions. After the hotheaded Portius works himself up into a frenzy over drawing the "tyrant's blood," Brutus admonishes him:

> Stay, Portius, stay—let reason calm thy passions,
> Let us not sully by unmeaning actions,
> The cause of injur'd freedom; this demands
> A *cool, sedate* and yet *determin'd* spirit.[78]

Once his passions have been tempered, Portius replies: "I'll go and soothe the boistrous [sic] multitude, / Calm all their souls, and make them act like freemen."[79] Here one glimpses Warren's own implicit patrician prejudices and republican theory of a top-down, hierarchical model of mass resistance, for it is true that Warren and her coterie made invidious distinctions between itself—as a representative voice of schooled republicanism, of "reason"—and the unruly, motley masses: "Boston's whig leaders used the annual Boston Massacre orations to establish hegemony over the local populace by focusing on the figure of the orator."[80] On the other hand, Whig leaders were, to a great extent, also forced to "catch up with the crowds," as Dick Hoerder explains, by sanctioning their actions *ex post facto* when it was convenient to do so: the crowds taught elites how to enact democratic assembly and forced them to make political compromises sensitive to their needs.[81] This sheds light on Warren's ambivalence about the Boston crowds. Although the strongly affected multitudes of enthusiasm need strong Whig leaders to keep them in line, Warren does not so much dismiss the revolutionary passions of the crowd as she does channel them for morally inculpable ends—she polices enthusiasm by juxtaposing "noble passion," or *true enthusiasm*, and the ignoble passion of an excessive fervor for freedom, or *false enthusiasm*.

When *The Adulateur* ends on the tragic chord of Rapatio's late defeat of the patriots, the closing oration repeats the injunction that the crisis is at hand, directing us back to the beginning in a play that is about nothing but the act of beginning: at every instant, the epigram pre-faces us, in the "pause of life," and we are still inside a tragedy that is "now acted" *de novo*. But that's not to say that the play's tragic chord sounds lugubrious or hopeless: on the contrary, the specters of enthusiasm, accumulating in the recent past of unjust deaths, invigorate, once more, the indomitable cause of "the good old spirit." The play is *provisionally* a tragedy but it means to awaken those specters who have already claimed independence in advance (the past prophesies, in the sense of reads or compels, a future), just as Brutus claims said independence in his speech after victorious resistance to Rapatio in Act III, Scene III. When he tries to speak, Brutus is, at first, *"interrupted with an universal hout [sic, shout]"* before effusing:

> Oh! what a burst of joy was that—there broke
> The warm effusion of an heart that feels
> In virtue's cause. Gods! what a throb of pleasure!
> To look around this vast, this crouded hall
> And hail them freemen—what tho' some have bled,
> Unhappy victims—what tho' I have wept,
> And struggl'd hard to rescue thee, my country,
> This glorious harvest richly compensates
> For dangers past—nature looks gay around me,
> And all creation seems to join my joy.[82]

Here Brutus illuminates, in inchoate Romantic rhetoric, the convulsive triad: first, enthusiasm is a convulsive affect of bursting and throbbing, an immanence of creative spirit, manifested in response to an unimpeachable cause; second, enthusiasm is a convulsive address delivered over to transfigured crowds—or, it is a collective phenomenon of plenary being embodied in a "universal shout"; third, enthusiasm is an antidote to the convulsive context of historical slavery and the mourning occasioned by it. This scene serves as *The Adulateur's* event of momentary liberation, lost as soon as it occurs, but which will serve to galvanize all further resistance efforts: "While thou my country, shall again revive, / Shake off misfortune, and thro' ages live."[83] In a defiant act of prolepsis, Brutus claims a future enthusiasm already lived in his imagination and a "theatre of action" in which the patriots will themselves play tomorrow's specters, resurrected once again for the performance of dissent.

A Kind of Bee-Hive: Swarms of Enthusiasm in *The Pennsylvania Magazine*

Published from January 1775 to July 1776, the crucial nineteen months of the colonial crisis that ended with the Declaration of Independence (and printed in its last issue), *The Pennsylvania Magazine; or, American Monthly Museum* is an important source essential to any discussion of an emergent American literature for at least the following reasons: its immense success relative to the time period ("With 1,500 subscribers, the fat issues achieved a larger circulation than that of any previous American magazine"),⁸⁴ its editor and occasional author, Thomas Paine, for whom the magazine served as an apprenticeship and experimental context for developing his unique polemical style,⁸⁵ and, most important for my argument, its promulgation of a public in print revolt, that is, its endorsement of political enthusiasm in terms contiguous with *The Adulateur*.⁸⁶

A public in print revolt is the precise antithesis of ideal periodical culture in eighteenth-century thought. As *Pennsylvania Magazine* publisher Robert Aitken originally intended for his publication, a periodical strives for "strict impartiality"—a *dis*interested public—nonpartisan so as to "avoid giving offence" [*sic*] to any reader.⁸⁷ In its strong etymological sense, the *Museum* should be an institution devoted to the cultivation of national genius through the liberal pursuit of high achievement in the arts and sciences, but as Aitken explains, the Muse does not take up residence in a climate of enthusiasm. While giving credit for the magazine's favorable reception to the "laudable spirit" of the public, which supports the "improvement of arts and sciences in America" and patiently bears "with present infirmities in expectation of future strength," Aitkin admits that publishing a periodical in the present hour has many disadvantages, and "the principal difficulty" lies in the political climate: the crisis with Britain does not facilitate the spirit of genius that thrives only in the "fruitful soil of *Peace,* and in the fostering sunshine of *Constitutional Liberty.*"⁸⁸ No, since the "intersting [*sic*] struggle for *American Liberty*" preoccupies "every heart and hand," men and women of "leisure and abilities" do not apply to the Muses; they do not turn their attention to the Muse-um.⁸⁹ The independence movement compromises, perhaps precludes, the antienthusiastic ideal of a sober, scientific public devoted to things "useful and entertaining" that Aitken nevertheless will insist is necessary.⁹⁰ Note the paradox: due to the political crisis, there's a need for an independent American periodical, yet, for the very same reason, such a periodical is *impossible,* or rather, it cannot possibly fulfill its own aims. As a result, it will be an altogether different kind of periodical—a periodical of enthusiasm.

Or at least that would be the perspective of Thomas Paine with his "uncommon *phrenzy,*" his "effusions of a distempered brain," his political views which resemble "the reveries of some brain-sick enthusiast."⁹¹ Paine chiefly edited and anonymously contributed many original pieces to the *Pennsylvania Magazine* from January to August or September 1775, and his colorful, contentious, grossly partisan stamp on the first nine issues is markedly apparent. No doubt he was responsible for the rise in subscriptions, namely because he orchestrated the issues around the political crisis. By 1775 a culture of political enthusiasm had ripened: "The resort to force in 1774 and 1775 was more clearly revolutionary than it had been at the time of the first tea parties. In 1773, as during the resistances of 1765–6 and 1768–70, force was used to oppose a limited exertion of British authority. By 1775, the validity of that authority as a whole was contested."[92] Accordingly, with each new issue of the *Pennsylvania Magazine*, Paine outdoes himself in contesting such authority. Especially after the Battles of Lexington and Concord in April of 1775, the verve and punch of the magazine climaxes in the May through September issues, only to return to a much duller, pedantic exhibition of writings for its ensuing life, a few exceptions notwithstanding.

In January 1775's "To the Publisher of the Pennsylvania Magazine," Paine (the most likely author of the anonymous piece)[93] articulates his own theory of the periodical as the essential apparatus for influencing "the manners and morals of a people" either with "the streams of vice or virtue," offering a decidedly interested axiom that a periodical is, for good or bad, a form of tenacious seduction: "Like a lover, it woos its mistress with unabated ardour, nor gives up the pursuit without a conquest."[94] In case one were to mistake this as an ill-conceived, offhand metaphor, Paine ends his essay by conceptualizing the periodical as a "swarm" product of inviting nectar: "I consider a magazine as a kind of bee-hive, which both allures the swarm, and provides room to store their sweets. Its division into cells gives every bee a province of its own; and though they all produce honey, yet perhaps they differ in their taste for flowers, and extract with greater dexterity from one than from another. *Thus* we are not all PHILOSOPHERS, all ARTISTS, nor all POETS."[95] In a synthesis of "Utility and Entertainment,"[96] the periodical allures the senses but also provides work. It is a site for labor that stores up sweets so that the swarms can feed off every bee's talents. Like *The Adulateur*, readers are to be converted into lovers of liberty and contribute to that liberty with their own actions, but unlike *The Adulateur*, Paine's hive theater of periodical action does not require a single voice of authority or an elite presence to regulate the swarms: a bee both receives and gives instruction. Paine sees the periodical as the ideal agent for unity within difference, and popular representation is an emergent property of all the hive's cells. While the periodical materials are apparently devoted to cultivating the aesthetic judgment or "taste" for "flowers" and "honey," underscored by the enlistment of liberal vocations, the *Pennsylvania Magazine* uses essays and poetry in order to contribute to the ongoing political resistance movement. In point of fact, this turns out to be the useful point of the labor. Every one of the cells plays a part in fomenting and defending anticolonial rebellion. In the process, the print swarm invents its own literature of dissent. To take an exemplary case, the July 1775 issue includes poetic and prose allegories about "vice and ruin"[97] convulsing domestic harmony, historical anecdotes on imperial and monarchical corruption as well as English war savagery, humorous or allegorical essays of cultural criticism on English–American relations and methods for winning war, satirical works on English politics, and direct propaganda in support of the impending war effort. If one analyzes the three propaganda pieces, two of which are attributed to Paine, it is apparent how the politics of enthusiasm figures centrally in the ethos of 1775.

As a celebration of Congress Sunday, the colonial fast day that took place on July 20, 1775, the anonymously authored "On the Late Continental Fast" declares the corporate action of fasting and prayer to be a symbolic gesture of unity for a people "oppressed with grief" at the "present calamities," as the "attempt is made to subject the numerous inhabitants of this extensive continent, and their innumerable posterity for ages to come, to the arbitrary impositions of an external power."[98] While fast days had their roots in the Puritan Revolution,[99] many considered the 1775 Continental Fast, promoted especially by Calvinist New England ministers, to confirm an American Union; the day "long lingered in Christian memory as perhaps the most glorious moment of the Revolution, if not of American history," and yet the event was not so much a "pious union, but a civil union" informed by pious values.[100] Since Parliament will not listen to the petitions of its aggrieved children, the continental fast "petitions to the throne of heaven; where no prime minister shall obstruct or suppress our earnest applications."[101] This unmediated appeal to God as an ultimate transpolitical civil authority belongs to the higher-law enthusiasms that helped to forge a language for natural rights, and this also shows us something crucial about dissenting publics in 1775: religious communal practices were not excluded from the public forum on politics but rather find their place here as an active participant in the American Museum. When the author reflects, "How exceedingly solemn is the idea of the thousands and ten thousands inhabitants of a country eighteen hundred miles in extent united in one important cause, at one and the same time suspending all their various occupations in life, and, at one and the same time with fasting and prayer prostrating themselves before the God of their worship," this sentiment both reflects the said political unity of action and calls it into existence, disseminating "the idea" that unites readers who may or may not have participated in the protest, effectively including them in it.[102] The *Pennsylvania Magazine* works in tandem with the fast to consolidate the ideals of American collective action.

"On the Late Continental Fast" needs to be read alongside the other propaganda pieces composed by Paine in the same issue—the essay "Thoughts on Defensive War" (by "A Lover of Peace") and the song poem "Liberty Tree" (by "Atlanticus"). The former takes up argument against Quaker pacifism, an argument that Paine would popularize in *Common Sense* the following year. Although a lover of peace himself, Paine argues that, in the face of an "unprincipled enemy," "nothing but arms or miracles can reduce them to reason and moderation."[103] Paine then gives a quasi sermon on the bound relationship between religious and civil liberty: "political as well as spiritual freedom is the gift of God through Christ," and again, "spiritual freedom is the root of political liberty."[104] The historical development of political liberty, Paine explains, is the exoteric manifestation of the historical development of spiritual liberty; conversely, where there has been religious tyranny, there has been political tyranny and vice versa. Since spiritual and political freedom are mutually constitutive, to defend the one is to defend the other: "Political liberty is the visible pass, which guards the religious. It is the outwork by which the church militant is defended."[105] Paine's invocation of the church militant is revealing: this concept derived from the "Oliverian spirit" of spiritual and political warfare that, in the Great Awakening era, Calvinist ministers embraced anew as part of the "Work of Redemption"; by the early 1770s, the Revolutionary Church Militant was "conceived as a last battle with a monarchical Antichrist."[106]

The above issues also come to bear on Paine's song poem "Liberty Tree," which refers, of course, to the elm that stood near Boston Common and served as a popular symbol of political resistance to the Crown. Paine's pastoral song fable describes the Liberty Tree as an "exotic" "temple," planted by the Goddess of Liberty, for all who adore liberty, in "one spirit" and "one friendship."[107] In other words, the Liberty Tree is a kind of out-of-doors church, a plant of spiritual democracy, linking, like the continental fast and the church militant, lovers of liberty together.

That's why, prior to the current crisis and convulsive context, its inhabitants were "unvex'd with the troubles of silver and gold, / The cares of the grand and the great," but alas: "the tyrannical powers, / King, Commons, and Lords, are uniting amain, / To cut down this guardian of ours."[108] As part of the defensive outwork, of the rites of dissent, Paine's song, finally, addresses all—"the far and the near"—in the closing lines to "unite with a cheer, / In defence of our *Liberty tree*."[109]

As in every issue, the *Pennsylvania Magazine* ends with the "Monthly Intelligence," a section on the latest political news, with primary documents and official statements from both sides of the Atlantic. In the July issue, one finds "A Declaration by the Representatives of the United Colonies of North-America, Now Met in General Congress at Philadelphia, Setting Forth the Causes and Necessity of their taking up Arms." This "Declaration" recapitulates in sterling political rhetoric all of the July issue's previous arguments presented to us in various forms and genres. The British Crown has given the colonies only two choices: "resistance by force" or "voluntary slavery."[110] Now it is clear that the *Pennsylvania Magazine* has been building up an argument to defend the former.

Thus, Paine's contributions to the *Pennsylvania Magazine* as both editor and author ought to be seen as part of a broader attempt to experiment with a print form of political enthusiasm. This culminates in the January 1776 publication of *Common Sense*, a work well known for its sermonic style and emphatic call to action. Eric Foner claims that "much of the Paineite rationalist thought can be viewed as an expression in secular terms of ideas which the evangelicals viewed through the lens of religion" (namely the idea of a civil millennium), but the above examples, I think, show the extent to which Paine was comfortable using religious vocabulary and invoking colonial religious traditions to the point of suspending the difference between "secular" and "religious" thought. It would be more appropriate to say that Paine's essays, poems, and pamphlets reflect a shift in emphasis foregrounding a political enthusiasm—civil redemption—that, speaking "the language of millennialism," adapts the Christian heritage, the "Oliverian spirit," to the experimental demands of the revolutionary present.[111] This surely would have been part of the context for John Adams's response to *Common Sense*, namely, that Paine's unicameral vision of government would be liable, like any individual, to "fits of humor, starts of passion, flights of enthusiasm";[112] and William Smith of New York echoes: "The Author of Common Sense is a political Enthusiast. He has made others so."[113] In her poem "Upon Reading a Book

Rites of Dissent 85

Entituled [sic] Common Sense," Hannah Griffitts labels Paine an "Oliverian" who has "confounded" all "Orders" and made the "impartial Press, most partially maintain'd."[114] Enthusiasm, finally, serves to explain both a wild affective means of persuasion and a wild political position—they are two sides of the same coin.

Three months after the publication of *Common Sense*, in the April 1776 issue of the *Pennsylvania Magazine*, both Warren's and Paine's enthusiasm become a point of contention in the lead article, "Dialogue on Civil Liberty," a transcription of a January 1776 debate at a public exhibition in Nassau Hall (Princeton). Speaking on the proper ethical comportment for patriots in the convulsive crisis of the present hour ("an alarming season" of "dark and gloomy aspect"), the anonymous speaker, D***, conjures Warren's specter by invoking the "the unbroken spirit of a Brutus or Cassius" and the "sanctity of Cato's life" as historical examples of the virtuous and absolute right to resist tyrants, reinforced by a stanza from none other than Addison's *Cato*.[115] Subsequently, D. defends enthusiastic affect as a corollary of the convulsive crisis on terms very much in sympathy with Paine: "Do not blame me for the ardor of my zeal. The subject authorises [sic] it, the situation of affairs demands it. Fervency of spirit and promtitude [sic] of action are first rate virtues in themselves, when they are not employed in an unrighteous cause.—We have certainly some enemies to American liberty, who cover their lukewarmness under the plausible terms of prudence and moderation."[116] In response to D., the conservative, apparently Loyalist voice of prudence and moderation, F***, rejoins that D.'s "language of blustering and rhodomontade" betrays an ignorance of judgment and experience; it has its origins in the "high and ranting manner of speaking on the subject of civil liberty" lately seen in contemporary literature: "I imagine you have been lately reading some of the pompous encomiums upon civil liberty, or inflammatory invectives against Hutchinson and Gage, contained in the news-papers."[117] This statement is a perfect example of how patriot political oratory and print cultures were understood to work in tandem—as types of enthusiastic rant.

Finally, the last speaker, H***, comes to the defense of D., and by extension, of literatures of enthusiasm as well; H. argues that virtue and happiness in society depend so much upon popular liberty that "I do not hesitate to prefer, not only the confusion of anarchy, and the uncertainty of a new settlement, but even extermination itself, to slavery rivetted [sic] on us and our posterity." This view also informs H.'s defense of the en-flamed mobs that Loyalists point to in order to sully the unimpeachable principles of civil liberty; while the late mobs certainly have "sometimes a way of administering justice not over-delicate," the present case justifies them for the following reason: "they [the tumults of dissenters] are of no consequence unless the whole body of the people join in them; and I will not easily believe that it is possible to unite the whole, if numerous and distant, unless when the oppression is universal, and as soon as this happens resistance is necessary, and the convulsion is salutary."[118] In other words, the independence movement—and its convulsive politics, willing to risk anarchy—is a kind of exponentially endowed and popularly supported mob, justified by its universal shout of oppression and, I would add, inflamed by the ardent zeal of enthusiastic speeches and publications, doubled by the bee-hive of mob dissent—the *Pennsylvania Magazine*.

The Spirits Dart: Throngs of Enthusiasm in Phillis Wheatley

By the time her poem "To His Excellency General Washington" was published in the April 1776 issue of the *Pennsylvania Magazine*, the West African Bostonian and freed slave Phillis Wheatley (emancipated in 1773) had already established her reputation as an extraordinary poetical genius, dating back to her popular 1770 broadside elegy, "An Elegiac Poem, On the Death of... George Whitefield," written in honor of the arch-religious enthusiast of the eighteenth century. Earlier in 1770, during the occupation of Boston, Wheatley also composed one of the first, albeit unpublished, poems on violent conflict with colonial authorities, "On the Death of Mr. Snider Murder'd by Richardson." That the seventeen-year-old Wheatley eulogizes the young Christopher Snider, whose death provoked public outrage leading up to the Boston Massacre, as "the first martyr for the cause" against the "grand Usurpers," "fair freedoms foes," shows that a precocious concern about the precipitating political crisis lies at the root of her poetic vocation.[119] Wheatley's earliest version of the Whitefield elegy (Variant 1) shows a similar concern:

> When his [Whitefield's] AMERICANS were burden'd sore,
> When streets were crimson'd with their guiltless gore!
> Unrival'd friendship in his breast now strove:[120]

These lines ask us to read the elegy in the convulsive context of the Boston Massacre. Wheatley alludes to the fact that Whitefield, while in Boston on his last American preaching tour, delivered a sermon expressing pity for New England and the Bostonians.[121]

My contention is that if "Wheatley increasingly came to believe that the colonial struggle for freedom from Britain would lead to the end of slavery in the former colonies,"[122] then her Whitefield elegy and Washington encomium of 1776 exhibit signs of this belief from the vantage point of political enthusiasm. As such, Wheatley's poetry also represents a further radicalization of enthusiasm[123] compared to the works of Warren and Paine even though, for that very reason, Wheatley, speaking from a disenfranchised position, had to be rhetorically subtle in her convulsive address to readers. The critical consensus among scholars is that Wheatley's poetry deftly presses literary classicism, orthodox Puritan piety, and the republican culture of sentiment into the service of a black liberation politics and powerful antislavery critique.[124] If that is so, then, along the axis of enthusiasm, she occupies the same structural position in relationship to poetry as Warren does in relationship to drama and Paine does in relationship to the periodical. My point is that she translates revival enthusiasms into black rites of dissent while redeploying poetic conventions for insurgent ends, and one can see this in the homology between Wheatley's enthusiastic religious sensibility in her 1770 Whitefield elegy and enthusiastic revolutionary sensibility six years later in her Washington panegyric, both of which orbit around the convulsive affect of democratic throngs.

With regard to the Whitefield elegy, Wheatley scholars have not fully appreciated that, although George Whitefield was not an abolitionist, governmental authorities and slave owners held his egalitarian (equality of souls) revival movement de facto responsible for slave insurrections and popular anarchy, dating back to the so-called Negro Plot of 1741.[125] The same Wonderful Wandering Spirit of the Great Awakening that I discussed in chapter 1 was also said to manifest itself in the "Itinerant Way" that Harvard College condemned in its testimony against George Whitefield and his "enthusiastic Turn, utterly inconsistent with the Peace and Order, if not the very Being of these Churches of Christ."[126] Revival preachers such as Whitefield had no "lawful call" to preach, thus "destroy[ing] the ecclesiastical constitution established by the laws of this government."[127] Not only that but his preaching itself seemed more like popular theater than sermon: the dramatic, "aggressive uncontainability"

FIGURE 2 *Enthusiasm display'd: or, the Moor Fields congregation.* Library of Congress, Prints & Photographs Division, LC-USZ62-137507 (b&w film copy neg.).

of his speech at "revivals provoke[d] a base theatricality among a markedly antibourgeois cross section of society."[128] Consequently, critics saw the religious convulsions of revival enthusiasm as implicit rallies for the political convulsions of mob enthusiasm. Take, for instance, a 1739 parody of Whitefield in the print *Enthusiasm display'd: or, the Moor Fields congregation*, shown in figure 2.

Given that Whitefield held revivals at Moorfields, then an area of open land in London known for its popular amusements and public vendors, but also for its footpads, gay taverns or brothels, and generally low, licentious character,[129] it was easy to draw the conclusion that his ministry was cut from the same cloth: the scene of scantily clad women and hawkers in this image depicts enthusiasm as a seedy religious version of exploitative, cheap mercenary interests, which is why the woman to the right of Whitefield hands over her moneybag as the female figures of "Hypocrisy" and "Deceit" prop up the preacher. A lot more could be said about this image, but for my purposes, the poem written below it cuts to the point; its author writes that "Enthusiasm ... draws behind him ye deluded Throng," leading to extreme political consequences:

Rites of Dissent 89

> The Plot still thickens when ye Play's begun,
> As Thirty-nine approaches forty-one,
> The baleful Consequence our Fears avow,
> For what was Peters once, is WH—D now.

As a traveling player, Whitefield went on tour in 1739 to America (his first trip there) with a proposed return to England in 1741, and, according to this broadside print, religion was only a pretense: the author sees Whitefield as the return of Hugh Peter (or Peters), the notorious radical minister during the English Civil War who was executed as a regicide. It would seem that Whitefield's tour of America, just like his services in Moorfields, served to mobilize and incite political rebellion, despite what Whitefield said to the contrary. Again, religious enthusiasm represents a mob politics of subversion and civil war in disguise. Thirty years later, Whitefield's sympathy with the antibourgeois cross section of the Boston mob in the Massacre only corroborated the point, and it should also not be forgotten that numbered among the dead was the Massacre's first victim, the African-Indian American, Crispus Attucks, a primary figure of the dissenting rabble from whom Boston Whigs often distanced themselves (though, as I showed earlier, John Hancock includes Attucks by name among the spectral patriotic dead).[130]

In Variant 1 of the Whitefield elegy (the version published in Boston), Wheatley first marks the absence of the preacher as the death of the revival: "We hear no more the music of thy tongue / Thy wonted auditories cease to throng."[131] That the dissolution of musical speech is also the dissolution of the throng eulogizes Whitefield as the conductor of public enthusiasm. Through heroic couplets, Wheatley often establishes a set of critical correspondences between concepts such as "tongue" and "throng," and the same strategy underlies the subsequent couplet's parallel syntax: "Thy lessons in unequal'd accents flow'd! / While emulation in each bosom glow'd."[132] A lesson relates to emulation, accents to bosoms, and flowing to glowing such that Wheatley offers a theory of enthusiastic transmission between language and affective embodiment, from ideas to bodies and from articulation to action. Furthermore, the call-and-response between speaker and audience, tongue and throng, becomes a formal way for Wheatley to conceive the call-and-response of the rhyming couplet. She treats religious encounter as the harmony between speech (convulsive address) and the active body (convulsive affect).

After depicting Whitefield's ascent into heaven, Wheatley shifts the emphasis of the poem to the political implications of his religious enthusiasm. This begins with the aforementioned "friendship" Whitefield showed toward America, qualified by Wheatley as follows:

> The fruit thereof was charity and love
> Towards *America*—couldst thou do more
> Than leave thy native home, the *British* shore,
> To cross the great Atlantic's wat'ry road,
> To see *America's* distress'd abode?[133]

Wheatley enjambs the first quoted line (line 18) so as to collapse the difference between religious virtues and political ones; charity and love are formally independent, marked as Christian virtues, but then in the continuation of her thought, rolling over into the next line, we see that to express "charity and love" is to empathize with America's political plight. Rather than treat America as an insubordinate pocket of the Empire, rather than reinforce a vertical relationship between the colonies and the Crown, Whitefield participates in a horizontal transatlantic movement of affectionate democracy. Or, as the patriot Presbyterian minister Nathaniel Whitaker stated in his own 1770 Whitefield eulogy, a *Funeral Sermon*, "He was no less a friend to the civil liberties of mankind. He was a patriot, not in shew, but reality, and an enemy to tyranny. He abhorred episcopal oppression" and was "greatly concerned for the liberties of America."[134] Wheatley devotes the rest of the poem to establishing precisely the democratizing, even antislavery, undercurrents of the sermon and revival. That Whitefield did "Inflame the soul, and captivate the mind" was an effect of his desire to "see *America* excell" through a radical inclusiveness: "He freely offer'd [the Saviour] to the num'rous throng,"[135] as Wheatley words it in the 1773 version from *Poems on Various Subjects, Religious and Moral*. But the most important lines read as follows:

> Take HIM, "my dear AMERICANS," he said,
> Be your complaints in his kind bosom laid:
> Take HIM ye *Africans*, he longs for you;
> Impartial SAVIOUR, is his title due;
> If you will chuse to walk in grace's road,
> You shall be sons, and kings, and priests to GOD.[136]

First, Wheatley directly quotes Whitefield, but then ends the quotation and proceeds to summarize his sermon in verse form; as a result, Whitefield's and Wheatley's voices have blended. The poem morphs into a sermon itself, with Wheatley now as our preacher who tries to convert her audience to the cause of American freedom. But not only American freedom: while the throng of America is emphatically generic, absent of any invidious distinctions, at the same time Africans belong to a separate category than Americans. Africans and Americans should be united and equal, but without forgetting that the former do not *belong* to America. Like Whitefield, Wheatley encourages a democratic revival far in excess of geopolitical boundaries; accordingly, the impartiality of religious enthusiasm emphasizes that Whitefield's message short-circuits racial prejudice, which is also linked to the liberation politics of the Boston resistance movement.

All the same, just as in death "WHITEFIELD wings, with rapid course his way" to Zion, so does his offer of salvation pertain *solely* to the "heart" as an otherworldly revolution, divorced from the material conditions of slavery about which Whitefield was anything but impartial.[137] On this last point, Carla Willard cogently reads the Whitefield elegy as an exemplary case of what she calls "paradoxical praise"; as in all of her hero encomiums, Wheatley celebrates the "*emancipatory* power" of the slave-holding Methodist icon to throw into negative relief that power's hypocrisy with regard to his "acts in life" and the one who speaks the poem.[138] I would add that Wheatley also borrows Whitefield's own pulpit strategy of self-authorization through "humble self-enlargement,"[139] that is, a strategy of self-effacement that allows Wheatley to be an ecstatic conductor or medium of emancipatory power herself.

The same can be said for Wheatley's panegyric to the slave-holding George Washington. Six years later, her vision of George Whitefield's revival theater finds its counterpart in her vision of George Washington's revolutionary theater. Reflecting a shift in emphasis from heavenly to earthly redemption, a terrestrial apostrophe to Mother Earth replaces the celestial destination of the Whitefield throng, thereby altering the tone of Wheatley's poetry from one of spiritual consolation to political tragedy (the convulsive context of tyranny): "See mother earth her offspring's fate bemoan."[140] In her prefatory letter to George Washington, Wheatley states that his appointment as Generalissimo of the American army, "together with the fame" of his "virtues," have "excite[d] sensations not easy to suppress," inducing her to play a part in the "great cause" and its "success" through poetry, but also, in a symbiotic relationship, by inspiring Washington's "great theatre of action" itself.[141] In a strong sense, one can read the poem as a convulsive address to Washington and other war participants.

The poem's opening lines read, "Celestial choir! enthron'd in realms of light / Columbia's scenes of glorious toils I write."[142] Wheatley crafts the couplet so that her writing is a *predicate* of the crisis and its theatrical scenes, emphasizing not merely the primacy of the events and the poet's ancillary, affected role but, more radically, that the poem will transform "light" into writing and a "choir" or throng into "scenes"— that is, the celestial into the terrestrial and the sacred into the civil domain, abrogating the difference between them in the process. Her song now channels but also encourages the revolutionary throng. One can see this again in lines 13 and 14: "Muse! bow propitious while my pen relates / How pour her armies through a thousand gates." Wheatley's pen and the armies are two sides of one action and event, much like the tongue and throng in the Whitefield revival. In rites of dissent, light imagery ceases to be a mere figure for the contemplation of sublime nature and a serene Apollo, but, like the "spirits" of the Imagination that "dart" through "glowing veins" in her great poem, "On Imagination," the political light of Columbia now "flashes dreadful in refulgent arms" as a military activity conducted by Washington.[143] What would normally be a sublime scene of terribly divine nature is here an enthusiastic scene of terribly divine revolt. Since the Revolution consists of "scenes before unknown!," by implication, the poem claims an unprecedented task: to give language to the political enthusiasm of "freedom's cause."[144] In the reflexive symbiosis between author and subject matter, "song" and "throng," Wheatley endows the Revolutionary War effort with a language of enthusiasm just as Washington embodies it with his actions.

Even more radical, Wheatley admonishes Washington in lines 25 through 28:

> Thee, first in place and honours,—we demand
> The grace and glory of thy martial band.
> Fam'd for thy valour, for thy virtues more,
> Hear every tongue thy guardian aid implore!

In line 25, Wheatley includes herself in a collective body ("we") hoping to be liberated by the armies, which cannot but refer to the black population for whom she speaks. Moreover, by having "we demand" occupy the same line as "Thee," a forced horizontal exchange, a demand of recognition, occurs in the bold public address to Washington that offsets the

Rites of Dissent 93

conventional deference to a superior even while the dash marks the social gap or separation between Washington and the public (especially the slave population). For the same reason, line 27 suggests that while Washington may have "valour," his "virtues" are of more importance to the poet; in other words, the political-ethical stakes of Washington's actions matter most, not his heroic deeds. Wheatley wishes to remind Washington that "every tongue" wants his aid: the American Revolution ought to have global significance and redeem the "hopes" of all the "nations,"[145] including African peoples. In this sense, the "tongue" of Wheatley preaches a sermon on political enthusiasm directly to George Washington even as the public "we" for whom she speaks represents a political throng of enthusiasts circulating around Washington.

Not incidentally, Wheatley's poem to Washington is strategically placed in the April 1776 issue of the *Pennsylvania Magazine* before the "Monthly Intelligence," which, in this edition, begins with "*The Address of the Hon. Council and House of Representatives, to his Excellency* George Washington, *Esq; General and Commander in Chief of the forces of the United Colonies*," an official recognition of praise for Washington's recent liberation of Boston followed by his reply. Washington celebrates not his own actions but the pleasure that the "happy event" brought to the people.[146] At least in print, Phillis Wheatley's name is attached to this event as part of the throng of enthusiasm.

Cry for Liberty: Trials of Enthusiasm

For Mercy Otis Warren and Thomas Paine, the ideals of the American Revolution had been compromised by 1787 when the Constitution was adopted and all but negated by 1794 when the Jay treaty was signed, reestablishing an economic alliance with Great Britain on the latter's terms and, in effect, abandoning "long-standing liberal principles of neutral rights [which] seemed to betray the Franco-American Alliance of 1778."[147] According to many critics and observers, the emergent Federalist program and "the elite founding fathers had waged—and won—a counter-revolution against popular democratic ideals."[148] Even Loyalists understood the new Republic as an obstruction to the political enthusiasm unleashed by the colonial crisis. Take Jonathan Boucher's dedication to his friend George Washington in his 1797 critique of the War of Independence, *A View of the Causes and Consequences of the American Revolution*:

SIR,

> IN prefixing your name to a work avowedly hostile to that Revolution in which you bore a distinguished part, I am not conscious that I deserve to be charged with inconsistency.... As a British subject I have observed with pleasure that the form of Government, under which you and your fellow-citizens now hope to find peace and happiness... has, in the unity of it's [sic] executive, and the division of it's [sic] legislative, powers, been framed after a British model. That, in the discharge of your duty as head of this Government, you have resisted those anarchical doctrines, which are hardly less dangerous to America than to Europe, is not more an eulogium on the wisdom of our forefathers, than honourable to your individual wisdom and integrity.[149]

Boucher goes on to admire Washington's support of religion and morality, especially his resistance to the "din and uproar of Utopian reforms" promulgated by "modern revolutionists," probably referencing not only the French Revolution but also the Democratic-Republican Societies of the 1790s and the president's successful campaign to squelch the Whiskey Rebellion of 1791–94. One should note that participants in the latter rebellion were convinced that "state and national governments were undermining equality and democracy to enrich and empower a handful of moneyed men."[150]

The embattled political terrain of the early Republic should be kept in mind when evaluating the fate of Warren, Wheatley, and Paine as voices of political enthusiasm. In 1788, the anti-Federalist Warren anonymously published *Observations on the New Constitution, and on the Foederal and State Conventions*. Therein, she emphasizes that post-Revolutionary politicking and its consolidation in the Constitution is a "degradation" that demands redress "before they [patriots] are compelled to blush at their own servitude, and to turn back their languid eyes on their lost liberties."[151] The late ratification, distilled to its essence, amounts to the decision "that we must have a master," with a "many-headed monster" government, and the ingenuous coinage of the term "*Federal Republic*" equivocates about the true purpose of reinstating "*aristocratic tyranny*" and the "*uncontrouled despotism*" which will result from it.[152] In Warren's opinion, unless the people generally consent to it, the Constitution ought "to be thrown out with indignation, however some respectable names have appeared to support it"[153]—including George Washington.

Rites of Dissent 95

Two years later, Warren dedicated her first published collection of works signed in her name, *Poems, Dramatic and Miscellaneous* (1790), to none other than George Washington, a dedication which on the surface defers to the splendor of his virtuous character and heroic accomplishments, but in a text that obsesses over the corruption of republics ("*weeping the absurd* FOLLIES *of the* DAY")[154] in actuality Warren intends to admonish Washington about the true meaning of the late "convulsion that has been felt from the eastern borders of the Atlantic, to the western wilds."[155] Washington did not learn the lesson. After the Jay Treaty was signed, Warren exclaimed, "Alas, humiliated America!"[156] The suppression of the Whiskey Rebellion and the inexplicable military forays against Native Americans—"the wanton attempt of government to exterminate the simple tribes or drive them from their native inheritance," as Warren put it[157]—outraged her further, to say nothing of the personal loss that she suffered (the death of her son Winslow in the 1791 Battle of the Wabash) as a result of the army's incursions against the Northwestern tribes.

As a self-proclaimed citizen of the world, or "planetary revolutionary,"[158] Thomas Paine shared many of Warren's disappointments about the Federal Republic, especially U.S. foreign policy with Britain and France during the French Revolutionary Wars. Paine's infamous 1796 *Letter to Washington*, written while in jail under Robespierre's reign, went so far as to call the first president a "hypocrite," a "treacherous" Rapatio, "swallowing the grossest adulation" out of vanity, like that "speller after places and offices," John Adams.[159] The late "double politics"[160] of Washington's administration courts the favors of aristocratic vice while pretending to act in good democratic faith. The Jay Treaty with England, or to be precise, Jay's note to Grenville, was a "satire upon the declaration of independence"; when it reached the public, "every well affected American blushed with shame."[161] Although Paine once upheld Washington as the paragon of revolutionary virtues, even dedicating *Rights of Man* to him, "the politics of Washington had not then appeared"[162] to prove him mistaken in his judgment. Washington's present appearance leaves the world wondering whether he's an "APOSTATE, or an IMPOSTER," whether he "abandoned good principles" or "ever had any"[163]—in other words, whether Washington betrayed the enthusiasms of the Revolution or ever embraced them.

As for Phillis Wheatley, while no further record of communication exists between her and George Washington before her premature death in 1784, she obviously did not live to see the black American Revolution that she desired. We know her position from the oft-quoted 1774 comment that she made to the Mohegan Reverend Samson Occom about the "strange Absurdity of their Conduct whose Words and Actions are so diametrically opposite. How well the Cry for Liberty, and the reverse Disposition for the Exercise of oppressive Power over others agree,—I humbly think it does not require the Penetration of a Philosopher to determine."[164] Whereas George Washington praised Phillis Wheatley as a great poetical talent, Thomas Jefferson sullied her reputation in *Notes on the State of Virginia* (1785, 1787), published in English a year after the first American edition of Wheatley's *Poems on Various Subjects, Religious and Moral*. One should take a more serious look at Jefferson's reasons for snubbing Wheatley: "Among the blacks is misery enough, God knows, but no poetry.... Religion indeed has produced a Phyllis Whately; but it could not produce a poet. The compositions published under her name are below the dignity of criticism."[165] I suggest that one substitute "enthusiasm" for "religion" in order to understand what Jefferson implies in his historical context. He rejects black popular dissent, informed by revival enthusiasms, against said institutional "misery." Wheatley poses a threat to the genteel, elitist values that underwrite both Jefferson's paternalistic vision of white supremacy and his defense of classical poetics.

Thus, contrary to the Federalist assumption, naturalized by the 1820s, that the American Revolution was a "unique and completed event"[166] never to return, a rite of passage fulfilled and absorbed by the Constitution, political enthusiasts in the post-Revolutionary era saw the fledgling United States as an antagonist to the Spirit of '76—the American Revolution was not yet completed. I have been making a case for a certain body of literature that formalizes rites of dissent as revolutionary constituent power; however, born of a context-bound convulsive crisis, a convulsive address to political throngs, and a convulsive affect that privileges intensive democratic society in the making, literary rites of dissent, or literatures of enthusiasm, when they have not been drained of their enthusiastic aspirations, have often, like Wheatley, been beneath the dignity of criticism. After the Revolution that they helped to produce, such writers belonged nowhere—but their "cry for liberty" would be taken up again in the decades to come.

CHAPTER THREE

Shaking Hands with the Prophet
The War of 1812 and Native American Enthusiasms

> My Father—I have informed you what we mean to do; and I call the Great Spirit to witness the truth of my declaration. The religion which I have established, for the last three years, has been attended to by the different tribes of Indians in this part of the world. The Indians were once different people; they are now but one. They are all determined to practice what I have recommended to them, that has come immediately from the Great Spirit, through me.
>
> —TENSKWATAWA to William Henry Harrison, 1808

Few Americans remember, much less commemorate, the War of 1812. As the title of a *USA Today* article stated plainly on the event of the war's recent bicentennial, "USA shrugs as Canada goes all out."[1] But why? Most explanations highlight that, while it chronicles a decisive moment of political self-definition for Canada (successfully defending its boundaries from U.S. incursion), the War of 1812 was for the United States, at best, an epilogue to the American Revolution and, at worst, an unnecessary war and failed invasion that it was lucky to survive. Append to this that the War of 1812 belongs to that awkward period of the early republic when, amidst the presence of stronger European powers in North America, Anglophile and Anglophobic Americans were divided over the "trans-Atlantic Englishness [that] existed everywhere in the Americans' culture,"[2] and one begins to see that amnesia and apathy about the war stem in large part from its repulsion of the logic of American exceptionalism.

But there is an even shadier—and I think, more compelling—reason that American history has repressed the War of 1812: namely, that it was a means to sever British political connections with Native American nations in the western territories so that the United States could carry out its expansionist policies without impediment after decades of deadly military conflict on the frontier. To be sure, in the Old Northwest, the rise of a factional coalition of American Indians, outraged by U.S. claims on the Ohio territory via the contested 1795 Treaty of Greenville and the

1809 Treaty of Fort Wayne, represented the most formidable obstacle to westward expansion. Inspired by its most recent ancestor, the Northwestern confederation of United Indian Nations (forged in the wake of the American Revolution), the new pan-Indian movement that we typically associate with the Shawnee chief, Tecumseh, mobilized an organized multiethnic confederacy against American settler colonialism throughout the continent, with allies extending far into the Old Southwest. Whites would come to call the epicenter of the movement "Prophetstown" (in Indiana territory) after its spiritual leader, the brother of Tecumseh, Tenskwatawa, or "the Shawnee Prophet,"[3] who radicalized a long and developing tradition of nativist prophecy and its basic political program— "challenging tribal boundaries, altering Indian identity, inventing a strategy of resistance against Anglo-American expansion."[4] Consequently, the United States demonized the Shawnee Prophet as a dangerous fanatic, the key figure around whom the domestic crisis and impending war with England centered. As Gordon Wood explains, "Many Americans initially saw the war as a way of dealing with the problem of the Indians in the Northwest."[5] And that is, in fact, the only war the Americans ultimately won. Alan Taylor sums up the War of 1812 accordingly: "Although the Americans lost the northern war to conquer Canada, they won the western war to subdue Indian resistance."[6]

But if the War of 1812 has been largely removed from our national memory, then so has the literature written in response to it, making the era "an unrecognized gap in American literary history."[7] In this chapter I will explain (and partially fill in) this gap by showing how, in the literary archive, the political enthusiasm of the American Revolution discussed in chapter 2 is transmitted, in the War of 1812 era, to Native America and its struggle against the imperial tyranny of the emergent United States. Of course, insofar as it was "a continuation of the struggle about Indian land and who was to get it,"[8] the American Revolution also adversely affected Native American nations, embroiling them in the conflict and throwing their communities and settlements into crisis. Nevertheless, the patriot movement for inherent sovereignty required Native America to get off the ground. As Helen Carr puts it, the critique of monarchical tyranny and arbitrary power, leveled in the name of a "return to the original liberty and equality that belonged to natural man," rhetorically depended upon the "virtues of the Indian" as emblematic of the natural state, while simultaneously relying upon a notion of progressive (white) civilization that naturalized the subordination and dispossession of American Indians: "the binary contrast represented by the 'Indian' and the 'European'—nature/culture, origin/decay, and lawlessness/tyranny—was resolved by the 'American', the mediating and superior term."[9] In order to be "Native Americans," the term post-Revolutionary America reserved for its white citizens, it was necessary to view American Indian societies as anachronistic forerunners, as "legitimating ancestors,"[10] to American republicanism, which is why, in Philip Deloria's terms, "playing Indian"[11]—"displacing the history of actual Native peoples by inhabiting representations of Indians"[12]—becomes such a pervasive motif of American cultural practice.

But we ought to draw the obvious conclusion from the above: the American Revolution was a kind of disavowed and denied Native American Revolution. Gordon Sayre contends that, in the colonial wars of North America, "literary and artistic expressions of the resistant native are often not voices of the Other heard from across a cultural divide but rather an imperial culture employing its own timeworn tropes of dissent."[13] In a revolutionary context, I would add that American culture's officially sanctioned tropes of dissent tend to belie, to alienate, the anti-imperial enthusiasms that originally informed them, and that's partly why a resistant Native such as the Shawnee Prophet becomes "the ultimate other, the alien savage,"[14] spawned from a tribe of "renegades and terrorists,"[15] or, as Robert Montgomery Bird memorably called the Shawnees in his popular frontier romance *Nick of the Woods* (1837), those "evil-minded Shawnee creatures."[16] Furthermore, tropes of the resistant Native—or to be more specific, the Indian enthusiast—betray the fact that the American Revolutionary event, while it may have introduced a novel egalitarian principle in political history, nevertheless did not include Native America in its truth procedure, and yet, because an event's meaning and ramifications outstrip its empirical outcomes, it was possible to apply that "universal" principle in the post-Revolutionary era to the rights of Native America. Oppositely, the United States opposed the indigenous confederacy's enthusiastic dissent *against* imperialism by "playing Indian" once again in its repeat performance of the American Revolution with England; War of 1812 literature brings this truth to light. This historical and literary example, then, provides a crucial insight into the political role that enthusiasm played in early national ideology regarding Native America.

For the same reasons, this chapter will also make the case that War of 1812 literatures do not so much *politically remove Native Americans* from history as they do *remove a Native American politics*. By calling attention to this fact, I echo Native American scholarship that privileges indigenous struggles for self-determination and tribal sovereignty.[17] Recent historians of the Shawnees, for instance, emphasize that, culturally and nationally, "transience, mobility, and alliance" lie at the core of what it means to be a Shawnee, not as a passive, depoliticized response to colonial violence in what has been called the "Shawnee diaspora," but as a creative and critical aspect of Shawnee nation building in the larger campaign for indigenous autonomy vis-à-vis the virulent forces of colonialism.[18] Historically, this has played out as an internal Shawnee affair over the best means to secure the future of their heterogeneous communities. For instance, with regard to the multitribal revitalization movement, which included Delawares, Wyandots, Miamis, Ojibways, Ottawas, Potawatomis, Kickapoos, Menominees, Sauks, and Meskwakis, the Shawnees were certainly cynosures of political and cultural life, but we are primarily talking about a band of Ohio Kispokos and Pekowis who dissented from Mekoche Shawnee leadership, refused to join the latter's settlement at Wapakoneta, and articulated a different and divisive geopolitical vision: "When both federal officials and Wapakonetan leaders sought to consolidate Native peoples under distinct tribal governments, the Prophet claimed that it was not important whether one was a Shawnee or an Ottawa. The essential thing was to be an Indian."[19] It is not my goal—nor is it within my rights or ability—to adjudicate the historical decisions made by Ohio Indians, but rather, taking my cue from Mark Rifkin's "negative approach to self-determination," which concentrates itself on the anti-imperial critique of U.S. policy and jurisdiction with respect to Native communities,[20] I wish to point out, first, how the persistent language of enthusiasm in the War of 1812 era played a crucial part in American objections to any militant struggle for indigenous sovereignty in order to avoid the unthinkable—a Native American revolution against the United States on the same grounds (an insufferable neocolonialism) that the United States claimed in its war with England. Second, apropos of what Craig Womack terms the "interrelationship between the political and spiritual" in his discussion of Red Stick Upper Creek traditionalists (it's worth pointing out here that the Shawnee Prophet and Tecumseh had clan identities in both Shawnee and Creek society, and the Red Sticks were formidable adherents of the Prophet's movement),[21] the concept of political enthusiasm as I have discussed it thus far did index, if through an ideological screen, the innovative anticolonial activities of nativist-centered prophetic culture.

In the next section, I provide more historical contextualization of enthusiasm as an important term for understanding the controversy surrounding the American Indian confederacy and the Shawnee Prophet. Subsequently, I argue that, in a literary reconstruction of the War of 1812 and its antecedents,[22] three obscure historical novels—Samuel Woodworth's *The Champions of Freedom* (1816), Don Pedro Casender's *The Lost Virgin of the South* (1832), and James Strange French's *Elkswatawa* (1836)—do the cultural work of demarcating (unsuccessfully) white patriotic enthusiasm from Native fanaticism (or religious enthusiasm). It becomes apparent that a pro-American vision of the War of 1812 requires the white imagination to both inhabit and displace, absorb and alienate, Native American enthusiasms. As my final section demonstrates, this is a political perspective explicitly articulated in *A Son of the Forest* (1829, 1831), the autobiography of Pequot Indian William Apess. In response to the War of 1812, Apess was unique for his outright defense of enthusiastic politics as a democratic expression of Indian constituent power against white imperialism.

The Rival Powers of a Sham Prophecy and a Real American Bullet: Enthusiasm and the Shawnee Prophet

The Shawnees developed a notorious reputation as a "warlike, predatory"[23] people after suffering a series of abuses in the eighteenth century. To highlight only a few important moments in Shawnee history, their early allies, the French, betrayed them by ceding their lands to the British at the termination of the French and Indian wars, then the British followed suit at the termination of the American Revolution. On the eve of the Anglo-American civil war, as white settlers—including Daniel Boone—ravaged their communities in Kentucky with impunity, the Shawnees (and Mingos) lost (more land after) Lord Dunmore's War (Tecumseh's father was killed in this conflict), then two of their most esteemed chiefs, Cornstalk and Moluntha, both of whom advocated for peaceful accommodation with the United States, were flagrantly murdered during the Revolutionary War. Meanwhile, the Americans forced the Shawnees to cede tribal lands east of the Ohio River. It was no wonder, then, that a Shawnee delegation said the American Revolution was "the greatest blow that could have been dealt us,"[24] and that over the next decade the Northwestern confederation continued efforts to curtail frontier settlement and military presence beyond negotiated treaty lines. It defeated the U.S. Army at the 1791 Battle of the Wabash (or St. Clair's Defeat) only to eventually lose to the army of "Mad" Anthony Wayne at the 1794 Battle of Fallen Timbers, which resulted in the cession of the Ohio territory to the United States via the 1795 Treaty of Greenville.[25] A few years earlier, as reported by U.S. emissary and Mahican Hendrick Aupaumut in an epic 1792 multitribal conference, a Shawnee delegate of the confederacy stated their political position to the Five Nations as follows: "The United States have laid these troubles, and they can remove these troubles. And if they take away all their forts and move back to the ancient line, then we will believe that they mean to have peace, and that Washington is a great man."[26]

As an outgrowth of this convulsive context, the Prophet's movement must be understood as a political body responding to disaffection over a series of treaties that it did not acknowledge as legitimate and a series of outrages for which they never received redress, but it also speaks to a renewed attempt among American Indians of the Northwest Territory to preserve an indigenous vision of land tenure, what Mohawk Joseph Brant had referred to as "the Dish with One Spoon." Lisa Brooks connects "the Dish" to the recurrent Native metaphor of the "common pot": "The conceptualization of a cooperative, interdependent Native environment emerges from within Native space as a prominent trope in the speeches and writings of the eighteenth and nineteenth centuries, reflected in the metaphor of the 'common pot.'"[27] This establishes the convulsive context for the emergence of nativist prophecy, which Shawnee tradition encapsulates in the so-called Legend of Greed, a variant of which Tenskwatawa apparently told to Charles Christopher Trowbridge: "the white man asked us for a small piece of land,—a piece that a string cut from a buffalo-hide would reach around. We told him, 'Certainly, we will gladly make you so small a grant as that!' whereat the white man began to cut a very small strip from the edge of the hide, cutting around it. This he kept doing, going round and round, until the hide was all converted into a very long string that surrounded a large piece of land."[28]

After his calling by the Master of Life in 1805, the Prophet gives a convulsive address to his community that demands a collective (popular) conversion of the convulsive context. Colin Calloway summarizes some crucial aspects of the Prophet's vision:

> He renounced his life of debauchery and gave up drinking.... He preached that the Master of Life had chosen him to spread a new

religion among the Indians. They were to return to their old ways and traditional values and renounce the things that had made them weak and corrupt. Indian people might continue to deal with the British, French, and Spaniards, but they must avoid contact with Americans.... They must abstain from alcohol, reject Christianity, cast off the white man's clothing, and stop using his tools.... They should practice communal ownership of property and reject the individual accumulation of wealth the Americans pursued. Indians should not resort to violence against Indians, whether tribes against tribes or husbands against wives.... They should pray morning and evening to the Master of Life, using prayer sticks Tenskwatawa provided, and they should throw away their medicine bundles that, like their shamans, had failed them in their time of need.[29]

The Prophet's revitalization movement, then, responds directly to a U.S. political context; all the new practices are meant to defensively quarantine the tribe from imperial conversions but also to enact self-criticism.

In his 1830 captivity narrative, John Tanner writes about his encounter with the Prophet when the latter spread his revelations to the Ojibwas, and if Tanner's testimony can be trusted, the Prophet administered four strings of beans, made out of his flesh, and each person in attendance was "expected to take hold of each string at the top, and draw them gently through his hand. This was called shaking hands with the prophet, and was considered as solemnly engaging to obey his injunctions, and accept his mission as from the Supreme."[30] Tanner himself finds the Prophet so convincing that a "serious enthusiasm which prevailed among them so far affected me that I threw away my flint and steel, laid aside my medicine bag, and, in many particulars, complied with the new doctrines."[31] A "serious enthusiasm" about the Prophet's message means both converting to a new religious practice and a new form of social self-embodiment: by shaking hands with the Prophet, one comes into direct contact with him, one absorbs his vision; there is no separation between him and his audience.

Moreover, the Prophet's convulsive address is grounded in communal revival practices of convulsive affect. At Greenville, where he founded his first spiritual center before moving to Prophetstown in 1808, the Prophet kept his disciples "in a state of religious exhilaration. On almost every evening they assembled in the council house to listen to the Prophet's new revelations and to dance and sing in celebration of their deliverance."[32] After Tecumseh spread the Prophet's message to the Creeks in the Old Southwest, one Natchez Indian reported that "Tecumseh's new war songs and dances, was sung and danced in all the towns on the Tallapoosy,"[33] and this was the means by which the Prophet and his adherents forged further alliances and rebuffed enemies. For example, having learned many of their rituals from Tecumseh and his companion Seekaboo (a prophet of Creek or Creek-Shawnee ancestry), including shaking hands with the prophet, the Red Stick Creek "prophets sought through ecstatic singing and dancing to summon up sacred power of such force that their enemies, intimidated by this new reality, would drop their weapons in fear."[34] This amounts to a performance of enthusiasm that, like the rites of dissent in the repertoires of the American Revolution, is at once political mobilization and sacred-creative expression, not excluding ceremonial objects such as the Prophet's pictographic "sacred slabs"[35] or the effigies of himself that he circulated to his followers from afar ("Contact with the figure, and shaking hands with it by means of the string of beans, indicated acceptance of his authority").[36]

Furthermore, "enthusiasm" as such needs to be seen as an intercultural performance that does not presuppose a pure cultural or ethnic source. By virtue of the long historical transactions between Native and white communities, nativist prophets such as Tenskwatawa "were influenced by alien ideas conveyed to them by missionaries and other spokesmen of the Christian religion. They all borrowed from its teachings and rejected its claims."[37] But a testimony such as John Tanner's points to the fact that a reverse influence also occurred, and it would be worth interrogating further to what degree Native American religions in the Americas are a vital subtext to the historical critique of enthusiasm itself, especially given that a "pattern" of "charismatic prophet" movements overwhelms the early colonial record.[38] Moreover, nativist prophets were most amenable to enthusiastic Christian sects (most obviously, the Quakers) that did not always seek to convert them. Take, for instance, a Shaker visit to the Shawnee Prophet, recorded in the journal "*A Journey to the Indians*" (in "Miami near Lebanon, Ohio, 3d. month 1807"). At least as reported, this remarkable cultural exchange results in a sense not of indigenous or white otherness respectively, but of common identity, both religions recognizing themselves in the other, namely through a shared charismatic form of worship defined by immediate inspiration, ecstatic dancing, a message of reform and renunciation, and a kind of folk communism—in short, religious enthusiasm. Without understanding what the Prophet says in his religious meetings, the Shakers nevertheless believe that "he sensibly spake by the power of God—his solemn voice, grave countenance, with every motion of his hand & gesture of his body, were expressive of a deep sence [sic] & solemn feeling of eternal things."[39] Inversely, while mainstream American society rejects the Shakers, "we are all of them by these poor *Shawneese* both discerned & comprehended"; and in their departing letter to the Prophet, the Shakers proclaim to him, "*Brother*, we believe that the same *good spirit* is working in you & in us, which has told us how to put away all wicked ways & be a *good people*."[40] In his 1832 account of Native Americans, *Indian Biography*, B. B. Thatcher goes so far as to state as a matter of fact (falsely of course) that the Shawnee Prophet taught the "*principles*" of the Shakers, and Tecumseh adopted their celibate "*practices*" in his "matrimonial life."[41]

But Shaker communities of the early nineteenth century were, more broadly, participants in the democratic upswing of the Second Great Awakening, a revival enthusiast movement that "marked the beginning of the republicanizing and nationalizing of American religion."[42] According to Gordon Wood, the Second Great Awakening was "more evangelical, more ecstatic, more personal, and more optimistic" than the First Great Awakening of the eighteenth century, and this was a reflection of the enthusiasms introduced by American Revolution—"The Revolution released torrents of popular religiosity and passion into American life. Visions, dreams, prophesying, and new emotion-soaked religious seeking acquired a new popular significance."[43] If bound political and religious ideals of sovereignty informed post-Revolutionary white society, so did they inform Shawnee culture on its own terms; as the Reverend David Jones reported of them, "they look on it that GOD made them free—that one man has no natural right to rule over another. In this point they agree with our greatest *politicians*, who affirm that a ruler's *authority extends* no further than the PLEASURE of the people, and when any exceeds that power *given*, it may be justly asked, by what authority doest thou these things, and who gave thee that authority—whether in church or state?"[44] In other words, the fierce independence and dissenting actions of certain Shawnees, for which enthusiasm is a euphemism or conceptual shorthand, belong to a shared and recognizable theory of constituent power as the right to oppose any constituted authority in the event that it exceeds its own limitations of power.

Thus, far from representing an instance of fanatical otherness to the mainstream currents of American religion and politics, the Shawnee Prophet's practices fit rather harmoniously into the culture of the Second Great Awakening. That's why, when Benjamin Drake, in his 1841 popular biography *Life of Tecumseh, and of His Brother The Prophet* reports that, in 1807, one month after the Shaker visit, "Tecumseh and his brother had assembled at Greenville about four hundred Indians, most of them highly excited by religious fanaticism," this fanaticism is meant generically to describe a cultural disposition, a category of religion, familiar to readers.[45] Thomas Jefferson even echoes one of the core definitions of the enthusiast when he appraises the Prophet as follows: "*He pretended to be in constant communication with the great spirit.... I concluded ... that he was a visionary, inveloped [sic] in the clouds of their antiquities, and vainly endeavoring to lead back his brethren to the fancied beatitudes of their golden age.*" But there was "little danger" in this, thought Jefferson, until the enthusiasm became a platform for political dissent and the British found the Prophet "corruptible"; which is to say, once the Prophet's religious enthusiasm articulates itself in direct opposition to the United States, the "visionary" becomes a "rogue."[46]

Against a popular mythology that by and large persists, historians now agree that the Prophet, not Tecumseh, was the spiritual leader and prime mover of the confederacy. A fabricated narrative, told by white commentators, of divided aims between the brothers, the one patriotic and valorous, the other religious and demagogic, reinforced this historical distortion.[47] As a kind of public face of the movement, Tecumseh led the military and diplomatic wing of his brother's teachings.[48] For example, he famously spread the Prophet's message in his southern tour of 1811–12—"one of the most ardent efforts on behalf of eighteenth and nineteenth-century pan-Indianism," and "a significant prelude to Indian participation in the War of 1812."[49] At a council on May 15, 1812, after the anticonfederacy Potawatomi government called Tenskwatawa a "*pretended prophet*," Tecumseh, in defense of his brother, rebuked the "*pretended chiefs of the Potawatomis and others, who have been in the habit of selling land to the white people that did not belong to them.*"[50] Given, therefore, that Tecumseh would have seen himself as a delegate of the confederacy, one can read his oratory as another instance of the performance of enthusiasm, obviously in a highly mediated (translated) sense that does not assume the literal authenticity or authority of its transmission.

In a recorded September 1811 speech to the Choctaws and Chickasaws, two tribes with longstanding allegiances to the United States, Tecumseh first asserts the convulsive crisis of Native American life: "The whites are already nearly a match for us all united, and too strong for any one tribe alone to resist; so that unless we support one another with our collective and united forces; unless every tribe unanimously combines to give a check to the ambition and avarice of the whites, they will soon conquer us apart and disunited, and we will be driven away from our native country and scattered as autumnal leaves before the wind."[51] Tecumseh also has little patience for those who disbelieve in this context: "But what need is there to speak of the past? It speaks for itself and asks, 'Where today is the Pequod? Where the Narragansetts, the Mohawks, Pocanokets, and many other once powerful tribes of our race?' They have vanished before the avarice and oppression of the white men, as snow before a summer sun."[52] He then proceeds to the convulsive address: "Sleep not longer, O Choctaws and Chickasaws...in false security and delusive hopes," and later, "Be no longer their dupes. If there be one here tonight who believes that his rights will not sooner or later, be taken from him by the avaricious American pale-faces, his ignorance ought to excite pity, for he knows little of the character of our common foe."[53] Like Jefferson in the Declaration of Independence, Tecumseh subsequently lists the many grievances and abuses that Native American nations have suffered, hammering home what he earlier calls the "just cause of liberating our race from the grasp of our faithless invaders and heartless oppressors."[54] As for convulsive affect, one has to imagine the event of such a speech, like that described in the account of pioneer Samuel Dale, the "Daniel Boone of Alabama," who said of Tecumseh's visit to the Creek nation: "His eyes burned with supernatural luster, and his whole frame trembled with emotion; his voice resounded over the multitude—now sinking in low and musical whispers, now rising to its highest key, hurling out his words like a succession of thunderbolts.... Its [his countenance's] effect on that wild, superstitious, untutored, and warlike assemblage may be conceived: not a word was said, but stern warriors, the 'stoics of the woods', shook with emotion, and a thousand tomahawks were brandished in the air. Even the Big Warrior, who had been true to the whites, and remained faithful during the war, was, for the moment, visibly affected, and more than once I saw his huge hand clutch, spasmodically, the handle of his knife. All this was the effect of his delivery."[55]

But despite Tecumseh's militant promotion of Native American rites of dissent, it was the Shawnee Prophet who came to symbolize uncompromising, religiously self-authorized—and thus savagely enthusiastic—intransigence toward U.S. settler colonialism, though this was often displaced onto his putative alliance with the British. In many of his reports, the governor of the Indiana Territory and military foe of the Prophet, William Henry Harrison, concludes that so many tribes have come "under the influence of the prophet" because the Prophet has come under the influence of the British emissaries for war.[56] Harrison apparently stated to the Shawnees in 1807, "My Children, this business must be stopped. You have called in a number of men from the most distant tribes, to listen to a fool, who speaks not the words of the Great Spirit, but those of the devil, and of the British agents."[57] This serves two convenient purposes: to deny the confederacy any legitimate grievances or mature political program and to build a claim for the imminent war against England. At the same time, these comments betray that the United States rightly understands the Prophet to be a political foe and focal point in a territorial struggle waged over the fate of the American West.

All of the above issues crystallize in the 1811 Battle of Tippecanoe, William Henry Harrison's so-called victory over the confederacy at Prophetstown and a conflict from which Tecumseh was absent. Benjamin Drake ventriloquizes a conversation in the aftermath of the battle in which Tecumseh chastises his brother as a coward and false prophet for instigating war while he (Tecumseh) was on his southern tour. In fact, Harrison had aimed to preemptively attack Prophetstown. The battle was inevitable. Neither did the event decisively dissolve the confederacy, Prophetstown, or the Prophet's reputation and spiritual power as popularly narrated by Harrison himself and others.[58] Drake's biographical fiction of the Tippecanoe affair best exemplifies how the antebellum imagination interpreted the "defeat" of the confederacy as the defeat of indigenous enthusiasm. Most saliently, Drake narrates the Battle of Tippecanoe as a war between "the rival powers of a sham prophecy and a real American bullet."[59] Having apparently placed a sacred spell on the confederates in order to make them immune to harm, the Prophet assured his comrades of a victory, but the American bullet breaks the spell of Native American enthusiasm for which the Prophet stands: "His magic wand was broken, and the mysterious charm by means of which he had for years, played upon the superstitious minds of this wild people, scattered through a vast extent of country, was dissipated forever.... He had, moreover, nimble wit, quickness of apprehension, much cunning and a captivating eloquence of speech. These qualities fitted him for playing his part with great success; and sustaining for a series of years, the character of one inspired by the Great Spirit."[60] Now the confederacy reveals the "real" nature of its constituency—"the most worthless and vicious portion of the tribes," or, as one review cited by Drake describes them, "outcasts, vagabonds and criminals . . . brought together by the novelty of the preacher's reputation, by curiosity to hear his doctrines, by the fascination of extreme credulity, by restlessness, by resentment against the whites, and by poverty and unpopularity at home."[61] It was the vocational talents of the folk preacher, then, that held this rude band of unhappy outsiders together, and only the "credulous fanaticism"[62] of the Native American masses rendered the Prophet powerful. But after the Battle of Tippecanoe, even in the case of Tecumseh, "that *ardent enthusiasm* which for years had sustained him, in the hour of peril and privation, was extinguished"[63] by the "real American bullet." The death of ardent enthusiasm is the death of the Native American confederacy, a point that will be taken up further in literary reflections on the Prophet and the War of 1812.

A Warm Zeal for the Independence of their Nation: Native American Enthusiasm in War of 1812 Fiction

Elkswatawa; or, The Prophet of the West (1836), by "Virginia's Unknown Novelist," James Strange French, may be the only antebellum work of fiction to exclusively advertise by title the Shawnee Prophet (Elkswatawa was an alternate spelling of his name).[64] French's apparent aim to appreciate and judiciously apologize for "those unfortunate champions of Indian liberty, whose conduct and characters, owing to the animosity excited in the minds of the frontier settlers by a series of harassing hostilities, have been generally misrepresented, and painted by the hand of prejudice, in the darkest and most odious colours,"[65] as he says in the novel's preface, at first gives the impression that a southerner from Jerusalem, Virginia, who helped to quell the Nat Turner rebellion, will take up the cause of the Shawnee Prophet in a fair treatment of his history. One feels encouraged when French adds that he spent time in the West, and the "names and deeds" of its "celebrated individuals . . . became familiar to me as household words, and I felt myself able to appreciate more justly" their "talents and policy."[66] Chapter 1 shows promise in this regard.

Therein, French gives a scathing historical backstory for the Prophet's appearance on the novel's stage, beginning with "the powerful dictating to the powerless" (the Treaty of Greenville), of "one encroachment [that] was but the prelude to another," in the history of white contact with the western tribes: "patient endurance availed them nothing, suppressed murmurs were at first heard, then hoarser remonstrances, and finally out they spoke, talked of right and wrong, and denounced the whites as grasping and unjust, till the sparks of vengeance which were to kindle up a flame among the tribes, were then first blown abroad."[67] After the Treaty of Greenville, the Shawnees were especially aggrieved; and since that time the young Tecumseh and Tenskwatawa "had been constantly brooding over the wrongs of their country" until the latter finally arose: "Then came the tidings that a Prophet had arisen, who held daily converse with the Great Spirit, and ruled the tribes with an absolute sway. With this annunciation, the clouds of discontent, which had so long lain scattered in the horizon, began to unite, and settle in darkness over the west. At this period we commence our narrative."[68] One still has the impression here that French intends to establish narrative sympathy for the Prophet.

But with the commencement of the narrative, the reader realizes that French has a very different project in mind than chapter 1 suggests. The product of an accumulated rage, the Prophet is like a terrible plague brought on America for its sins, but for all that, he's still a plague, a devil unleashed by white colonialism, and a devil who must be exorcised. The novel quickly shifts to the gothic mode, and the Prophet becomes a familiar savage, the evil Indian, who holds the novel's maidenly protagonist, Gay Forman, in captivity as her paramour and our chivalric hero, Richard Rolfe, attempts to rescue her. When we enter Prophetstown, French offers his reader a typecast portrait of the Prophet and Tecumseh respectively: whereas the former was of "a dark and ferocious countenance, who spoke not, but sate apart, brooding on the visions of his own fancy"—that is, whereas the Prophet was an enthusiast—the latter had "an ease of manner, and a grace which marked him one of nature's nobles."[69] In an inventive dramatization, French goes on to imagine a time, in 1806, when Tecumseh and Tenskwatawa artfully contrive their revitalization movement as a means to create "one mind" among the western tribes. The Prophet is not a truly religious individual; instead, he stages his fanaticism: "Superstition must do our work," said Elkswatawa, "and by it we must master them. We must excite their fears. We must seem to work

Shaking Hands with the Prophet 111

miracles. We must see into the future, and the red men must be troubled until they say, 'behold the agents of the Great Spirit!' When we have done this, we lead them as we please."[70] This is the critic's skeptical translation of the indigenous convulsive address. French divorces the Prophet from the thoughtless tribes en masse and transforms his enthusiasm—his violence of passion, his elevation of fancy—into an expedient means to political despotism. Moreover, Tenskwatawa must play the Prophet because Tecumseh could never pull off the stage act: "No, brother; you are wise above most of the red men in the gift of speech. Your words flow sweet as honey from the hive. But you cannot dissemble. I can. I am the Prophet, you are my convert, and as such, must paint to them what they were before the stranger came among them, and make their misfortunes a judgment from the Great Spirit on account of their dissensions and evil deeds."[71] In the Prophet's mouth, French reduces the entire history of indigenous resistance to such demagogic dissimulation: "[King] Philip and Pontiac endeavoured to do what we intend; they failed, yet the earth trembled under their operations. I have studied their histories. Many Prophets have arisen in days past and been for a time all powerful. I have considered their plans, I have learned their tricks, their deceptions, their practices; gathering something from all I will perfect my character, and form my medicine bag, and with it will I trouble the red men, and they shall know no quiet until the same spirit animates every wandering tribe."[72] As a plot device, French's interpretation of the Prophet solidifies his and Tecumseh's tragic fate, since, by imitating King Philip and Pontiac, the Prophet repeats their failures. He assumes the role, "aware of its weakness," and not as a "fanatic believing what he preached, and led on by a bigoted zeal."[73] This explanation makes very little sense: the Prophet, by his own account, knows that other prophets and their followers have power only "for a time" before their inevitable destruction, and yet he decides to repeat their tragedy anyway.

Since the anonymous Indian masses are the genuine fanatics, in contrast to the Prophet's fully rationalized political enthusiasm, they ultimately become the weakness that dooms the confederacy; in French's Battle of Tippecanoe, "the warriors succeeded in forcing the Prophet to give them immediate battle," not vice versa. But this in turn fuels the Prophet's sense of self-importance. Now "determined to fight," Tenskwatawa reassures the warriors of the Great Spirit's promise to give them victory: "The fiat of Heaven itself could not have inspired them with more confidence."[74] Here, French imports the contemporaneous dictionary definition of enthusiasm as a vain confidence of divine favor or the extravagant hope and confidence of success. This enthusiasm follows from French's earlier vision of a Native American ceremony (a kind of gothic revival) where the tribes are converted into fanatics after messengers "invite the red men to hear him [the Shawnee Prophet] preach and expound the doctrines of the Great Spirit," down in a "Haunted Cavern" of "rude gothic grandeur," the best place for him to "affect singularity."[75] The "crowd" naturally responds to the Prophet's convulsive address and, henceforward, lives under his spell, ready to indulge "in all the unrestrained freedom of wild revelry."[76] The careful choice of words in these passages—preaching, affect, crowds—shows the extent to which out-of-doors religious publics and revival enthusiasm easily function as a popular image for implicit political terrorism.

In Volume II, the Prophet's "dark and midnight meetings" with the indigenous "multitudes" continue, only now the reader sees a further reason why French needs to invalidate cultures of enthusiasm: it allows him to undercut the confederacy's parity with the United States, for "as an explanation of his motives for continual preachings, and for sending far and wide his disciples, as he termed them, he [the Prophet] stated that he wished, in imitation of the United States, to form a union of all the tribes, for their own mutual benefit and advantage."[77] Although he rightly discerns the connection between nativist prophecy and American Indian nation building, French cannot accept their compatibility and makes the easy move of discrediting the latter by way of the former. As in Edmund Burke's critique of Richard Price (discussed in chapter 1), religious sermonizing and a politics of liberty can never mix. This is also implied by an earlier passage: "His opinions were seized upon with avidity, and propagated with impassioned zeal; and that they were to produce any other effect, than merely to better the conditions of the Indians, no human being could foresee."[78] Here is the double bind: that the Prophet falsely taught his followers that he intended to better their lives, not lead them into savage war, excites them to such a degree that they insist on going to savage war anyway, without bettering their lives. Would the right thing have been to candidly lead them to war? Of course not. Savage war—that is, Native American political dissent—is illegitimate by definition, but so is telling the "crowd" that they should work for their own benefit and advantage. For French, despite conceding the insufferable ills of U.S. imperialism in his prefatory remarks, no Native American politics exists so long as it is a politics for and constituted by Native Americans.

From the Kantian viewpoint highlighted in chapter 1, the Shawnee Prophet is thus a figure analogous to Oliver Cromwell. A strong and interested affection, a delusional fervor for freedom, corrupts his otherwise admirable sublimity of mind, leading him into the error of putting impossible political notions into action. On this point, the novel ends with the following literary explanation of the Prophet: "That power [of the Prophet's persuasion] must have been great, and a great mind alone could have created it, which enabled him to lead as he pleased, the lawless band of Indians who generally accompanied him; which enabled him, like Prospero, who, by the wave of his wand, called up tempests from the vasty deep, at his bidding, to lash his followers into the fury of a raging storm, or hush them when excited, into quiet deep as that of a sleeping child."[79] But this fantastical character assessment allows us to marvel at the Prophet, as a kind of Byronic superhero, and to appreciate, even while we cannot condone, his brooding enthusiasm. One wishes that French might have followed through on the implications of his political translation of the Prophet into Prospero, a removed king in exile, who conjures that tempest to restore his throne from criminal usurpers. The comparison is even more interesting when we remind ourselves that, in the Shawnee Prophet's account of his revelatory vision, he says that the Great Spirit created an Island for his people: "The Great spirit then opened a door, and looking down they saw a white man seated upon the ground. He was naked, and destitute of hair upon his head or his body and had been circumcised. The great Spirit told them that this white man was not made by himself but by another Spirit who made & governed the whites & over whom or whose subjects he had no control. That as soon as they reached their Island and had got comfortably situated, this great white spirit would endeavour to thwart his designs."[80] This adds an entirely new dimension to Benjamin Drake's assertion that the Prophet's "magic wand was broken": the great white spirit expropriates the enchanted island of prophetic enthusiasm, a figure of speech for the political autonomy of Northwestern American Indians.

While *Elkswatawa* may be the only U.S. novel devoted to the history of the American Indian confederacy up until the Battle of Tippecanoe, Samuel Woodworth's 1816 novel *The Champions of Freedom, or The Mysterious Chief, A Romance of the Nineteenth Century, Founded on the Events of the War, Between the United States and Great Britain, Which Terminated in March, 1815* may be the only U.S. novel of the era to chronicle the War of 1812 itself in any great detail. Famous for his poem-cum-ballad "The Old Oaken Bucket" (1817), Woodworth was a minor journalist, poet, playwright, and librettist affiliated with Washington Irving's Knickerbocker circle. *Champions of Freedom*, Woodworth's sole attempt at the novel, blends War of 1812 historical events and a romantic bildungsroman about George Willoughby, a boy reared in the western wilds who grows up to be a soldier in the war—a champion of freedom.

The most memorable character of the novel, however, is an anonymous, undead Miami Indian, "the Mysterious Chief," who inspires George's patriotic actions. The backstory is as follows: in the 1794 Battle of Fallen Timbers, Major George Willoughby, a decorated war hero of the American Revolution who served under George Washington with a "romantic enthusiasm for arms," and who "in the enthusiasm of his feelings . . . vowed to devote his future life and services to Freedom and Washington," has his right hand severed in battle so that he can no longer wield the sword of Washington that he vowed to never to relinquish.[81] Lying on the field of battle, a dead Miami chief, as an oracular corpse, then says to him, "You have a son, to redeem your vow,"[82] in reference to the simultaneous birth of his son back home. In honor of his hero, the Major names his son George Washington Willoughby. At the time of the novel's events, Major Willoughby now has a portrait of the Miami chief (given to him by an artist in the field) that he hangs on the wall in his house in the Ohio Valley where he settles his family. On Lake Erie, the Willoughbys live in perfect harmony with benevolent indigenous tribes, and George becomes "quite an accomplished savage" himself— in the noble sense, of course.[83] For my purposes, it's important to note that all of the events are framed around the problem of genuine versus false enthusiasm, the former tied to the military patriot's defense of America, what Woodworth calls George Willoughby's "general glow of patriotic enthusiasm," whereas false enthusiasm, attached specifically to Quaker pacifism by Major Willoughby, refers to any "spiritual enthusiasm" that makes no distinction between an ideal state of perfection—say, political peace—and the pragmatic necessity of war for a sinful, divided humanity;[84] as Major Willoughby puts it, "enthusiastic delusions" lead one to invoke "ideal virtues that cannot be practised."[85] Here too a real American bullet—a genuine enthusiasm—goes to war against a sham spirituality.

At a crucial moment in the novel, while George attends a masquerade anniversary party, a guest in a friar's costume accosts him. When the guest removes the costume, he reveals himself to be an American Indian chief—the "exact counterpart of the picture [of the Miami chief] in major Willoughby's possession." When George mentions this to him, the chief responds, "I have nothing to do with *pictures* or *copies*. I am an *original*. You are my pupil, and the day fast approaches when the lessons I shall teach you must be put into practice in your country's defence. Even now the tomahawk is suspended; the ambush is laid."[86] The Mysterious Chief, then, is not in disguise: he appears to be an original, resuscitated chief of the American Indian confederacy. Meanwhile, as we soon learn, he also appears to Major Willoughby, first in a dream: the Miami chief, now alive and well, hands the Major his sword on the field of battle, but, when he mishandles it and the sword falls from his hands, the Major wakes up to discover that his real sword has indeed fallen off the hook. Then in a repetition of the dream, the Mysterious Chief enters, picks up the sword, gives it to the Major again, and informs him about the Battle of Tippecanoe, the same event alluded to in the above message to George: "The Wabash will run with human blood before the dawn of morning. Even now the ambush is laid, the tomahawk raised, and the scalping-knife sharpened. Treachery lurks round the white men's camp. A prophet strikes at the heart of your country: and all this is but the bloody prelude to a long and more dreadful contention, the result of which will depend on that of the approaching battle. *If the valor of white men foil the treachery and ferocity of the cruel foe, then the Champions of Freedom will conquer in the subsequent contest with a mighty empire.* If not—Washington has lived in vain, and the blood of patriots flowed for nothing."[87] In the latter appearance of the Mysterious Chief, the lesson is identical: no dream figure, an "original" chief, the selfsame chief whom Major Willoughby killed, sends a warning about the Shawnee Prophet, referred to elsewhere by Major Willoughby as the "pretended prophet."[88] One also learns here that the first prophecy of the oracular corpse establishes George Willoughby's destiny—to defend the United States in the War of 1812 just as Major Willoughby did in the American Revolution. The Mysterious Chief not only prophesies the Battle of Tippecanoe but, importantly, reads it both as a postlude to the American Revolution and a prelude to the War of 1812, and a decisive one at that: a loss at the Battle of Tippecanoe entails a retroactive loss of the American Revolution and a tragic outcome to the War of 1812. Woodworth views the War of 1812 primarily as a battle against the Native confederacy and specifically the Shawnee Prophet, who strikes at the heart of the United States.

Woodworth's choice to resurrect a dead Miami chief and have this chief admonish white men to take up the cause of George Washington in order to defeat the confederacy to which the chief himself belonged is outrageous, to say the least. The ending is even more so. After the United States and its champions of freedom have valiantly defended their liberty, the Mysterious Chief makes a final appearance to George and declares the following moral: "Think of me as an *ALLEGORY*—and let it be recorded in your journal, that it is the duty of every parent to believe that his children are *specially* destined by Heaven for a life of *peculiar usefulness*—in order that he may be thereby induced to prepare them for such a life. I repeat—that, as the instrument of Heaven, I achieved every victory which graces your Journal; because (let it be recorded) whenever Americans would succeed, either in peace or war, their counsels must be actuated and their heroes inspired by the—*Spirit of Washington*."[89] This eccentric conclusion still does not explain why the "Spirit of Washington" has mysteriously come to reside in and revive the dead Miami chief. In *The National Uncanny* (2000), Renée Bergland reads the Mysterious Chief as "actually George Washington himself, appearing as a spectral Indian."[90] But no mention is made of the actual George Washington, only his "spirit," so that if a ghost appears in this scene, it is Washington's, not the Indian chief's.

There are at least two other ways to read this conclusion. First, the Miami chief, as a substitute American ancestor, stands for the genuine enthusiasm tallied by George Washington (Willoughby), the white man's symbolic Indian hero. More concretely, this might speak to the historical fact that the famous Miami chief Little Turtle, while he led the Northwestern confederation to victory in St. Clair's Defeat, wished to make peace as Wayne's army advanced upon them in 1794 and relinquished leadership to the Shawnee commander, Blue Jacket; he also began to work with the United States in the aftermath of Fallen Timbers and did not ally himself with Tecumseh and the Prophet's movement. At any rate, the Mysterious Chief, whether he symbolizes Little Turtle or not, either realizes that the Spirit of Washington—let us call it the spirit of enthusiasm—is destined to prevail over the western tribes (Washington's spirit cannot lose, says the allegory) or that he always had true enthusiasm in him although he did not know it in life. In this reading, Bergland's claim that the conclusion "establishes Indian ghosts as

Shaking Hands with the Prophet 117

fathers of their country, thereby constituting young Americans as the children and spiritual heirs of the Native Americans," still holds good, but her claim that the "transformation of the Indian ghost into the spirit of the first president works to remove Indians completely from the text—they were never really there at all"—does not.[91] There is no true removal of the American Indian here.

A better reading of Woodworth's concluding "displacement" of Native Americans requires us to be more attuned to the significance of the Battle of Fort Wayne and Tippecanoe. If Woodworth "removes" anything, it is the American Indian confederacy's defensive war of independence against the United States; in other words, it is the "Great Spirit" of American Indian nations—their own "patriotic enthusiasm"—that has been ghosted. The dead Miami chief truly did imbibe the Spirit of Washington, which is why, in an unconscious slip on Woodworth's part, unless he ingeniously intends it through a narrative of veils, the Mysterious Chief holds Major Willoughby's sword *in his dream*, as if at Fallen Timbers the chief was already fighting with the sword of Washington, on the side of liberty. In Major Willoughby's nightmare, the sword of Washington is turned against him (he cannot hold it), a perfect image of the War of 1812's counterrevolutionary cause. Thus, the Spirit of Washington, via the Miami chief (in essence, a nativist prophet), wants to "play Indian" in order to be fighting on the right side in the War of 1812. Woodworth, in an act of narrative transference, translates the confederacy's self-defense against U.S. imperialism into the United States' self-defense against a savage West, and the mystery of the prophetic chief lies in the unfathomable idea for white Americans that American Indian nations might be the thwarted champions of freedom.

This is a perspective that becomes explicit in one of the most jagged, motley, and unorthodox antebellum historical romances, uniquely devoted to the War of 1812's southern theater, *The Lost Virgin of the South, An Historical Novel, Founded on Facts, Connected with the Indian* [Creek] *War in the South, in 1812 to '15* (1831, 1832), an obscure novel attributed (without certainty) to either the Alabama publisher Wiley Conner or Reverend Michael Smith, but authored pseudonymously by the Spaniard "Don Pedro Casender."[92] In a wild, labyrinthine plot that tours the reader not only through the Old Southwest but also through Spain and France before terminating in New York, the story mainly revolves around the titular "lost virgin of the South," Calista Ward, the young daughter of an English colonel and Spanish lady, who is taken captive by a band of

Seminoles on the eve of the Creek War after her family shipwrecks off the tip of Florida. The unexpected significance of the title makes for the easiest entry into the novel's political landscape: given the captivity narrative, one might assume that Casender tells the story of a woman's adventurous struggle to survive the hostile and chaotic forces of the savage South, and this assumption would be correct, only the savages turn out to be Andrew Jackson's "licentious soldiers" who, it is assumed, will rape Calista (and indeed an unsuccessful attempt is made during the Battle of Tohopeka or Horseshoe Bend).[93] This is all the more remarkable considering that Andrew Jackson and his forces entered the war in order to subdue the Red Stick Upper Creeks after they decimated Fort Mims on the Alabama River "espousing the creed of Tecumseh and his brother."[94] While these Creeks are certainly portrayed as the "hostile Indians," the novel mostly represents southern Native communities as a refuge for European exiles from both Continental tyranny (during the Napoleonic Wars) and white America, a theme that becomes radicalized in a conversation between one of the novel's heroes, the ex-priest Don Ricardo Duville, playing an "incognito" Indian, and Andrew Jackson's aide, the Presbyterian preacher and Indian hater Mr. Blackburn. Duville indicts the American cause against Native American nations in the War of 1812 as a theological-political imperialism on par with the "religious and political fanaticism"[95] of King Ferdinand VII of Spain and Bonapartism more generally in Europe. In other words, what the Willoughbys consider true enthusiasm is here understood as national fanaticism.

But if *Lost Virgin* couches the War of 1812 as a U.S. war of fanaticism, it criticizes the Shawnee Prophet and the American Indian confederacy on similar terms:

> This [the Creek] war seems to have been commenced partly by the influence of the agents of the Northern Indians, who were on the point of a war in connection with the British in that quarter.
>
> An artful imposter about this time had sprung up among the Shawnees of the North, who, by passing for a prophet of the Great Spirit, who had commissioned him, acquired astonishing influence among them. His brother Tecumseh, who became so famous in the war of the North ... was sent to the Southern Indians to incite them to hostility also.... He told the [Creek Nation] Indians of the great power and riches of the English, who would succor them, even to the subjection of the United States.[96]

In this passage Casender explains away indigenous resistance as ancillary to British interests, part and parcel of a cynical struggle for "power and riches." Once again, that Tenskwatawa passes as a prophet affirms the cultural ideology of the enthusiast as one who marshals religious authority in the service of ignoble political ends. Likewise, converts to the religion of the Shawnee Prophet, the hostile Creeks, "believed as their prophets had told them, that the Great Spirit was on their side," inducing them to obtain "arms and ammunition at Pensacola from the Spaniards"[97] and commence the Fort Mims Massacre. Casender sees indigenous enthusiasm and colonial militarism as two sides of the same coin, but he ultimately gives the confederacy no agency or outlook of its own: "These Indians are rendered mad by British influence. . . . Yet all this wrong and misery, blood shed [sic] and death, of white and red men is to be attributed to the bad policy of the governments of Britain and the United States."[98] Less than two decades after the War of 1812, Casender more or less agrees with today's historians on the "status quo ante bellum" established by the 1814 Treaty of Ghent: "both parties will end as they began, without any benefit resulting to either,"[99] though the British did grant a "belated victory" to the United States by "abandoning impressment and leaving the Indians to their American fate."[100]

In other places, however, Casender not only blames the outbreak of indigenous enthusiasm on American and British policies but also implicitly justifies said enthusiasm and the right to resist imperial encroachments. For example, when arguing against the aforementioned Mr. Blackburn on the point of Native American war "cruelties," Duville forcefully states: "How . . . would the American white people justify the conduct of the Indians, if they being the strongest, should invade their country and destroy them, because some white people should have happened to commit similar depredations, as is alleged against some of our red brethren? Did ever any civilized nation make a cause of war against another whole nation and take their land, because of the depredations of a few? No."[101] It is therefore hard not to hear a double and ironic voice at work in other passages, such as when the narrator details the Battle of New Orleans (whereby the U.S. successfully defended the city from British seizure) as follows: "It is in accordance with the principles of justice and the rights of man, to war against an invading foe. It is pure patriotism to defend the land of one's birth and one's home. But it is sinful to become the invaders for money, and a robbery of the rights of man to compell [sic] him to become an invader!"[102] But if that's the case, the Duville passage above precisely intends to position Native America as a coalition of nations at patriotic war against an "invading foe."

In another significant passage, the narrator confronts the problem of the Indian enthusiast directly, this time in reference to a Creek prophet and ally of the confederacy, Monohoe, and his war against "invading white foes": "Whether any of these persons were really inspired or not, *with any spirit other than a warm zeal for the independence of their nation, and a strong belief that the great spirit would assist them in its maintenance*, we will not pretend to say—Yet little doubt can be entertained, but that they believed, that they had the direction of the Almighty communicated to them, by dreams, visions &c. Such persuasions are entertained by many persons of a religious turn of mind—who would not wish a comparison of their intellectual faculties to be made with Monohoe's."[103] Notice that the narrator suspends judgment on the authenticity of Native American enthusiasm so as to highlight two germane points—first, that the ethos of inspiration, whether true or false, conceals a more important affective desire and struggle for indigenous sovereignty and national independence; and second, that such enthusiasm, even if delusional, would be no argument for Native American savagery since it is a common "turn of mind" among religious persons, including those who wrongly view themselves as superior to or more civilized (at least intellectually) than Native American prophets.

Despite these apologies for indigenous sovereignty, Native American political resistance still cannot be affirmed as such; instead, Casender closes out the novel calling the United States a land "where political and religious freedom prevail" and "government was not prostituted to the vile purposes of avarice, superstition, bigotry and religious fanaticism,"[104] even though the thrust of the narrative tends to demonstrate otherwise. Still, as in *Elkswatawa* and *Champions of Freedom*, American Indians are not truly removed from the text in *Lost Virgin*, only their warm zeal for the independence of their nations—that is, their true enthusiasm. And yet such a fervor for freedom is surely the most compelling leitmotif of this otherwise sprawling and confused story. We, as readers, are more likely to give Calista's adopted Seminole father, Ropaugh, the last word on the novel's political agenda as he dies "from the malice of the white people against their colored brethren."[105] He says on his deathbed, "Oh! could all the white people believe that the Indians were their own brothers and sisters indeed, as they surely are, all having one great father; they would deal more tenderly with them, like as the good people called

Quakers did in the North with the Indians; then there was no war amongst them—good will begets good will, and love begets love—and this is pleasing to the great spirit to see all his red, white and black children live together in peace, on this wide and rich land, where there is room enough for all."[106] In the spirit of Ropaugh, *The Lost Virgin* is a strikingly radical work of fiction for 1832, but to various degrees, all of the above War of 1812 novels, from the Prophet Prospero to the Mysterious Chief to the Incognito Indian, articulate Native America's rightful claim to enthusiastic dissent even while they deny it.

Let the Thing Be Changed: William Apess as Political Enthusiast

The writings of the Pequot Indian and Methodist minister William Apess not only affirm a nativist-centered, pan-Indian politics of enthusiasm but also inaugurate a Native American textual tradition of enthusiastic dissent in English. I prefer to think of this as Apess's unique intellectual contribution to a broader transnational culture of revolutionary enthusiasm (and literatures of enthusiasm): like many of his contemporaries, Apess employs an "alternative separatist rhetoric" of prophetic, antiracist protest, but specifically to oppose "a hegemonic Puritan identity"[107] that he associates with the Manifest Destiny philosophy of U.S. Empire and American Indian removal policy. With regard to the American Indian confederacy and nativist prophecy, I agree with Joshua David Bellin that Apess's works are "rearticulations—revivals—of the nativist politics of identity that originated in the century before his," including the Radical Indigenism of the revitalization movements, and that it is a mistake to view his Methodism as a compromise of such a politics, if only because it was "precisely the nature of the prophetic tradition to *transmit* Indianness by *transforming* it."[108] While scholars have devoted much attention to the way that Apess, as a "transcultural individual,"[109] conceives of his Nativeness and Christianity as mutually constitutive and mutually informative, always with an eye toward the vigorous assertion of indigenous political sovereignty,[110] my own position is that, rather than focus on the politics of his identity, we should underscore the identity of his politics. If the American Indian confederacy represents the evental force, the revolutionary rupture, of a novel maxim of Native equality and unity, then Apess carries out the truth procedure of articulating its ultimate ramifications. However, to stake his claim as a modern intellectual of "universal" history (including within it the unrepresented, excluded reality of Native American history), Apess synthesizes, he tallies, he innovates upon, the many and varied cultural forms of enthusiasm—religious and political, derived from both indigenous and Euro-American traditions—compatible with democratic progress and anti-imperial critique. In this sense, William Apess transmits or interprets the tongue of enthusiasm for both white and Native peoples (though not exclusively for them)—he labors for an enthusiasm in common.

Although Apess's first work, *A Son of the Forest: The Experience of William Apess, a Native of the Forest* (1829, 1831), can be easily mistaken for a standard Christian conversion narrative, an account of the Pilgrim's progress from a life of sin to salvation, upon closer inspection his autobiography rewrites Christian typology on indigenous political terms: the path begins with the "sinful" convulsive context of white America but leads to the freedom or "salvation" of the Native American forest. In the beginning of *A Son of the Forest*, Apess gives us a short genealogy of his family in order to point to acts of "treachery" and the "violation" of "inherent rights" practiced against his people, the Pequot, dating all the way back to King Philip with whom he claims blood affiliation.[111] Already this is a communal narrative rooted, on the one hand, in the violence of colonialism (for which Apess further blames the disintegration of his nuclear family) and, on the other hand, in a patriotic history of indigenous resistance (for which King Philip stands). Apess's own life story merely represents one more articulation of said violence and resistance in a new logic of its appearance (the past as condition, the present as agent). This is why, when he tells us about his formative experiences as a bound-out servant of various white households, Apess carefully chooses his language, emphasizing the "spirit of obedience" instilled in him by his educators and reinforced through continual beatings and racially motivated persecutions; then, in defiance of all three of his families (the Furmans, the Hillhouses, the Williamses), Apess performs a "grand act of disobedience"[112] again and again by attending evangelical meetings, first of the "Christians," probably a dissenting Methodist congregation, and later of the "*noisy Methodists*" proper. It is at these meetings that Apess, "affected even unto tears," hears an enfranchising doctrine, a convulsive address, an egalitarian maxim for the first time: "I felt an assurance that I was included in the plan of redemption with all my brethren."[113] Linked to this assurance, Apess finds common ground with what he views as Methodist alienation from the mainstream, culturally elite Congregational communities to which his last two prominent and politically powerful families belong: "The power of the Holy Ghost moved forth among the people—the spirit's influence was felt at every meeting.... In a little time the work rolled onward like an overwhelming flood. Now the Methodists and all who attended their meetings were greatly persecuted." For Apess, to convert to enthusiastic Christianity, to experience the convulsive affect of Holy Ghost revival, is to convert to a *doctrine of disobedience* for which "age, sect, color, country, or situation made no difference,"[114] and he is further confirmed in this doctrine when he suffers abuse from the Williams family "in consequence of my being a Methodist."[115]

Apess, however, soon lapses from Christian piety and runs away from home before joining the U.S. Army (during the War of 1812) where he takes up the "wickedness of the soldiers." Here he inserts this choice piece of criticism: "Now, my enlistment was against the law, but I did not know it; I could not think why I should risk my life and limbs in fighting for the white man, who had cheated my forefathers out of their land."[116] That the United States illegally dispossessed his people (by military force no less) and illegally enlisted him to fight in its war are connected actions in Apess's mind: they are both operations of a seamless historical imperialism, yesterday and today. More important, Apess's sinful debauchery and ignorance, his *hamartia*, blinds him to the evil of his military service. Assigned to the army "destined to conquer Canada," Apess then states unequivocally that the War of 1812 was also an attempt to take a people's land: "They thought it a great thing to march through the country and assist in taking the enemy's land."[117] It is not that the U.S. Army indirectly relates to the land stolen from his ancestors; the United States is a land conqueror by definition, the selfsame culprit of Native American dispossession. The plight of Native American nations and Canada in the War of 1812 are part of the same historical narrative.

After the war, the Army adds insult to injury by failing to reward Apess with the "forty dollars bounty money and one hundred and sixty acres of land"[118] that he was promised for his services. He was illegally enlisted in the war and then illegally forgotten. Apess comments, "But I could never think that the government acted right toward the '*Natives*,' not merely in refusing to pay us but in claiming our services in cases of perilous emergency, and still deny us the right of citizenship; and as long as our nation is debarred the privilege of voting for civil officers, I shall believe that the government has no claim on our services."[119] Intentionally or not, this critique has more scathing implications than one might realize when one recalls that the stated reason for the U.S. declaration of war on England in the War of 1812 was that the latter did not respect U.S. sovereignty by continuing to impress American soldiers in the British navy as subjects of the Crown. By the same logic, Americans impressed individuals from sovereign American Indian nations into its war, even though they were not American subjects or citizens of the United States. If English impressment of American soldiers was neocolonialism, then so was American impressment of indigenous peoples. On this point, is it also striking how Apess uses the language of "our nation" for Native America; by extension, the War of 1812 ought to be grounds for united American Indian nations corporately declaring war on the United States. That's why Apess is careful to mime the strict thinking of American ideology here, such as when he observes that "many a brave man fell—fell in the defense of his country's rights."[120] In this way, Apess points to the endless hypocrisy of the United States when Native Americans likewise claim such a defense. This becomes explicit when he transitions from the War of 1812 to a sweeping interpolated paragraph on Native American dispossession at the beginning of chapter 6:

> No doubt there are many good people in the United States who would not trample upon the rights of the poor, but there are many others who are willing to roll in their coaches upon the tears and blood of the poor and unoffending natives—those are ready at all times to speculate on the Indians and defraud them out of their rightful possessions. Let the poor Indian attempt to resist the encroachments of his white neighbors, what a hue and cry is instantly raised against him. It has been considered as a trifling thing for the whites to make war on the Indians for the purpose of driving them from their country and taking possession thereof. This was, in their estimation, all right, as it helped to extend the territory and enriched some individuals. But let the thing be changed. Suppose an overwhelming army should march into the United States for the purpose of subduing it and enslaving the citizens; how quick would they fly to arms, gather in multitudes around the tree of liberty, and contend for their rights with the

last drop of their blood. And should the enemy succeed, would they not eventually rise and endeavor to regain liberty? And who would blame them for it?[121]

In context, this passage (which sounds very much like Duville in the *Lost Virgin*) must be read as Apess's reflection on the War of 1812 as a campaign of aggression, not only against Canada, but also against American Indian nations in the West; conversely, for those Native Americans, including members of the American Indian confederacy who fought with the British, it was a war of resistance to tyranny.

After leaving the Army, Apess moves from place to place and job to job before he stays with some of his "brethren" (probably Mohawks) in the woods of the Bay of Quinte on Lake Ontario, the first time in Apess's life that he communes with other Native peoples—and this experience marks a narrative volta, a conversion moment, a dramatic *anagnorisis* in the autobiography. When he recalls, "I then turned my eyes to the forest, and it seemed alive with its sons and daughters," Apess ascribes spiritual agency to the forest, which claims him as its son. Lisa Brooks reads this moment as Apess's participation in the reclamation of Native space and the indigenous struggle for the common pot: "In reclaiming his identity as a 'son of the forest,' he [Apess] recovered a conceptual interdependence. The son reclaimed the forest as the place of his birth and the pot that sustained him, thereby reclaiming his identity as a 'Native,' in accordance with Wzokhilain's sense of being human and being born of this land.... Although he had been separated from his Native community ... the land still recognized him as one of its own."[122] The forest scene is important, moreover, because Apess subsequently makes comments that, on first consideration, read like a concession to the Christian civilizing mission of the heathen Indian. Against those who do not believe in the capacity of Native Americans to "improve" themselves, Apess marshals this evidence to the contrary: "The forests of Canada and the West are vocal with the praises of God, as they ascend from the happy wigwams of the natives. We see them flocking to the standard of Emmanuel."[123] Once again, the divine forest is the active subject of Native revitalization, if only because, as Apess explains elsewhere, Native Americans are God's chosen people, descendants of the ten lost tribes of Israel, "brought out of the wilderness of sin into the Canaan of Gospel Liberty."[124] In effect, Apess wants to reclaim, to steal back, Christianity *as* indigenous. Nevertheless, the tenor of this rhetorical argument indisputably participates in the regulative work that we have seen time and again in the cultural criticism of enthusiasm: Native religion finds its redeemed expression in Christian faith, although it is the experience of the forest itself that sets Apess on a course of devotion until he finally feels the "awakening power"[125] of the Holy Spirit at a Methodist camp meeting and turns revival preacher himself. When Apess speaks directly to the reader at the end of his autobiography, enjoining us, the "brethren," to look "at the natives of the forest ... [who] will occupy seats in the kingdom of heaven before you," it becomes clear that Apess has been preaching to us all along: in his convulsive address, the reader has been asked to convert to a "*new* doctrine"[126] of enthusiasm that includes the songs and shouts of forest revivalism.

The political stakes of Apess's religious doctrine of enthusiasm are more pronounced in *The Increase of the Kingdom of Christ: A Sermon* (1831). Here we are taught that Christ's kingdom—a proindigenous kingdom—collides with the "kingdoms of this world," the latter ruled over by the "rich" and "powerful," "while the poor are enslaved and doomed to much servile drudgery." And if the American Indians descend from the lost tribes of Israel, does not the "great American nation [have] reason to fear the swift judgments of heaven on them for nameless cruelties, extortions, and exterminations inflicted upon the poor natives of the forest?"[127] The increase of Christ, therefore, implies the increase of Native American freedoms. That's why, as proof of the millennial spirit of revivalism from the days of "Wesley, and Whitefield, and Edwards" to the present, the "tribes of the wilderness are [now] in motion," but this motion will ultimately necessitate "revolutions, changes, and the shaking of the nations."[128] Once exported to and claimed by Native America, enthusiastic revival will lead to political revolution: the Gospel of Canaan Liberty and the Gospel of Political Liberty are two sides of the same indigenous enthusiasm.

That *A Son of the Forest* is designed to be a collective narrative of the Native American experience helps to explain why Apess adds a short anthology of texts on Native American history, with his own commentary and annotations, in the *Appendix*, which is approximately the same length as the autobiography itself. By Apess's own account, the appendix is at least as important to the work as his personal narrative; he makes room for it by abridging his own story: "Believing that some general observations on the origin and character of the Indians, as a nation, would be acceptable to the numerous and highly respectable persons who have lent their patronage to his work, the subscriber has somewhat abridged 'his life' to make room for this Appendix."[129] Why does Apess place "his life" in quotation marks? Probably because he sees it as merely exemplary, an appendix or footnote to the American Indian "nation"; in other words, Apess has his "experience," but it is subordinate to the generic appellation, "a son of the forest." This is significant once Apess explicitly attaches the American Indian confederacy to his own story. He quotes approvingly from De Witt Clinton, who writes, "They [the 'very ancient men'] derive however some consolation from a prophecy of ancient origin and universal currency among them, that the men of America will, at some future period, regain their ancient ascendancy and expel the man of Europe from this western hemisphere. This flattering and consolatory persuasion has enabled the Seneca and Shawnee prophets to arrest, in some tribes, the use of intoxicating liquors, and has given birth, at different periods, to attempts for a general confederacy of the Indians of North America'."[130] And when he turns to Christian missions among Native tribes, Apess includes a testimony of successful and hospitable communications with the Shawnees, "the most savage of the Indian nations," but supplements this by referring to David Brainerd's opinion of a "devout and zealous reformer" among the American Indians of New England: "He was considered and derided by the other Indians as a precise zealot, who made an unnecessary noise about religious matters, but in Mr Brainerd's opinion, there was something in his temper and disposition that looked more like true religion than anything he had observed among other heathen Indians."[131] Thus, in the decades after the War of 1812, William Apess incorporates both the confederacy and nativist prophecy into his own autobiography and heritage of "true religion," transmitting pan-Indian nationalism in the process.

As many critics have noted, by the time that he publishes his two late works, *Indian Nullification of the Unconstitutional Laws of Massachusetts Relative to the Marshpee Tribe; or, The Pretended Riot Explained* (1835) and *Eulogy on King Philip, as Pronounced at the Odeon, in Federal Street, Boston* (1836), Apess had discovered the limits of Methodism after he "came to experience racism and exclusion as he struggled first to become licensed and later to be accepted as a preacher among white Methodists."[132] Consequently, Apess begins to foreground Native history, community, and politics in his last publications. For my purposes, this shift is significant because a distinctly political enthusiastic rhetoric now outstrips the religious rhetoric of the early works, as Apess forcefully asserts the right of Native America to claim a revolutionary heritage of resistance to tyranny—a Native American constituent power. Interestingly, in his galvanizing role as leader of the Mashpee movement for sovereignty over its tribal lands, Apess ends up occupying the role of the Shawnee Prophet for his critics; they call him a "*pious* interloper" and "hypocritical *missionary*" who leads his "ignorant, deluded followers" to "declare their independence of the laws of Massachusetts, and to *arm themselves* to defend it."[133] Although he does not, in fact, encourage the Mashpees to take up arms, Apess does appropriate the language of the American Revolution to prove the point that U.S. jurisdiction over the American Indian amounts to "slavery," and, speaking on behalf of the Mashpees, states that anyone who thinks otherwise they consider "Tories, hostile to the Constitution and the liberties of the country."[134] Accordingly, in *Eulogy on King Philip*, Apess forces his audience—including us—to admit the necessity of Native American Revolution: "Let every friend of the Indians now seize the mantle of Liberty and throw it over those burning elements that has [sic] spread with such fearful rapidity, and at once extinguish them forever.... We want trumpets that sound like thunder, and men to act as though they were going at war with those corrupt and degrading principles that robs one of all rights, merely because he is ignorant and of a little different color.... Give the Indian his rights, and you may be assured war will cease."[135] The boldness of *Eulogy* lies, finally, in its convulsive address to the "children of the Pilgrims"[136] to claim the ideals of the American Revolution *for the first time*. This also means that the sons of Pilgrims will claim "true religion" for the first time. Apess's rewriting of the Puritans, past and present, as the "pretended pious," with a "pretended zeal for religion and virtue," ironically leverages the same antienthusiasm rhetoric leveled against the Shawnee Prophet, but only to insist on a higher doctrine of political enthusiasm that commissions this categorical imperative: all "lovers of liberty" must take a "stand" for Native American independence.[137]

CHAPTER FOUR

The Revival of Revolt
Conjure, Slave Insurrection, and the Novel of Enthusiasm

> I believe in insurrections—and especially those of the pen and of the sword.
> —JOHN S. ROCK, 1860

Whereas chapter 3 highlighted the importance of enthusiasm to Native American projects of dissent in the context of the War of 1812, this chapter highlights, in the same respect, the importance of enthusiasm to black projects of dissent, albeit in a broader context of slavery and abolitionism in the black Atlantic. Taken together, a study of enthusiasm helps us to see the overlapping—but culturally distinct—strategies of resistance among indigenous and black communities in their respective confrontations with Western imperialism before the Civil War, as well as the way such enthusiasms participate in—but I would say correct—the bourgeois revolutionary heritage of the French and American Revolution as I explored those events in chapters 1 and 2.

Thomas Wentworth Higginson's five essays on slave insurrection, published in the *Atlantic Monthly* in the 1850s and 1860s but eventually compiled together in *Travellers and Outlaws* (1889), best introduce the themes that I want to explore in this chapter. Therein, the Transcendentalist clergyman, author, and Civil War commander of the first regiment of freed slaves compels us to listen to discrete liberation events as part of the same historical symphony—including the maroon insurrections of Jamaica and Surinam; the American, French, and Haitian Revolution; the Gabriel Prosser plot of 1800 in Virginia and the Denmark Vesey plot of 1822 in South Carolina; the Caucasian War (against imperial Russia, 1817-64) and the November Uprising or Cadet Revolution of 1830-31 in Poland; the Nat Turner or Southampton Insurrection of 1831 and John Brown's raid on Harper's Ferry in 1859; and finally, the American Civil War. One statement best encapsulates Higginson's reading of antislavery revolt history: "Each time did one man's name [a revolt leader] become a *spell* of dismay and a *symbol* of deliverance. Each time did that name eclipse its predecessor, while recalling it for a moment to fresher memory: John Brown *revived* the story of Nat Turner, as in his day Nat Turner recalled the vaster schemes of Gabriel."[1] A spell of dismay, a symbol of deliverance, a revival of revolt stories: these interwoven concepts will be something of a leitmotif in this chapter.

Higginson, though, also refers the reader to a pervasive cultural practice of real spells, ritual symbolism, and revivalism in black insurrection history—that "spell of dismay" and "symbol of deliverance" known as conjure, especially the religious and medical practice of West African slaves in the Caribbean—obeah. For Higginson, the practice of conjure is, first and foremost, a nonspecific moniker for secret slave society, interchangeable with a generic "freemasonry." Committed to his own "strange enthusiasm,"[2] Higginson had good reason to be drawn to such societies: he led a surprise attack of abolitionists in 1854 to rescue Anthony Burns from a federal courthouse after his arrest under the Fugitive Slave Act, and he was part of the Secret Six who backed John Brown's scheme to invade the South.[3] In "The Maroons of Jamaica," Higginson says this about the famous Coromantee maroon leader, Cudjoe: "Cudjoe, like Schamyl [the Avar leader of Muslim tribes in the Caucasian resistance], was religious as well as military head of his people; by Obeah influence he established a thorough freemasonry among both slaves and insurgents."[4] He later adds that the maroon Jamaicans, in their "savage freedom," "practised Obeah rites quite undiluted with Christianity."[5] In "The Maroons of Surinam," Higginson mentions that "their worship was obi-worship";[6] and in "Gabriel's Defeat," while he makes no mention of obeah, Higginson does say that one of the conspiracy's recruits, Ben Woolfolk, confessed that "he had been asked by a negro named Colonel George whether he would like to be made a Mason," ultimately to join Gabriel by oath in a secret "plan of insurrection."[7] One learns from the deposition of this 1800 insurrection plot that George told Woolfolk "it was not a free-mason society he wished him to join, but a society to fight the white people for their freedom."[8] In "Denmark Vesey," Higginson calls attention to Vesey's accomplice, the conjure man Jack Purcell, or "Gullah Jack," who "wielded in secret an immense influence" on the black community of Charleston: as a guru in the art of invincibility, "he was very good at beating up recruits for insurrection."[9] And last but not least, in "Nat Turner's Insurrection," Higginson compares Turner's infamous "religious hallucinations" to those of the German mystic Jacob Böhme, or Boehme, and offers that at least one person "attributed it [the Southampton Insurrection] to Free-Masonry."[10] Taken as a whole, Higginson's

The Revival of Revolt 131

analysis forges inextricable links between secret societies, African spiritualism, and slave insurrection across a wide (geographical) range of black struggles for emancipation, yet without sealing these struggles off from the revolutionary forces shaping Europe and the Americas at large.

In historical context, circum-Atlantic black Freemasonry did indeed pose a threat to slavery.[11] Not only were black Freemason societies in the eighteenth century a means of creating transatlantic, diasporic affiliations, but a "rapprochement [also existed] between West African secret societies and European Freemasonry"[12] as the latter was exported throughout the West Indies. Especially in the French-Haitian context, where Freemasonry was associated with Jacobinism and antigovernment conspiracy, Vodou could be described as "a sort of religious and dancing masonry"[13]—that is, an Africanized Freemasonry. One American critic would go so far as to say, "Let Freemasonry once spread its baneful influence thoroughly amongst the slaves of our Southern and Western States, and the scenes of St. Domingo would be sunk into insignificance, compared with those which would follow."[14] The explicit language of masonry employed in Gabriel's rebellion is telling on this point, yet this seems to be an instance that speaks more to what James Weldon Johnson referred to as "the freemasonry of the race," a phrase that Corey Walker glosses to mean, among other things, "the requisite knowledges, practices, and habits inculcated within a particular stratum of a marginalized group that are used to cognate and navigate the social and political structures of the dominant society."[15] While Freemasonry has been a vital historical institution to men of African descent, "the freemasonry of the race" transcends the organization proper to describe the "rituals of race" among black cultures of invisibility.[16]

For my purposes, "the freemasonry of the race," as informed by conjure religion, is a place to locate the politics of enthusiasm specific to black history and culture of the slavery era. On this point I follow Theophus Smith, who argues that conjure is a "form of ritual speech and action," simultaneously a real "system of communication" and a "literary or cultural metaphor," "that circumscribes black people's ritual, figural, and therapeutic transformations of culture."[17] According to Smith, through various permutations, conjure characterizes any "literary-religious expressions ... [meant] to induce material transformations of reality for enslaved people in America."[18] But if I have anything new to contribute to studies of American slave resistance, it is to situate conjure culture within the longstanding and elastic debates over revolt enthusiasm that

I have discussed in previous chapters. That enthusiasts were often defined by two refusals—the "refusal to accept forms of authority outside the self" and the refusal "to discipline the body"[19]—takes on an intensely literal value with respect to the material conditions of slavery, where the acceptance of authority and bodily discipline means subordination to the machinations of that enslavement. A privileged expression of refusal among slaves, conjure is a veritable synonym for enthusiasm applied to black life, especially given that, as Houston Baker Jr. notes, conjure (according to the OED) can also mean "conspiracy" (or to plan by conspiracy), the invocation of supernatural power ("The exercise of magical or occult influence"), or transformation through fanciful words *as if* by magic ("*Conjurer*: One who performs tricks with words")[20]—in short, conjure is a black "mythomania" that critics often understood as a "sickness of the imagination and feelings."[21]

In an analysis of enthusiasm, the example of conjure is crucial, furthermore, for at least two reasons articulated by Toni Wall Jaudon in "Obeah's Sensations: Rethinking Religion at the Transnational Turn" (2012). First, what Jaudon calls "obeah fictions"—diverse, multigenred accounts of obeah in literatures about the Americas—displace Christianity as the central frame of reference for studies of early American religion and literature. Second, these fictions point not only to the "transnational connections" and currents of early American religion but also to a historical reappraisal of religion itself as "a thickly lived set of connections to the material that allows the subject to access something outside of the nation-state—that orients the individual otherwise."[22] In a sense, this chapter gives one answer to Jaudon's question, "What would an Americanist literary study look like that took obeah fictions, and the sense perceptions they ambivalently recorded, as the model for the world in which American literatures intervened and to which they responded?"[23] My claim is that such an intervention and response often resulted in a cultural translation of conjure religion (including but not exclusive to obeah) that went by the appellation of "enthusiasm," and that the enthusiast was precisely that slave who, like the obeah practitioner, tried to make novel "connections between the body and the world" through a convulsive means of expression.[24] The literary study that Jaudon calls for must foreground and appreciate black cultures of enthusiasm.

More specifically, my task in this chapter is to show how certain literatures of enthusiasm orbit around a "conjure aesthetics" wedded to slave revolt. In the terms that I have established for such literatures, slavery obviously constitutes the black convulsive context, the crisis that demands immediate response; tricks with words, literary expressions for social transformation, spells of dismay, or symbols of deliverance constitute the black convulsive address; and the revival of revolt (the revival matrix of black community that I will discuss below) constitutes the convulsive affect of black emancipatory action. After establishing that enthusiasm is the key to understanding the cross-fertilization of black cultural/political/aesthetic forms and insurrectionary historical projects, my central argument emerges: conjure aesthetics sets the terms for the antislavery novel of enthusiasm. This argument presupposes Laura Doyle's contention in *Freedom's Empire* (2008) that the rise of the Anglo-Atlantic novel—and the narrative of liberty in modernity—had the African-Atlantic experience and the "understory of race" as its dialogized background.[25] More to the point for American studies, if one intends to take seriously Eric Sundquist's classic "account of antebellum literature defined along the axis of revolution and slavery," that is, "black slave revolution,"[26] then it is necessary to show how the antebellum novel and black enthusiasm mutually inform one another. Certain novels, referring explicitly to the history of slave revolt, beg to be read, in both form and content, through the lens of black enthusiasm—they deserve to be read as novels *of* enthusiasm.

In the next section, I establish the historical background for reading conjure and slave insurrection as a species of enthusiasm absorbed by fiction writers. Subsequently, I analyze two prose works as examples of the antislavery novel of enthusiasm—Harriet Beecher Stowe's *Dred* (1856) and Martin Delany's *Blake* (1859–62). Both Stowe and Delany turn novel writing itself into an enthusiastic contact zone (of call and response) with the reader, soliciting us to speed up the political crisis of slavery through direct intervention. But from Stowe to Delany, one also sees a progressive movement from a highly mediated, indirect novelization of black enthusiasms to a direct and explicit experiment in writing the African-American novel of enthusiasm as a narrative revival of revolt, which is to say, as a ritual speech and action for inciting political transformation.

The *Unheimlich* Slave: Conjure, Romanticism, and the Novel of Enthusiasm

The practice of conjure was a common denominator in the cornucopia of religions introduced to the West through the slave trade. As a correlate to the belief, in "the traditional religion of West Africa," that "the power of the gods and spirits was effectively present in the lives of men, for good or ill, on every level—environmental, individual, social, national, and cosmic,"[27] enslaved Africans would have generally ascribed to a core vision that, via ritual, "human beings would be able to tap supernatural power for manifold purposes."[28] As a special delegate of said power, the conjurer facilitates material transformations of reality. But conjure religions have also been called "danced religions," namely religions that apprehend divinity or divinities through rituals of song and dance.[29] In his genealogy of African-American music and the black church, W. E. B. Du Bois makes one of the earliest claims on what "characterized this religion of the slave,—the Preacher, the Music, and the Frenzy."[30] As one former slave, Robert Anderson, put it, "Practically all of their [slave] songs were accompanied by a motion of some kind ... the weird and mysterious music of the religious ceremonies moved old and young alike in a frenzy of religious fervor."[31] In connection with "the frenzy of a Negro revival" that he attends, Du Bois essays that the "church was not at first by any means Christian nor definitely organized; rather it was an adaption and mingling of heathen rites among the members of each plantation, and roughly designated as Voodooism"; he goes on to colorfully conjure obeah as the slave's war against the "dark triumph of Evil over him. All the hateful powers of the Under-world were striving against him, and a spirit of revolt and revenge filled his heart. He called up all the resources of heathenism to aid,—exorcism and witchcraft, the mysterious Obi worship with its barbarous rites, spells, and blood sacrifice even, now and then, of human victims."[32] Perhaps it is needless to say that the above practices diagnostically belong to what antebellum culture considered enthusiasm: "Wherever the slaves practiced their religion ... it was characterized by physical and spiritual enthusiasm and involvement."[33]

Anything *but* a benign opiate, such physical and spiritual enthusiasm and involvement, throughout the black Atlantic, ritually developed in opposition to white colonialism. In Jamaica, West African slaves who brought "the secret and the hidden" arts of the obeah sorcerer (*obayifo*) over with them were inordinately hostile toward their enslavers,[34] and the obeah practitioner was known to use his or her medicinal knowledge on occasion to poison slave owners and incite rebellion. In Tacky's Rebellion of 1760, a Jamaican obeah man (Tacky) apparently believed that his potion protected him and his fellow slaves against death: any bullets fired would be returned to the enemy.³⁵ Twenty years later, contemporaneous with the American Revolution, folk hero and bandit Jack Mansong, with obeah-bag paraphernalia, "ascended above SPARTACUS," in the words of Benjamin Moseley, and established a maroon society of escaped Jamaican slaves.³⁶ By 1781, the *Code Noir* of Jamaica included a more stringent clause outlawing the practice of obeah (with penalty of "death or transportation"), punishing not merely the congregation of slaves or acts of poisoning but also the supposition of "any Negro or other slave who shall pretend to any supernatural power,"³⁷ an articulation, it should be noted, that strictly overlaps with the modern definition of the enthusiast. Henceforth, the government prohibits enthusiasm itself: slaves can have no access to divinity. One Anglican minister in Jamaica summed up nicely what obeah stood for, practically, to colonialists: "Obeah, and death, are synonymous."³⁸ The report from the *House of Commons Sessional Papers* on obeah in 1789 denigrated it as so many "Feathers and Trumperies," a practice of impostures and tricksters, a craft of lepers, "sunk from the land of the living."³⁹ Obeah: or, a perpetual night of the living dead slaves.

The North American colonies were not immune from the horrors of insurrectionary black magic either. As early as the eighteenth century, fears over the practice of slave poisoning led to laws in South Carolina outlawing the activities of conjurors.⁴⁰ Walter Rucker explains why: "Conjurers very often were leaders or major figures in slave rebellions. Claiming command over esoteric forces, they were seen as integral to the success of slave revolts.... They [slave insurgents] believed, with little question, the ability of these spiritualists to determine the outcome of events through arcane means."⁴¹ In his classic work *Black Culture and Black Consciousness* (1977), Lawrence Levine cites sources confirming that one slave usually acted as an oracle for the others, and "slave music, slave religion, slave folk beliefs—the entire sacred world of the black slaves— created the necessary space between the slaves and their owners and were the means of preventing legal slavery from becoming spiritual slavery."⁴² Thus, one can see how the convulsive context of slavery situates black *marronage* and conjure culture both as a site of refusal to the plantation labor economy and as a space for a ritual convulsive address to and for black peoples, encouraging them to actively resist or overturn that economy.

If black enthusiasm under slavery was characterized by "the presence of a compelling communal ethos ... which threatened continually to transform observers into participants,"⁴³ then, at the intersection of rituals of race and rituals of rebellion, so was slave revolt. Take the suggestive report about the South Carolina Stono Rebellion of 1739: "Several Negroes joined them [an assembly of twenty slaves], they calling out Liberty, marched on with Colours displayed, and two Drums beating, pursuing all the white people they met with, and killing Man Woman and Child.... They increased every minute by new Negroes coming to them, so that they were above Sixty, some say a hundred, on which they halted in a field, and set to dancing, Singing and beating Drums, to draw more Negroes to them, thinking they were now victorious over the whole Province."[44] As this description tends to confirm, if slave religion established "instantaneous community," "creating an expanded universe" with "confidence in the possibilities of instantaneous change," especially through a unique "song style, with its overriding antiphony, its group nature, its pervasive functionality, its improvisational character, its strong relationship in performance to dance and bodily movement and expression,"[45] then this sensibility also holds true for a critical theory of slave insurrection: the primary features of black music inform the extemporaneous, ad hoc actions of slaves during a revival moment of insurrection, and it's not without reason that, at slave services, "the tumult often resembled that of an excited political meeting."[46] Slave insurrection enacts the very political freedoms that the rituals of religion concomitantly express, and this follows as a corollary of a worldview that does not separate the secular and the sacred, political and spiritual freedom.

However, like conjure and freemasonry, the language of enthusiasm with regard to slave culture and black religion must be seen as historically specific as it is heuristically appropriate for at least the following reason: enslaved Africans, increasingly converted to Christianity with the rise of the evangelical movement in the eighteenth century, played a defining role in the shaping of white religious expression, especially those "noisy, enthusiastic [camp] meetings" of the eighteenth- and nineteenth-century revival movement.[47] Yvonne Chireau's account of black magic in African-American religion pivots around the historical connections between conjure and revival Christianity: "Yet from slavery days to the present, many African Americans have readily moved between Christianity, Conjure, and other forms of supernaturalism with little concern for their purported incompatibility."[48] And as Albert Raboteau notes, "the situation of the camp-meeting revival, where enthusiastic and ecstatic religious behavior was encouraged, presented a congenial setting for slaves to merge African patterns of response with Christian interpretations of the experience of spirit possession, an experience shared by both blacks and whites."[49] According to Chireau, these "patterns of response," for both "Africanized forms of Protestantism" and "African-based religions elsewhere," "put great emphasis on ecstatic behaviors, spirit revelations, supernatural healing, and antisorcery ritualism."[50] At the same time, we should not perpetuate the notion that slaves adopted and adapted evangelical Christianity organically, because of its "particular attractiveness to people of color," so as to overlook the "compound historical, political, economic, cultural, regional, and denominational factors" involved,[51] nor do I wish to promote a homogeneous phenomenon called "black enthusiasm" that flattens out the religious, cultural, and geopolitical differences among heterogeneous populations. I prefer to see enthusiasm in Jared Hickman's terms as a modern "metacosm," that is, as a creative "attempt" on the part of both European and non-European peoples after 1492 "to articulate a 'global' conception of life" within a metaphysical and enchanted horizon of meaning, as diverse religious epistemologies interface for the first time through colonial encounter and try to make sense of the world accordingly.[52] Hickman makes the convincing claim that the category of "race" itself in the colonial imagination was informed by a theological vision whereby "'religious' and 'racial' othering work in tandem to such a degree as to be inseparable,"[53] and he includes African conjure as a key example. Contrariwise, obeah was also "a frame through which Afro-Caribbeans interpreted European religious and medical practice," as they struggled "to rework their existing knowledge to provide some protection in a new, terror-filled setting."[54]

My point is that the modern concept of enthusiasm itself accrued racialized connotations against the backdrop of black and indigenous religions and their representations. In the U.S. context, it is no coincidence, as I have argued elsewhere, that the definitions of enthusiasm in the first edition of Webster's *Dictionary* (1828) are the precise terms used in the cultural criticism of Nat Turner—the slave enthusiast par excellence—three years later, and just as G. W. F. Hegel would draw a conceptual distinction between the unspiritualized "physical enthusiasm" of African religion and the superlative "spiritual enthusiasm" of the French Revolution in order to dissociate black peoples from progressive history in the Age of Revolution,[55] so must we see that the Kantian attack on constituent power discussed in chapter 1 precludes the right of slaves to both throw off their chains and to enact their freedoms through the rituals of race embodied by their historical religions.

That's why the problem of black enthusiasm, according to its critics, concerns not only the pollution of white society by the influx of African religions but also the pollution of slave culture by the influx of modern revolutionary ideals. Obviously, the Haitian Revolution is the historical crystallization of this anxiety, an explosive example of what happens when you mix Enthusiasm and Enlightenment. When Vodou priest Dutty Boukman led a slave revolt against the white man's god, helping to spark the movement for Haitian independence, this was no isolated incident—it was yet another symptom of the widespread progress of black enthusiasms.[56] Then, as a fallout from the Haitian Revolution, refugees from Saint-Domingue, spread throughout the Atlantic, "became carriers of new doctrines" of liberty to diverse black populations, free and enslaved.[57] Even the Anglo-American and European polemics against French Revolutionary enthusiasms need to be understood in the context of the Reign of Terror attributed to black Haitians who imbibed French doctrines, a revolutionary nightmare waiting to be unleashed in the U.S. by its own black Jacobins.[58] Higginson, for instance, cites a newspaper of 1800 that reads, "It is evident that the French principles of liberty and equality have been effused into the minds of the negroes, and that the incautious and intemperate use of the words by some whites among us have inspired them with hopes of success."[59] To be sure, Gabriel Prosser's revolt was inspired by the contemporaneous Haitian Revolution and meant to spare the liberty-loving French (but interestingly, also the Quakers and Methodists), and Denmark Vesey (himself a former Haitian slave) chose Bastille Day for his revolt and planned to sail to Haiti. As Edwin Clifford Holland put it candidly in an honest proslavery admission, "Let it never be forgotten that our Negroes are freely the JACOBINS of the country; that they are the ANARCHISTS and the DOMESTIC ENEMY: the COMMON ENEMY OF CIVILIZED SOCIETY, and the BARBARIANS WHO WOULD, IF THEY COULD, BECOME THE DESTROYERS OF OUR RACE."[60]

Moreover, conjure religion played an influential, if understated, role not only in the discourse of modern revolution but also in the development of Anglo-American Romanticism. For example, Alan Richardson traces the cultural influence of obeah on the British Romantic movement in the arts and argues that its feverish currency as an intriguing "superstition" in Britain reflected anxieties over England's imperial power in the Atlantic. British ambivalence over obeah spoke to the latter's double significance as both a "tangible threat and an empty show of power which would dissipate when confronted by civilized superiority."[61] This ambivalence expressed itself most explicitly in the abolitionist campaign and its wish to simultaneously "inspire pity as well as fear in relation to enslaved Africans"; as Richardson sums up, "Obeah can evoke the slaves' legitimate grievances as well as the illegitimacy of their means for redressing them."[62] Black "magic" was a kind of primitive sublime that, though false, powerfully worked among its believers as a "symbol of deliverance." Premiering in London in 1800, the same year as the London publication of William Earle's novel *Obi; or, the History of Three-Fingered Jack*, John Fawcett's pantomime *Obi; or, Three-Finger'd Jack* popularized the story of the Jamaican slave bandit and the mysterious practice of obeah. In a review of the drama, the *Morning Herald* exclaimed that Jack's character, the "Black Hecate, of Jamaica," was "likely, from the force of its magic, to throw [its] spells all over the town."[63] The play on words aside, here one sees how the culture of conjure translates for English audiences into a mesmerizing aesthetic experience even while the play, with its anti-Jacobin sympathies, may otherwise strategically oppose abolitionism.[64] By contrast, William Earle's depiction of Three-Fingered Jack as a tragic and Herculean folk hero corresponds to the "pro-Jacobin aspirations regarding figures such as Toussaint L'Ouverture"[65] though it betrays that ambivalence of fascination described by Richardson with regard to obeah. As a kind of epistolary meta-novel recording the physical and mental struggle of the Jamaican George Stanford to write the impossible history of Three-Fingered Jack, Earle's *Obi* offers a narrative of conjure that reflexively becomes the conjure of narrative, the mimetic double of obeah. In Letter 1 to his English friend Charles, George tells us that "the name of Jack ... perpetually buzzed" in his "ears": "I start and stare about in expectation of seeing the three-fingered one make his appearance."[66] Jack "acts as a spell upon my senses," George goes on to say, taking possession of him and conducing him to tell the story of this "bold and daring defender of the Rights of Man": "The image of Jack haunts me, and I am loath to drop my pen, until I have concluded his history."[67] In short, as an enthusiastic historical medium, George authors his romantic tale under the spell of Jack's conjure power and, through imaginative fancy, also conjures and textually transmits Jack's insurrectionary obeah—his evental enthusiasm.

In the U.S. context, Harriet Beecher Stowe takes an analogous approach to her fictional version of the American Three-Fingered Jack, Dred, in her eponymous 1856 romance, a character primarily inspired by that "great enthusiast" Nat Turner.[68] Stowe was unique among her contemporaries for recognizing a connection between en vogue Romantic ideals and the enthusiasms of insurrectionary slaves. A long quote from *Dred* proves the point:

> There is a twilight-ground between the boundaries of the sane and insane, which the old Greeks and Romans regarded with a peculiar veneration [classical enthusiasm]. They held a person whose faculties were thus darkened as walking under the awful shadow of a supernatural presence; and, as the mysterious secrets of the stars only become visible in the night, so in these eclipses of the more material faculties they held there was often an awakening of supernatural perceptions.
>
> The hot and positive light of our modern materialism, which exhales from the growth of our existence every dew-drop, which searches out and dries every rivulet of romance, which sends an unsparing beam into every cool grotto of poetic possibility, withering the moss, and turning the dropping cave to a dusty den—this spirit, so remorseless, allows us no such indefinite land. There are but two words in the whole department of modern anthropology—the sane and the insane; the latter dismissed from human reckoning almost with contempt. We should find it difficult to give a suitable name to the strange and abnormal condition in which this singular being, of whom we are speaking, passed the most of his time [Dred].
>
> It was a state of exaltation and trance, which yet appeared not at all to impede the exercise of his outward and physical faculties, but rather to give them a preternatural keenness and intensity, such as sometimes attends the more completely-developed phenomena of somnambulism.[69]

Stowe codes the dialectic of sober reason and drunken exaltation as the dialectic not of sanity and insanity (which she dismisses) but of materialism and spiritualism, further positioning both Dred and romance in a middle ground, in an "indefinite land," suspended between these polarities, where rational cognition and ecstatic perception become mutually affirmative and generative copartners. Like a muse, Dred points back to—buttresses even—Stowe's own ethos and identity as a romancer of "poetic possibility." They are both leagued in opposition to modern anthropology. Her comments surely allude, furthermore, to Nathaniel Hawthorne's famous description of romance in *The Scarlet Letter* (1850) as he performs his own withdrawal from the custom house, in preference for "domestic scenery" drenched in "magic moonshine." In that context, Hawthorne allows the "imaginative faculty" to discover that "neutral territory, somewhere between the real world and fairy-land, where the Actual and the Imaginary may meet, and each imbue itself with the nature of the other."[70] In the spirit of Hawthorne, Stowe sees enthusiasm as at one with such a maroon space, an intervallic void of darkened caves and mysterious secrets. She outlines, in nineteenth-century terms, the conjunction of black enthusiasms and Romantic literary sensibilities. When she says of Dred, "There were elements in him which might, under other circumstances [namely, emancipated ones], have made him a poet," Stowe understands that a visionary prophet such as Nat Turner, whose "fertility of ... imagination," by everybody's account, made him unfit as a slave and whose "enthusiasm ... terminated so fatally to many both white and black,"[71] shares a cultural sensibility with a Hawthorne or an Emerson.[72] No doubt Turner also believed that "nothing great was ever achieved without enthusiasm." In *Moby-Dick* (1851), Melville's sailor-preacher, Father Mapple, may cry out "with a heavenly enthusiasm," "Delight is to him—a far, far upward, and inward delight—who against the proud gods and commodores of this earth, ever stands forth his own inexorable self.... Delight,—top-gallant delight is to him, who acknowledges no law or lord, but the Lord his God, and is only a patriot to heaven,"[73] but to a Three-Fingered Jack or Nat Turner, the proud gods and commodores of this earth are slave owners and the acknowledged law of the earthly patriot slavery itself.

For modern readers, that "strange and abnormal condition" of the twilight mind which Stowe attributes to Dred registers as "the uncanny." Indeed, since Freud's classic essay "The 'Uncanny'" (1919), the association between Romantic art and "primitive" magic or animism has been a common and problematic one. By now one hardly needs a reminder that the philological roots of the word "uncanny" in German, *unheimlich*, which literally translates as "unhomely," denote not only the unfamiliar, the strange, the haunted, and the wild, but also the opposite—the familiar, the intimate, the concealed, the domestic, the secretive; furthermore, it can refer to the magical ("The *heimlich* art") and even the conspiratorial. In Freud's terms, the uncanny is therefore a phenomenon ambivalently homely and unhomely, designating a familiar but repressed history or desire that ought to have remained a secret but has surfaced and returned to one in a fearful form.⁷⁴ Pushed beyond psychoanalysis, the uncanny remains a suggestive way to think about the black presence in the Americas under the conditions of slavery, a foreign presence that subverts the domestic, homely identity of white imperial nationhood and yet founds, enables, and sustains it intimately as its very interior and essence. This is how Priscilla Wald approaches the uncanny in *Constituting Americans* (1995), calling it a signal of disturbance that "can generate or disrupt" a "narrative of identity," especially an American identity and the dominant modes of narrating the American experience, but that also speaks to "the sense of estrangement expressed as ill-fitting selfhood by individuals excluded from the terms of full and equal personhood and the uncanniness they represented within the official stories."⁷⁵ In the terms of this chapter, the historical reality of secret slave societies—and the ever-present anticipation or fear of black insurrection—forms the uncanny context for literary Romanticism.

I would ask us to further understand the uncanny in the manner of Jacques Derrida's concept of "the secret," as outlined in "I Have a Taste for the Secret" (1997, 2001 in English). The secret refers, most basically, to a structured relation to the future, a secret *of* the future, that cannot be predicted or governed, and a "singularity of the here and now" without presence or home, a temporal uncanny that demands a decision, a negotiation of an immanent and untotalizable context, which "implies a wager—that is, a certain way of giving ourselves over to not-knowing, to the incalculable."⁷⁶ Derrida adds that, within a "totalitarian space," "Belonging—the fact of avowing one's belonging, of putting in common—be it family, nation, tongue—spells the loss of the secret."⁷⁷ Accordingly, with regard to slavery, the *heimlich* designates the domestic empire of enslavement and the *unheimlich* "the freemasonry of the race," both the structure of not belonging to—subtracting from—the home, nation, domestic slavery, and the structured relation to a future emancipation for black peoples, who must make decisions and take risks, often insurrectionary ones, when it required an uncanny imagination to project and enact emancipation in excess of slavery as a matrix of social being and knowledge. In less theoretical or more historical terms, one could call a "literature of the secret," after James Scott, the "*hidden transcript*" of a subordinated group—an "infrapolitics" enacted through "offstage speeches, gestures, and practices," often in material "zones of refuge"—which opposes the official, codified "public transcript" of the dominating group. The hidden transcript should be seen as "*a condition of practical resistance rather than a substitute for it*," as it lays the breeding ground for a "charismatic act" of open defiance that attempts to abolish the public transcript.[78] Seen from the point of view of Atlantic slave cultures, conjure enthusiasm looks very much like a living, ritual literature of the secret that also participates in a "circum-Atlantic interculture" of performance—"the adaptive creativity produced by the interactions of many peoples"—that traverses Euro-American cultural traditions and African ritual expressions.[79] Black enthusiasm is itself such an interculture of religious, political, and aesthetic performance.

Before turning to two examples of the American's novel engagement with black enthusiasm, it behooves me to say in what sense the novel represents, if only theoretically, an ideal conjure medium. In the terms of Georg Lukács, the Romantic novel primarily posits the antagonism between the individual's spiritual autonomy or ideal life and the disenchanted external world; as "an expression of transcendental homelessness," the novel's heroes, who do not belong, must "sometimes fall prey to the power of the demon and overreach themselves in ways that have no reason and cannot be explained by reason, challenging all the psychological or sociological foundations of their existence."[80] In this sense, a "disillusioned romanticism" is, structurally speaking, the plight of the narrative slave whose desire for freedom is frustrated, often defeated, from the start by slavery's prohibitions on human freedom, and yet in the case of the slave insurgent, such as Three-Fingered Jack or Dred, we still have an instance of an older idealism's "heroism of militant interiority,"[81] capable of transforming desire into action, only with the double intensification that these characters represent, not the allegorical, but the real historical forces of militant resistance to slavery.

Although he emphasizes the heteroglossic, polyvocal expressions of social reality represented in the novel, Mikhail Bakhtin likewise thinks of the genre as one intimately related to a historical problematic. He writes that the novel incorporates and introduces into other genres "a living contact with unfinished, still-evolving contemporary reality (the openended present)," and thus reflexively, a novel is a "genre-in-the-making" just as it is a representation of history-in-the-making.[82] That the novel is woven out of the "unconcluded process" of history, "where there is no first word (no ideal word), and the final word has not yet been spoken,"[83] makes it, de facto, a literature of the secret: the novel, at its best, is uncanny because it asks us to involve ourselves in the indeterminate present, to invent or imagine—to conjure—solutions beyond what our reality admits. But for the same reasons, the ideal novel privileges "free improvisation" and spontaneity, in an engagement with social reality in the process of becoming. This has parity with the "improvisatory character" of black revivalism outlined above, and as I'll show momentarily, it was possible for novelists to incorporate black enthusiasms into the formal mechanisms of their narratives. Moreover, Bakhtin historicizes the novel itself as an art form shaped by "street songs, folksayings, anecdotes, where there was no language-center at all."[84] In *Rabelais and His World* (1965), he describes how the folk carnival culture of the dominated, as incorporated by the ideal novel, builds a "second world and a second life outside officialdom," that is, in my terms, creates a maroon space of the secret devoted to the "world's revival and renewal."[85] The carnival, like black enthusiasm, is "by no means a purely artistic form nor a spectacle and does not, generally speaking, belong to the sphere of art. It belongs to the borderline between art and life. In reality, it is life itself, but shaped according to a certain pattern of play"; "Carnival is not a spectacle seen by the people; they live in it, and everyone participates because its very idea embraces all the people. While carnival lasts, there is no other life outside it."[86] Or, as Paul Gilroy argues with regard to modern black history, "it is the moment of jubilee that has the upper hand over the pursuit of utopia by rational means."[87] For a similar reason, Bakhtin argues that, in the best novels, the reader does not have the luxury of detachment, since it "portray[s] an event on the same time-and-value plane as oneself and one's contemporaries," such that "we encounter the specific danger inherent in the novelistic zone of contact: we ourselves may actually enter the novel."[88] In my language, the novel's convulsive context, address, and affect must be our own if it is to be enthusiastic. A novel of enthusiasm will draw us into a ritual speech and action of historical transformation.

By establishing affinities between the novel and enthusiasm, I mean only to specify how the novel lends itself—and opens itself up—to forms of representation that can be mobilized in the service of black dissent. It is obviously not the case that there is something inherently black and enthusiastic about the novel or that there is something inherently novelistic about black expression and enthusiasm, but it is possible to coordinate the aesthetic presuppositions of certain novels and black cultures of enthusiasm in the antebellum era. I adduce this, at least, from two antebellum works of American fiction—Harriet Beecher Stowe's *Dred* and Martin Delany's *Blake*—which exemplify the antislavery novel of enthusiasm.

Dread Fellowship: Enthusiasm as Insurrectionary Revivalism in Harriet Beecher Stowe's *Dred*

By the time Harriet Beecher Stowe publishes *Dred: A Tale of the Great Dismal Swamp* (1856), insurrection fictions have become a pervasive aspect of national life. In 1939, historian Harvey Wish called attention to the "Slave Insurrection Panic of 1856," when tales of Gabriel Prosser, Denmark Vesey, and Nat Turner consistently circulated as part of unconfirmed insurrection rumors from Delaware to Texas.[89] While overshadowed by *Uncle Tom's Cabin* (1852), *Dred* was nevertheless "one of the most popular novels of the time, selling upwards of 200,000 copies during the nineteenth century."[90] As Robert Levine observes, Stowe's second major novel revises or complicates the domestic portrait of slaves in her more famous work by turning "the plantation novel upside down": "Domesticity and sympathy go only so far in *Dred*, a novel that ultimately asks its readers to consider slavery from the point of view of black revolutionaries lurking in the recesses of the Dismal Swamp."[91] For this reason, one can read *Dred*, as the noncanonical case of enthusiastic affect and the maroon revolt novel, against the grain of *Uncle Tom's Cabin*, as the canonical case of sentimental affect and the domestic reform novel.

The shift in perspective from *Uncle Tom's Cabin* to *Dred* deserves some explanation: certainly, the debate between Martin Delany and Frederick Douglass on *Uncle Tom's Cabin* led Stowe to reconsider her hallowed vision of slave martyrdom and support of Liberian colonization, while her reading of William Cooper Nell's *The Colored Patriots of the American Revolution* (1855), for which she wrote the introduction, exerted a palpable influence on her late appreciation for black revolutionary history. But as the sectional crisis reached a white heat in the interval between the two works of fiction, Stowe may have also decided, on her own terms, that the abolition of slavery would eventually require direct resistance and war, a position, however unwonted and understated, that was not completely alien to the world of *Uncle Tom's Cabin*. Sure, Uncle Tom tells Cassy that murdering Simon Legree and making a home of the swamp is "wickedness,"[92] but Eliza Harris's husband George advocates for black fugitive resistance and declares his independence with the same love of liberty, Stowe tells us, as a contemporaneous Hungarian freedom fighter. More important, in the closing remarks of *Uncle Tom's Cabin*, Stowe adumbrates, arguably already *begins*, *Dred* by pointing to the impending apocalyptic judgment on slavery concomitant with the Church of Christ's redemption. After quoting Biblical prophecy on the destruction of the oppressor, she writes: "Are not these dread words for a nation bearing in her bosom so mighty an injustice? Christians! every time that you pray that the kingdom of Christ may come, can you forget that prophecy associates, in dread fellowship, the *day of vengeance* with the year of his redeemed?"[93] Furthermore, this day of vengeance entails a political revolution that Stowe articulates as a convulsive crisis: "This is an age of the world when nations are trembling and convulsed. A mighty influence is abroad, surging and heaving the world, as with an earthquake. And is America safe? Every nation that carries in its bosom great and unredressed injustice has in it the elements of this last convulsion."[94] My sense is that Stowe was already open to the view that, if the United States refused to abolish slavery through peaceful means (out of an ethics of sentimental Christian sympathy), then it would be abolished through militant means (out of an ethics of Christian judgment that properly deserves to be called enthusiastic). This latter sentiment becomes the dominant motif of *Dred*. Thus, when she writes in the preface to the latter, "Never has there been a crisis in the history of this nation so momentous as the present,"[95] Stowe believes the "last convulsion" is at hand.

That Stowe's *Dred* places the center of abolitionist morality not in the domestic sphere but out in the howling wilderness among insurgent maroons who preach death and judgment to sentimental empire poses many problems for our conventional understanding of Stowe, not to mention the very ethos of antebellum American women's fiction. If Stowe's path from domesticity and martyrdom to *marronage* and militancy "constitutes a lost chapter in the history of abolitionist literary representation," as Martha Schoolman argues, it can be no coincidence that this secret—repressed—history dovetails with the "geographic uncanny" represented therein.[96] The uncanny Harriet Beecher Stowe of the Great Dismal Swamp "explores various models of public, democratic sociopolitical organization; introduces the potential for organized, violent, slave insurrection as viable means of securing freedom; and challenges the liberal individualist foundation of contemporary U.S. society and its basis in private property."[97] I wish to stress, though, that Stowe imagines this *unheimlich* "heterotopic space" of the "uncontained and uncontainable—the unknown"[98] as an enthusiastic domain of revival democracy drawing its resources from black cultures of conjure. While both Justine Murison and Caleb Smith have called attention to the tradition of enthusiasm that informs *Dred* (Murison through the filter of medical language and the antebellum theory of nervous disorders, Smith through the filter of legal language and antebellum rhetorics of condemnation),[99] I underscore the black religious and insurrectionary practices represented in the novel and argue for a more emphatic vision of the novel *as* enthusiastic. Murison mentions that Stowe, in *A Key to Uncle Tom's Cabin* (1853), reduces African religion (the practice of magic and obeah) to a distinct "nervous organization," a racial susceptibility to mesmeric influence,[100] and I would add that, in an ambivalence typical of Stowe, her ultimate point here is to applaud and appreciate the unique religious expressions, the spiritual enthusiasms, of the slave population, of course, so long as they are "acted upon by the powerful stimulant of the Christian religion,"[101] the "true enthusiasm" of Biblical revelation. More to the point, her defense of black enthusiasm in this discussion involves the example of a former slave who, under the influence of a divine voice, promptly obeyed the call to flee his bondage.

The character, Dred, is himself such a divine voice in the eponymous novel. When he first speaks (in chapter 28), the narrator forces the reader to encounter Dred as the characters do at a camp meeting by concealing his identity; a "deep voice" speaks from the "swampy thicket" as though it were, without qualification, the voice of God, and a God of judgment on slavery at that.[102] Dred is the embodiment of black enthusiasms: he calls Harry—and any black reader who occupies his position—a slave for living on the subordinate terms of white society, and, as he sings a "wild camp-meeting hymn, much in vogue in those parts," "a wild, exultant fulness of liberty ... rolled in the note," which has the intended effect of inspiring Harry to rebellion: "There was an uprising within him, vague, tumultuous, overpowering; dim instincts, heroic aspirations; the will to do, the soul to dare; and then, in a moment, there followed the picture of all society leagued against him."[103] Dred's revivalism brings to the surface the contradiction between the feeling of liberty and the state of slavery. Stowe plays on the double meaning of "uprising" to make the point: the feeling of enthusiasm rises up in the individual, but it also enacts a spirit of uprising or rebellion, the desire to act out and oppose the society leagued against Harry. Stowe further emphasizes that, while a revival hymn may be in "vogue" for the white audience, the "armies of

God" metaphor at work in Dred's song ("*Brethren, don't you hear the sound? / The martial trumpet now is blowing; / Men in order listing round, / And soldiers to the standard flowing*")[104] translates for the slave as a militant call to join a coming rebellion. This passage amounts to Dred's convulsive address to all readers to participate in the spiritual-political slave revolt against tyranny.

But in her delineation of Dred, Stowe also connects his enthusiastic disposition to African conjure: that individual with "the largest and keenest vitality" develops, through a "sympathy and communion with nature," instinctive abilities to master and affect his or her surroundings with what are considered "peculiar magical powers."[105] While problematic as a biologized stereotype of African peoples, this description nevertheless echoes what Chireau refers to as "the concept of *force vitale*, an omnipresent energy" articulated in "traditional African cultures": "The power of this life force was believed to dwell within organic and inorganic objects, in the elements of nature, and in the bodies of all animate things,"[106] only some individuals—conjurors—are endowed with the capacity to appropriate this life force and do things with it for the community. Dred's grandfather, Stowe explains, was an African sorcerer who "discovered in the boy this peculiar species of temperament," glossed as mesmeric clairvoyance, a faculty which the narrator does "not pretend" to understand but speculates that it could be an undiscovered attribute that is to the future as memory is to the past, or some "sensuous organization" that "endows them [conjurors] with something of that certainty of instinctive discrimination which belongs to animals."[107] These popular naturalistic musings, finally, serve as an explanation for the fact that "Dred was under the inspiring belief that he was the subject of visions and supernatural communications,"[108] a strict definition of the enthusiast that Stowe roots in a cultural anthropology of conjure religion.

The racial embodiment of conjure notwithstanding, Stowe ultimately incorporates black enthusiasm into her novel in order to positively historicize slave insurrection. Dred, for instance, turns out to be Denmark Vesey's son, born of a woman who belongs to the Mandingo, a people, according to Stowe, "distinguished for intelligence, beauty of form, and an indomitable pride and energy of nature."[109] Like Nat Turner, Dred was taught that he could never be a slave, and as a youth he killed his overseer in a fight, "made his escape to the swamps, and was never afterwards heard of in civilized life."[110] No doubt Stowe intends for us to read "civilized life" as trenchant irony (later Dred jokes about the civilizing influences of slavery), but even so, nothing prepares the reader for Stowe's most inspired prose when she turns her alternately approbative and disturbed attention to the uncanny Dismal Swamp, that "immense chain of swamps, regions of hopeless disorder, where the abundant growth and vegetation of nature, sucking up its forces from the humid soil, seems to rejoice in a savage exuberance, and bid defiance to all human efforts either to penetrate or subdue." Prima facie, it might seem from this passage that the swamp has a negative valence but this is complicated when Stowe adds that such "twine[d] and interlace[d]" growths attest to the "solitary majesty of nature" and its "endless vitality and stimulating force."[111]

Rather strangely, Stowe goes on to establish a homology between the Dismal Swamp and enthusiastic revival culture, though the latter, as a democratic public space, has the unique potential to overcome an America divided by race. This is mimicked in the novel's form, since the camp meeting revival scene ends Volume I and serves as a mediating space between the Gordon (Canema) plantation (where the first half of the novel is mostly set) and the Dismal Swamp at the beginning of Volume II. I read this narrative arc as Stowe's self-conscious, even pedagogical, way of paying her respects to domestic sentimentalism before introducing out-of-doors enthusiasm as her new privileged site of democratic cultural and constituent power. At any rate, Stowe represents the camp meeting as a sunny, religious, cross-racial analogue to the Dismal Swamp: "The world is as full of different minds and bodies as the woods are of leaves, and each one has its own habit of growth," says the novel's sage protagonist, Edward Clayton, as he preaches to his sister Anne on the virtues of enthusiasm: "You would have well-trimmed trees and velvet turf. But I love briers, dead limbs, and all, for their very savage freedom.... Unite any assembly of common men in a great enthusiasm,—work them up into an abandon, and let every one 'let go,' and speak as nature prompts,—and you will have brush, underwood, briers, and all grotesque growths; but, now and then, some thought or sentiment will be struck out with a freedom or power such as you cannot get in any other way. You cultivated people are much mistaken when you despise the enthusiasms of the masses. There is more truth than you think in the old 'vox populi, vox Dei.'"[112] Let me accent that "a great enthusiasm" *produces* the human swamp world and that the swamp here becomes an objective correlative, not a mere symbol, for democratic assembly.

But what Clayton gives with one hand he takes away with the other. Not only does he never participate in the enthusiasm of the masses with which he identifies himself, disavowing his own cultivated position as the spectator and cultural critic of the revival, but in the same speech, as part of one continuous sentiment, he demarcates white spiritual enthusiasm from black physical enthusiasm: "No, let the African scream, dance, and shout, and fall in trances. It suits his tropical lineage and blood, as much as our thoughtful inward ways do us."[113] It should be noted that the narrator does not completely agree with Clayton on this point, or at least he or she serves as his corrective by whitening the "tropical lineage" at the camp meeting. For example, the preacher, Father Bonnie, deploys a wild "discourse...like the tropical swamp, bursting out with a lush abundance of every kind of growth—grave, gay, grotesque, solemn, fanciful, and even coarse caricature, provoking the broadest laughter. The audience were swayed by him like trees before the wind."[114] The art of revival preaching requires "pressing into the service all the great life forces and influences of nature," with "poetic skill," to harmonize religious sentiment and the "American landscape," which gives "the human system such an intense consciousness of life."[115]

As for black fugitives in the Dismal Swamp, the novel's most consistent position turns out to be a difference not in racial essence but in political context. Insurrection is only a *politicized revivalism*—that is, the slave's revivalism. Dred's name not only stands for the most obvious pun on his uncanny role as "an object of dread among overseers";[116] it also was a name common among Africans, "generally given to those of great physical force"[117]—in other words, to conjurors. Dred is mostly a name, though, for the "rude poetry" of popular enthusiasms, and in turn, this poetry is derivative—a kind of emergent property—of Stowe's natural philosophy: "There is no principle so awful through all nature as the principle of *growth*. It is a mysterious and dread condition of existence,"[118] but one that serves as both the material site—configuration—and the metaphorical site—poetic figuration—of rebellious slave culture as Stowe sees it. Lest we think Stowe opposes this dread or assigns it solely to slaves, the camp meeting, once again, makes the swamp of human souls into a kind of unconscious folk democracy. Stowe makes the connection for us through the repetitious language of awfulness, dread, and mystery: "There is always something awful in the voice of the multitude. It would seem as if the breath that a crowd breathed out together, in moments of enthusiasm, carried with it a portion of the dread and mystery of their own immortal natures. The whole area before the pulpit, and in the distant aisles of the forest, became one vast, surging sea of sound, as

The Revival of Revolt 151

negroes and whites, slaves and freemen, saints and sinners, slave-holders, slave-hunters, slave-traders, ministers, elders, and laymen, alike joined in the pulses of that mighty song."[119] In a sovereign moment of enthusiasm, master–slave distinctions are abrogated and all breathe, all exist, as one, participating together in the univocal, but overwhelming, chorus of ecstatic community. Moreover, the narrator believes enthusiastic affect to be a cipher for "immortal nature," to which he or she is drawn: after listening to one of the spirituals sung by Father Dickson for a dying slave girl, Emily, the narrator, moved by the tragic scene, loses him- or herself in exclamatory evangelical ejaculations.[120] Our narrative has been drawn into the sphere of enthusiasm, and by proxy so have we as readers. Not only that but elsewhere the narrator serves as our guide into the swamp and walks us through it step by step like one familiar with the passage: "It would seem impossible that human foot could penetrate the wild, impervious jungle; but we must take our readers through it, to a cleared spot."[121] This turns the novel into a form of enthusiastic participation as we finally enter a contact zone with Dred. Stowe collapses the representation of Dred into a relationship with Dred: by reading, we have become involved in a black maroon society.

If any ambiguity about the swamp's affirmative nature remains, it is removed when the narrator represents the Bible—a text "prolific of insurrectionary movements, under all systems of despotism"—as an "oriental seed, an exotic among us,"[122] properly belonging to the Dismal Swamp, just as Afro-Christian folk practice sometimes viewed the Bible as the preeminent conjure book—"as a talisman or amulet, on the one hand, and as a source of conjurational spells, incantations, or prayers on the other . . . for invoking extraordinary powers in order to reenvision, revise, and transform the conditions of human existence."[123] When "planted back in the fiery soil of a tropical heart, it [the Bible] bursts forth with an incalculable ardor of growth," and even "in the soil of the cool Saxon heart the Bible has thrown out its roots with an all-pervading energy," the selfsame energy of Dred said to kindle "the current of enthusiasm" in him.[124] The Bible, like the swamp and the revival (all of which constitute a metonymic chain or cluster of enthusiastic signifiers), also has an "intense sympathy with nature."[125] This becomes even more interesting when Stowe adds political revolution to the cluster of concepts; not only does she say that the same "indefinite stimulating power" of the Bible inheres in "the mingled wail and roar of the Marseillaise," but she also states that Denmark Vesey's insurrectionary schemes (interchangeable with Dred's) were of the same kind that "purchased for our fathers a national existence."[126] But if this is the case, there's nothing exceptionally African or even American about the Dismal Swamp of Souls.

In the development of Volume II, Stowe's *Dred* leaves behind the exoticizing language of (black) religious enthusiasm and transforms Dred into the heroic slave of a more politicized variant of enthusiasm; symmetrically, the narrator begins to boldly preach revolutionary Enlightenment. Dred now commands Harry to read not the Bible but the Declaration of Independence to other slaves at their secret meeting, the same Harry who has recently written to Edward Clayton of Dred's father: "Denmark Vesey was a *man!* His history is just what George Washington's would have been, if you had failed. What set him in his course? The Bible and your Declaration of Independence."[127] Despite speaking the language of revolution, Dred nevertheless doesn't lose his belief in the "perfectness of his own religious enthusiasm, his absolute certainty that he was inspired of God, as a leader and deliverer," and this becomes, in part, his tragic flaw, a point which the narrator qualifies at Dred's funeral: "But he who lies here so still and mournfully in this flickering torch-light had struggling within him the energies which make the patriot and the prophet. Crushed beneath a mountain of ignorance, they rose blind and distorted; yet had knowledge enlightened and success crowned them, his name might have been, with that of Toussaint, celebrated in mournful sonnet by the deepest thinking poet of the age."[128]

So as it turns out, Dred is *not* an actual patriot or prophet, if only because he lacked "knowledge," the kind of knowledge that makes for the "deep thinking" poetry of William Wordsworth here invoked, and for an abolitionist politics that still sees the African race as a "slow-growing plant."[129] This crucial passage finds Stowe participating in the long historical critique of enthusiasm: only a reasonable (educated, enlightened) state of mind, capable of properly channeling the fervor for freedom into the upright enthusiasms of the poet, patriot, and true prophet, can curb the primal excesses of unrefined, if divinely sanctioned, enthusiasm. Nevertheless, Stowe reveals two things about her political thinking: first, enthusiastic energies, if coupled with "knowledge," make the revolutionary patriot/prophet; and second, these energies made the Haitian Revolution. To Stowe, Dred is an unsophisticated Toussaint L'Ouverture.

In the last analysis, Stowe's political sympathies lie with her heroine, Anne Clayton, who preaches a "levelling doctrine"[130] without compromise, but one that consists in educating and rearing her slaves for an ascendant right to freedom. Still, when confronted with the objection that educated, well-treated slaves became insurrectionary in Charleston, Anne retorts "that the best-developed and finest specimens of men have been those that have got up insurrections in Italy, Austria, and Hungary";[131] and moments prior to the novel's denouement, she rebuffs the pragmatic, power-hungry Frank Russel, for whom democracy is a mere pacifier to conceal the operations of "an oligarchy, and the mob... its standing army," in the following terms: "All that nobleness and enthusiasm which has animated people in all ages for liberty cannot be in vain."[132] Then she recites part of the French revolutionary anthem, "La Marseillaise," before exclaiming, "It is not *my* liberty, nor *our* liberty, but the *principle* of liberty itself, that they strove for."[133] Through the voice of Anne Clayton, Stowe makes a concerted effort to associate slave insurrection with global liberation movements of enthusiasm.

But no slave revolution occurs in the novel. It dies with Dred. And even though Stowe replaces the African colonization politics of *Uncle Tom's Cabin* with an exodus politics to the North, her democratic imagination exposes its limits as the novel concludes. In a disappointing image of black utility, we learn that, on Edward Clayton's Canada settlement, the former slave revolter, Hannibal, "instead of slaying men, is great in felling trees and clearing forests." The dissenting slave makes for the ideal laborer, while his educated superior, Harry, "is rapidly acquiring property."[134] Obviously this conclusion echoes the standard platform that emancipated slaves will productively contribute to a liberal capitalist economy, but the problem remains that Stowe does not imagine a way for black or white communities to actively abolish slavery. On the other hand, why should she be expected to? Even if only as a threat, slave insurrection remains significant for Stowe because it eloquently articulates an enthusiasm for freedom following from the right to revolution generally recognized by Americans at large; in that sense, Dred has the last word of the novel: "'Let us die, then!' said Dred. 'What if we do die? What great matter is that? If they bruise our head, we can sting their heels! Nat Turner—they killed him; but the fear of him almost drove them to set free their slaves! Yes, it was argued among them. They came within two or three votes of it in their assembly. A little more fear, and they would have done it'."[135] To Stowe, fear of the black enthusiast is itself politically productive—the Great Insurrection Panic pushes abolitionism forward. But from the Haitian Revolution to Denmark Vesey's plot to Nat Turner's Rebellion, *Dred* also resurrects these events of self-authored freedom as a constituent memory of black enthusiasm for the present hour, as a proclamation that slaves have wanted, want, and will want their liberty at any cost.

White Gaps and Black Magic: The Gospel of Enthusiasm in Martin Delany's *Blake*

Martin Delany's *Blake; or the Huts of America* (1859–62) establishes Harriet Beecher Stowe as the dialogic background of its narrative by using a quatrain from her poem "Caste and Christ" for the epigraph of each of its two parts. This commonplace poem—about Christ siding with slaves against their masters—was published in *Autographs for Freedom* (1853), a collection of antislavery essays, stories, and poetry edited by Julia Griffiths, which includes Frederick Douglass's *The Heroic Slave*, William G. Allen's "Placido" (an homage to the Cuban revolutionary and poet), and James Monroe Whitfield's apocalyptic poem "How Long?" Delany echoes all of these latter voices in *Blake* as well—the novel is his own autograph for freedom. In comparison to *Dred,* if Volume II of Stowe's novel accents a fugitive politics of the Dismal Swamp that ends with the successful foundation of a Canada commune, so does *Blake* in Part I, as if to suggest that black *marronage* and exile—now accomplished by the "enlightened" heroic slave himself, Henry Blake, who leads his friends and family on the Franks plantation to Canada after spreading the gospel of insurrection throughout the slave states—ought to be the mere first movement of black enthusiasm. The second movement has yet to be written: in Part II, Blake travels to Cuba, where he and his comrades plan and coordinate a large-scale black rebellion unimaginable to Stowe.

Undoubtedly *Blake* is the "most radical black novel of the nineteenth century," as Bernard Bell claims, and this has much to do with the fact that it was "intended primarily for a black rather than a white audience, and [thus] his hero is a young black Cuban revolutionary, not an American mulatto or a pious old slave."[136] As such, I read *Blake* as the only antebellum novel of black enthusiasm *for itself*, and, accordingly, it creates a model of black politics that circulates outside of national parameters. Within the United States, as Andy Doolen argues, Delany represents the Dismal Swamp as the organizing center of black resistance, as a "sacred revolutionary ground" "claiming African Americans as the real heirs to the universal right of revolution";[137] however, Delany also sees the hopelessness (made apparent by Stowe) of delimiting black revolution therein, within the dismal belly of the beast, a problem that he circumvents by shifting the locus of slave resistance to Cuba.

But if Delany's narrative forms a bridge across the Dismal Swamp to Cuba, the question becomes how he transposes and extends the politics of conjure and a literature of enthusiasm in doing so. Two plot facts begin to answer this question. Whereas Dred erects his home in the confines of the Dismal Swamp, Blake, as a figure for black diasporic consciousness, has no home: he does not belong anywhere and becomes instead the unconfined Wandering Slave, with Cuba serving more as a geographical depot and bunker than his native land. And whereas conjure in *Dred* refers to the spiritualized, if physically vital, enthusiasms of a wild, subterranean "immortal nature" (a *depth model* of the swamp uncanny), conjure in *Blake* refers solely to the political—which is not to say secular—enthusiasms of black community opened up through diasporic communication (a *network model* of the itinerant uncanny). In this production of black geopolitical space, the depth and network models are two different "scales of identification," to use Hsuan Hsu's terminology, for the "counterhegemonic scale jumping" of black politics "discontiguous with national boundaries" in their dominant or imperial form.[138] The one functions as a subtractive, insular counternational space, a geographical lacuna, missing on a map, but also as a cultivated microhabitat. Contrariwise, as a nomadic, diffuse, and hemispheric space—more like a virtual grid of black connections, including the swamp itself—the other model relates more to what Homi Bhabha, by way of Frantz Fanon, calls "the zone of occult instability" and "transnational dissemination," or "DissemiNation," to describe a migratory people-in-the-making, dwelling in the political *unheimlich*.[139]

Yet the above observations hardly explain why and how Delany uniquely conceived such a project of occult black internationalism, nor do they allow us to comprehend his African "familial reconstruction" that, despite its critique of colonialism, invokes a "black Atlantic patriarchy" positing a "necessary relationship between nationality, citizenship, and masculinity."[140] Delany's belief in Freemasonry best clarifies these issues, and I agree with Corey Walker that the novel is also the "preeminent example of an African American literary appropriation of the culture of Freemasonry for revolutionary ends."[141] Many people know that Freemasonry was the elite gentleman's club par excellence throughout the eighteenth century, and this was no different for its black chapter, but the evolution of Freemasonry in the nineteenth century deserves further elucidation: while eighteenth-century Freemasonry promulgated the culture and ideals of rational Enlightenment, post-Revolutionary Freemasonry often participated in the culture and ideals of evangelical Protestantism and Romantic spiritualism by emphasizing the organization's pre-Enlightenment roots in hidden wisdom and spiritual mystery as well as by transforming its rituals into a cultic practice of sublime feeling.[142] As I mentioned in my opening remarks, Freemasonry was one form of secret society whereby the black community could leverage cultural power and respond to its convulsive context: it offered "supranational citizenship," a vision of cosmopolitan black nationalism, to disenfranchised African Americans and facilitated—in the black diaspora—an "international network of cultural and commercial exchanges and interests."[143] Moreover, as part of an emergent pan-African ideology, black Freemasons such as Martin Delany stressed the genealogical origins of Masonic thought—a preslavery culture of high black civilization in the ur-home of Egypt and Ethiopia; only, in Delany's own imperious platform, African Americans now needed to recolonize and recivilize Africa.[144] With this context in mind, one might expect that Delany would be sensitive to legacies of African religion and culture while, as an elite intellectual, he would also work to reinscribe said legacies in a more "enlightened" *Weltanschauung*. *Blake* bears out this position.

I suggest that one read Part II of Delany's *Blake* as the political-revolutionary sublation of conjure society and slave religion represented in Part I, superseding the belief in an occult magic of supernatural pretenses but preserving its imaginative adherence to a magnitude of unheard-of, uncanny, emancipatory works. Or, put in other terms, the black political enthusiasm of Part II both displaces and incorporates, abolishes and fulfills, the religious enthusiasm of Part I. While this does function for Delany as a secularist critique of what he sees as counterprogressive black superstition, it does not mean that the political composition of enthusiasm for him has no sacred dimension; on the contrary, it's an attempt on his part to enact a "progressive" form of religiosity that *foregrounds* political causes—namely, emancipation—but also recognizes the importance of conjure enthusiasm to black history and culture. Through the interaction of heterogeneous black characters struggling to compose a workable model for their historical becoming, the novel—as a genre-in-the-making—allows Delany to depict black enthusiasm-in-the-making, and signifying on religious folk culture is one way that he does this. For example, Delany riffs on the black identification with the Children of Israel who wait for their Moses to deliver them from slavery, which of course Moses ultimately does by parting the Red Sea with his magic staff. In African-American conjure religion, Moses was—in the words of Zora Neale Hurston—"honored as the greatest Conjurer."[145] As Theophus Smith further explains, "Moses-the-conjuror . . . is [often] mimetically related to God-as-conjuror and to reality as conjurational."[146] But in his 1853 address on the *Origin and Objects of Ancient Freemasonry*, Delany also appeals to Moses as a father of Masonic wisdom, and a "*fugitive* slave" at that.[147] In a kind of mock epic mode, at once humorous and didactic, Delany's narrative Moses, the disenchanted Blake, will now lead his people through "the white gap" with the magic staff of cash that he teaches slaves to steal from their masters.[148]

However, the novel does not sustain, at least not consistently, its Enlightenment program of educating slaves in the rational technologies of self-conjured freedom. In the early part of the novel, Henry Blake certainly declares his dissent from the pacifying Christianity of his fellow slaves, but only to later "renew his faith and dependence upon Divine aid, when falling upon his knees he opened his heart to God, as a tenement of the Holy Spirit."[149] Waffling between satire and sincerity, Delany ambiguously exploits the vocabulary of Christianity for an unambiguous end: the abolition of slavery. To start an insurrection becomes Blake's leap of faith, and his accomplice, Andy, a Baptist preacher, says a prayer for the success of it. Then, after Blake first reveals his plan—the Good News of insurrection—in the following terms, "I now impart to you the secret, it is this: I have laid a scheme, and matured a plan for a general insurrection of the slaves in every state, and the successful overthrow of slavery!," the slaves, as if at a church service listening to the preacher, respond with enthusiastic alacrity: "'Amen!' exclaimed Charles. 'God grant it!' responded Andy."[150] As Blake continues to establish his "black Masonic network in the slave South,"[151] the most interesting narrative aspect of the novel is that, while we as readers overhear the news *of* the secret plan for an insurrection, we never overhear the plan itself as Blake whispers it to his confidantes and they cry "Eureka!" This preserves the immanent structure of black enthusiasm: at a revolt revival-in-the-making, in the convulsive address between black participants, Delany keeps in reserve the maroon conspiracy, the hidden transcript ("silent communion") that asks the reader either to join in (to make contact with the events) if he or she wishes to know the secret, to imagine and invent it herself, or to be fearful of the clandestine *how* and *when* of the impending event. In the political revival, Blake breaks spontaneously into a song that establishes his and the novel's *evangel*: "Insurrection shall be my theme! / My watchword 'Freedom or the grave!'"[152]

Furthermore, the visit to the Dismal Swamp in Part I gives Blake a chance to directly engage with the culture of conjure as an essential expression of his theme and watchword. In chapter 24, "A Flying Cloud," Blake, prior to entering the swamp, visits South Carolina and meets "one of the remaining confidentials and adherents of the memorable South Carolina insurrection," and when the old man learns of Blake's plan, he exclaims: "Dis many a day I been prayin' dat de Laud sen' a nudder Denmark 'mong us! De Laud now anseh my prar in dis young man!" Next, when Blake nears the Dismal Swamp in North Carolina, he also meets "old confederates of the noted Nat Turner" and refers to that geographical space as an "entirely new element," a fertile breeding ground for the coming insurrection: "Finding ample scope for undisturbed action through the entire region of the Swamp, he continued to go scattering to the winds and sowing the seeds of a future crop, only to take root in the thick black waters which cover it, to be grown in devastation and reaped in a whirlwind of ruin."[153] Here Delany capitalizes on popular American fears of black insurrection: uncanny slave revolt incubates in the Dismal Swamp, and, horror of all horrors, it's a general conspiracy led by a Caribbean slave. In the Dismal Swamp itself, the "boldest black rebels" live and hold the names of "Nat Turner, Denmark Veezie, and General Gabriel" in "sacred reverence; that of Gabriel as a talisman."[154] This establishes, in effect, a relationship between storytelling, political resistance, and conjure: by turning the name of Gabriel, like the name of Three-Fingered Jack, into the magic obeah fetish, into a spell of dismay, Delany interprets conjure as a revolt revivalism and a dynamic symbol of freedom. This is reinforced when Gamby Gholar, a "noted high conjurer and compeer of Nat Turner," claims to have been waiting for Blake, having prophesied his appearance; Gholar then performs an elaborate ritual with his "goombah" fetish, gives a talisman to Blake, and, like the obeah man in Tacky's Rebellion, says it will keep him from harm: "Take dis, meh son, an' so long as yeh keep it, da can' haum yet, dat da can't."[155] My sense is that Delany sees conjure as a kind of folk revolutionary and utopian fiction. For instance, when Gamby Gholar and his

The Revival of Revolt   159

allies claim to "have been patriots in the American Revolution"[156] and Maudy Ghamus, a high conjuror, says that he and Gabriel, who was born in 1776, fought together in the Revolution, these tall tales and anachronisms serve both a creative and a critical function: on the one hand, in act of prolepsis, they project backward a black revolution that has *yet* to come, a black revolution seen as continuous with the American Revolution; and, on the other hand, they project backward the revolutionary repressed of the American Revolution itself, criticizing it for its prohibition on black enfranchisement but through a narrative in which it was already a black American Revolution as it should have been.

Still, Delany can appreciate conjure only insofar as he demystifies it. We soon learn that, in a highly codified political system, with fourteen-year appointments and a "supreme executive body called the 'Head'," the goal of the high conjuror, ostensibly "to create new conjurers, lay charms, [and] take off 'spells'," is actually to obtain "revenue" "for keeping up an organized existence in this much-dreaded morass—the Dismal Swamp."[157] Delany outs the conjurer for selling indulgences, so to speak, but in the practical service of maintaining the freemasonry of the race: he wants to filter the militant content out of conjure practice and leave behind the dross of superstition. Thus, after the "Head" christens Blake an official high conjurer himself, "licensed with unlimited power" to work wonders "for their deliverance," and Blake leaves the swamp to hide out with a friend in Richmond, Delany includes the following passage so as to make the conjure revival of revolt unmistakable, in a new—plain, concrete—logic of its appearance: "when developing his [Blake's] scheme, the old material extinguished and left to mould and rot after the demonstration at Southampton, was immediately rekindled, never again to be suppressed until the slaves stood up the equal of the masters. Southampton—the name of Southampton to them was like an electric shock."[158] Southampton marks the convulsive event of 1831 and its affective resurrection in the present (the "electric shock"), as Blake revives and relays the prophet Nat Turner's convulsive address to other slaves about the secret scheme of insurrection: that's what matters, not the religious outfit of the old material. For the same reason, Delany has no problem accommodating black magic, since, as Blake puts it to Charles in their dialogue on conjure, "It makes the more ignorant slaves have greater confidence in, and more respect for, their headmen and leaders," and "we must take the slaves, not as we wish them to be, but as we really find them to be," by whatever means necessary "to gain our freedom."[159]

As if to reinforce the point, in the next chapter Mammy Judy and Daddy Joe, as "ignorant slaves," express greater confidence in Blake himself because they think his explanation of how to pass through the white gap (via the compass) must be occult conjure knowledge—"Wy, you is conjure, sho'nuff,"[160] says Mammy Judy. Once again, Delany riffs on the conjure tradition, only his "magic" fetish does not merely inspire confidence but allows the slave to emancipate him- or herself through a critical piece of technology. In contradiction to his earlier sentiment, however, Blake doesn't always take the conjurers as he finds them: "'Now you see, boys,' said Henry, 'how much conjuration and such foolishness and stupidity is worth to the slaves in the South. All that it does, is to put money into the pockets of the pretended conjurer, give him power over others by making them afraid of him; and even ... the High Conjurors ... are depending more upon me to deliver them from their confinement ... than all their combined efforts together. I made it a special part of my mission, wherever I went, to enlighten them on this subject.'"[161] Like critics of enthusiasm before him, Delany invokes a negative definition of the black enthusiast—one who pretends to have special communication with the divine—only to shore up another positive definition, a rational enthusiasm, whereby Blake himself is the "deliver" or Messiah, the Enlightened conjure man, the negation and realization of conjure. And yet, like Kant (in chapter 1), Blake allows himself to sit on the border and transgress the boundaries of true enthusiasm, if only for a moment, when he later exchanges conjure secrets "concerning dog charming" with his "native African" friend Grande.[162]

In Part II of *Blake*, it becomes increasingly clear that Delany thinks of the black poet or artist as the genuine article and agent of enthusiastic transmission, exemplified by the Afro-Cuban song poet and political radical Gabriel de la Concepción Valdés, or Plácido, Blake's cousin and accomplice. Delany (anachronistically) incorporates the historical figure of Plácido (who was executed in 1844), as he does many songs and poems, so that black legacies of rebellion and creativity are part of the novel's zone of contact with a living, unfolding historical reality: he thereby wishes to remind the reader of the communal and aversive context in which black song and poetry circulates. On this point, William Wells Brown summarizes the significance of Plácido as follows: "The imaginative brain of the poet produced verses which the slaves sung in their own rude way, and which kindled in their hearts a more intense desire for liberty. Placido planned an insurrection of the slaves, in which he was to be their leader and deliverer; but the scheme failed.... His songs are still sung in the bondsman's hut, and his name is a household word to all. As the *Marseillaise* was sung by the revolutionists of France, and inspired the people with a hatred to oppressors, so will the slaves of Cuba, at a future day, sing the songs of their poet-martyr, and their cry will be, 'Placido and Liberty.'"[163] Similarly, one statement by the narrator in *Blake* best describes the importance of Plácido's song poetics as Delany sees it: "In poetry he wrote them [the "great principles" of resistance] in sentiments of song, enigmatically, though comprehensively. These words, though softly and fearfully spoken—as if in thunder tones—were indelibly impressed on every heart, while the sentiments of song, like a lightning flash, ran through every mind the length and breadth of the island."[164] Aesthetic language (poetry) is to song as thunder is to lightning as message is to medium or, finally, as reason is to enthusiasm. The weight of this passage falls on the power of song to transmit to "every mind" the convulsive affect—the "electric shock"—of emancipatory action-in-the-making.

The revival of black revolt reaches its apogee in "Entertainment at Carolus Blacus," chapter 69, antecedent to Blake's declaration of war in the next chapter, "I am for war—war upon the whites," which receives a "universal shout of response" and cries of "Amen!" as the "greatest enthusiasm prevailed, though prudently controlled within due bounds."[165] This declaration of enthusiastic independence seems indeed prudent compared to the prior entertainment scene when Plácido leads the singing of a ballad set to the words of the poem "Yes! Strike Again That Sounding String" by Delany's friend, the U.S. poet James M. Whitfield. First and foremost, the poem admonishes us to play and sing the music of the "fiercest passion" and "wildest numbers," music not of "joy and gladness" nor of peace but of the "tempest roaring / Across the angry foaming deep." And then this quatrain:

> Sing of the lightning's lurid flash,
> The ocean's roar, the howling storm,
> The earthquake's shock, the thunder's crash,
> Where ghastly terrors teeming swarm.

From there the poem breaks out into an unchecked call for violence and revels in the fantasy of "human gore," before concluding with the sentiment that only such a song could "an echo wake" in the speaker's "crush'd and sad" soul and "shake" the "direful impressions" which "threaten now to drive" him "mad."[166] After the assembly bows with "silent devotion" in response to the ballad, the narrator then relays that their "justification of the issue"—the swarm's right to a bloody judgment—is predicated on their "indisputable right with every admixture of blood, to an equal, if not superior, claim to an inheritance of the Western Hemisphere,"[167] and Delany includes Native Americans here as a "colored race" belonging to the coming insurrection.

But precisely at this point, when the novel has nowhere else to go if Henry Blake, the General-in-Chief of the Army of Emancipation of the Oppressed Men and Women of Cuba, does not begin to realize the work of the "greatest enthusiasm," *Blake* stalls or defers its own trajectory and suspends the critical pressure that it has accumulated (that is, unless the presumably missing final six chapters of the novel would have proved otherwise). But I do not agree with the critical refrain that the novel's plot is necessarily *incomplete* without the insurrection: "It is safe to say that the missing revolution deflates many readers' enthusiasm for the novel."[168] After all, the pugnacious caterer Gofer Gondolier already takes this perspective in the last chapter: "But we're neglecting our murdered brother there [referring to Plácido, who has been viciously beaten by a bookseller], disputing about them serpents which the Scriptures told us long ago should have their heads mashed."[169] By this Gondolier probably means to indirectly criticize the novel's hero: "Blake during the whole of these scenes was grave and sober, having nothing to say."[170] As if in response to Blake's silence, Gondolier, "who had no scruples in assuming to himself this particular duty of political dispensation," decides that he will be commander if nobody else will, and it's he who has the last word of the novel: "Woe be unto those devils of whites, I say!"[171] The missing revolution, then, has been written into the novel as part of Blake's and the Army of Emancipation's failure, and the "deflation" of enthusiasm therefore demands another interpretation; I would even like to suggest that the discordant ending is one of the novel's greatest strengths.

Recall Bakhtin's idea that the novel makes the center of its activity not the past but the future and a participation in historical becoming; as part of the dialogic interaction between the text and its reader, "we encounter the specific danger in the novelistic zone of contact: we ourselves may actually enter the novel." Then look at *Blake*'s ending again. Nothing would cheat black enthusiasm more than to represent an *incomplete* emancipation as if it had already been realized. Unlike Stowe's happy image of black reconciliation at the end of *Dred* (in which the slave rebel must be either killed or exiled), Delany, both by refusing to let the insurrection occur *in* the text and by ending on a tragic chord of antiblack violence, makes his novel a literary *prelude* to and *projection* of emancipation that purposefully accents the convulsive crisis of black inactivity such that, in his convulsive address to the reader, it is necessary for historical actors to take the baton as part of a new "political dispensation," to carry on Blake's theme of insurrection, and to *complete the novel*. In other words, the novel is only a call that sows the seeds but the reader, having traveled with Blake and attended the revival meetings, must respond and reap the harvest as the secret subject of all future enthusiasm. Only a critic and reader, not a participant and actor, can miss this point: the novel's ending means to set the reader into motion—to incite, not to deflate, enthusiasm for the "missing revolution." It's a kind of insurrectionary maieutic method designed to elicit not knowledge but action from the reader. While it's certainly plausible that Delany wishes to spotlight not revolutionary violence but "responsible black leadership,"[172] I see the closing chapters as a strategic detachment from Blake's authority so that the convulsive crisis can be afforded its fullest weight: *Blake* then becomes another symbolic talisman of deliverance, a conjure text and watchword for reviving revolt.

In an 1875 comment on "negro music," the author and musician Sidney Lanier reports that a man named Dick, while singing, all of a sudden "changed his tune" with an "*allegro!*" tempo: "*Da capo*, of course, and *da capo* indefinitely; for it ends on the dominant. The dominant is a chord of progress: no such thing as stopping."[173] In musical vocabulary, *da capo* is a directive to a performer to go back to the beginning, to revive, to replay a composition, and, as Lanier tells us, to do so indefinitely, for every ending of a song informs the musician that progress has not been *finally* made, that the song must be sung again and quickly so, *allegro*. The same applies to the antislavery novel of enthusiasm, especially to *Blake*—there's no such thing as ending the blues narrative until liberation has been achieved. The novel of enthusiasm may be incomplete, but it ends on the dominant chord of progress—*da capo*.

CHAPTER FIVE

The Free State of Whitman
John Brown, the Civil War, and the Dis-memberment of Enthusiasm in the 1860 Leaves of Grass

> And for the Union with Slavery no manly person will suffer a day to go by without discrediting disintegrating & finally exploding it. The 'union' they talk of, is dead & rotten, the real union, that is, the will to keep & renew union, is like the will to keep & renew life, & this alone gives any tension to the dead letter.
>
> —RALPH WALDO EMERSON, 1856

In the last chapter, I introduced Thomas Wentworth Higginson's position that both John Brown's 1859 attack on Harper's Ferry and the American Civil War represent further extensions of a revolutionary tradition including the Atlantic Revolutions and a blinding series of antislavery insurrections. This final chapter amplifies that claim by focusing on the arch-literary enthusiast of the era, Walt Whitman, or rather, the Walt Whitman of "the fractured state"[1] who primarily surfaced in the 1860 *Leaves of Grass* on the eve of the Civil War but also appeared intermittently in singular poems throughout his career. This Whitman crystallizes in the underappreciated cluster "Songs of Insurrection" from the 1871–72 and 1876 *Leaves of Grass*. I read these six poems—three of which were originally published in 1860—as Whitman's definitive poetry of enthusiasm.

Why 1860? One can broach this question by noting that the 1860 *Leaves* was published in the same year (and by the same publishers) as another work, James Redpath's *Echoes of Harper's Ferry*, an anthology of speeches, poems, essays, and letters mostly devoted to defending and eulogizing the recently executed John Brown. My contention is that Brown and Whitman share a legacy of political enthusiasm as Abraham Lincoln polemically defined it in his criticism of Brown: "An enthusiast broods over the oppression of a people till he fancies himself commissioned by Heaven to liberate them."[2] For Whitman, 1859–60 was a historical moment that demanded the political enthusiast. In "Year of

Meteors. (1859–1860.)," a poem that depicts John Brown's execution, Walt Whitman dubs 1859 to 1860 a "brooding year!" and a "year of forebodings!"[3] for a United States that was trying to save its name from irony. That "Year of Meteors" was published in *Drum-Taps* (1865) as a "retrospective," highlighting the pivotal "contest" for the presidency and John Brown's execution,[4] points to Whitman's understated adoption of a (then) controversial ideology: namely, that Lincoln and Brown were active prefigurations of the Civil War and agents of emancipation. Whitman shares Herman Melville's view that "Weird John Brown" was the "meteor of the war."[5]

In 1859–60, however, when it was far from clear that liberty would be victorious, Walt Whitman was forced to confront the possibility that his poetic vocation of chanting triumphant democracy would come to an end: "Must I change my triumphant songs? said I to myself; / Must I indeed learn to chant the cold dirges of the baffled? / And sullen hymns of defeat?"[6] Hence the significance of John Brown's execution: it was a historical sign for Whitman of the crucifixion of democracy in the United States. In "Year of Meteors," Whitman announces that he "stood very near" the old man at the scaffold and remained silent, but now he "would sing" of Brown as part of the "deeds and signs" of this critical year, the portent of which nobody grasps.[7] Yet, as he "gleam[s]" with these deeds and signs, Whitman becomes a John Brown meteor himself, falling from the heavens:

> Year of comets and meteors transient and strange!—lo!
>   even here, one equally transient and strange!
> As I flit through you hastily, soon to fall and be gone,
>   what is this book,
> What am I myself but one of your meteors?

A meteor "dropt in the night," Whitman's book-cum-self is a vertiginous fragment born along by convulsive events and shooting through space as part of the "huge meteor procession."[8] But if Brown's death "will make the gallows as glorious as the cross,"[9] as Emerson put it (an image that Whitman celebrated)[10], then in the context of the poem's publication in *Drum-Taps*, Brown arguably becomes the first of many broken soldiers in Whitman's phalanx of the dead to wear "the face of the Christ himself; / Dead and divine, and brother of all."[11] Regardless, "Year of Meteors" marks a distinct shift in Whitman's politics that retrospectively calls attention to the historical conditions concurrent with the publication of the 1860 *Leaves of Grass*. Here we first meet a Whitman who conceptualizes democratic ideals, not in the robust terms of spiritual manifest destiny or American exceptionalism, but in terms of rare and contingent meteors of liberation that land and die instantaneously without any promise of success or recognition by the nation.

To help explain Whitman's hymn to political meteors, some biographical context is in order. Between 1856 and 1860, Whitman had become entangled with and embraced by the most radical wing of abolition enthusiasts who shared John Brown's passion for "the primacy of the act."[12] Ted Genoways's study of Whitman's "quicksand years" details the many indirect connections Whitman had to John Brown through his friendship with Brown's most adamant supporters: most notably, Whitman was in attendance with his friends James Redpath and William Thayer at the 1860 hearing of Frank Sanborn after his arrest for aiding John Brown in the attack on Harper's Ferry. Redpath and Thayer came armed, ready to kidnap Sanborn if convicted, and Whitman was there to help them escape.[13]

It is not only the enthusiasms of radical abolitionism, however, that account for Whitman's more pronounced dissenting politics around this time. Michael Moon points to the influence that "sex radicals" in the New York City bohemian scene (orbiting around Pfaff's Tavern) had on Whitman in 1860, the year that Moon "see[s] as the culminating one in Whitman's brief but intense career as a visible and public bohemian."[14] Although critics have thoroughly examined Whitman's bohemian-inspired "free love" vision of a "homosexual republic"[15] that "releases erotic potentialities into every register of social life,"[16] this vision's relationship to the year of meteors and the sectional crisis has remained obscure and tenuous. In fact, we cannot understand the one without the other, and where love and politics intersect, it is not so much a circumscribed homosexuality that is at stake in Whitman but, supervening on his homosocial affections, an intimate desire to "introduce the stranger" and the transient and strange as such—"a queer, queer race, of novel fashion" and "new ways and days."[17] As I will argue in this chapter, the 1860 Whitman attempts to weave both John Brown–style democratic revolt and a queer, queer politics ("in the nineteenth-century sense of unpredictable, unusual, and unconventional")[18] into an unheard-of model of political enthusiasm, but it is Whitman's misunderstood incorporation of the former that this chapter specifically explores.

Of course, any time that one tries to extract and stabilize Walt Whitman's politics or identity or poetic ethos, both in general or in a specific edition of *Leaves*, it is always possible, as Whitman himself warned us, to adduce evidence to the contrary (he is all things, and infinitely variable), a problem compounded by the accretive, palimpsestic nature of his project whereby each ensuing edition of *Leaves*, though a singular work of art, both archives and recontextualizes, preserves and revises, earlier stages of self and composition. My thesis on the Whitman of the 1860 *Leaves* does not assume an absolute difference from prior or later manifestations, but I do believe, like Michael Moon, that "cultivated disintegrations"[19] play a special role in this version of *Leaves*, that is, in the 146 new poems written for the edition as well as in Whitman's alterations to the previously published material. While I don't wish to claim exceptional status for this body of poetry, I do admit to sympathizing with Roy Harvey Pearce's influential thesis that the 1860 *Leaves* represents the most redeemable Whitman, albeit for very different reasons.[20] Apropos of the "Enfans d'Adam," "Calamus," and "Leaves of Grass" cluster, the 1860 *Leaves* is often correctly viewed as Whitman's poetry of the finite and contextual, of real first person experience, as opposed to the bombastic, limitless, and totalistic rhetorical mode that one customarily associates with the American bard. For the same reason, readings of this edition often accent—but in my estimate, wrongly—either a depoliticized Whitman who turns to private love poetry, sometimes glossed as a "*Poetry of Loss*,"[21] or a politicized and amorous Whitman who emphasizes a patriotic love and national cohesiveness defined by male affection and erotic attachment. For example, many of the articles in the *Huntington Library Quarterly*'s wonderful 2010 volume devoted to the 1860 *Leaves* in honor of the sesquicentennial testify to the endurance of these positions, some critics essaying on discrete issues of sex and love, others on existential crisis and pensiveness, while David Reynolds argues that Whitman's "Calamus" love aims to heal the sectional divide through an affectionate Unionism.[22] I take up argument with this last claim and Reynolds's position elsewhere that "Whitman sought to provide America with healing and reconciliation through poetic language" whereas "[John] Brown sought to purge America of its greatest injustice through military action."[23]

Betsy Erkkila has been one of the most compelling voices in articulating the stakes of Whitman's politics qua politics, and her contextualization of the 1860 Whitman-in-crisis is the point of departure for my own reading. As she explains, after the election of James Buchanan in 1856, Whitman's faith in the Union "totality" broke down, and simultaneously, after the poor sales of the 1856 edition of *Leaves*, so did Whitman's belief that his poetry would bind the nation together. Whitman's politics, then, shifted toward the left around this time; in particular, in the wake of the 1857 economic depression and disputes over "the extension of slavery, Whitman retreated from the politics of manifest destiny that had led to his earlier support of the Mexican war and President Polk's expansionist policies."[24] Erkkila goes on to suggest that, circa 1858–59, Whitman turns to private love poetry not only because of a tortured love affair gone bad but also because of "his crisis of faith in the 'grandeur of the States'," a crisis that Erkkila reads as a symbolic secession on Whitman's part: "At a time when the South was threatening to secede from the Union and when the country's political administration seemed determined to save the Union by making slavery rather than freedom the law of the land, Whitman enacts a kind of private secession by severing himself from the political sphere";[25] Whitman "seceded from the democratic en masse."[26] But if Whitman secedes from the political sphere, how is it that Erkkila sees the 1860 "Calamus" poems as "Janus faced, expressing a separatist impulse toward a private homosexual order at the same time that they invoke a national and global community of democratic brotherhood"?[27] Strictly speaking, her answer is that the 1860 *Leaves* betrays a profound ambivalence, a competing tendency to resolve Whitman's personal crisis and restore his faith in democratic union on the one hand, and to voice a heartfelt sense of both public and private fracturing on the other hand. Still, Erkkila reads a brazenly militant poem in the 1860 *Leaves* such as "France, The 18th Year of These States" as sympathetic to John Brown's revolutionary judgment on slavery: this is verse about the political sphere par excellence.[28]

How, then, can a depoliticized and separatist swerve toward erotic privacy coexist with a prorevolutionary "national and global community"? This chapter proffers an answer to this question. The stumbling block lies in automatically associating secession—or disunion—with the Confederacy and the "fractured state" of Whitman's crisis with a withdrawal from public politics; on the contrary, abolitionists, including Whitman, thought of John Brown's actions and the impending Civil War as a meteoric attempt to fracture and secede from a slave-chattel Union and to subtract from the constitutional tyranny of slavery, thereby releasing alternative democratic possibilities occluded by existing legal and nationalist frameworks. Our canonical view of Whitman as the poet of generic pluralism and democratic harmony does not allow for what I believe to be the case in 1860: Whitman enacts a politics of civil dismemberment that shatters juridical and national Unionism in the name of an extra-legal, affectionate form of Unionism claimed by enthusiasts for liberty and them alone.

Furthermore, Whitman's politics of dismemberment expresses itself as enthusiastic literature. As a writer of his convulsive context (especially the sectional crisis of 1859–60), Whitman defines his poetic vocation opposite the political machinations and social divisions of the troubled fifties; he would later say that the three pre-Lincoln administrations of Fillmore, Pierce, and Buchanan proved that despotism was an inherent potentiality of the U.S. political system.[29] In response, Whitman sought to therapeutically remedy national ills in a directly political engagement. As a writer of the convulsive address, Whitman wants to establish direct contact with his reader in an outrageously affectionate manner, to remedy the convulsive context through an insurgent form of affiliation and love. And finally, as a writer of convulsive affect, Whitman privileges ecstatic communities, or embodied, dynamic, and experimental publics that invent a democracy-in-the-making through collaborative exchange, only I will show that the Whitman of political enthusiasm does so with his comrades alone, not with everyone. I am arguing for a view of Walt Whitman—that is, a singular Whitman—not as the national bard of American Unionism and integralism who speaks for all and heals the nation's fragmentation, but of American dismemberment and sectarian internationalism who speaks only for the enthusiast and a camaraderie based *upon* a "fractured state."

Rather than conceive of civil dismemberment as a mere concept for political crisis and disunion, Whitman composes a model of subjectivity and affection based on the whirl and contest of the vertiginous self flitting through space in a meteor procession of liberty. In order to conceptualize more concretely the conjoined "themes of political *and* sexual revolution,"[30] dismemberment and queer sexuality, in the 1860 poetry, it will help to keep in mind what queer and disability theorist Robert McRuer sees as the "thoroughly interwoven" systems of "compulsory able-bodiedness" and "compulsory heterosexuality"; so-called sexual and physical normalcy have been historically articulated together to deny social access to both homosexuals and impaired persons who are equally viewed as effaceable deviants or aberrations.[31] Although it is well known that Whitman, as a Civil War nurse, was fixated on impaired soldiers and war fragmentation, the disability motifs in his composition of intimate—civil war—nationhood have not been adequately explored, and yet they hold the key to Whitman's understanding of the Union body politic as expressed through his relationship to bodies generally. In the next section, I discuss the discursive politics surrounding the Civil War and situate John Brown's enthusiasm in relation to it. Enthusiasm enacts a "fractured state," a will to political dismemberment, in the name of democracy, which Whitman embraces in his 1860 poetry, as I show in the subsequent section. Next, I move to a close reading of Whitman's "Songs of Insurrection" in order to tease out Whitman's enthusiastic politics in detail, especially his international vision of enthusiasm. This sets up my concluding evaluation of Walt Whitman's struggle to square both Union victory in the Civil War and the carnage that it produced with the ideals of the enthusiast.

Ordinances of Dismemberment: Of Union Disability and John Brown's Burning Fragment

Historically, societies threatened by deterioration, destruction, and civil strife have often been problematically compared to mutilated bodies. As David Mitchell puts it, "Because disability has served primarily as a metaphor for things gone awry with bodily and social orders (as opposed to the inherent mutability of bodies themselves), there is a cumulative material impact on cultural attitudes toward disabled people in general. Disability proves an exceptional textual fate in that it is deployed in literary [though not only literary] narrative as a master metaphor for social ills."[32] Influentially, Mitchell and Sharon Snyder coin the term "*narrative prosthesis*" to describe the "perpetual discursive dependency upon disability" as a "narrative device—an artistic prosthesis" on which "literary narratives lean for their representational power, disruptive potentiality, and analytical insight."[33] Often this prosthesis functions as a "desire to compensate for a limitation or to reign in excessiveness," and to "resolve or correct" a "deviance marked as abnormal or improper in a social context."[34] As such, while people with physical impairments suffer directly from a culture that limits social access to those without "normate" bodies, disability—as an ideology and imbedded rhetoric—refers to the "social process that turns an impairment into a negative," especially by conceptualizing disability as a condition of abjection, dysfunction, abnormality, and illness.[35] Hence the project of disability theory as Lennard Davis conceives it: "Disability studies demands a shift from the ideology of normalcy, from the rule and hegemony of normates, to a vision of the body as changeable, unperfectable, unruly, and untidy."[36]

In the context of the Civil War and its "Piles of solid Moan," as Emily Dickinson phrased it,[37] the rhetoric of disability is an obsessive theme, and Civil War narratives, on both sides of the Mason-Dixon, exhibit a willful opposition to a compromised and dissociated, internally broken national body, framed in terms of a horror over U.S. disability. At a formative moment in Civil War narration, Abraham Lincoln, in his 1865 Second Inaugural Address, claims that the Confederacy threatened the body of the Union with two separate acts of violence. The first was the spread of slavery, that moral cancer God willed "to remove" through the "terrible war."[38] Yet, Lincoln nevertheless insists that if slavery had remained benign, that is, localized in the South, the all-tolerant Union would not have interfered: "To strengthen, perpetuate, and extend this interest was the object for which the insurgents would rend the Union, even by war; while the government claimed no right to do more than to restrict the territorial enlargement of it." The second act of violence was, therefore, the Confederate attempt to excise the South from the national body. As Lincoln admits, Southern diplomats did not ask for war; they wished to "*destroy*" the body politic "without war—seeking to dissolve the Union."[39] Lincoln's First Inaugural Address describes secession as illegal "anarchy" because, if the body can be arbitrarily split and torn, the law of national sovereignty—"the majority principle"—does not exist. In the Union narrative, the South is a limb with no autonomous power to amputate itself from the Union body on which it is dependent; were this not the case, any minority of the Union, or of the "new confederacy" for that matter, could choose to "arbitrarily secede again, precisely as portions of the present Union now claim to secede from it."[40] National Unionism does not permit experimental rearrangements or admit impairment of the body politic.

Even though the Confederacy had a different narrative of the Civil War in which the relation of part to whole was inverted, it too struggled for an ideal of whole-bodied unionism: secession meant the amputation of an insidious and superfluous Northern limb from its own sovereign and independent political union. In his Inaugural Address to the Confederacy, Jefferson Davis says that the "perverted" purposes of the Union, with its "hostile opposition" and "wanton aggression," demand the "remedy of separation" for a "people united in heart, where one purpose of high resolve animates and actuates *the whole*."[41] By identifying the North as a malign appendage, the Confederacy claims to be a replete national body or Union in its own right, the true representation and faithful interpreter of the "Constitution formed by our fathers."[42] In both Union and Confederate narratives, then, the other is construed as a dangerous supplement to bodily integrity, and the outcome of the war would determine control of the metaphor of the body's territorial arrangement.

Few people know that Lincoln's argument from anarchical dismemberment turned out to come true in the state of Alabama. In February 1861, Montgomery became the official capital and Cradle of the Confederacy, but either later that year or in early 1862, in a stagecoach stop called Looney's Tavern, Union-loyal residents of Winston County, Alabama created the so-called Free State of Winston and declared their right to secede and remain neutral in the conflict. Echoing Lincoln, they defended their decision as follows: "If ... a state can lawfully and legally secede or withdraw, being only a part of the Union, then a county, any county, being a part of the state, by the same process of reasoning, could cease to be a part of the state."[43] But the Confederacy did not buy this argument: it conscripted pro–Unionists into service in its own illegal rebellion and resorted to bloody acts of suppression in order to enforce Confederate centralism, a boldfaced example of the internal social contradictions to claiming a Southern wholeness. Throughout the South, internal popular resistance to fighting was detrimental, arguably fatal, to the Confederate cause. Elsewhere, Western Peace Democrats, decrying Lincoln's war for abolition as they saw it, considered forming a "Northwest Confederacy" that would ally with the South,[44] but the most explicit case of political dismemberment occurred with the secession of Western Virginia (now West Virginia) from the Confederacy, its Free State adopting what was called an "ordinance of dismemberment."[45]

Even though the aforementioned dismemberment metaphors for civil disunion imply, if thought through consistently, an act of violence against oneself, Civil War discourse often split the narrative into a contest of two autonomous bodies. According to the painter Francis Carpenter, who resided at the White House during Lincoln's presidency, Lincoln made a comment in which he relocated the "diseased limb" of the Union to another body altogether: "I have sometimes used the illustration ... of a man with a diseased limb, and his surgeon. So long as there is a chance of the patient's restoration, the surgeon is solemnly bound to try to save both life and limb; but when the crisis comes, and the limb must be sacrificed as the only chance of saving the life, no honest man will hesitate."[46] Lisa Long quotes this passage in *Rehabilitating Bodies* (2004) as example of the "corporeal rhetoric of the national body deployed before and during the war era," but she reads Lincoln's metaphor as an example of the South "figured as an infected appendage" of the Union body.[47] On closer examination, the "diseased limb" to which Lincoln refers is the institution of slavery that had to be sacrificed in order to save the Union patient, and yet the schizophrenic quality of civil war betrays Lincoln since this metaphor leaves the role of historical surgeon confused and indeterminate. It is hard, perhaps impossible, not to read the Union North as the surgeon and the Confederate South as the patient with the diseased limb. In this case, Lincoln certainly evokes two distinct figures, scrupulously sparing the North the dangerous status of amputee, which is understandable given that wounded soldiers in the Civil War rarely survived amputation surgery. Most died within twenty-four hours of the operation.[48] But the metaphor is confusing precisely because it seems to unwittingly subvert the very thing for which the Union was fighting—the image of one national body. The problem becomes one of two irreconcilable and inconsistent visions: the South cannot rend the Union, at least not by seceding, if North and South are already dissociated. This doctor/patient trope participates in narrative prosthesis (with the South as amputee), effectively saving an uncompromised, able-bodied vision of the Union.

But any way one looks at it, during the Civil War, as one doctor put it after Manassas, "the whole country, from Manassas Junction to Richmond in one direction, and to Lynchburg in another, was one vast hospital."[49] And as one industrialist later argued, in explaining the postbellum debt that the government owes to disabled veterans, "the mutilated soldier" must be seen as a sacrifice for a larger vision of whole-bodied nationalism—"to save the nation from dismemberment" was the true aim of the Civil War.[50] This accords with Elaine Scarry's view that war apologizes for the destruction and disappearance of bodies through national narratives about the "imaginary body of a colossus."[51] For those destroyed bodies of the Civil War, a whole-bodied spiritualism, buttressed by a strong sense of nationalism, often served as an antidote to abjection. For instance, in her *Hospital Sketches* (1863), Louisa May Alcott narrates the comical exclamations of one impaired sergeant who sees heaven and bodily perfection as one and the same state: "Lord! what a scramble there'll be for arms and legs, when we old boys come out of our graves, on the Judgment Day: wonder if we shall get our own again? If we do, my leg will have to tramp from Fredericksburg, my arm from here, I suppose, and meet my body, wherever it may be."[52] Or, as the fictional war amputee, George Dedlow, puts it in Silas Weir Mitchell's 1866 short story "The Case of George Dedlow," "to lose any part [of the body] must lessen this sense of his [a man's] own existence." A "fraction of a man," like "some strange larval creature," Dedlow finds consolation at a séance when his missing limbs speak to him from their spectral place in the United States Army Medical Museum, metaphysically reuniting with his body.[53] Such whole-bodied spiritualism reveals a pronounced antipathy, not for violence or personal impairment—popularly regarded as a proud mark of war heroism—but for disability at the level of personal identity, a perfect example of "compulsory able-bodiedness."

Given that neither the Union nor the Confederacy fought *for* the freedom of slaves, the abolition enthusiast occupies a curious position, a *tertium quid*, in Civil War narration, at odds with and disdained by both Union and Confederate ideologues. Such abolitionists were by no means committed Unionists. In a view shared by many, Frederick Douglass said of Lincoln's early compromises on slavery: "But if the Union can only be maintained by new concessions to the slaveholders; if it can only be stuck together and held together by a new drain on the Negro's blood ... then ... let the Union perish, and perish forever."[54] Some Republicans thought it would be better to let the Southern states secede "like a limb lopped from a healthy trunk, wilt and rot where she falls."[55] Lincoln said in 1862, "If I could save the Union without freeing *any* slave I would do it, and if I could save it by freeing *all* the slaves I would do it; and if I could save it by freeing some and leaving others alone I would also do that,"[56] but the abolition enthusiast took the inverse position: if I could save the slave without destroying the Union I would do it, and if I could save the slave by destroying the Union I would do it; and if I could save the slave by destroying some but not all of the Union, I would also do that. Radical abolitionism cares not at all for a model of political affiliation based on able-bodied Unionism, and it is the only position that embraces and enacts a will to civil dismemberment in the name of justice toward the slave.

More than any other event, John Brown's raid on Harper's Ferry in 1859 had a momentous, unparalleled impact in inspiring and fomenting civil dismemberment. As one journalist from the *Richmond Enquirer* put it, "The Harper's Ferry invasion has advanced the cause of disunion, more

FIGURE 3 "Worship of the North." Special Collections and College Archives / Musselman Library, Gettysburg College.

than any other event that has happened since the formation of its Government."⁵⁷ According to David Reynolds, John Brown and his pikes "epitomized the twin horrors of Northern aggression and slave revolts," and in Confederate rhetoric, the Civil War was a conflict between fanatical enthusiasm (the "Ur-source of subversiveness: New England Puritanism") and conservative civilization (a constitutionally sound, traditional Southern society).⁵⁸ That John Brown's raid was sometimes thought to be, as Edward Everett said, "an attempt to do on a vast scale what was done in St. Domingo in 1791, where the colored population was about equal to that of Virginia," also situates the event within the black revolutionary heritage discussed in the previous chapter: at any rate, the "motives and aims" of John Brown are "those of an enthusiast."⁵⁹ For Southerners, even Lincoln was, despite himself, "an Abolitionist; a fanatic of the John Brown type; the slave to one idea, who . . . would override laws, constitutions, and compromises of every kind."⁶⁰ In other words, Lincoln's "negro mania"⁶¹ for freedom led him to become an apologist for revolutionary constituent power. You can see this position in all its complexity in the Confederate political cartoon "Worship of the North" (see figure 3).

In the center, one views the image of a naked white male (probably representing the Union) sacrificed on an altar that reads from top to bottom as follows: NEGRO WORSHIP, SPIRIT RAPPING, FREE LOVE, WITCH-BURNING, SOCIALISM, ATHEISM, RATIONALISM, and, at the base in much larger font, PURITANISM. Behind the altar is a bust of Abraham Lincoln. To the side and swelling the ranks, one sees many popular abolitionists of the day, including Harriet Beecher Stowe, organized into a mob, and above all else, a statue of John Brown holding a spear and facing a shrine with a naked, simian-like depiction of what is meant to be a black man with pikes emanating radially from his body. This strangely contradictory litany of Northern enthusiasms speaks to the way that John Brown and Abraham Lincoln were connected, in the Confederate imagination, to black insurrection on a large scale and the liberal subversion of social order broadly; but it also continues to invoke the historical critique of enthusiasm by representing this abolitionist mob as an out-of-doors public of religious maniacs, so uncompromising and willing to sacrifice the Union in the name of liberty, derivative of what even John Brown's admirers considered his Cromwellian stature.[62]

As an anthology of abolition enthusiasms and "negro mania" riding over laws, constitutions, and compromises of every kind, *Echoes of Harper's Ferry* can be read as a sustained attempt to vindicate enthusiastic dismemberment as opposed to de jure Unionism and constituent power as opposed to constitutional form. The anthology's perspective can perhaps be succinctly summed up by the statement of a black woman from Indiana in her letter to John Brown: "You have rocked the bloody Bastile [sic]."[63] To be sure, many texts in *Echoes* clearly see John Brown's actions as a sign of a coming civil war couched in the language or invoking the culture of revolutionary enthusiasm. In his opening Dedication to General Fabre Geffrard, the President of Haiti, as well as in his subsequent Preface, James Redpath claims that the raid on Harper's Ferry belongs to a larger transnational black liberation movement. By posting the event and book to Haiti, Redpath calls attention to "our Union" as anything but a "free Republic,"[64] that is, as anything *but a de facto Union*. Moreover, Redpath clarifies that *Echoes* does not eulogize a hero but attempts to "fan the holy flame that their [Brown and his accomplices'] action kindled, until, becoming a consuming fire, it shall burn up, with thoroughness and speed, every vestige of the crime of American Slavery." In short, Redpath wants to foment a revolution: "to bring to a speedy issue the approaching and Irresistible Conflict between Slavery and Freedom."[65] Likewise, Henry David Thoreau, in "A Plea for Capt. John Brown," believes that the event ought to "create a revival," namely for John Brown's "truth, clear as lightning, crashing into their obscene temples";[66] and in a letter to Francis Jackson, Theodore Parker speaks of John Brown's insurrection as portentous of a Second American Revolution: "What a stormy time you are having in America! Your cradle was rocked in the Revolution, and now in your old age you see the storm of another Revolution beginning: none knows when and where it shall end."[67]

In his polemical and colorful fashion, abolitionist and firebrand Wendell Phillips best delineates the counterintuitive logic of the enthusiast's justice-making claims. In his speech "The Lesson of the Hour" (1859), Phillips argues that John Brown speaks to the "impulsive, enthusiastic aspiration" in the Yankee, "something left to us from the old Puritan stock; that which made England what she was two centuries ago [in the English Civil War]; that which is fated to give the closest grapple with the Slave Power to-day."[68] He also wittily exclaims, "Virginia, the commonwealth of Virginia! She is only a chronic insurrection.... She is a pirate ship.... What I say is this: Harper's Ferry was the only government in that vicinity."[69] If political Unionism means the preservation of institutional injustice, then, for Phillips, it apologizes for a lawless state of constitutional insurrection against black peoples, and John Brown's attack assumes the rightful duty of a government—to protect its constituents from tyranny. Finally, when he claims that Harper's Ferry is not the constituted American Revolution, "Saratoga and Yorktown," but the constituent power of "those who flung themselves, at Lexington, few and feeble, against the embattled ranks of an empire, till then thought irresistible," Phillips encourages the overthrow of the American government "in behalf of justice and liberty"; "Harper's Ferry is the Lexington of to-day."[70] If the American government now deems it necessary to execute John Brown for his liberation politics, it does so just as the British government deemed it necessary to subdue the colonies during the American Revolution: Phillips reminds us that "George Washington, had he been caught before 1783, would have died on the gibbet, for breaking the laws of his sovereign."[71] John Brown's "impulsive, enthusiastic aspiration" may be written off as "fanaticism" but the lesson of history is this: "What is fanaticism to-day is the fashionable creed to-morrow."[72]

John Brown's critics (included in *Echoes*) also see his action as a fomentation of civil dismemberment but of course judge it illegitimate for precisely that reason. As one example, the lawyer Charles O'Conor makes the following comment in a Union-meeting speech: "We never would have attained to the wealth and prosperity as a nation which is now ours, but for our connection with these very much reviled and injured Slaveholders."[73] In other words, the South is a vital member of the Union body, connected to it as an essential and salubrious source of national life. Henry Ward Beecher's 1859 sermon echoes this sentiment, but first by excoriating Brown's dismemberment politics: "The surprise of the whole nation, at a recent event, is itself the best evidence of the isolation of that event. A burning fragment struck the earth near Harper's Ferry. If the fragment of an exploding aerolite had fallen down out of the air, while the meteor swept on, it would not have been more sudden, or less apparently connected either with a cause or an effect!"[74] An event, a burning fragment, a singularity without publicly warranted causes or effects: this underwrites Beecher's view of Brown's action as both courageous and wrong ("His soul was noble; his work miserable").[75] A political meteor defies any "normate" concept of the Union body: "These sovereign States are united to us, not by any federal ligaments, but by vital interests, by a common national life." And yet, as is well known, Beecher himself deplores the institution of slavery and advocates for its eventual abolition. Just like Kant with his desire for constitutional Enlightenment without revolution (see chapter 1), Beecher lobbies for slavery to end through constitutional means. When he says that "I am bound by the great law of love to consider my duties towards the slave, and I am bound by the great law of love also to consider my duties towards the white man who is his master! Both are to be treated with Christian wisdom and forbearance,"[76] Beecher speciously denies that, in the case of the Fugitive Slave Law, for example, those duties are in direct contradiction to one another, that one's duty toward the slave, as John Brown believed, might mean liberating him from the master at whatever cost. The common national life invoked above can refer only to interstate commerce wedded to an ideology of national sovereignty that trumps any divisive politics of emancipation from below or outside the juridical order. Yet it is precisely on the contested point of "vital" Unionism that Walt Whitman's poetics of enthusiasm intervenes.

My Body No More Inevitably United:
Hospitality as Enthusiastic Dis-Memberment

Not surprisingly, many Southerners saw Walt Whitman's poetry as another instance of wild and fanatical Northern enthusiasms. A review of Whitman from 1860 in the *Southern Literary Messenger* makes him out to be the poster boy for Northern literary radicalism, couched in the language of disease, when it speaks of the "spasmodic idiocy of Walt Whitman. The smart scribblers who compose the better part of the Northern literati, are all becoming infected with the new leprosy—Whitmansy."[77] Even William Thayer, in an 1860 letter to Whitman, refers to Whitman's common reader as a "fanatic."[78] Like all of Thayer and Eldridge's books, *Leaves* was largely suppressed in the South as incendiary material, but denunciations of Whitman's poetry were continental in scope. When one review from the *Critic* (a London journal) lashes out at Whitman's "republican insolence, his rank Yankeedom," and acerbically offers that his poetry could only be written in "a nation from which the spirit-rappers sprung,"[79] it mimes the rhetoric of fanaticism in the "Worship of the North" cartoon.

If not commissioned by Heaven, at the very least, self-commissioned as one who sees God in "the faces of men and women" and his "own face in the glass,"[80] Walt Whitman has a closer relationship to John Brown's brooding enthusiasm than critics have assumed. In a generic sense, to call Whitman an enthusiast hardly seems noteworthy;[81] but when he actually uses the term, Whitman tends to have a very specific idea in mind. As early as 1839, in "Talk to an Art-Union" (delivered as a lecture in 1851), he essays on "the mighty deeds written in the pages of history—deeds of daring, and enthusiasm, devotion, and fortitude," performed by "great rebels and innovators" who are "not merely artists, they are also artistic material."[82] The artist as transdisciplinary rebel and innovator must be cross-referenced with Whitman's late comment on the enthusiast in "Slang in America" (1885): "The Hebrew word which is translated *prophesy* meant to bubble up and pour forth as a fountain. The enthusiast bubbles up with the Spirit of God within him, and it pours forth from him like a fountain. The word prophecy is misunderstood. Many suppose that it is limited to mere prediction; that is but the lesser portion of prophecy. The greater work is to reveal God. Every true religious enthusiast is a prophet."[83] Enthusiasm is that unblocked flow of sovereign states adequate to the revelation of God and authorized by the innovative self. As is well known, Whitman wished (for us all) to "tally all antecedents" and take over the role of "fading religions and priests," which was incidentally the goal of the 1860 *Leaves of Grass*, his "evangel-poem of comrades and of love,"[84] his new Bible for and of America: "This *Leaves of Grass* was to inaugurate a new American religion, which cleared away the staid detritus of empty ritual,"[85] an enthusiastic pretense if there ever was one. Whitman boldly asserts in "Gods," "All heroisms, deeds of rapt enthusiasts, / Be ye my Gods."[86] And in "Years of the Modern," another poem originally about the crisis of impending Civil War and first published in *Drum-Taps* as "Years of the Unperformed," Whitman declares the following:

> No one knows what will happen next, such portents fill the days and nights;
> Years prophetical! the space ahead as I walk, as I vainly try to pierce it, is full of phantoms;
> Unborn deeds, things soon to be, project their shapes around me,
> This incredible rush and heat, this strange ecstatic fever of dreams
>   O years![87]

For Whitman, prophecy does not involve the clairvoyant prediction of things future, but on the contrary, the immanent projection of possible deeds and a queer future, forged out of the ecstatic fever of dreams.

A clearer example of Whitman bubbling forth with enthusiasm can be found in the 1860 poem "Apostroph." When Whitman cries, "O days by-gone! Enthusiasts! Antecedents!," he sandwiches the line between, "O whirl, contest, sounding and resounding! I am your poet, because I am part of you" and "O vast preparations for These States! O years!"[88] In sympathy with his definition of the enthusiast above, here the poetic enthusiast is seen as a vessel or medium—a fountain—of the convulsive whirl and contest, "free and ecstatic," but also notice that this poem resonates with the image of meteors flitting through space in "Year of Meteors." The enthusiast's role is to open up the blind present to a more democratic future and to enact that very future by binding people together ("I, ecstatic, O partners! O lands! with the love of lovers tie you").[89] Thus, circa 1860, when he claims that the "dependence of Liberty shall be lovers" and the "continuance of Equality shall be comrades," because "lawyers," "an agreement on a paper," and "arms" allow no democratic world to truly cohere, and when he preaches that the "centuries, and all authority" are "to be trod under the foot-soles of one man or woman!"[90]

Whitman sums up, on his own terms, the antinomian heritage of democratic constituent power and expresses the selfsame spirit of political enthusiasm that motivated illegal actions such as John Brown's. This is further apparent in "O Star of France," about the Franco-Prussian War (1870–71) and the Paris Commune of 1871. Here Whitman celebrates precisely those enthusiasts who feel themselves commissioned by the spirit of liberty to free the oppressed:

> The struggle and the daring, rage divine for liberty,
> Of aspirations toward the far ideal, enthusiast's dreams of brotherhood,
> Of terror to the tyrant and the priest.[91]

Enthusiasm projects and then attempts to realize the "dreams of brotherhood," but this requires the whirl and contest of a "rage divine" and a subtraction of institutional blocks to democracy. I take this to be Walt Whitman's basic concept of enthusiasm, and it is one that eventually led him to create the "Songs of Insurrection"; yet, three of these six poems—"To a Certain Cantatrice," "Walt Whitman's Caution," and "France"—were originally published in the 1860 *Leaves*, a fact that forces us to account for this singular year of meteors in Whitman's career.

As I have suggested, radical abolitionism's influence best explains this fact, and a similar logic of civil dismemberment works in Whitman's new poetry as it does in *Echoes of Harper's Ferry*, only Whitman does not thereby give up his lifelong desire to forge a democratic union of comrades. Instead, he insists on the following proposition: if an ethics of able-bodied Union power leads to the destruction of real bodies, then an ethics of disabled Union power ought to lead to the hospitable inclusion of all bodies and the creation of democratic political bodies. But if that is the case, we can no longer think of dismemberment, like disability, as an abject metaphor for civil war or a physical condition of the amputee. Here dismemberment—let me be clear, understood as a way of thinking about identity and the political-ethical relations between parts and wholes, *not* the destructive effects of war or physical impairment—works analogously to deconstruction, which Jacques Derrida, in his later writings, consistently reformulated in terms of the practice of hospitality. For Derrida, hospitality refers to the unconditional law of responsibility to the other beyond every coercive legal order and duty, economy and debt, "a hospitality invented for the singularity of the new arrival, of the unexpected visitor," whereby one says "occupy me, take place in me, which means, by the same token, also take my place."[92] In sum: "Hospitality is the deconstruction of the at-home; deconstruction is hospitality to the other, to the other than oneself, the other than 'its other,' to an other who is beyond any 'its other.'"[93] With regard to political community, Derrida urges us to think of unity not in terms of circumscribed nations without openness closed in on themselves but in terms *of* openness to the other: "dissociation is the condition of community, the condition of any unity as such" and not an opposition to it.[94] In the same respect, Whitman's *dis*-memberment is the condition of membership, the condition of any affectionate Unionism as such, but this presupposes a positive vision of the hospitable individual and the body politic "as changeable, unperfectable, unruly, and untidy."

Between 1856 and 1860, when the Union was clearly not reading or writing the "poem" of affectionate democracy, Whitman accepts radical abolitionism's conviction that political hospitality requires opposition to any concept of Unionism standing in the way of the "new City of Friends."[95] He turns this into the theme of the 1860 *Leaves* by announcing his revolt against the tyrannical "majority": "Mind you the the [sic] timid models of the rest, the majority? / Long I minded them, but hence I will not."[96] By the same logic, he ceases to define democracy in terms of colluding specimens in an intricated web of vital, able-bodied nature as he tends to do in the 1855 and 1856 editions of *Leaves*; instead, he emphasizes a mode of intimate exchange defined, not by the functional and spectacular capacities of physical or national bodies, but by self-otherness, singular relationships, and queer affections. This results in the self's dis-memberment as the very possibility for enthusiastic community, a community derived from coordinated fragments and their extrinsic, situated relations.

Take "Calamus 8," a poem that appeared only in the 1860 edition. In the first four lines, Whitman rehearses his career and former desire to expansively embrace all peoples and places. Then he tells readers everywhere to "take notice":

> [. . .] That you each and all find somebody else to be your singer of songs,
> For I can be your singer of songs no longer—One who loves me is jealous of me, and withdraws me from all but love,

> With the rest I dispense—I sever from what I thought would suffice me, for it does not—it is now empty and tasteless to me,
> I heed knowledge, and the grandeur of The States, and the example of heroes, no more,
> I am indifferent to my own songs—I will go with him I love,[97]

Whitman admits that his former belief in a generic partnership, with slave and slave-owner alike as it were, and his bardic role as cheerleader of the nation do not constitute love, since love requires an exclusive commitment to a certain other or others, and an attendant severance or dismemberment from "the rest," that is, the totality of readers and the nation. One has to read this, however, as a performative declaration of independence, a convulsive address: each and all of us have been told directly to find our own singer of songs just as Whitman has found his own love, or better yet, that we imagine ourselves in the place of the lover who withdraws with Whitman. On this basis, a disjunctive synthesis of democratic unity through a common separation occurs. This is Whitman's ordinance of dismemberment, a kind of Free State of Whitman for civil war Unionism.

"Calamus 16," a poem that was also never included in any subsequent editions of *Leaves*, reinforces this interpretation of number "8." The poem reads in its entirety:

> 1. Who is now reading this?
>
> 2. May-be one is now reading this who knows some wrong-doing of my past life,
>   Or may-be a stranger is reading this who has secretly loved me,
>   Or may-be one who meets all my grand assumptions and egotisms with derision,
>   Or may-be one who is puzzled at me.
>
> 3. As if I were not puzzled at myself!
>   Or as if I never deride myself! (O conscience-struck! O self-convicted!)
>   Or as if I do not secretly love strangers! (O tenderly, a long time, and never avow it;)
>   Or as if I did not see, perfectly well, interior in myself, the stuff of wrong-doing,
>   Or as if it could cease transpiring from me until it must cease.[98]

Once again, this poem establishes a disjunctive unity between Whitman and the reader; we connect to Whitman because we reject him as he rejects himself, and we too harbor hidden or singular loves for strangers—notably, for some, a secret love for Whitman. The first line implicates us all as strangers and makes the exchange between poet and reader an intimate one, since I may be the only reader and I am addressed as a possible kind of reader whom Whitman invites. Yet, our divorce from or secession with Whitman is to be the paradoxical grounds for our affection—as an odd reader, "whoever you are, flush with myself,"[99] one joins Whitman in a dis-membership.

Of the 1860 dismemberment poems, the most important (and famous) is surely "As I Ebb'd with the Ocean of Life," or "Leaves of Grass 1" in the cluster of 1860. In this poem, Whitman walks along the shores of Long Island and contemplates debris in the ocean waves washing onto the shore. The ocean of life, that "fierce old mother" as he calls her, "cries for her castaways,"[100] her rejects, materialized in the form of debris. As he observes the "chaff, straw, splinters of wood, weeds, and the sea-gluten, / Scum, scales from shining rocks, leaves of salt-lettuce, left by the tide," Whitman reflexively posits himself:

I, too, but signify, at the utmost, a little washed-up drift,
A few sands and dead leaves to gather,
Gather, and merge myself as part of the sands and drift.[101]

And later: "I too am but a trail of drift and debris, / I too leave little wrecks upon you, you fish-shaped island."[102] But this objective image of dis-memberment also takes on subjective dimensions as the Whitmanian ethos of able-bodied language is wrecked and undermined:

O baffled, balked,
Bent to the very earth, here preceding what follows,
Oppressed with myself that I have dared to open my mouth,
Aware now, that, amid all the blab whose echoes recoil upon me,
    I have not once had the least idea who or what I am,
But that before all my insolent poems the real ME still stands
    untouched, untold, altogether unreached,
Withdrawn far, mocking me with mock-congratulatory signs and bows,
With peals of distant ironical laughter at every word I have written
    or shall write,
Striking me with insults till I fall helpless upon the sand.[103]

On first consideration, these lines seem to point to an abject notion of disability, but in fact the "real" Whitman—of irony, mockery, and laughter—enjoys and posits the dis-membered ebb and flow of the self's drift, mocking what Whitman calls his "insolent poems." The abjection invoked is the mere illusion of a Whitman who has misidentified himself with poetic able-bodiedness. Once broken, Whitman can merge with the drift. He now posits agitation and conflict with himself, submitting himself to a Free State of self-dissolution. That's why in the sixteenth stanza of the poem Whitman's excitement mounts over his dissipated state and his poetry of accreted word-tufts:

> We, loose winrows, little corpses,
> Froth, snowy white, and bubbles,
> ....
> Tufts of straw, sands, fragments,
> Buoyed hither from many moods, one contradicting another,
> ....
> We, capricious, brought hither, we know not whence,
>   spread out before You, up there, walking or sitting,
> Whoever you are—we too lie in drifts at your feet.[104]

Whitman apprehends himself as a queer, queer assemblage, in an experience of self-fracturing that nevertheless takes the form of a collective identification and participation with the world around him. This leads us back to the first stanza where Whitman says that he's "seized by the spirit" which "stands for all the water and all the land of the globe"[105]—that is, for planetary exchange, a global community of drift.

The phrase "whoever you are" in the last line occurs twenty-five times in the 1860 *Leaves*, and it is clear from surrounding poems that "whoever you are" most often refers to or includes the reader, the single individual who must, as in the lines above, receive the fragments of the transient and strange Whitman in a dis-membered bond of the affections. One on one, we are always asked to receive Whitman hospitably as a comrade and stranger of flitting moments and to decide whether we also "celebrate the need of comrades."[106] If we will not do so, "Put me down, and depart on your way,"[107] Whitman insists. It would be a mistake to read the above poems as instances of withdrawal from the "democratic en masse" or as unqualified dejection; on the contrary, the masses continue to be a presence in the new 1860 poetry as does Whitman's ecstatic love for them. Whitman balances out his determined negativity (which I have accented above) with gestures of contact and intimacy with the reader, most of all when he turns *Leaves* itself into a passing kiss:

> We must separate—Here! take from my lips this kiss,
> Whoever you are, I give it especially to you;
> *So long*—and I hope we shall meet again.[108]

The implication is that we host Whitman and Whitman hosts us but only insofar as we lie at each other's feet in a dis-membered, never fixed, bond of hospitality.

Taken alone, the aforementioned poems of a dis-membered Whitman have no determinate enthusiastic politics per se. The question becomes how the 1860 persona translates into directly political terms. I read the above poems as an insurrection of the affections on par with Whitman's insurrection against the Union, a kind of Free State of Whitman, the convulsive political context of which summons a new form of identification through the convulsive affect of lovers and comrades. The key is to read this poetry in light of the 1860 lines: "Let others promulge the laws—I will make no account of the laws, / Let others praise eminent men and hold up peace—I hold up agitation and conflict."[109] This statement might have been lifted directly from a pro–John Brown argument: only the one who instigates dis-memberment, subtracting from an unjust peace and eminence, can be a true comrade of the oppressed. Moreover, Whitman wants us to see that a collective makes sense only as a dis-membered and aleatory form of unruly togetherness; his term for this is the "ensemble of the world"[110] in the strong double sense of the French cognate for togetherness within multiplicity. The affectionate mode, once politicized, is expressed as dissent: "And I will make a song for the ears of the President, full of weapons with menacing points, / And behind the weapons countless dissatisfied faces."[111] While he does continue to curse anyone who would "dissever the Union," Whitman now admits to the fragility of the body and denies the teleology of that Unionism: "Singing the song of These, my ever united lands—my body no more inevitably united, part to part, and made one identity, any more than my lands are inevitably united, and made ONE IDENTITY."[112] This is a perfect example of a political ensemble in which Unionism occurs as an emergent property of symphonic coordination, a constituent power of the united affections, not as an a priori or de jure Unionism. Characteristically, Whitman writes lines that superimpose the dis-membered self onto a dis-membered Union in a positive but unpredictable program of democracy to come: "And how these of mine, and of The States, will in their turn be convulsed, and serve other parturitions and transitions."[113] Just as Whitman will be convulsed, broken, and reassembled, so will the United States, and this is what Whitman sees as the ethics of the impending Civil War indexed here in the future tense. Progressive Unionism demands the fracturing and reconfiguration of political bodies.

To a Foiled Walt Whitman: Songs of Insurrection

The Whitman of enthusiastic dis-memberment crystallizes in his six poems "Songs of Insurrection," as he grouped them in the 1871 and 1876 centennial editions of *Leaves*. Three of these poems were originally written for the 1860 edition ("Walt Whitman's Caution," "France, The 18th Year of These States," "To a Certain Cantatrice"), two at earlier moments but with significant alterations in the 1860 edition ("Europe, The 72d and 73d Years of These States" in 1850, "To a Foil'd European Revolutionaire" in 1856), and one for the new 1871–72 edition ("Still Though the One I Sing," a poem I will bracket for now and discuss in the epilogue). Four of the six poems concern European subjects, and only one addresses the United States, an indication that Whitman's dis-memberment politics of enthusiasm is part and parcel of a broader self-stylized cosmopolitanism[114] that, in my view, reaches a *summit* in 1860.

Let me begin with "Walt Whitman's Caution," later named "To the States," a short tristich that reads as follows:

> To The States, or any one of them, or any city of The States,
>   *Resist much, obey little*,
> Once unquestioning obedience, once fully enslaved,
> Once fully enslaved, no nation, state, city, of this earth, ever
>   afterward resumes its liberty.[115]

At various scales, from nation to state to city, the smaller political or civil body subtracts from the larger one to which it belongs: a city can resist a state, a state the nation. However, as one zooms in on the micro-level of the city, we reach the earth ("all the water and all the land of the globe") as the generic ground of political liberty, as liberty's condition of possibility. Although the poem begins by addressing the United States, the concluding lesson atomizes the nation as another monad of a universal truth applicable to all political communities. The italicized emphasis on dis-obedience coincides with dis-memberment of the social body: the whole has no internal integrity or essence. Liberty and civil fragmentation coincide in Whitman's Free State.

To resist much and obey little is the theme of all the "Songs of Insurrection." In "France, The 18th Year of These States," Whitman commemorates the end of the French Revolutionary Tribunal in 1794. It may seem like a curious decision to turn to the French Revolution during the "year of meteors" but the poem explains why: by keeping alive the "latent music" of historical revolution through his songs, Whitman believes that "some chansonniers"[116] in France will understand him. Presumably Americans will not. Himself a chansonnier for a new war of "Liberty!," Whitman can "hear already the bustle of instruments—they will soon be drowning all that would interrupt them."[117] But the primary addressee of the poem is "ma femme," liberty (also apostrophized in "Calamus 5" as "ma femme," "O Democracy")[118] and Paris the secondary subject of Whitman's "love." The song to France, finally, serves as an enthusiastic conduit or transmission between historical memory and historical futurity: "And from to-day, sad and cogent, I maintain the bequeath'd cause, as for all lands."[119] In the interstice between the past and the future, the poetic subject of enunciation inhabits a space of sadness, the dismembered Whitman, balked and defeated, but the "GREAT year and place" of the French Revolutionary event continues to inspire the song and the future manifestation of that song politically "for all lands."[120] Despite the moment of crisis, the anamnesis of a new political order, from then to now, says Whitman, "swells me to joyful madness," that is, to enthusiasm, and now he "will run transpose it in words, to justify it,"[121] so that it can be claimed again in another context. The cause is "for all lands" in the same sense that the "earth" grounds the political sequence of "Walt Whitman's Caution": the event has a universal destination, inclusive of all. France is only a terminal, a node or point, like Whitman himself, through which the traffic of enthusiasm has passed.

With its love missive to chansonniers, "France" gives us a clue as to how to read the most anomalous "Song of Insurrection" from 1860, "To a Cantatrice" (later "To a Certain Cantatrice"), a tribute to Whitman's favorite opera singer, Marietta Alboni, who performed at various New York venues in her 1852–53 tour of the United States. A great lover of the *bel canto* style, Whitman claimed to have seen all of her performances,[122] and, in an unpublished manuscript from 1858 or later, "Italian Singers in America," he clarifies the political import of the renowned contralto: "All persons appreciated Alboni—the common crowd quite as well as the connoisseurs. We used to go in the upper tiers of the theatre, (the Broadway,) on the nights of her performance, and remember seeing that part of the auditorium packed full of New York young men, mechanics, 'roughs,' &c., entirely oblivious of all except Alboni."[123] And in "A Visit to the Opera," Whitman says that Americans would have to learn from the Italians in order to produce any worthwhile singers.[124] Far from advocating for a brute nativism, Whitman clearly views opera as one of his higher models for an art that both cultivates and absorbs the masses, but as the passage above suggests, he also sees the opera a classless space, a microcosm of the democratic crowd, that orbits around Alboni. Placed strategically between "To The States, To Identify the 16th, 17th, or 18th Presidentiad" (one of Whitman's angriest, most disaffected poems on the state of the U.S. government) and "Walt Whitman's Caution," Whitman's short verse for Alboni reads in the 1860 edition:

> HERE, take this gift!
> I was reserving it for some hero, orator, or general,
> One who should serve the good old cause, the progress and freedom of the race, the cause of my Soul;
> ["Some brave confronter of despots, some daring rebel;" added in the 1871 version and all subsequent versions]
> But I see that what I was reserving belongs to you just as much as to any.[125]

Read in conjunction with "France," the gift-poem for Alboni doubles Whitman's gift of love for Lady Liberty: perhaps the cantatrice even becomes metonymic for the latter. This would explain why Whitman refuses to address her by name. Instead, the austere, aphoristic quality of the poem directs the reader to contemplate not Alboni but, as in "Walt Whitman's Caution," a political lesson—in this case, the relationship between song and insurrection, art and politics. Yet Whitman does not explain his logic; as a unilateral address, the poem shuts the reader out of an intimate secret between Whitman and the cantatrice. She is the single lover who separates Whitman, and all who adore her, from the rest. Whitman only posits the hermetic thesis that one might be tempted to limit democratic insurrection to traditional (masculine) figures of militancy but says that this would be a mistake: the singer participates in the insurrectionary cause of democracy. This also reflexively refers to Whitman himself ("the cause of my Soul"), especially as the character in "France" who encourages the "insurrection *of* song"—an art devoted immediately to championing democratic politics, certainly, but inversely, also a politics that will have to be true to Whitman's dithyramb of "joyful madness."

The two older "Songs of Insurrection" prefigure and amplify the ideas and arguments of the 1860 poems. First published in the *New York Daily Tribune* of June 21, 1850, under the title "Resurgemus," "Europe, The 72d and 73d Years of These States" was one of Whitman's earliest poems about another year of meteors, 1848, and it was included in every edition of *Leaves*. As such, it is the sort of poem that warns us not to identify Whitman with an easy, homogeneous Americanism. The various versions of "Europe" also provide a unique window into the evolution of Whitman's stylistic choices and political thought. While the original periodical version has traditional stanzas, line breaks, and formal diction, the wild 1855 *Leaves* version demolishes orthodox verse construction in ways familiar to any reader of Whitman. He crunches two or three lines from the original into one so that the stanzas spread out horizontally and read like broken paragraphs or aphoristic blocks of text; also, he often splices ellipses in between lines instead of the standard comma. On the page, these choices create a sense of open space without a center that marks the ebb and flow, the discontinuous wave, of punchy flashes and discrete images instead of a continuous, internally coherent stream of text leading downward. Still, a certain kind of continuity is implied by the ellipses: they capture the sense that Whitman quickly records actions without time to pause, caught up in a stream of events, but unable to keep up with them as they become lost in the space of the ellipse. This further reflects Whitman's attempt to make poetic form mimic political content. The time of writing has become dis-membered. For example, whereas the first two lines of the last stanza from the original 1850 version read, "Liberty, let others despair of thee, / But I will never despair of thee,"[126] the 1855 version reads on one line, "Liberty let others despair of you.... I never despair of you."[127] In the latter, liberty no longer needs to be formally separated from the rest of the line: without the comma between "Liberty" and "let," the alliteration rolls off the tongue without pause and the line quickens its pace, barreling toward the "I" that is no longer subordinated to liberty in a separate line as in the original. Accordingly, liberty has ceased to be invoked with the archaic, formal pronoun and becomes a familiar comrade. There is an equality between liberty and the self, formally marked through the balance between the two lines that now face each other but, via the ellipse, without collapsing into one statement, either—they are dis-membered together. By crunching the two lines so that "I" immediately counteracts the others who despair, the same others who fall into the void of the ellipse, Whitman bodies forth his war against despair.

Placed in context, the above line has the utmost significance: it refers the reader back to the defeat of the revolutionary movements and the deaths occasioned by the 1848 uprisings. Whitman envisions a veritable specter of revolution haunting Europe, a "Shape" that resembles Poe's Red Death, "Vague as the night, draped interminably, head front and form, in scarlet folds, / Whose face and eyes none may see."[128] While the first three variants (through 1856) have the line "Yet behind all, lo, a Shape,"[129] in 1860 the line reads "Yet behind all, hovering, stealing—lo, a Shape,"[130] but in 1867 and all subsequent variants, "hovering" becomes "lowering." Thus, whereas in 1855–56 the Shape merely *is*, in 1860 its shadow has begun to appear and hover ominously while "stealing" connotes the dis-memberment politics of secession or subtraction: the revolution will extirpate the tyrant. In 1867, the change to "lowering" signifies, in juxtaposition to "hovering," not a specter of revolution but its descent or actualization, while simultaneously capturing the sense of a threatening or angry storm/appearance. Surely the 1867 change updates the poem for the post–Civil War era when the specter had lowered in Whitman's view, thus attaching the Civil War to the spirit of 1848 that walks "over the earth." This specter doesn't terminate with a specific historical event, nor can it be stopped by defeat or death: as in the song "John Brown's Body," the spirit of revolution, the spirit of the martyred dead, "live[s] in other young men, O kings!," "live[s] in brothers, again ready to defy you!"[131] And more radically:

9. Not a grave of the murdered for freedom, but grows seed for freedom, in its turn to bear seed,
    Which the winds carry afar and re-sow, and the rains and the snows nourish.

> 10. Not a disembodied spirit can the weapons of tyrants let loose,
>   But it stalks invisibly over the earth, whispering, counselling, cautioning.[132]

In the 1855 version, Whitman places no commas between the last three gerunds, as if to suggest that they exist as one action or as continuous actions, sounded by the chant of the dactyls (*whis*-per-ing *coun*-sel-ing *cau*-tion-ing), steady and confident, but increasing in gravity from the soft tone of a whisper to the serious urgency of a caution, as the spectral spirit of the dead revolter for freedom intimately addresses and instructs us as a comrade.

If "Europe" has a message, then, it's that all revolt fertilizes the ground for further revolt, propelled forward by past defeats or the historical memory of victories as in "France." In order to receive the "disembodied spirit" as a guest, to be hospitable to it, one has to carry on the struggle. In the last three lines, Whitman imagines the spirit of revolt as akin to a messiah who will return like a thief in the night:

> Is the house shut? Is the master away?
> Nevertheless be ready—be not weary of watching,
> He will soon return—his messengers come anon.[133]

We must be ready, at any moment, to host and be hosted by "ma femme," the insurrectionary spirit of liberty. Moreover, that spirit's concealment and invisibility—held in abeyance by a democratic eclipse—directly parallels Whitman's ethos in the "Calamus" poems. Whitman reserves his song for the beloved brothers and sisters of dis-memberment who will defy tyrants. Not just any reader can be a comrade. And last of all, only now do we fully understand why Whitman understands the "earth" as a breeding ground of revolt: it is a rather hackneyed metaphor for continuous revolution as a global insurrectionary crop that dies and revives.

Thematically, "Europe" is a sister poem to "To a Foil'd European Revolutionaire," first published in the 1856 *Leaves* and arguably the best poem out of the "Songs of Insurrection" (also the only one to use the phrase). This poem has a modest but interesting evolution in the various editions of *Leaves*. It was first named "Liberty Poem for Asia, Africa, Europe, America, Australia, Cuba, and The Archipelagoes of the Sea," but changed to "To a Foiled Revolter or Revoltress" in 1860. Notice that this emendation of address moves drastically from the "totality" to a singular, intimate perspective which nevertheless remains geographically generic, unlike the title's later epistolary address to a "European Revolutionaire" beginning in 1871. Corresponding changes occur within the poem in the later versions. But rubbing against the grain of its Europeanization, the 1871 version includes a new parenthetical comment expressing Whitman's affiliation with revolters everywhere:

> 3 (Not songs of loyalty alone are these,
> But songs of insurrection also;
> For I am the sworn poet of every dauntless rebel, the world over,
> And he going with me leaves peace and routine behind him,
> And stakes his life, to be lost at any moment.)[134]

Why the European revolutionary then? Probably one has to see this as occasioned by historical events: in 1871, Whitman also published "O Star of France!" in the *Galaxy*, a poem that, after its appearance in *As a Strong Bird on Pinions Free and Other Poems* (1872) and *Two Rivulets* (1876), was incorporated into the same cluster ("Autumn Rivulets") as "To a Foil'd European Revolutionaire" in the final 1881 arrangement of *Leaves*.

For my purposes, the point I wish to emphasize is that the 1860 version, "To a Foiled Revolter or Revoltress," newly includes three final sections (or Whitmanian Bible verses) that reflect Whitman's dis-memberment poetics and encourage insurrectionary sacrifice, not so much in the clichéd terms of heroic martyrdom, but as a commitment to experimentation, as an exploratory risk, without any ideological guarantees or assurance of success. Here is one example:

> 8. I do not know what you are for, (I do not know what I am for myself, nor what anything is for,)
> But I will search carefully for it in being foiled,
> In defeat, poverty, imprisonment—for they too are great.[135]

In this encomium for balked democracy, addressed to the likes of the foiled revolter, John Brown, who stakes his life, to be lost at any moment, as the "prison, scaffold, garrote, hand-cuffs, iron necklace and anklet, lead-balls, do their work,"[136] Whitman emphasizes once again that the enthusiast, suspended in the abyss of a convulsive crisis, acts without positive support, unable to see the role that he and others ultimately play but making this the groundless ground of democratic affiliation. Even if liberty were wiped from the earth and foiled, it would still have been necessary to side with self-loss and dis-memberment on her behalf instead of the victorious whole: "COURAGE! my brother or my sister! / Keep on! Liberty is to be subserved, whatever occurs."[137] What we do know is that the revolter or revoltress cannot be party to "tushes of power—soldiers, cannon, penal statutes"[138]; no, he or she risks something for liberty from a powerless situation, without any institutional backing, and Whitman posts this message to all "the superb lovers of the nations of the world" threatened by those who are "elated at the sight of slaves."[139] In the depressing present, we, the lovers, still have reason to hope, for immutable liberty remains ever and always a virtual condition of life, a political truth, waiting to be hosted again, even if on a deep historical or cosmic time scale:

2. What we believe in waits latent forever through Asia, Africa, Europe, North and South America, Australia, Cuba, and all the islands and archipelagoes of the sea.

3. What we believe in invites no one, promises nothing, sits in calmness and light, is positive and composed, knows no discouragement,
    Waits patiently its time—a year—a century—a hundred centuries.[140]

At least in this poem, Whitman is the poet not of manifest U.S. destiny but of latent international destiny.

Unpent Enthusiasm: Of Civil War Hospitality

Walt Whitman initially saw the Civil War as an event continuous with his "Songs of Insurrection." This is apparent not only in "Year of Meteors" but also in another early poem from *Drum-Taps*, "The Centenarian's Story," written from the standpoint of a war volunteer of 1861–62 in Washington Park, Brooklyn as he assists a veteran of the 1776 Battle of Long Island (or Brooklyn). Whitman's "chansonnier" makes another appearance in the poem in order to make the link to "France" explicit; once again, Whitman sings of historical revolution—this time, the American—as an inspiration for the political present. The specter of George Washington and the Battle of Brooklyn hover by way of an old Centenarian's narrative of the events; importantly, this was a battle that Washington lost. When Whitman, or the war volunteer, asks the veteran, "Why do you tremble and clutch my hand so convulsively?"[141] the latter answers that the Battle of Brooklyn has come back to life for him in the present: in other words, as I interpreted the "Terminus" from this poem in my introduction, the Civil War is another revolutionary struggle for freedom in a new logic of its appearance, but, like the American Revolution itself, its outcome cannot be determined in advance. Not only that but a Union defeat retroactively means the failure of the American Revolution and its principles.

With regard to the Civil War itself, however, Whitman never expressed much interest in war battles or quelling rebellion; what he loved about it initially was the "unpent enthusiasm"[142] and ecstatic camaraderie that seemed to fulfill the objective of the 1860 *Leaves*. One can see this clearly in the following lines from the *Drum-Taps* poem "As I Lay with My Head in Your Lap, Camerado": "Dear camerado! I confess I have urged you onward with me, and still urge you, without the least idea what is our destination, / Or whether we shall be victorious, or utterly quell'd and defeated."[143] That the "shock electric" of the secession (or perhaps the bombardment of Fort Sumter in the early hours of April 12, 1861) took people away from a work economy and tore off the "costumes of peace"[144] attracted Whitman to the cause, but even if the Confederacy quelled and defeated the Union, a meteor of enthusiastic liberty would have announced itself.[145]

But the outcome of the Civil War ultimately restored Whitman's faith in the United States and breathed new life into his mission to become the poet of America: one consequence of this was that a renewed vision of both able-bodied nationalism and able-bodied selfhood began to populate his poetry again. As critics such as David Simpson and Robert Scholnick have shown, Walt Whitman's work, taken as a whole, certainly reveals a pronounced (national and individual) able-bodiedness.[146] I have been making a case for a different view of Walt Whitman, but a singular Whitman who was indeed "transient and strange," perhaps as much to himself as to us. A noticeable transformation already occurs by 1861 if the poem that he wrote for that year is any indication: "Eighteen Sixty-One" is the "robust year" of the "masculine voice," the "strong man erect,"[147] and rising with that man a Whitman who would cease to be dis-membered.

Nevertheless, Whitman remained aware that the Civil War birthed a new Union that had never been itself, a Union produced *through* dis-memberment. In *Democratic Vistas* (1871), he famously proclaims that the nation (to be exact, Civil War soldiers fighting for liberty) proved itself by "fearful tests—the wound, the amputation, the shatter'd face or limb, the slow hot fever, long impatient anchorage in bed, and all the forms of maiming, operation and disease. Alas! America have we seen, though only in her early youth, already to hospital brought."[148] And when, in "The Real War Will Never Get in the Books" from *Specimen Days* (1882), he argues that "the marrow of the tragedy [was] concentrated in those Army Hospitals—(it seem'd sometimes as if the whole interest of the land, North and South, was one vast central hospital, and all the rest of the affair but flanges ...)"[149] Whitman does not delineate a United States on the verge of being broken up, but a States amputated, maimed, and shattered. For him, Unionism is dis-abled: it emerges out of the historical hospital.

Analogously, when he volunteered as a nurse in the Civil War hospitals, Whitman continued to claim a model of enthusiasm based on a largesse of the affections. One cannot overlook those touching passages in *Specimen Days* where he writes letters for the wounded or gives gifts in a spirit of honor to the amputated: "Charles Miller, ... very bright, courageous boy, left leg amputated below the knee; next bed to him, another young lad very sick; gave each appropriate gifts. In the bed above, also, amputation of the left leg; gave him a little jar of raspberries."[150] Whitman does occasionally exhibit an able-bodied and parasitical mentality in relationship to the wounded ("I remain in capital health and strength and go every day, as before, among the men in my own way, enjoying my life and occupation more than I can tell"),[151] but for this I think we should at least partially forgive him as a pragmatic necessity of the ugly and difficult working conditions, to say nothing of the mortal horrors, in war hospitals. The Whitmanian joie de vivre is part of the job: "In my visits to the hospitals I found it was in the simple matter of personal presence, and emanating ordinary cheer and magnetism, that I succeeded and help'd more than by medical nursing."[152] Besides, another famous Civil War nurse, Louisa May Alcott, adopts the same persona in her writings. In the short story "The Brothers" (1863), she explains why: "But in a hospital one learns that cheerfulness is one's salvation; for, in an atmosphere of suffering and death, heaviness of heart would soon paralyze usefulness of hand, if the blessed gift of smiles had been denied us."[153] Indeed, Alcott's *Hospital Sketches* complements Whitman's tableaus written from the standpoint of a working nurse: "The sight of several stretchers, each with its legless, armless, or desperately wounded occupant, entering my ward, admonished me that I was there to work, not to wonder or weep; so I corked up my feelings, and returned to the path of duty."[154] Later Alcott needs a "businesslike air" to complete her tasks and articulates the need in hospital camps for "strong, properly trained, and cheerful men"¹⁵⁵ like Walt Whitman to attend to suffering patients. One wounded soldier in her narrative appreciates that the hospital is a "jolly place" or, Alcott phrases it, a service for "making of the hospital a home"¹⁵⁶—a space of hospitality.

Furthermore, Whitman's celebratory poetic vision of the Civil War was by no means one-dimensionally triumphalist in tone or perspective. Take "Lo, Victress on the Peaks," a poem in which, after six lines honoring victorious "Libertad," Whitman concludes:

> No poem proud, I chanting bring to thee, nor mastery's rapturous verse,
> But a cluster containing night's darkness and blood-dripping wounds,
> And psalms of the dead.¹⁵⁷

This example illustrates Whitman's struggle to reconcile a will to Civil War liberty and the blood-dripping wounds that result from it: he chooses a delicate stoicism. Rapturous enthusiasm, in such a case, would be inhumane, but failure to appreciate the cause of liberty for which the soldier died would be no less so. A politics of enthusiasm, then, does not refer to a particular emotional state or pathos of expression, only to a particular sort of affective commitment, in this case, a Unionism defined by emancipatory popular loves. For the same reason, if one has any criticism to make of Whitman's Civil War, it's that Louisa May Alcott chose to labor in the hospitals as a "red-hot Abolitionist,"¹⁵⁸ whereas Whitman tended to submerge and sometimes altogether disavow the racial underpinnings of the Civil War. All the same, Whitman—as political enthusiast—did unmistakably embrace the liberation of slaves in the name of a better Unionism like his hero Lincoln. He called the Emancipation Proclamation "a marked and first-class event,"¹⁵⁹ insisted that the Civil War and its results proved "that popular democracy, whatever its faults and dangers, practically justifies itself beyond the proudest claims and wildest hopes of its enthusiasts," and, as for the ones emancipated by that enthusiasm and event, Whitman was also pleased to learn of African-American soldiers, "men [who] look well," sporting "great names" such as "John Brown."¹⁶⁰

Epilogue
The Tramp and Strike Question: Terminal Enthusiasms

What happens to the politics of enthusiasm in the aftermath of the Civil War? It would be impossible to give a neat and definitive answer to this question, if only because I have argued for a view of enthusiasm sutured to singular events, manifesting itself relative to a convulsive context. There is no narrative of enthusiasm in general. Yes, I have made the case for a consistent formal structure to enthusiastic expression, but its historical content has to be assessed on a case-by-case basis, or an event-by-event basis as it were. Needless to say, for the minoritarian groups represented in this study, the "mania for freedom" certainly does not exhaust itself in the Civil War era. Although the future of enthusiasm for such groups lies beyond the scope of my analysis, I would, however, like to briefly consider one tributary, one inlet, of enthusiasm which follows from the Civil War itself: "The outcome of the war and the nearly dozen years of tumultuous struggles during 'Reconstruction' ultimately secured the social and political conditions for industrial capitalist development in the 'Gilded Age'"[1] and a "new America of big business, heavy industry, and capital-intensive agriculture that surpassed Britain to become the foremost industrial nation by 1880."[2] Out of this situation arises a new convulsive context orbiting around the intensifying problem of labor and money, immiseration and economic inequality.

In the terms of the Union dis-memberment politics discussed in chapter 5, the prosthetic goal of Reconstruction, as the name implies, was to put a war-torn nation back together again. As Abraham Lincoln said about "reconstruction" after Lee's surrender, "We simply must begin with, and mould from, disorganized and discordant elements."[3] Whether we're talking concretely about a burgeoning prosthetic industry (with "a vision of American society in the near future for which the boundary between bodies and machines has become ambiguous")[4] that emerged as a response to the large number of disabled veterans, "enabling them to walk and work again,"[5] or more broadly about the reunification of the North and South on the terms of progressive industrialization, the national project of economic and technological advance (a prosthetic nationhood) absorbs and transforms the politics of enthusiasm in the postbellum

United States. If the traumatic death toll of the Civil War by and large demystified the "romantic, glamorous idea of war"[6] that Americans held before the conflict, I would suggest that the same holds true for any romantic, glamorous idea of enthusiasm, a shift in sentiment that Herman Melville captures in his poem "A Utilitarian View of the Monitor's Fight" from *Battle-Pieces and Aspects of the War* (1866):

> Hail to victory without the gaud
> Of glory; zeal that needs no fans
> Of banners; plain mechanic power.[7]

While never relinquishing the minimal enthusiastic creed of emancipation ("Those of us who always abhorred slavery as an atheistical iniquity, gladly we join in the exulting chorus of humanity over its downfall"), Melville nevertheless saw "Law on her [Civil War America's] brow and empire in her eyes."[8] The times have changed, and *"Orpheus' charm is vain"*[9]—this was Melville's message, perhaps, to a certain Walt Whitman and all artists that we now need more austere and intransigent, principled and negative, forms of enthusiasm—we need literatures of enthusiasm without the gaud of glory.

Much postbellum American literature, under the banner of what would come to be called literary "realism," certainly seems to echo Melville. Take the first American novel about the Civil War, John W. De Forest's *Miss Ravenel's Conversion from Secession to Loyalty* (1867), which narrates the convulsive event as a historical bridge from romantic pastoralism to pragmatic urbanism. In the novel's final pages, the hero Edward Colburne typifies the modern American man of tomorrow: "His responsibilities will take all dreaminess out of him, and make him practical, industrious, able to arrive at results," and this is all for the good: such a man will now be "the soldier citizen: he could face the flame of battle for his country: he can also earn his own living.... It is in millions of such men that the strength of the Republic consists."[10] The new practical and industrious man of business, of plain mechanic power, steals his fire from the valor of the Union soldier, but conspicuously not a disabled one, as De Forest in this passage confirms the way that "the term 'able-bodied' workers came to be interchangeable with able-bodied citizens."[11]

In sympathy with De Forest and his prosthetic vision of nationhood, Walt Whitman's postbellum poetry concisely illustrates the historical transformation of enthusiasm in the Reconstruction era and the Gilded Age. No longer does Whitman cry for martial music, "Beat! beat!

drums!"; instead, he celebrates the convulsive beat of the locomotive: "Thee in thy panoply, thy measur'd dual throbbing and thy beat convulsive."[12] At the same time, Whitman had his reservations about the unquestioned connection between progressive democracy and technological industry, and his own enthusiasm for the latter was predicated on the hope that it would create the material conditions for a hospitable economy of global human exchange: "The earth to be spann'd, connected by network, / . . . The lands to be welded together."[13] In a late note, Whitman calls the unprecedented "materialistic, political and money-making successes" of the United States mere "pre-successes," the "indispensable foundations—the *sine qua non* of moral and heroic (poetic) fruitions to come," though minus these fruitions, "a gross materialistic prosperity" alone would amount to national "failure": American materialism "has not advanced the standard of humanity a bit further than other nations."[14]

But what do we do if "gross materialistic prosperity" threatens to undermine our democratic polity? Whitman seriously considers this question in an undelivered lecture (composed sometime before 1882) on the problem of poverty called "The Tramp and Strike Questions": "If the United States, like the countries of the Old World, are also to grow vast crops of poor, desperate, dissatisfied, nomadic, miserably-waged populations, such as we see looming upon us of late years—steadily, even if slowly, eating into them like a cancer of lungs or stomach—then our republican experiment, notwithstanding all its surface-successes, is at heart an unhealthy failure."[15] The "immense capital and capitalists" are "a sort of anti-democratic disease and monstrosity," Whitman says elsewhere, and, if this disease wins out, it will retroactively prove that the "American Revolution of 1776" was "simply a great strike, successful for its immediate object."[16] The Tramp and Strike Question, then, is really the Poverty and Revolution Question. Not only that but Whitman now defines revolution itself as a strike against poverty: "The French Revolution was absolutely a strike, and a very terrible and relentless one, against ages of bad pay, unjust division of wealth-products, and the hoggish monopoly of a few, rolling in superfluity, against the vast bulk of the work-people, living in squalor."[17] One of Whitman's other private notes on the Tramp and Strike Question reads as follows:

> The most important bearings of this questo [sic] on the fact that humanity in the U S is being divided merged more and more

Epilogue 201

definitely into two marked divisions, the vast masses of employed persons, poor, ignorant, desperate, & dissatisfied/

& the luxurious rich describe them without gloves/

The class, middle class, American men, good stock—are growing less and less.[18]

And again: "the great point (perhaps) is that instead of a *homogeneousnes* [sic] of race, & a common platform to start from, we are rapidly dividing off into two densely colored classes, the few the capitalists, the great companies & owners, very hoggish with enormous advantages (in finance & privilege) & the bulk of the p [cuts off, but implies "people"]."[19] This last sentence fragment, whether intended as such by Whitman or not, reads suggestively: an absent, unspeakable, or dwindling people have become divorced altogether from the luxurious rich. And, in the above block quote, Whitman scrambles the class schema of "top" and "bottom" according to a numerical hierarchy: the poor are on "top" as the dominant class, then the rich, and finally the dying middle class sits on bottom.

As he nearly always did, Whitman, against the dialectic of rich and poor, apotheosizes "the aggregate of its middling property owners"[20] as an "average" race of ideal Americans, as if said property owners were anticapitalists who do not aspire to accumulate gross wealth or exist by virtue of the same marketplace dynamics responsible for the growing class divide. What Whitman fails to understand in his social criticism is that capitalist economies do not work for the "average." They produce extremes: "the *growth of capital* and the *increase in the proletariat* appear, therefore, as interconnected—if opposed—*products* of the same process."[21] Then again, maybe he did understand that in his own way. In another fragment from Whitman's notes on the Tramp and Strike Question, it's as if he gestures toward an anticapitalist solution to the problem, or at least acknowledges its political existence: "The Communists of France—the radicals &   of the British Islands—the Socialists?   of Germany—the   of the United States   —(Tramp & Strike question)."[22] Taken at face value, this note merely presents an offhand list of the groups taking up the Tramp and Strike Question, but, in the context of his other writings on the subject, it's hard not to read this as his affirmative conclusion that communist and socialist movements in the present hour now carry the baton of the revolutionary historical process (once again, if we read this fragment formalistically, the United

States has no people taking up the question or at least no nameable people). As I have mentioned more than once, Whitman wrote "O Star of France," perhaps specifically with the Communists of France in mind, in order to celebrate the "enthusiast's dreams of brotherhood": this indicates to me that Whitmanian enthusiasm in the postbellum era pertains directly to the problem of wealth and poverty, to the Tramp and Strike Question.

But if I am correct about Whitman's post–Civil War fascination with anticapitalism, this hardly amounts to a surprising phenomenon in the United States of the 1870s and 1880s—a period not only of rapid development and economic growth but, as part of the same process, also of mass worker strikes and protests, part and parcel of a Progressive Movement that included the emergence of American labor unions and popular interest in socialist or otherwise anticapitalist ideas. In American literature, from Rebecca Harding Davis's *Life in the Iron Mills* (1861) to Upton Sinclair's *The Jungle* (1906), it is well known that a certain strain of literary fiction takes up the Tramp and Strike Question in order "to protest against conditions deemed harmful to society and to initiate and advance more equitable social arrangements."[23] Lindsay Reckson has recently made the case for a "repressed enthusiasm at the very heart of realist aesthetics," by which she means that "ecstatic performance" continues to haunt American fiction once the "enthusiastic fervor" of the antebellum era has been "naturalize[d] and diffuse[d],"[24] but the same argument could be made for the tradition of protest derived from the political enthusiasms discussed in this book.

There is at least one unrepressed popular example of postbellum literature, however, that candidly invokes the legacy of enthusiasm as I understand it, and that is Edward Bellamy's bestseller *Looking Backward 2000–1887* (1888). Unique for inspiring a formidable political movement (the Nationalist Clubs of 1888–96), Bellamy's novel is one part utopian romance and one part socialist tract (though he never used the *s*-word), but it also draws upon the resources of Christian millenarianism, the Social Gospel Movement of the late nineteenth century, and the evangelical heritage of the Great Awakenings in its imagination of a future for the United States without tramps or strikes.[25]

In the year 2000, the prefatory remarks of the "author" (to the letter, it's as if Bellamy strangely projects himself into the future) plainly introduce the moral of the story to the reader. Cast in the entertaining fashion of a "romantic narrative," the novel will illustrate the "social contrasts between the nineteenth and twentieth centuries" in order to teach the reader the historical lesson that speedy and thoroughgoing political transformations do in fact occur—that human advancement is always possible. The former age (Bellamy's age) could not imagine the termination of the "ancient industrial system, with all its shocking social consequences," though they readily accepted such a convulsive event once the logical basis and benefits of nationalized industry were well understood: this fact, says the author, ought "to moderate the enthusiasm of reformers who count for their reward on the lively gratitude of future ages!"[26] What does "moderate" mean here? Given the author's point of view, it hardly makes sense to say that the sublime lesson of social progress should chasten or diminish the enthusiasm for reform; therefore Bellamy probably refers to that other sense of the word "moderate" meaning to preside over or lead—in other words, the historical lesson ought to guide, give direction or confidence to, reformers; they should have an expectant faith in the rationality of their commitments, which future ages will commemorate and take for common sense. At the same time, Bellamy may also imply that enthusiasm need not express itself desperately or immoderately: reformers can proceed with a sober conviction that the future will corroborate their as yet unrealized ideals. Even if Bellamy's didacticism is a little on the nose, the artifice of the novel's temporality, its manipulation of a voice speaking from the future, has a powerful rhetorical effect: whereas our "author" asks his contemporaries at the end of the second millennium to look backward and celebrate the advent of enthusiastic humanity, his nineteenth-century readers have to reverse the reading process by looking forward, virtually commemorating that revolution which has yet to happen, or more to the point, that enthusiasm which presently has no reward, no foundation, no people. Bellamy thereby admonishes his reader to occupy the position of that future reformer—or author—who, once upon a time that is actually tomorrow, claimed the constituent power of a people's revolution.

Since I cannot discuss *Looking Backward* in any great depth, let me simply highlight that "Mr. Barton's Sermon" in chapter 26 unambiguously calls attention to Bellamy's self-conscious understanding of the role that enthusiasm plays not only in projecting but also in actualizing future political possibilities. First the preacher, like the author in the preface, reflects on the radical disparities between "the dreary hopelessness of the nineteenth century, its profound pessimism as to the future of humanity" and "the animating idea of the present age," which is "an enthusiastic conception of the opportunities of our earthly existence, and the unbounded possibilities of human nature."²⁷ An antidote to historical hopelessness and pessimism, enthusiasm—always projective, open-ended, forward looking—is the animating force, the political *élan vital*, of Bellamy's ideal society, but Mr. Barton also makes it clear that enthusasm was the *primum mobile* of the revolution itself: "To wonder at the rapidity with which the change was completed after its possibility was first entertained is to forget the intoxicating effect of hope upon minds long accustomed to despair. The sunburst, after so long and dark a night, must needs have had a dazzling effect. From the moment men allowed themselves to believe that humanity after all had not been meant for a dwarf, that its squat stature was not the measure of its possible growth, but that it stood upon the verge of an avatar of limitless development, the reaction must needs have been overwhelming. It is evident that nothing was able to stand against the enthusiasm which the new faith inspired."²⁸ Thus, enthusiasm is both the sufficient cause and catalyzing effect of social transformation, or in the terms of my discussion in chapter 1, both the "in-streaming causing power" of Emerson and the moral response of Kant for the "new faith" of the redeemed captives—it is the constituent power of living democracy that founds and continues to animate the constituted order.

As one learns in greater detail from Bellamy's fictional sequel *Equality* (1898), if an emancipated society is ever to exist, then the hearts and minds of average Americans must themselves be transformed via a "tidal wave of humane enthusiasm," what Bellamy elsewhere calls "the enthusiasm of humanity."²⁹ This is how the revolution occurred: as already noted, first "the plan of a nationalized industrial system, and an equal sharing of results, with its promise of the abolition of poverty and the reign of universal comfort" did not take hold with the masses because "it seemed too good to be true." However, once the masses grasped the scientific rationale of the new system, thanks to the "revolutionary propaganda" of the anticapitalist party, "the hope of the multitude grew into confidence, and confidence flamed into a resistless enthusiasm," that is, into a "popular enthusiasm" for the revolution, which drove the movement "irresistibly forward from the moment that the prospect of its success became fairly clear to the masses."³⁰ Subsequently, "to cap the climax" of this enthusiasm, a corresponding outbreak of "religious emotion" occurred. Dr. Leete explains "The Great Revival" to Julian as follows: "The Great Revival was a tide of enthusiasm for the social, not the personal, salvation, and for the establishment in brotherly love of the

Epilogue 205

kingdom of God on earth which Christ bade men hope and work for. It was the general awakening of the people of America in the closing years of the last century to the profoundly ethical and truly religious character and claims of the movement for an industrial system which should guarantee the economic equality of all the people."[31] Enthusiasm, finally, is to anticapitalism as revival is to revolution—the former terms (enthusiasm/revival) refer to the constituent affections and popular fervor for "economic equality," the latter (anticapitalism/revolution) to the constituted event and political structure of that equality.

Moreover, the revival enthusiasm of Bellamy's future society will have been part of a historical concatenation of emancipatory events. This is made clear in Bellamy's postscript to the second edition wherein he contends that *Looking Backward* is not only a "forecast ... of the next stage in the industrial and social development of humanity";[32] it also belongs to a historical genealogy of evental politics including the unlikely birth of the American Republic and the convulsive termination of U.S. slavery. And now we see a new event on the horizon: "Not only are the toilers of the world engaged in something like a world-wide insurrection, but true and humane men and women, of every degree, are in a mood of exasperation, verging on absolute revolt, against social conditions that reduce life to a brutal struggle for existence, mock every dictate of ethics and religion, and render well-nigh futile the efforts of philanthropy.... [T]he barbaric industrial and social system ... is shaking the world with convulsions that presage its collapse."[33] But as the protagonist of the novel, Julian West, learns when he dreams of returning to the nineteenth century and preaching the absurd follies of capitalism, the "enthusiasm of reformers" for the average nineteenth-century American translates into the politics of a " 'Madman!' 'Pestilent fellow!' 'Fanatic!' 'Enemy of society!' "[34] Tomorrow's true enthusiasm is today's false fanaticism.

Insofar as *Looking Backward* announces itself, vis-à-vis an articulated convulsive context, as the very revolutionary propaganda interpolated into its history of the coming revolution, projecting, encouraging, disseminating the convulsive affect of "popular enthusiasm," the novel deserves to be included in "literatures of enthusiasm." It is important to note, though, that Bellamy places such a high premium on enthusiasm because he believes the infectious spirit of mass democratic revivalism alone—converting everybody, rich and poor, to the cause—can obviate the need for a violent revolutionary solution to the problem of capitalism, or, for an excessive and lawless manifestation of enthusiasm that contradicts the peaceful and rational conditions of true moral reform. On the other hand, in a passage cited above, Bellamy retains the language of "world-wide insurrection," lodged against the unjust industrial system, and appears to sympathize with "absolute revolt," only he means to offer what he thinks of as a more constructive platform and harmonious vision—a rational enthusiasm—for confronting and remedying the convulsive context of the Tramp and Strike Question.

Walt Whitman read *Looking Backward* (or at least part of it) in 1889. We learn this from his close friend and literary executor, the socialist Horace Traubel, who encouraged Whitman to pick up Bellamy's novel. According to Traubel, earlier in 1888 he asked Whitman if he had any sympathy for the English socialism of William Morris and his (Whitman's) friend Ernest Rhys, to which Whitman replied, "Lots of it—lots—lots. In the large sense, whatever the political process, the social end is bound to be achieved: too much is made of property, here, now, in our noisy, bragging civilization—too little of men. As I understand these men they are for putting the crown on man—taking it off things. Ain't we all socialists, after all?" Then this exchange: "But about their political program—how about that?," asks Traubel. Whitman responds, "Of that I'm not so sure—I rather rebel. I am with them in the result—that's about all I can say."[35] It's in this context that Traubel and another correspondent, the Bellamyite journalist and poet Sylvester Baxter, began to recommend Bellamy to Whitman. But he did not, finally, share their love of the novel after giving it a look: "I can't say I am ravished with it: but it has a certain sort of interest."[36] In a later conversation, Whitman spoke positively of Sylvester Baxter's reporting but qualified that he could not get behind the latter's enthusiasm for Bellamy ("he is enthusiastic over Bellamy's book"), namely because he did not believe that the "Henry Georgian Socialism, Anarchism, Schools" platform alone would answer to the diversity of reform needed "from all quarters."[37] Before we draw the simple conclusion that Whitman could not go so far as to identify himself with Traubel's and Baxter's politics (why not take seriously his claim that he's with the socialists "in the result"?), it might be worth considering that Whitman's reservations, as he himself notes, have more to do with his radical contemporaries' "political program" than with socialist ideals as such, and here I would accent above all else Whitman's interesting declaration in the conversation above, "I rather rebel." What does this mean? To my mind, it implies Whitman's unflinching devotion to militant rites of dissent in the revolutionary heritage and a corresponding suspicion of all utopian projects such as Bellamy's that, true to the prosthetic nationalism of the post–Civil War United States, envision a homogeneous society, a political consensus, defined by an "industrial army."[38]

This is where the "Songs of Insurrection" cluster, introduced in the 1871 *Leaves of Grass* and maintained in the 1876 centennial edition, becomes relevant: Whitman's remark "I rather rebel" speaks to the fact that he believed that the abolition of economic injustice, like the abolition of slavery, would not occur through successful propaganda and a peaceful social revival, as is made clear in the unpublished introduction and prefatory remarks that he wrote for the cluster: "Not only are These States the born offspring of Revolt against mere overweening Authority. . . . but seeing ahead for Them in the future, a long, long reign of Peace, with all the growths, corruptions and tyrannies & fossilisms of Obedience, (accumulating, vast folds, strata, from the rankness of continued Prosperity and the more and more overshadowing and insidious grip of Capital,) I feel it worth while to keep well up, & vital even such ideas as the following [no period]."[39] The six "Songs of Insurrection," then, were grouped together with an eye toward a future revolution that Whitman thought might be necessary to overturn capitalist corruption. As I showed in chapter 5, these particular poems also have an unmistakable global vision, perhaps because Whitman already had in mind, as he states in the 1876 preface to the centennial *Leaves*, the "glory of Labor, and the bringing together not only representatives of all the trades and products, but, fraternally, of all the Workmen of all the Nations of the World."[40] But if the "Songs of Insurrection" cluster primarily looks forward to a (future) labor revolution, it also assembles a historical lineage of democratic revolt from poems that span Whitman's entire career. Even in his apostrophe to the "Spirit Whose Work is Done," originally published in *Sequel to Drum-Taps* (1865–66), Whitman asks that the insurrectionary spirit of the Civil War never die:

> Leave me your pulses of rage—bequeath them to me—fill me with currents convulsive,
> Let them scorch and blister out of my chants when you are gone,
> Let them identify you to the future in these songs.[41]

Against the grain of prosthetic nationhood, Walt Whitman—or rather, an occasional Walt Whitman—writes the Civil War not as the termination of convulsive politics giving way to the spirit of industrial reunification but as a song of insurrection that will inspire future revolutionary projects.

With the above context in mind, let me end this study of enthusiasm by analyzing the one "Song of Insurrection" that I did not discuss in chapter 5, the only new (post–Civil War) poem written for the cluster: "Still Though the One I Sing." The original version reads:

> STILL, though the one I sing,
> (One, yet of contradictions made,) I dedicate to Nationality,
> I leave in him Revolt, (O latent right of insurrection! O quenchless, indispensable fire!)[42]

The grammatical structure of this tristich is subtly disorienting. Without the parenthetical commentary, it reads: "Still, though the one I sing, / I dedicate to Nationality, / I leave in him Revolt." What precisely does the poem dedicate to Nationality? And why does this dedication occur in the same line with a parenthetical phrase about a contradictory One? One reading is that Whitman dedicates the "One, yet of contradictions made" to Nationality: dominant "Nationality" (in the foreground of the poem) has as its ancillary background the "One," only this is offset (or contradicted?) by the fact that Whitman privileges the "One, yet of contradictions made" as the first subject of the line. The use of parentheses, in this sense, formally reinforces the theme of insurrectionary latency (if not contradiction as well). The third line then clarifies the nature of the One's contradiction: marked by capitalization and the line break, the order of Nationality and the order of Revolt contradict each other on a vertical axis, which is to say, the latent right of insurrection emerges from below as a volcanic, Promethean principle to disturb the Nationality that sits on top of it visually in the poem. This reading accords with the most obvious translation of the poem's message: even though he still sings for the unity of the nation, Whitman nonetheless dedicates to and leaves in nationhood the right to revolt ("I dedicate to Nationality, I leave in Nationality, Revolt"), if only because Unionism—the One of Nationality—has built into itself many internal contradictions. Insurrection against the nation is paradoxically constitutive of progressive Unionism, and the contradiction is that Whitman dedicates the convulsion of Nationality to Nationality. But why? First and foremost, because he sings of the "one," that is, Whitman does not sing a song *of* Nationality but a song of the one, implying a subordination of the nation to oneness as well as their inequality: the superlative one exceeds the nation by sitting on top of it visually in the poem.

However, the "one" in the first line is not capitalized: it might mean a single one or a collective one, but given that Whitman uses a singular pronoun ("him") to refer ambiguously to either the "one" or "Nationality," it is impossible to choose. Nevertheless, another plausible interpretation is that the poem reads: "Still, though the one I sing, I leave in him Revolt." If one will not grant this reading (which poses new problems for the awkward dedication to Nationality), the poem certainly forces the reader to see a repetition between the "one" in the first line and the capitalized "One" in the second line, as if the singular "one" is synecdochic for the collective or metaphysical "One" and vice versa. This may indeed be how Whitman intends it, in the sense of the following unpublished fragment, "The Law is grand," housed in the Berg Collection at the New York Public Library: "When the whole combined force of the nation is champion for one human being, outraged in his rights of life or liberty, no matter of what color, birth or degree of ignorance or education he or she may be, then the law is grand."[43] This statement is very close in spirit to the following lines from the 1860 poem "Says": "With one man or woman—(no matter which one—I even pick out the lowest,) / With him or her I now illustrate the whole law."[44] In 1871 and 1876, at least, the liberation and coordination of singularities, of ones, is still the sum goal of Whitman's politics: as long as Nationality does not champion each and every one, the order of Revolt must remain an inherent aspect of political life.

But given the international scope of the other "Songs of Insurrection," what if Whitman implies a cosmopolitan thesis by subordinating "Nationality" to the "one" or "One" (the human nation)? Hence the dedication of the latter to the circumscribed nation or ethnic-political body: the "one" trumps all politics of nationhood, and the indispensable fire of revolt, the spirit of enthusiasm, must have a universal or generic horizon as its enabling condition. In "Song of the Exposition," a poem also first appearing in 1871 under the title "After All, Not to Create Only," Whitman invites the United States to accept its own foreignness:

But hold—don't I forget my manners?
To introduce the stranger, (what else indeed do I live to chant for?)
    to thee Columbia;
. . . .

> Fear not O Muse! truly new ways and days receive, surround you,
> I candidly confess a queer, queer race, of novel fashion,
> And yet the same old human race, the same within, without,[45]

From the future comes a queer, queer race and a novel hospitality that is both inside and outside nationality. To introduce the coming stranger to Columbia and to dedicate to her a future revolt: a parity exists between these sentiments. Although Whitman still leaves open whether the One's contradictions can or should ever be resolved or not and on what terms, what could be more dangerous than pretending to reconcile the One with itself as if he understood the future stranger of new ways and days? Unlike Bellamy, Whitman does not presume to grasp from what quarter, what party, what platform, or what social body true reform will come, nor by what precise means, nor in what era. As a kind of enthusiastic categorical imperative, he merely claims the right to dissent. I take the ambiguity of "Still Though the One I Sing" to be its greatest strength, for it stays within the horizon of Whitman's present while announcing an open promise for the future: politically, it asks us not to allow unity to become despotic and crush the right to resistance and, philosophically, not to allow the One to be one with itself as long as a gap exists between the order of Nationality and what it *ab-jects* or *rejects*. Whitman demurs. But he has articulated the clearest, most foundational, politics in Jacques Rancière's terms: "Politics exists when the natural order of domination is interrupted by the institution of a part of those who have no part.... It defines the common of the community as a political community, in other words, as divided, as based on a wrong that escapes the arithmetic of exchange and reparation. Beyond this set-up there is no politics. There is only the order of domination or the disorder of revolt."[46]

Walt Whitman does not merely bequeath to the future the latent right of insurrection; he also bequeaths to us his "Songs of Insurrection" for an unexpected future of democracy that he cannot foresee, a future claimed by latent peoples whom he cannot foresee, and a future of enthusiasm that he cannot foresee, at the terminal point of his own poetry: "What is known I strip away.... I launch all men and women forward with me into the unknown."[47] In an unpunctuated present, the song of insurrection—a latent, international music—is dedicated to all tomorrow's queer, queer enthusiasms.

Notes

Introduction

1. Carlyle, *French Revolution*, 70, 101.
2. For scholarship on enthusiasm, see especially Tucker, *Enthusiasm*; Beiser, *Sovereignty of Reason*; Heyd, *"Be Sober and Reasonable"*; Knox, *Enthusiasm*; Klein and La Vopa, *Enthusiasm and Enlightenment in Europe, 1650–1850*; Lovejoy, *Religious Enthusiasm in the New World*; Taves, *Fits, Trances, and Visions*. For literary considerations of enthusiasm, see Irlam, *Elations*; Hawes, *Mania and Literary Style*; Rosenberg, *Critical Enthusiasm*; Mee, *Dangerous Enthusiasm* and *Romanticism, Enthusiasm, and Regulation*; Goldsmith, *Blake's Agitation*; and Orianne Smith, *Romantic Women Writers*. In American literary criticism, see Herd, *Enthusiast!*, which takes a broadly formalist approach to enthusiasm as a condition of poetic composition and to the enthusiast as "a circulator of thoughts, a person who keeps ideas and values moving," linking together such diverse figures as Ralph Waldo Emerson, Ezra Pound, Henry David Thoreau, James Schuyler, Herman Melville, and Frank O'Hara (5).
3. Lincoln, *Speeches and Writings*, 541.
4. Whitman, "Apostroph," line 39, *Leaves of Grass and Other Writings*.
5. Comay, *Mourning Sickness*, 25.
6. Hawes, *Mania and Literary Style*, 1.
7. "Coulter on Wall Street Protests."
8. Burke, *Reflections*, 156.
9. Arendt apologizes for the deliberative character and making of the American Revolution as against the French Revolution, and Negri defends the more progressive, radical character of the latter. While he famously argues for the "radicalism" of the American Revolution, Gordon Wood, in *The Radicalism of the American Revolution* (1992), really ends up associating said radicalism with the unanticipated democratic consequences of the Revolution while the Revolution itself remained moored to a genteel republicanism. Ultimately Wood identifies an antinomy between Enlightened republicanism and egalitarian commercialism, an irreconcilable conflict between cosmopolitan, disinterested, but elitist Enlightenment: and bourgeois, capitalistic, but popular or equal-opportunity democracy. As for Bercovitch, I briefly assess his views in chapter 2.
10. Burke, *Letter from the Right Honourable Edmund Burke*, 17, 12.
11. Ibid., 12.
12. Ibid., 12–13.
13. I have taken this information from Erdman, *Blake*, 1–19.
14. Burke, *Letter from the Right Honourable Edmund Burke*, 13.
15. Pocock, "Radical Criticisms," 48.

16. Ibid., 51.
17. Burke, *Reflections*, 262.
18. Ibid., 158.
19. Ibid., 123, 159.
20. Ibid., 161.
21. Ibid., 256, 213.
22. Lovejoy, "'Desperate Enthusiasm,'" 219.
23. Bouton, *Taming Democracy*, 4.
24. Cappon, *Adams-Jefferson Letters*, 346–47.
25. Mee, *Romanticism*, 14.
26. Imlay, *Emigrants*, 31; Melville, *Pierre*, 128, 109; Sedgwick, *Hope Leslie*, 8, 189; Lippard, *Quaker City*, 446, 526.
27. Blake, *Complete Poetry and Prose*, 645.
28. See Erdman, *Blake*, 5–9.
29. Blake, "America," 1:1, 2:4, *Complete Poetry and Prose*. My citations of *America* follow the *Complete Poetry and Prose* arrangement of Plate: Line Number.
30. My numbering of the plates follows that of *The Complete Poetry and Prose of William Blake*.
31. Blake, "America," 2:8, 2:16, 2:10–17.
32. Ibid., 4:3, 4:7–9.
33. Tucker, *Enthusiasm*, 144–61.
34. Erdman, 24–25.
35. Blake, "America," 6:4–15.
36. Ibid., 15:5.
37. Ibid., 15:8.
38. Ibid., 16:15.
39. Ibid., 15:20–22.
40. Ibid., 15:25–26, 16:1.
41. Ibid., 15:23.
42. Rosenberg, *Critical Enthusiasm*, 15.
43. Giles, *Global Remapping*, 21.
44. Pease, *New American Exceptionalism*, 11.
45. Lionnet and Shih, "Introduction," 5, 8.
46. See Buck-Morss, *Hegel*.
47. Kaplan, *Anarchy of Empire*, 34.
48. Fisher, *Hard Facts*, 91.
49. Warner, *Publics and Counterpublics*, 56–57.
50. C. Smith, *Oracle and the Curse*, 4, xi.
51. See Ruttenburg, *Democratic Personality*; Fliegelman, *Declaring Independence*; Gustafson, *Eloquence is Power*; J. Brooks, *American Lazaraus*; Modern, *Secularism*.
52. Toscano, *Fanaticism*, xiii, xii.
53. Ibid., xxi.
54. See especially Asad, *Formations of the Secular*; Modern, *Secularism*; and Kaufmann, "Religious, the Secular, and Literary Studies."
55. Asad, *Formations of the Secular*, 25.

56. Modern, *Secularism*, 8.
57. See Taves, *Fits, Trances, and Visions*, 20.
58. Beiser, *Sovereignty of Reason*, 200–201.
59. Fessenden, *Culture and Redemption*, 61, 6.
60. Johnson, "Enthusiasm," *Dictionary*.
61. Webster, *American Dictionary*, 672.
62. Ibid.
63. Hume, *Essays*, 78.
64. Staël, *Germany*, 364, 360.
65. Berlant, "Intuitionists," 845.
66. Anderson, "Modulating the Excess," 166.
67. Freeman, "Enthusiasm," 5.
68. See Mee, *Dangerous Enthusiasm*.
69. Goldsmith, *Blake's Agitation*, 10.
70. Ibid., 9, 11.
71. Massumi, *Parables for the Virtual*, 28.
72. Ibid., 35.
73. Deleuze and Guattari, *Thousand Plateaus*, 256, 240.
74. Brennan, *Transmission of Affect*, 3, 1.
75. Ibid., 140.
76. Seigworth and Gregg, "Inventory of Shimmers," 3.
77. Brennan, *Transmission of Affect*, 8.
78. Gatens, "Privacy and the Body," 115.
79. Mee, *Romanticism*, 11, 50, 268.
80. Berlant, "Intuitionists," 845.
81. Felix Guattari, quoted in Bertelsen and Murphie, "Ethics of Everyday Infinities and Powers," 151.
82. Grossberg, "Affect's Future," 324.
83. See Zupančič, "Enthusiasm, Anxiety and the Event," for an interesting account of contemporary philosophy's interest in Kantian enthusiasm.
84. Lyotard, *Differend*, 168, 170. See also Lyotard, *Enthusiasm*.
85. Jameson, *Valences of the Dialectic*, 596, 610.
86. Badiou, *Logics of Worlds*, 76.
87. Badiou, *Theoretical Writings*, 145.
88. Badiou, *Ethics*, 44.
89. Badiou, *Being and Event*, 178–79.
90. Ibid., 234.
91. Ibid., 178.
92. Badiou, *Logics of Worlds*, 378, 66.
93. Badiou, *Metapolitics*, 141.
94. Ibid., 143.
95. Badiou, *Ethics*, 85.
96. Badiou, *Metapolitics*, 149, 146.
97. Loughlin and Walker, Introduction, 2.
98. Douglass, *Autobiographies*, 926–27.

99. Ibid.
100. Ibid., 928, 926.
101. Ibid., 927.
102. Ibid., 935.
103. Douglass, *Heroic Slave*, 49.
104. Ibid., 51.
105. Ibid.
106. Tomkins, *Shame and Its Sisters*, 180–81.
107. Berlant, "Intuitionists," 845.
108. Hatch, *Sacred Cause of Liberty*, 53.
109. Ruttenburg, *Democratic Personality*, 6.
110. Lovejoy, *Religious Enthusiasm*, 2.
111. Whitman, *Complete Prose*, 78, emphasis mine.
112. Whitman, "Calamus," 5:1, *Leaves of Grass, 1860*. My citations of the 1860 facsimile edition of *Leaves* follow Whitman's arrangement of Cluster or Poem Title, Number (if applicable): Verse.
113. Ibid., 5:5.
114. Ibid., 5:11.
115. Ibid., 5:7, 9–10.
116. Ibid., 5:10, 11.
117. Ibid., 5:15.
118. Whitman, "O Star of France," lines 9–10, *Leaves of Grass and Other Writings*.
119. Whitman, "The Centenarian's Story," lines 95–96, *Leaves of Grass and Other Writings*.
120. Whitman, *Notebooks*, 1:357.

Chapter One

1. Emerson, *Selected Writings*, 274.
2. Ibid.
3. Ibid., 418, 406.
4. R. Richardson, *Emerson*, 199. It should be noted that Richardson stresses the primary influence of Germaine de Staël on Emerson's concept of enthusiasm.
5. Coleridge, *Lay Sermons*, 23. See the editorial note on this page for Coleridge's source material.
6. Kant, *Observations*, 212–13.
7. Edwards, *Works of Jonathan Edwards*, 508–9.
8. Emerson, *Selected Writings*, 40, 42.
9. Ibid., 316.
10. See Brodhead, "Prophets in America ca. 1830"; and Scales, "Narrative Revolutions in Nat Turner and Joseph Smith."
11. Harding, "Symptoms of Liberty," 91.
12. Reynolds, *John Brown*, 17.
13. Samuel C. Cox, quoted in Reynolds, *John Brown*, 482.

14. Some of the most notable writings on the subject not discussed in this book but worth referencing include Meric Casaubon, *A Treatise Concerning Enthusiasme* (1655); John Locke, "Of Enthusiasm," in *Essay Concerning Human Understanding* (1690/1700); Anthony Ashley Cooper, Third Earl of Shaftesbury, *Letter Concerning Enthusiasm* (1708); John Wesley, *Sermon on Enthusiasm* (1750); Theophilus Evans, *The History of Modern Enthusiasm from the Reformation to the Present Times* (1752); John Langhorne, *Letters on Religious Retirement, Melancholy, and Enthusiasm* (1762); and Isaac Taylor, *The Natural History of Enthusiasm* (1829).

15. More, *Enthusiasmus Triumphatus*, 12.
16. Ibid., 30.
17. Ibid., 22.
18. Ibid., 17–19.
19. Pocock, "Enthusiasm," 10.
20. Tucker, *Enthusiasm*, 15.
21. Beiser, *Sovereignty of Reason*, 189. It should be emphasized that Oliver Cromwell notoriously crushed these radical sects, just as later, in the French Revolution, Robespierre suppressed what he called "outbursts of dangerous enthusiasm" within the Revolutionary movement (Robespierre, *Virtue and Terror*, 35). As Christopher Hill explains in his classic text, *The World Turned Upside Down* (1972), enthusiasts had a very different—more democratic—vision for English society than the Cromwellian one that was victorious. I highlight this to say that even though a figure such as Cromwell or Robespierre commonly becomes a symbol of enthusiasm, one needs to divorce the ideology of this symbolism from the historical person and wrestle with the internal contradictions whereby enthusiasm designates the excess to any constituted power, including the Protectorate or the Jacobin state.
22. Irlam, *Elations*, 24.
23. Barker-Benfield, *Culture of Sensibility*, 215.
24. Mee, *Romanticism*, 3, 50.
25. Ibid., 49.
26. Ibid., 3.
27. Irlam, *Elations*, 37.
28. Another influential example of this regulation at work occurs in Anthony Ashley Cooper, Third Earl of Shaftesbury's *Letter Concerning Enthusiasm* (1707), in *Characteristics*.
29. Voltaire, *Philosophical Dictionary*, 187.
30. Ibid.
31. Voltaire, *Les Oeuvres complètes*, 36:59.
32. Voltaire, *Works*, 4.2:239.
33. Voltaire, *Philosophical Dictionary*, 188.
34. Voltaire, *Works*, 4.2:241.
35. Voltaire, *Les Oeuvres complètes*, 41:127–28.
36. Ibid., 36:60.
37. Voltaire, *Philosophical Dictionary*, 188.
38. Ibid., 203.

39. Voltaire, *Les Oeuvres complètes*, 36:110.
40. Voltaire, *Works*, 5.1:25–26.
41. C. Taylor, *Secular Age*, 3, 299, 322.
42. Tucker, *Enthusiasm*, 89.
43. A. Alcott, "Orphic Sayings," 303–4.
44. Foucault, *Politics of Truth*, 129.
45. Kant, *Political Writings*, 58.
46. Ibid., 181.
47. Ibid., 182.
48. Ibid., 183.
49. Foucault, *Politics of Truth*, 94.
50. Kant, *Political Writings*, 185.
51. Ibid., 184.
52. Ibid.
53. Ibid., 81.
54. Loughlin and Walker, Introduction, 2.
55. See Loughlin, "Constituent Power Subverted," on English constitutional arguments over "real" versus "personal" sovereignty.
56. Negri, *Insurgencies*, 311.
57. Ibid., 11.
58. See W. Adams, 61–95.
59. Negri, *Insurgencies*, 149. The right of revolution, in modern political theory, is of course a key ingredient of John Locke's social contract theory in *Two Treatises of Government* (1689).
60. See Griffin, "Constituent Power," 49.
61. Fritz, *American Sovereigns*, 3–5. I regret not having access to Dana Nelson's *Commons Democracy* (2016) as I finished this book, but see her discussion of constituent power, "vernacular democracy," and the politics of participation therein.
62. Negri, *Insurgencies*, 24.
63. Ibid., 321.
64. Hawthorne, *Tales*, 239.
65. Ibid., 240.
66. Ibid., 241.
67. Ibid., 242.
68. Ibid.
69. Ibid.
70. Ibid., 243.
71. Ibid., 241.
72. Kant, *Political Writings*, 145.
73. Ibid., 118.
74. Robert Clewis, in *The Kantian Sublime and the Revelation of Freedom* (2009), lays out a clear and detailed version of this argument in relation to Kant's philosophy as a whole.
75. Kant, *Political Writings*, 146.

76. Ibid., 188.
77. Kant, *Conflict of Faculties*, 167.
78. Kant, *Gesammelte Schriften*, 7:92.
79. Kant, *Political Writings*, 188.
80. Kant, *Observations on the Feeling*, 28; *Gesammelte Schriften*, 2:221–22.
81. Kant, *Observations on the Feeling*, 57; *Gesammelte Schriften*, 2:251.
82. Kant, *Critique of the Power*, 154.
83. Kant, *Gesammelte Schriften*, 5:275.
84. Kant, *Critique of the Power*, 156–57, 154, 157.
85. Kant, *Political Writings*, 182.
86. Kant, *Gesammelte Schriften*, 7:85.
87. Burke, *Reflections*, 276.
88. Ibid., 94, 97, 157. Burke is of course referencing Price's 1789 sermon *A Discourse on the Love of Our Country*, which sparked the Revolution Controversy.
89. Ibid., 283–84.
90. Ibid., 165.
91. Pocock, "Enthusiasm," 9.
92. Beiser, *Sovereignty of Reason*, 188. In the most foundational philosophical text on enthusiasm, Plato's *Ion*, Socrates expresses skepticism about the aesthetic/religious performance of the professional rhapsode and inspired enthusiast, Ion. While he does not question the reality of divine (enthusiastic) possession, Plato makes Ion into an implicitly useless con man.
93. Lewis, *Ecstatic Religion*, 91.
94. Paine, *Collected*, 461.
95. Ibid., 467.
96. Ibid., 467–68.
97. Negri, *Insurgencies*, 3.
98. Paine, *Collected*, 513, 510.
99. Ibid., 452–53, 513.
100. Ibid., 454.
101. Wheelwright, "Fast-Day Sermon," 165, 161. See page 166 on the Matthew reference.
102. Miller, *Errand*, 5.
103. Ibid., 21.
104. Winthrop, "Short Story," 218.
105. Bercovitch, *Puritan Origins*, 93.
106. Cotton, "Sixteene Questions," 58.
107. Wheelwright, "Fast-Day Sermon," 162, 164.
108. Lang, *Prophetic Woman*, 7.
109. Winthrop, "Short Story," 230.
110. Wheelright, "Fast-Day Sermon," 165.
111. Winthrop, "Short Story," 253.
112. "Examination of Mrs. Ann Hutchinson," 343.
113. Winthrop, "Short Story," 230.
114. Ibid., 234.

115. Ibid., 205, 204.
116. Ibid., 213.
117. Ibid., 262.
118. "Examination of Mrs. Ann Hutchinson," 372.
119. Ibid., 342.
120. Ibid., 316.
121. Winthrop, "*Short Story*," 294.
122. In an unflattering critique of women in the literary marketplace, Hawthorne's early sketch "Mrs. Hutchinson" (1830) notoriously links Hutchinson's heresy to sentimental novelists and the women's movement of his own day. See Hawthorne, *Tales*, 18–24.
123. Bercovitch, *Rites of Assent*, 215.
124. Hawthorne, *Scarlet Letter*, 37.
125. Ibid., 76.
126. Ibid., 108, emphasis mine.
127. Ibid., 107.
128. O. Smith, *Romantic Women Writers*, 41–46.
129. Hawthorne, *Scarlet Letter*, 42.
130. Ibid., 61.
131. Ibid., 62.
132. Ibid., 63, 65, 89, 69, 89.
133. Ibid., 90.
134. Ibid., 129.
135. See Guelzo, "Literature of the Colonial Revivals of Religion."
136. A. Taylor, *American Colonies*, 339.
137. Ibid., 302–37, 422–24; Hoffer, *Cry Liberty*, 68, 119; Lepore, *New York Burning*, xviii, 53–55.
138. "Wonderful Wandering Spirit," 150.
139. Ibid., 147–48.
140. Ibid., 150–51.
141. Stiles, "Looking-Glass," 311.
142. Ibid.
143. Ibid., 315.
144. Brockwell, "Every Idle Untruth," 65.
145. Chauncy, "Heat and Fervour," 75.
146. Chauncy, "Seasonable Thoughts," 297.
147. Chauncy, "Enthusiasm Described," 231.
148. Chauncy, "Seasonable Thoughts," 302–3.
149. Chauncy, "Enthusiasm Described," 243.
150. Hawthorne, *Tales*, 84–85.
151. Ibid., 68.
152. Ibid., 86, 84.
153. Ibid., 84.
154. See Juster, *Disorderly Women*.
155. See O. Smith, *Romantic Women Writers*.

156. As Nina Baym explained decades ago, women's fiction, devoted to "the formation and assertion of a feminine ego," flourished from 1820 to 1870, in opposition to the antecedent culture—and literature—of sensibility and its promotion of passive womanhood enthralled to a male-dominated social order (12). The sentimental complex or habitus, far from reducible to a conservative model of feeling, deserves to be seen as a progressive offshoot of the culture of sensibility, a "gendering of sensibility" whereby women were able to draw upon the moral capital of the reformation of manners in order to push for equal rights and critique men's activities in the marketplace (Barker-Benfield, xvii). As a "reform literature" prescribing rules for how to "feel right" (Samuels, 5), sentimental expression, which many scholars have emphasized should also include men's literary culture (see Burgett, Chapman, Hendler), can be viewed as radical sensibility: it very often pushes reform politics and public sentiment to its limit by demanding a consistent moral doctrine of equality, especially when claimed by minority voices. As Julie Ellison puts it, "Slavery, revolution, and economic stratification became matters of public dispute through sentimental politics—that is, through the claim to suffering" (122). Nevertheless, without dismissing its many virtues, sentimental reform de rigueur mostly belongs to the regulatory process of bourgeois society, what Lori Merish dubs "sentimental materialism" "suited to a liberal-capitalist social order that privileged individual autonomy and, especially, private property ownership" (3), with all of the attendant problems that follow from this along race and class lines (see Samuels, *Culture of Sentiment*, for a wide range of classic articles that characterize the multivalent uses of sentimentality as discussed above). In Amy Kaplan's terms, domestic sentimentality was part and parcel of a "domestic empire" that the United States wished to extend intranationally and internationally—"a mobile and mobilizing outpost that transformed conquered foreign lands into the domestic sphere of the family and nation" (34, 25). If sentimental politics was, as Nina Baym observes, an agent of "social peace and civic stability" (xxviii), it also militated against any model of politics inviting "active antagonism, which threatens the *sense* in consensus" (Berlant, *Female Complaint*, 11). Most often, this antagonism—against domestic empire—designates precisely enthusiasm.

157. Coleridge, *Literary Remains*, 367.
158. Davidson, *Revolution and the Word*, 7, 72, 104.
159. Barnes, *States of Sympathy*, 2, 8.
160. For more on Pogson, see Kritzer, Introduction, 18–20; Ford, "Liberty Contained"; and Detsi-Diamanti, "Sarah Pogson's *The Female Enthusiast*."
161. Pogson, "*Female Enthusiast*," 147.
162. Ibid., 154, 167, 157.
163. Ibid., 163.
164. Ibid., 181.
165. "Art. XXVII," 451.
166. There is a long bibliography on Brown and gender, sex, and feminism. Without providing a list, I would simply refer the reader to Barnard, Kamrath, and Shapiro, *Revising Charles Brockden Brown*, 118–215, which includes influential

voices and relevant citations on the subject. On *Ormond*, also see Layson, "Rape and Revolution"; and Comment, "Charles Brockden Brown's *Ormond*."

167. Brown, *Ormond*, 116.

168. I'm thinking in particular of Stern, *Plight of Feeling*; and P. Lewis, "Attaining Masculinity."

169. Barnard and Shapiro, Introduction, xxx.

170. For example, the mother of the narrator, Sophia Courtland, after leading a profligate and prurient life, converts to Methodism and bewails her sins, but her adopted religious enthusiasm still sanctions the same antisocial egoism and lack of "restraint and moderation" that characterized her former state of dissipation. Her affected enthusiasm is evidence of a degenerative condition: "Her thought became, by rapid degrees, tempestuous and gloomy, and it was at length evident, that her condition was maniacal" (174). Here we meet in miniature *Ormond*'s version of the elder and younger Wieland in Brown's first and more famous novel, *Wieland; or The Transformation* (1798), just as the titular and demagogic patriarch, Ormond, who has the power of ventriloquism, recalls Carwin the biloquist. The common denominator of egregious enthusiasm in both novels is an antisocial, unmoored, self-indulgent "studious leisure, and romantic solitude" (*Wieland*, 310). To Brown, the willful individualism of the enthusiast translates into a solipsistic fanaticism of fancy but especially a vulnerability to the power of suggestion as well as the auto-suggestion of unbridled power.

171. Brown, *Ormond*, 153.

172. Ibid., 154.

173. Ibid.

174. On the "woman warrior" trope of the 1790s as connected to *Ormond*, see Gustafson, "Genders of Nationalism"; and P. Lewis, "Attaining Masculinity."

175. Brown, *Ormond*, 158.

176. Ibid., 164.

177. See Comment, "Charles Brockden Brown's *Ormond*," and Layson, "Rape and Revolution," on lesbianism in the novel.

178. Waterman, *Republic of Intellect*, 96. See Waterman for more on Brown's connections to Godwin and Wollstonecraft, and on the ways that the Friendly Club's "Enlightenment ideals of unregulated conversation and scientific progress came under attack by Anglo-American conservatives" (53).

179. Howe, *Birth-mark*, 149.

180. Dickinson, "1044," lines 1–4, 9–12, *Poems*.

Chapter Two

1. For a synthesis of criticism on the Revolution, see Gould, "Virtue, Ideology, and the American Revolution," and Young, Introduction.

2. Bercovitch, *Puritan Origins*, 89.

3. Bercovitch, *Rites of Assent*, 38.

4. Ibid., 30; *Puritan Origins*, 136.

5. Bercovitch, *American Jeremiad*, xliii; *Rites of Assent*, 53.

6. "Anglicization" is a coinage—and thesis—of John M. Murrin taken up by many other scholars. See, especially, the recent collection of essays, *Anglicizing America*, edited by Gallup-Diaz et al.; and Larkin, "Nation and Empire in Early US." On post-Revolutionary society and culture, see Tamarkin, *Anglophilia*.

7. Murrin, "England and Colonial America," 17.

8. See Linebaugh and Rediker, *Many-Headed Hydra*; Bouton, *Taming Democracy*; Nash, *Unknown American Revolution*; and Frank, *Constituent Moments*.

9. Quoted in Nash, "Social Change," 29. These are the words of Sir Francis Bernard, 1st Baronet, Governor of Massachusetts Bay from 1760 to 1769.

10. Twomey, "Jacobins and Jeffersonians," 314.

11. See Gustafson, *Imagining Deliberative Democracy*, 86–96. For a concise version of the argument for—and scholarship on—the centrality of oratory, as opposed to print, in the early American public sphere, see Gustafson, "American Literature and the Public Sphere."

12. For a wonderful summary and assessment of this scholarship, see Wood, "Religion and the American Revolution." I am thinking, in particular, of Bonomi, *Under the Cope of Heaven*; Clark, *Language of Liberty*; and Marini, *Radical Sects*.

13. Stauffer, "Foreword," xiv.

14. See Frank, "'Besides Our Selves.'"

15. Wood, "Disturbing the Peace," 20.

16. Kammen, *Season of Youth*, 41.

17. Stansbury, "Epigram," 6.

18. Querno, "American Times," 12; Odell, "Word of Congress," 48; Querno, "American Times," 2.

19. J. F. D. Smith, "Verses Written in Captivity," 107.

20. Leacock, "Fall of British Tyranny," 301; Brackenridge, "Battle of Bunkers-Hill," 265.

21. Trumbull, "M'Fingal," 3:45, 3:130, 3:144, 3:146, 3:210, 3:145, 3:46, *Satiric Poems*. These citations follow the arrangement Canto: Line Number.

22. Burke, "*To* Charles O'Hara," 232.

23. Oliver, "From *The Origin & Progress*," 52.

24. May, *Enlightenment in America*, 154.

25. Bloch, *Visionary Republic*, 53.

26. Burke, *Speech of Edmund Burke*, 17.

27. Ibid., 18.

28. Boucher, *View of the Causes*, 77.

29. Ibid., 60, 79.

30. Ibid., 79–80.

31. Ibid., 79.

32. Ibid., 81.

33. Hoerder, "Boston Leaders," 240.

34. Kornblith and Murrin, "Making and Unmaking," 43.

35. Gilman, *Theatrum Majorum*, 53.

36. See Wood, *Radicalism*, 90, 110–21.

37. Rosswurm, "'As a Lyen out of His Den,'" 279.

38. Pocock, "Radical Criticisms," 46.

39. Young, "English Plebian Culture," 200, 196. See Young's chapter, "Tar and Feathers and the Ghost of Oliver Cromwell: English Plebeian Culture and American Radicalism," in *Liberty Tree*, for a concise summary of the historical reception of Cromwell in Early America and the Revolutionary era.

40. Peters and McCormick, *General History of Connecticut*, 232.

41. Carla Mulford suggests the name might have "indicated a woman who ran a house of prostitution," satirizing the affair of John Hancock with Dorcas Griffiths (27).

42. Leacock, *First Book*, 70.

43. "Gouvernor Morris to Penn," 862.

44. Isaac, "Preachers and Patriots," 150.

45. Ruttenburg, *Democratic Personality*, 151, 194.

46. Quoted in Silverman, *A Cultural History*, 113.

47. Linebaugh and Rediker, *Many-Headed Hydra*, 234.

48. Middlekauff, *Glorious Cause*, 176.

49. Nash, "Social Change," 24.

50. Middlekauff, *Glorious Cause*, 177.

51. According to Benjamin Franklin V, there is "evidence in Warren's manuscripts that she composed most but not all of the 1773 text," although we don't know exactly what new material she authored; the old material constitutes "IV. ii, V.i, and V.ii–iii, exclusive of the last ten lines" (Introduction, viii). Some new scenes were "interlaced," as Warren put it, with her original ones (which already alluded to the Massacre); that the plagiarist was never discovered and Warren "took little interest in the subject" is, at least in part, a testimony to the collaborative and often anonymous project of seditious republican print (quoted in Anthony, *First Lady*, 83–84). See Sarkela, "Freedom's Call," for a reading of Warren's dramatic sketches in the context of their newspaper publication.

52. Shaffer, "Making 'an Excellent Die,'" 7. This quotation is specific to the article, but see Shaffer's *Performing Patriotism* for a detailed analysis of theater's relationship to Revolutionary American identity.

53. On Warren's belief in *theatrum mundi*, see J. Richards, *Theater Enough*, 224–26, 258–60, 287–91.

54. Weales, "*The Adulateur* and How It Grew," 106.

55. M. Warren, *Plays and Poems*, 3.

56. J. Richards, *Theater Enough*, 200.

57. Bailyn, *Ideological Origins*, 44.

58. J. Richards, *Theater Enough*, 184.

59. Ibid., 123.

60. Washington and Mifflin, "Speeches in the Continental Congress," 794.

61. M. Warren, *Plays and Poems*, 5.

62. Ibid., 6.

63. Ibid., 8.

64. Ibid., 12–13.

65. Ibid., 13.

66. Ibid., 15.
67. Ibid., 19.
68. Ibid., 20, 30.
69. J. Warren, *An Oration*, 756.
70. Gustafson, *Eloquence is Power*, 189, 164.
71. Hancock, *Oration*, 9.
72. Ibid., 19.
73. Ibid., 20.
74. Ibid., 11.
75. M. Warren, *Plays and Poems*, 23, 21.
76. Ibid., 15, 7.
77. Ibid., 15, 18, 14.
78. Ibid., 11–12.
79. Ibid., 12.
80. Gustafson, *Eloquence is Power*, 186.
81. Hoerder, "Boston Leaders," 265.
82. M. Warren, *Plays and Poems*, 22.
83. Ibid., 32.
84. Silverman, *A Cultural History*, 296.
85. See Keane, *Tom Paine*, 95–96; and Foner, *Tom Paine*, 72–73.
86. For another reading of the *Pennsylvania Magazine*, see Larkin, *Thomas Paine*. Larkin argues that Paine used the *Pennsylvania Magazine* to open up the public sphere to a wider, less elite audience and to redefine Americanness as "a matter of acting and thinking in specific ways, and by extension participation in the revolution also became a matter of everyday life" (45). Larkin, however, limits his analysis to the print sphere and emphasizes Paine's literary inventiveness. I am emphasizing, instead, the role that live enthusiastic publics play in the ethos of Paine's periodical work.
87. "*Publisher*'s Preface," 4.
88. Ibid., 3, 4.
89. Ibid., 4.
90. Ibid., 3.
91. Inglis, *True Interest of America*, vi, 21, 48.
92. Maier, *From Resistance to Revolution*, 244–45.
93. Throughout my discussion of the *Pennsylvania Magazine* and Paine, I am basing my attributions of authorship on Keane, *Tom Paine* (see 94–104).
94. "To the Publisher of the Pennsylvania Magazine," 10.
95. Ibid., 12.
96. Ibid., 10.
97. Aiken, "Miscellaneous Pieces in Prose," 328.
98. "On the Late Continental Fast," 309.
99. Middlekauff, *Glorious Cause*, 239.
100. Heimert, *Religion and the American Mind*, 404.
101. "On the Late Continental Fast," 310.
102. Ibid.

103. Lover of Peace, "Thoughts on Defensive War," 313. Note that Paine is the assumed author of this article.

104. Ibid., 314.

105. Ibid.

106. Heimert, *Religion and the American Mind*, 149–51, 411.

107. Atlanticus, "Liberty Tree," 328.

108. Ibid., 329.

109. Ibid., 329.

110. "Monthly Intelligence: London," 336.

111. Foner, "Tom Paine's Republic," 205.

112. Adams, *Portable*, 236.

113. W. Smith, "15 Novr 1776," 44.

114. Griffitts, "Upon Reading a Book," lines 6–9.

115. "Dialogue on Civil Liberty," 157–58.

116. Ibid., 159.

117. Ibid., 162, 159.

118. Ibid., 167.

119. Wheatley, "Elegiac Poem," line 2, 22, 27, *Complete Writings*. All subsequent citations of Wheatley's poetry from *Complete Writings* refer to the line number(s).

120. Ibid., 15–17.

121. Willis, "Phillis Wheatley," 166.

122. Carretta, Introduction, xxxiii.

123. The leading Wheatley scholar, John C. Shields, in his illuminating article, "Phillis Wheatley's Theoretics of the Imagination" (2011), argues that Wheatley's vision of the poetic imagination as the highest, self-authorizing faculty, "serving as the poet's reason," should be appreciated as a "revolutionary moment in the evolution of literary aesthetics," and this innovative perspective derives from the positive theories of enthusiasm preached by her influences and mentors, including Samuel Cooper, William Billings, Joseph Seccombe, and Mather Byles (367). This is another way of arguing that Wheatley was in the vanguard of enthusiastic culture and literature.

124. This is the thrust of nearly all the articles in Shields, *New Essays*. See also Erkkila, "Phillis Wheatley"; Aker, "'Our Modern Egyptians'"; O'Neale, "Slave's Subtle War"; P. Richards, "Phillis Wheatley"; Bennett, "Phillis Wheatley's Vocation"; Waldstreicher, "The Wheatleyan Moment"; J. Brooks, "Our Phillis, Ourselves."

125. See Lovejoy, *Religious Enthusiasm*, 206.

126. "Testimony of Harvard College," 341.

127. Connecticut Assembly, "Be It Enacted," 69.

128. Ruttenburg, *Democratic Personality*, 85; J. Richards, *Theater Enough*, 198.

129. See H. Wheatley, *London*, 561–62; Cruickshank, *London's Sinful Secret*, 62, 142.

130. See Gustafson, *Eloquence is Power*, 180–85.

131. Wheatley, "Elegiac Poem," 3–4, *Complete Writings*.

132. Ibid., 5–6.
133. Ibid., 18–22.
134. Whitaker, *Funeral Sermon*, 33–34. Whitaker himself intervenes on the debate over enthusiasm in this sermon.
135. Wheatley, "Elegiac Poem," 8, 28; "On the Death of the Rev. Mr. George Whitefield," 26, *Complete Writings*.
136. Wheatley, "Elegiac Poem," 39–44, *Complete Writings*.
137. Ibid., 14, 27.
138. Willard, "Wheatley's Turn of Praise," 243, 239.
139. Ruttenburg, *Democratic Personality*, 20.
140. Wheatley, "General Washington," 5, *Complete Writings*.
141. Wheatley, *Complete Writings*, 88.
142. Wheatley, "General Washington," 1–2, *Complete Writings*.
143. Wheatley, "On Imagination," 40; "General Washington," 4, *Complete Writings*.
144. Wheatley, "General Washington," 6, 3, *Complete Writings*.
145. Ibid., 33–34.
146. "Monthly Intelligence: New-England," 195.
147. Wood, *Empire of Liberty*, 197
148. Bouton, *Taming Democracy*, 4.
149. Boucher, *View of the Causes*, no page.
150. Bouton, *Taming Democracy*, 219–20.
151. Warren, *Observations on the New Constitution*, 3.
152. Ibid., 5, 7–8, 6.
153. Ibid., 22.
154. Warren, *Plays and Poems*, 246.
155. Ibid., v.
156. Quoted in Stuart, *Muse of the Revolution*, 232.
157. Quoted in ibid., 224.
158. Linebaugh, Introduction, vii.
159. Paine, *Letter to George Washington*, 42, 7.
160. Ibid., 30.
161. Ibid., 24, 28.
162. Ibid., 2.
163. Ibid., 42.
164. Wheatley, *Complete Writings*, 153.
165. Jefferson, "From *Notes on the State of Virginia*," 81.
166. Kammen, *Season of Youth*, 39.

Chapter Three

1. Hampson, "War of 1812 bicentennial."
2. Wood, *Empire of Liberty*, 643.
3. The Prophet's given name was Lalawethika; Tenskwatawa is his prophetic name, meaning the Open Door.

4. Dowd, *Spirited Resistance*, 129.

5. Wood, *Empire of Liberty*, 675.

6. A. Taylor, *Civil War of 1812*, 428.

7. Letter, "Reincarnating Samuel Woodworth," 691.

8. Calloway, *American Revolution in Indian Country*, 23.

9. Carr, *Inventing the American Primitive*, 52, 53.

10. Sollors, *Beyond Ethnicity*, 124.

11. See Deloria, *Playing Indian*.

12. Konkle, *Writing Indian Nations*, 39.

13. Sayre, *The Indian Chief as Tragic Hero*, 33.

14. White, *Middle Ground*, 519.

15. Calloway, *The Shawnees*, 74.

16. Bird, *Nick of the Woods*, 141.

17. Works that have influenced my perspective include Womack, *Red on Red*; Warrior, *Tribal Secrets*; Weaver, *That the People Might Live*; Konkle, *Writing Indian Nations*; and Bellin, "Red Routes: William Apess and Nativist Prophecy."

18. S. Warren, *Worlds the Shawnees Made*, 21. In addition to Warren, see Lakomäki, *Gathering Together*.

19. Lakomäki, *Gathering Together*, 144.

20. Rifkin, *Manifesting America*, 18.

21. Womack, *Red on Red*, 43.

22. Other relevant literary works not discussed here include George Longmore's *Tecumthe* (1824); Richard Emmons's *The Fredoniad* (1827) and *Tecumseh* (1836); John Richardson's *Tecumseh* (1828) and *The Canadian Brothers* (1840); George Colton's *Tecumseh* (1842); and George Jones's *Tecumseh and the Prophet of the West* (1844).

23. Howard, *Shawnee!*, 127.

24. Quoted in Calloway, *Shawnees*, 77.

25. On the "performance of consent" behind the Treaty of Greenville, see Cayton, "'Noble Actors' upon 'the Theatre of Honour.'"

26. Aupaumut, "*Narrative of an Embassy*," 121.

27. L. Brooks, *Common Pot*, 3. On the Northwestern confederation and "the Dish with One Spoon," see pages 121–27.

28. Howard, *Shawnee!*, 41–42.

29. Calloway, *Shawnees*, 130–31.

30. Tanner, *Falcon*, 146.

31. Ibid., 147.

32. Edmunds, *Shawnee Prophet*, 54.

33. Quoted in Sugden, "Early Pan-Indianism," 287.

34. Cave, *Prophets of the Great Spirit*, 165.

35. The Prophet's "sacred slabs" or sticks represented the universe of deities according to Shawnee theology—from top to bottom, Heaven, Thunderers or Gate Keepers of Heaven, Blue Sky, Sun, All Plant Life, an unknown symbol, Fowls and Animals of Earth and Air, Corn, Four Corners of the Earth, Trees, Lightning, Water, Earth, and Family (Howard, *Shawnee!*, 205–7).

36. Sugden, *Tecumseh*, 147.
37. Cave, *Prophets*, 5.
38. Wilson, *Earth Shall Weep*, 70.
39. Andrews, "Shaker Mission to the Shawnee Indians," 120. This article is a publication of the Shaker journal.
40. Ibid., 126.
41. Klinck, *Tecumseh*, 19.
42. Wood, *Empire of Liberty*, 582.
43. Ibid., 582, 600.
44. D. Jones, *Journal of Two Visits*, 54.
45. Drake, *Life of Tecumseh*, 91–92.
46. Cappon, *Adams-Jefferson Letters*, 299.
47. Edmunds, "Tecumseh, The Shawnee Prophet," 275; *Tecumseh and the Quest*, 84.
48. See Sugden, *Tecumseh*, 9–10, 127–28, 187–89.
49. Sugden, "Early Pan-Indianism," 273.
50. Quoted in Dowd, "Thinking and Believing," 327, emphasis original.
51. Cushman, *History of the Choctaw*, 248.
52. Ibid.
53. Ibid., 250.
54. Ibid.
55. Klinck, *Tecumseh*, 95–96.
56. Ibid., 52.
57. Ibid., 48.
58. See Cave, *Prophets*, 125–28; and Calloway, *Shawnees*, 144.
59. Drake, *Life of Tecumseh*, 152.
60. Ibid., 155–56.
61. Ibid., 222–23.
62. Ibid., 224.
63. Ibid., 234, emphasis mine.
64. For an introduction to James Strange French, see Curtis C. Davis's "Virginia's Unknown Novelist."
65. French, *Elkswatawa*, 1:v–vi.
66. Ibid., 1:v.
67. Ibid., 1:14, 18.
68. Ibid., 1:19, 22.
69. Ibid., 1:71–72.
70. Ibid., 1:199.
71. Ibid., 1:199–200.
72. Ibid., 1:201.
73. Ibid., 1:203.
74. Ibid., 2:205.
75. Ibid., 1:212, 215, 210.
76. Ibid., 1:242.
77. Ibid., 2:9.

78. Ibid., 1:210.
79. Ibid., 2:229–30.
80. Howard, *Shawnee!*, 37.
81. Woodworth, *Champions of Freedom*, 1:2, 3.
82. Ibid., 1:9.
83. Ibid., 1:28.
84. Ibid., 2:49, 1:49.
85. Ibid., 2:23–24.
86. Ibid., 1:143.
87. Ibid., 1:156–57.
88. Ibid., 1:161.
89. Ibid., 2:336.
90. Bergland, *National Uncanny*, 58. For another reading of *Champions of Freedom*, see Letter, "Reincarnating Samuel Woodworth."
91. Ibid., 59.
92. I am aware of only one engagement with the *Lost Virgin*, Philip D. Beidler's chapter, "'The First Production of the Kind, in the South': A Backwoods Literary *Incognito* and His Attempt at the Great American Novel," in *First Books*. Beidler provides a concise historical and literary introduction to *Lost Virgin* in order to show the "cultural work" that fiction of the Old Southwest performed in early America. Among other things, Beidler argues that the novel, as a strange hybrid genre, a "historical-gothic-sentimental-picaresque novel-romance," is an exercise in trying "to write a new literature apace with the rise of a new culture" so as "to beggar the possibilities of early American genre" (33).
93. Casender, *Lost Virgin of the South*, 1:52.
94. Sugden, "Early Pan-Indianism," 299. Also see Calloway, *Shawnees*, 152.
95. Casender, *Lost Virgin of the South*, 2:116.
96. Ibid., 1:18.
97. Ibid., 1:19.
98. Ibid., 1:105.
99. Ibid.
100. A. Taylor, *Civil War of 1812*, 435.
101. Casender, *Lost Virgin of the South*, 1:62.
102. Ibid., 2:32.
103. Ibid., 1:89–90, emphasis mine.
104. Ibid., 2:125–26.
105. Ibid., 1:46.
106. Ibid., 1:47.
107. Gustafson, "Nations of Israelites," 35.
108. Bellin, "Red Routes," 48, 55.
109. Peyer, *Tutor'd Mind*, 16–17.
110. See Bellin, *Demon of the Continent*, 71–97; Donaldson, "Making a Joyful Noise"; Gustafson, "Nations of Israelites"; Haynes, "'A Mark for Them All to ... Hiss at'"; and Tiro, "Denominated 'SAVAGE.'"
111. Apess, *On Our Own Ground*, 4.

112. Ibid., 11, 16.
113. Ibid., 18–19.
114. Ibid., 19.
115. Ibid., 22.
116. Ibid., 25.
117. Ibid., 26.
118. Ibid., 30.
119. Ibid., 31.
120. Ibid., 30.
121. Ibid., 31.
122. L. Brooks, *Common Pot*, 175.
123. Apess, *On Our Own Ground*, 34.
124. Ibid., 111.
125. Ibid., 41.
126. Ibid., 51, 19.
127. Ibid., 106.
128. Ibid., 104, 109, 107.
129. Ibid., 52.
130. Ibid., 73.
131. Ibid., 94–96.
132. Gustafson, "Nations of Israelites," 33.
133. Apess, *On Our Own Ground*, 227.
134. Ibid., 204.
135. Ibid., 307.
136. Ibid., 286.
137. Ibid., 304, 279, 277.

Chapter Four

1. Higginson, *Black Rebellion*, 186.
2. *Strange Enthusiasm* is the title of Tilden G. Edelstein's biography of Higginson. As Edelstein explains, Daniel Webster used the phrase in his aspersions against the brand of "dogmatic" abolitionism represented by Higginson (2).
3. McPherson, *Battle Cry of Freedom*, 119–20, 204.
4. Higginson, *Black Rebellion*, 120.
5. Ibid., 127–28.
6. Ibid., 166.
7. Ibid., 188–89.
8. Quoted in Walker, *Noble Fight*, 99.
9. Higginson, *Black Rebellion*, 230–31.
10. Ibid., 284, 322.
11. On anti-Freemasonry in American history, see David B. Davis, *Fear of Conspiracy*.
12. Walker, *Noble Fight*, 54.
13. Quoted in Buck-Morss, *Hegel, Haiti*, 65.

14. Quoted in Walker, *Noble Fight*, 194.
15. Ibid., 3.
16. Ibid., 48.
17. T. Smith, *Conjuring Culture*, 4.
18. Ibid., 147.
19. Klein, "Sociability, Solitude, and Enthusiasm," 160–61.
20. Baker, *Workings of the Spirit*, 69.
21. Ibid., 74.
22. Jaudon, "Obeah's Sensations," 717–18. For recent readings of obeah and a great summary of scholarship on the practice, see the special issue "Obeah: Knowledge, Power, and Writing in the Early Atlantic World," in *Atlantic Studies: Global Currents* 12.2 (2015), edited by Wisecup and Jaudon; and *Obeah and Other Powers: The Politics of Caribbean Religion and Healing* (2012), edited by Forde and Paton.
23. Ibid., 729.
24. Ibid., 733.
25. Doyle, *Freedom's Empire*, 5.
26. Sundquist, *To Wake the Nations*, 29–30.
27. Raboteau, *Slave Religion*, 11.
28. Chireau, *Black Magic*, 38.
29. Raboteau, *Slave Religion*, 15.
30. Du Bois, *Souls of Black Folk*, 155.
31. Quoted in Raboteau, *Slave Religion*, 65.
32. Du Bois, *Souls of Black Folk*, 161.
33. L. Levine, *Black Culture and Black Consciousness*, 42.
34. Moorish, *Obeah, Christ, and Rastaman*, 40.
35. Ibid., 41.
36. Moseley, "*Treatise on Sugar*," 165.
37. Quoted in Williams, *Voodoos and Obeahs*, 164.
38. Quoted in ibid., 177.
39. "*House of Commons Sessional Papers*," 173, 177.
40. Rucker, *River Flows On*, 111–13.
41. Ibid., 181.
42. L. Levine, *Black Culture*, 70, 80.
43. Ibid., 27.
44. "Account of the Negroe Insurrection," 14–15.
45. L. Levine, *Black Culture*, 25, 33, 40, 6.
46. Frederick Olmsted, quoted in L. Levine, *Black Culture*, 43. One could also understand this in Paul Gilroy's terms as the "continuity of art and life" in slave culture, a culture that did not divorce "aesthetic performance" and "struggles toward emancipation" (*Black Atlantic*, 57).
47. Quoted in Epstein, *Sinful Tunes and Spirituals*, 196.
48. Chireau, *Black Magic*, 12.
49. Raboteau, *Slave Religion*, 72.
50. Chireau, *Black Magic*, 68.
51. J. Brooks, *American Lazarus*, 24.

52. Hickman, "Globalization and the Gods," 156–57.

53. Ibid., 162.

54. Katharine Gerbner, quoted in Wisecup and Jaudon, "On Knowing," 132; Forde and Paton, Introduction, 5.

55. See Kilgore, "Nat Turner and the Work of Enthusiasm."

56. According to Raboteau, "Religion played a significant role in the early [Haitian] slave revolts led by Macandal and Biassou. Under one rebel leader, Hyacinthe, fifteen thousand slaves went into battle, supported by the belief that their chief had the power to render bullets harmless and confident that if they died on the field they would return to Africa. The revolt led by Boukman in 1791 was inaugurated by an awesome religious ceremony concluded by a blood pact. Though it would be wrong to view the Haitian War of Independence as a religious war, Sidney Mintz is right in stating that '*vaudou* surely played a critical role in the creation of a viable armed resistance by the slaves against the master classes'" (*Slave Religion*, 26).

57. Genovese, *From Rebellion to Revolution*, 94.

58. For more on the influence of the Haitian Revolution in the U.S. and Atlantic world, see Geggus, *Impact of the Haitian Revolution*.

59. Higginson, *Black Rebellion*, 197.

60. Quoted in Franklin, *Militant South*, 76.

61. A. Richardson, "Romantic Voodoo," 178.

62. Ibid.

63. Quoted in Reed, *Rogue Performances*, 103. The bracketed insertion is his.

64. See O'Rourke, "Revision of *Obi*," 286.

65. Aravamudan, Introduction, 42.

66. Earle, *Obi*, 69.

67. Ibid., 70, 68, 112.

68. "The Richmond Enquirer, Richmond, Virginia, 30 August 1831," in Tragle, *Southampton Slave Revolt*, 45.

69. Stowe, *Dred*, 273.

70. Hawthorne, *Scarlet Letter*, 29.

71. Turner, *Confessions*, 44–45.

72. Stowe, *Dred*, 446; Turner, *Confessions*, 44–45.

73. Melville, *Moby-Dick*, 54.

74. Freud, *Writings on Art and Literature*, 195–200.

75. Wald, *Constituting Americans*, 10.

76. Derrida, *Taste for the Secret*, 13.

77. Ibid., 59.

78. Scott, *Domination and the Arts of Resistance*, 4, 191, 20. For more on hidden and public transcripts, see Scott, *Domination and the Arts of Resistance*, 4–19. By "infrapolitics," Scott means "a wide variety of low-profile forms of resistance that dare not speak in their own name" (19). By "zones of refuge," or "shatter zones," Scott means "wherever the expansion of states, empires, slave-trading, and wars, as well as natural disasters, have driven large numbers of people to seek refuge in out-of-the-way places" (*Art of Not Being Governed*, 8).

79. Roach, *Cities of the Dead*, 5, 189.
80. Lukács, *Theory of the Novel*, 41, 90.
81. Ibid., 116, 117.
82. Bakhtin, *Dialogic Imagination*, 7, 11.
83. Ibid., 30.
84. Ibid., 273.
85. Bakhtin, *Rabelais and His World*, 6–7.
86. Ibid., 7.
87. Gilroy, *Black Atlantic*, 68.
88. Bakhtin, *Dialogic Imagination*, 14, 32.
89. Wish, "Slave Insurrection Panic of 1856," 206.
90. R. Levine, Introduction, ix.
91. Ibid., xvii.
92. Stowe, *Uncle Tom's Cabin*, 361.
93. Ibid., 408.
94. Ibid.
95. Stowe, *Dred*, 3.
96. Schoolman, "White Flight," 262, 269. For a fleshed-out version of Schoolman's reading of Stowe, see *Abolitionist Geographies*.
97. Karafilis, "Spaces of Democracy," 27.
98. Ibid., 40.
99. See chapter 4 of Murison, *Politics of Anxiety*; and chapter 5 of C. Smith, *Oracle and the Curse*.
100. Stowe, *A Key to Uncle Tom's Cabin*, 27.
101. Ibid., 28.
102. Stowe, *Dred*, 198.
103. Ibid., 200.
104. Ibid.
105. Ibid., 273–74.
106. Chireau, *Black Magic*, 38.
107. Stowe, *Dred*, 274–75.
108. Ibid., 274.
109. Ibid., 208.
110. Ibid., 209.
111. Ibid., 209–10.
112. Ibid., 245, 254–55.
113. Ibid., 245.
114. Ibid., 251.
115. Ibid., 258.
116. Ibid., 209.
117. Ibid., 208.
118. Ibid., 496.
119. Ibid., 250.
120. Ibid., 267.
121. Ibid., 239.

122. Ibid., 205, 211.
123. T. Smith, *Conjuring Culture*, 6.
124. Stowe, *Dred*, 210.
125. Ibid., 446.
126. Ibid., 446, 211.
127. Ibid., 451, 435.
128. Ibid., 496, 516.
129. Ibid., 328.
130. Ibid., 316.
131. Ibid.
132. Ibid., 534–35.
133. Ibid., 535.
134. Ibid., 544.
135. Ibid., 341.
136. Bell, *Afro-American Novel*, 51.
137. Doolen, "'Be Cautious of the Word "Rebel",'" 158–59.
138. Hsu, *Geography and the Production of Space*, 14.
139. Bhabha, *Location of Culture*, 55–56, 244, 199.
140. Gilroy, *Black Atlantic*, 25–26.
141. Walker, *Noble Fight*, 114.
142. Bullock, *Revolutionary Brotherhood*, 178, 260–72.
143. Walker, *Noble Fight*, 48.
144. R. Levine, *Martin Delany*, 185–86.
145. Quoted in Chireau, *Black Magic*, 25.
146. T. Smith, *Conjuring Culture*, 32.
147. Delany, *Documentary Reader*, 64.
148. Delany, *Blake*, 43.
149. Ibid., 69.
150. Ibid., 39.
151. R. Levine, *Martin Delany*, 195.
152. Delany, *Blake*, 44.
153. Ibid., 112.
154. Ibid., 113.
155. Ibid., 112–13.
156. Ibid., 113.
157. Ibid., 114.
158. Ibid., 115–16.
159. Ibid., 126.
160. Ibid., 134.
161. Ibid., 136–37.
162. Ibid., 172–73.
163. W. Brown, *Black Man*, 89–90.
164. Delany, *Blake*, 238.
165. Ibid., 290–92.
166. Ibid., 286.

167. Ibid., 287.
168. Doolan, "'Be Cautious of the Word "Rebel",'" 173–74.
169. Delany, *Blake*, 309.
170. Ibid., 311.
171. Ibid., 311, 313.
172. R. Levine, *Martin Delany*, 216.
173. Lanier, *Florida*, 30.

Chapter Five

1. Erkkila, *Whitman the Political Poet*, 129–54.
2. Lincoln, *Speeches and Writings*, 125.
3. Whitman, *Drum-Taps*, 51–52.
4. Ibid., 51.
5. Melville, *Battle-Pieces*, 11.
6. Whitman, *Drum-Taps*, 54.
7. Ibid., 51.
8. Ibid., 52. Whitman is also referring to a real meteoric phenomenon, the 1860 Great Meteor.
9. Quoted in R. Richardson, *Emerson*, 545.
10. Reynolds, *John Brown*, 367.
11. Whitman, *Drum-Taps*, 46.
12. Lerone Bennett Jr., quoted in Toscano, *Fanaticism*, 1.
13. Genoways, *Walt Whitman and the Civil War*, 35.
14. Moon, "Solitude, Singularity, Seriality," 309. Also see the book of essays devoted to Whitman and bohemianism, *Whitman among the Bohemians*, edited by Levin and Whitley.
15. Erkkila, "Whitman and the Homosexual Republic," 153–71.
16. Coviello, *Intimacy in America*, 155.
17. Whitman, "Song of the Exposition," lines 61, 64–65, *Leaves of Grass and Other Writings*. All subsequent citations of Whitman's poetry from *Leaves of Grass and Other Writings* refer to the line number(s).
18. Castiglia, *Interior States*, 14.
19. Moon, *Disseminating Whitman*, 146.
20. Pearce argues, "The Whitman of the 1860 *Leaves of Grass* would be a sage, a seer, a sayer. But he speaks of only what he knows directly and he asks of his speech only that it report fully and honestly and frankly" ("Whitman Justified," 41). Although he doesn't attempt to "justify" the 1860 *Leaves* as Whitman's poetic summit, Michael Moon, in his classic *Disseminating Whitman* (1991), observes that this Whitman uniquely privileges the limitations of the "real body" (131).
21. Bellis, *Writing Revolution*, 111.
22. In the *Huntington Library Quarterly* special issue, on sex and love, see Folsom, "'A spirit of my own seminal wet,'" and Thomas, "'Till I hit upon a name'"; on existential crisis and pensiveness, see D. Blake, "Whitman's Ecclesiastes," and

Price, "Love, War, and Revision"; for Reynolds's argument, see "'Affection shall solve every one of the problems of freedom.'"
  23. Reynolds, *John Brown*, 11.
  24. Erkkila, *Whitman the Political Poet*, 149.
  25. Ibid., 152–53.
  26. Ibid., 154.
  27. Ibid., 179.
  28. Ibid., 186.
  29. Whitman, *Complete Prose*, 260.
  30. Erkkila, "'To Paris with my Love,'" 21.
  31. McRuer, *Crip Theory*, 2.
  32. D. Mitchell, "Narrative Prosthesis," 24.
  33. D. Mitchell and Snyder, *Narrative Prosthesis*, 47, 51, 49.
  34. D. Mitchell, "Narrative Prosthesis," 20.
  35. L. Davis, *Bending Over Backwards*, 12.
  36. Ibid., 39.
  37. Dickinson, "704," line 9, *Poems*.
  38. Lincoln, *Speeches and Writings*, 687.
  39. Ibid., 686.
  40. Lincoln, *Speeches and Writings*, 220.
  41. "Davis' Inaugural," 58–59, 61, emphasis mine.
  42. Ibid., 61.
  43. Quoted in Dodd and Dodd, *Civil War in Winston County*, 3.
  44. McPherson, *Battle Cry of Freedom*, 593.
  45. Ibid., 298.
  46. Carpenter, *Six Months at the White House*, 76–77.
  47. Long, *Rehabilitating Bodies*, 20.
  48. Rutkow, *Bleeding Blue and Gray*, 32.
  49. Quoted in Rutkow, *Bleeding Blue and Gray*, 29.
  50. Quoted in ibid., 255.
  51. Scarry, *Body in Pain*, 71.
  52. L. Alcott, *Hospital Sketches*, 32.
  53. S. Mitchell, "The Case of George Dedlow," 220, 223, 215.
  54. Douglass, *Selected Speeches and Writings*, 428.
  55. The Chicago *Daily Tribune*, October 11, 1860, quoted in Stampp, *And the War Came*, 22.
  56. Lincoln, *Speeches and Writings*, 358.
  57. Quoted in Shanks, *Secession Movement in Virginia*, 90.
  58. Reynolds, *John Brown*, 14–15.
  59. Everett and Cushing, "Speeches at Faneuil Hall," 179; Norton, "To Mrs. Edward Twistleton," 185.
  60. Quoted in Reynolds, *John Brown*, 426.
  61. Quoted in McPherson, *Battle Cry for Freedom*, 768.
  62. Oates, *To Purge This Land*, 183, 237.

63. "Letters from Northern Women," 418.
64. Redpath, "Dedication," 3.
65. Ibid., 5.
66. Thoreau, "Plea for Capt. John Brown," 39, 31.
67. Parker, "Two Letters," 88.
68. Phillips, "Lesson of the Hour," 60.
69. Ibid., 51–52.
70. Ibid., 53.
71. Ibid., 58.
72. Ibid., 66.
73. O'Conor, "Speech," 289.
74. Beecher, "Sermon," 258.
75. Ibid., 262.
76. Ibid., 263.
77. Quoted in Genoways, *Walt Whitman and the Civil War*, 65.
78. Quoted in ibid., 74.
79. *Leaves of Grass Imprints*, 44.
80. Whitman, "Text of 1855 *Leaves of Grass*," 1279, *Leaves of Grass and Other Writings*.
81. At least three full-length studies have been written on Whitman's ecstatic politics: see Hutchinson, *Ecstatic Whitman*; Maslan, *Whitman Possessed*; and Sowder, *Whitman's Ecstatic Union*.
82. Whitman, *Complete Prose*, 372.
83. Ibid., 405.
84. Whitman, "Chants Democratic," 7:2, 1; "Proto-Leaf," 22, *Leaves of Grass, 1860*.
85. Stacy, Introduction, x.
86. Whitman, "Gods," 15–16, *Leaves of Grass and Other Writings*.
87. Whitman, "Years of the Modern," 24–27, *Leaves of Grass and Other Writings*.
88. Whitman, "Apostroph," *Leaves of Grass, 1860*.
89. Whitman, "Over the Carnage Rose Prophetic a Voice," 19, *Leaves of Grass and Other Writings*.
90. Whitman, "Calamus," 5:11, 1; "Chants Democratic," 2:14, *Leaves of Grass, 1860*.
91. Whitman, "O Star of France," 9–11, *Leaves of Grass and Other Writings*.
92. Derrida, *Of Hospitality*, 83, 123.
93. Derrida, *Acts of Religion*, 364.
94. Derrida, *Deconstruction in a Nutshell*, 15.
95. Whitman, "Calamus," 34, *Leaves of Grass, 1860*.
96. Ibid., 19:1.
97. Ibid., 8.
98. Ibid., 16:1–3.
99. Whitman, "Walt Whitman," 286, *Leaves of Grass, 1860*.
100. Whitman, "Leaves of Grass," 1:2, *Leaves of Grass, 1860*.

101. Ibid., 1:4.
102. Ibid., 1:10.
103. Ibid., 1:5.
104. Ibid., 1:16.
105. Ibid., 1:2.
106. Whitman, "Calamus," 1, *Leaves of Grass, 1860*.
107. Ibid., 3:3.
108. Whitman, "Leaves of Grass," 24, *Leaves of Grass, 1860*.
109. Ibid., 10:4.
110. Whitman, "Chants Democratic," 13:2, *Leaves of Grass, 1860*.
111. Whitman, "Proto-Leaf," 20, *Leaves of Grass, 1860*.
112. Ibid.; Whitman, "Chants Democratic," 4, *Leaves of Grass, 1860*.
113. Whitman, "Chants Democratic," 9, *Leaves of Grass, 1860*.

114. On Whitman's cosmopolitanism and internationalism, see especially Grünzweig, "'For America—For All the Earth'"; Leypoldt, *Cultural Authority*; and Thomas, *Transatlantic Connections*.

115. Whitman, "Walt Whitman's Caution," *Leaves of Grass, 1860*.
116. Whitman, "France, The 18th Year of These States," 5, *Leaves of Grass, 1860*.
117. Ibid.
118. Whitman, "Calamus," 5:15, *Leaves of Grass, 1860*.
119. Whitman, "France, The 18th Year of These States," 5, *Leaves of Grass, 1860*.
120. Ibid., 1.
121. Ibid., 5.
122. Stauffer, "Opera and Opera Singers"; T. Brown, *History of the New York Stage*, 394.
123. Whitman, *Notebooks*, 1:396.
124. Ibid., 1:394.
125. Whitman, "To a Cantatrice," *Leaves of Grass, 1860*.
126. Whitman, "Resurgemus."
127. Whitman, "Europe, The 72d and 73d Years of These States," 33, *Leaves of Grass and Other Writings*.
128. Whitman, "Europe, The 72d and 73d Years of These States," 5, *Leaves of Grass, 1860*.

129. To be precise, the 1856 version deletes "Yet" from the beginning of the line.

130. Whitman, "Europe, The 72d and 73d Years of These States," 5, *Leaves of Grass, 1860*.
131. Ibid., 8.
132. Ibid., 9–10.
133. Ibid., 12.
134. Whitman, "To a Foil'd European Revolutionaire," 1:3, *Leaves of Grass* [1871].
135. Whitman, "To a Foiled Revolter or Revoltress," 8, *Leaves of Grass, 1860*. This is not the entirety of the new lines.
136. Ibid., 4.

137. Ibid., 1.
138. Ibid.
139. Ibid., 6.
140. Ibid., 2–3.
141. Whitman, "The Centenarian's Story," 12, *Leaves of Grass and Other Writings*.
142. Whitman, "First O Songs for a Prelude," 39, in *Leaves of Grass and Other Writings*.
143. Whitman, "As I Lay with My Head in Your Lap Camerado," 10–11, *Leaves of Grass and Other Writings*.
144. Ibid., 17, 7.
145. My reading echoes and amplifies Michael Warner's view that Walt Whitman's Civil War does not always participate in the redeemer nation motif but instead leads us to contemplate an "immersion in fatality," a "trembling before history," especially by way of the "fatefulness of erotic exchange" (86–87).
146. Simpson highlights the nationalist-imperialist implications of Whitman's "metaphysic of wholeness" (182) in "Destiny Made Manifest"; and Scholnick emphasizes the eugenic implications of Whitman's poetics of "perfect health" (259) in "'How Dare a Sick Man or an Obedient Man Write Poems?'"
147. Whitman, "Eighteen Sixty-One," 13, 7, 4, *Leaves of Grass and Other Writings*.
148. Whitman, *Complete Prose*, 217.
149. Ibid., 81.
150. Ibid., 28.
151. Whitman, *Walt Whitman's Civil War*, 71.
152. Whitman, *Complete Prose*, 38.
153. L. Alcott, "The Brothers," 192.
154. L. Alcott, *Hospital Sketches*, 30.
155. Ibid., 31, 66.
156. Ibid., 86, 30.
157. Whitman, "Lo, Victress on the Peaks," 7–9, *Leaves of Grass and Other Writings*.
158. L. Alcott, *Hospital Sketches*, 33.
159. Whitman, *Notebooks*, 2:545.
160. Whitman, *Complete Prose*, 216, 420.

Epilogue

1. Post, *American Road to Capitalism*, 154.
2. McPherson, *Battle Cry of Freedom*, 452.
3. Lincoln, *Speeches and Writings*, 697.
4. Yuan, "Disfigurement and Reconstruction," 77.
5. Mihm, "'A Limb Which Shall Be Presentable in Polite Society,'" 292.
6. McPherson, *Battle Cry of Freedom*, 332.
7. Melville, *Battle-Pieces*, 61.

8. Ibid., 268, 162.
9. Ibid., 101.
10. De Forest, *Miss Ravenel's Conversion*, 468.
11. L. Davis, *Bending Over Backwards*, 111.
12. Whitman, "Beat! Beat! Drums!," 1; "To a Locomotive in Winter," 3, *Leaves of Grass and Other Writings*.
13. Whitman, "Passage to India," 32, 35, *Leaves of Grass and Other Writings*.
14. Whitman, *Complete Prose*, 521–22.
15. Ibid., 330.
16. Ibid., 337, 330.
17. Ibid., 330.
18. Whitman, *Notebooks*, 3:1154.
19. Ibid., 3:1155.
20. Whitman, *Complete Prose*, 221.
21. Marx, *Capital*, 1062.
22. Whitman, *Notebooks*, 3:1161.
23. Tichi, "Novels of Civic Protest," 394.
24. Reckson, "A 'Reg'lar Jim Dandy'," 76, 73.
25. See Connor, "Awakening of Edward Bellamy."
26. Bellamy, *Looking Backward*, 3.
27. Ibid., 170–71.
28. Ibid., 166.
29. Bellamy, *Equality*, 342, 381.
30. Ibid., 339.
31. Ibid., 340.
32. Bellamy, *Looking Backward*, 195.
33. Ibid., 196–97.
34. Ibid., 192.
35. Traubel, *With Walt Whitman in Camden*, 1:221–22.
36. Ibid., 5:407.
37. Ibid., 6:46.
38. Bellamy, *Looking Backward*, 150.
39. Whitman, *Notebooks*, 2:932–33.
40. Whitman, "Preface 1876—*Leaves of Grass* and *Two Rivulets*," *Leaves of Grass and Other Writings*, 658.
41. Whitman, "Spirit Whose Work is Done," 16–18, *Leaves of Grass and Other Writings*.
42. Whitman, "Still Though the One I Sing," *Leaves of Grass* [1871].
43. Whitman, "Law is grand."
44. Whitman, "Says," 24–25, *Leaves of Grass and Other Writings*.
45. Whitman, "Song of the Exposition," 60–61, 64–66, *Leaves of Grass and Other Writings*.
46. Rancière, *Dis-agreement*, 11–12.
47. Whitman, "Text of 1855 *Leaves of Grass*," 1134, *Leaves of Grass and Other Writings*.

Bibliography

"Account of the Negroe Insurrection in South Carolina." In *Stono: Documenting and Interpreting a Southern Slave Revolt*, edited by Mark M. Smith, 13–15. Columbia: University of South Carolina Press, 2005.

Adams, John. *The Portable John Adams*. Edited by John Patrick Diggins. New York: Penguin, 2004.

Adams, Willi Paul. *The First American Constitutions: Republican Ideology and the Making of the State Constitutions in the Revolutionary Era*. Translated by Rita and Robert Kimber. Lanham: Rowman & Littlefield Publishers, Inc., 2001.

Aiken, J. and A. L. "Miscellaneous Pieces in Prose." *The Pennsylvania Magazine; or, American Monthly Museum* 1 (July 1775): 327–28.

Akers, Charles W. "'Our Modern Egyptians': Phillis Wheatley and the Whig Campaign Against Slavery in Revolutionary Boston." *The Journal of Negro History* 60.3 (July 1975): 397–410.

Alcott, Amos Bronson. "Orphic Sayings." In *The Transcendentalists: An Anthology*, edited by Perry Miller, 303–15. Cambridge, MA: Harvard University Press, 1950.

Alcott, Louisa May. "The Brothers." In *To Live and Die: Collected Stories of the Civil War, 1861–1876*, edited by Kathleen Diffley, 191–208. Durham: Duke University Press, 2002.

———. *Hospital Sketches*. Edited by Bessie Zaban Jones. Cambridge, MA: Harvard University Press, 1960.

Anderson, Ben. "Modulating the Excess of Affect: Morale in a State of 'Total War.'" In *The Affect Theory Reader*, edited by Melissa Gregg and Gregory J. Seigworth, 161–85. Durham: Duke University Press, 2010.

Andrews, Edward Deming. "The Shaker Mission to the Shawnee Indians." *Winterthur Portfolio* 7 (1972): 113–28.

Anthony, Katherine. *First Lady of the Revolution: The Life of Mercy Otis Warren*. Port Washington: Kennikat Press, 1958.

Apess, William. *On Our Own Ground: The Complete Writings of William Apess, a Pequot*. Edited by Barry O'Connell. Amherst: University of Massachusetts Press, 1992.

Aravamudan, Srinivas. Introduction. *Obi; Or, the History of Three-Fingered Jack*, edited by Srinivas Aravamudan, 7–51. Ontario: Broadview, 2005.

Arendt, Hannah. *On Revolution*. Edited by Jonathan Schell. New York: Penguin, 2006.

"Art. XXVII." *The Anti-Jacobin Review and Magazine* 6 (May 1800): 451.

Asad, Talal. *Formations of the Secular: Christianity, Islam, Modernity*. Stanford, CA: Stanford University Press, 2003.

Atlanticus. "Liberty Tree." *The Pennsylvania Magazine; or, American Monthly Museum* 1 (July 1775): 328–29.
Aupaumut, Hendrick. "*A Narrative of an Embassy to the Western Indians, from the Original Manuscript of Hendrick Aupaumut, with Prefatory Remarks by Dr. B. H. Coates.*" In *Memoirs of the Historical Society of Pennsylvania*. Vol. 2. 61–131. Philadelphia: Carey, Lea & Carey, 1827.
Badiou, Alain. *Being and Event*. Translated by Oliver Feltham. London: Continuum, 2006.
———. *Ethics: An Essay on the Understanding of Evil*. Translated by Peter Hallward. London: Verso Press, 2001.
———. *Logics of Worlds: Being and Event II*. Translated by Alberto Toscano. London: Continuum, 2009.
———. *Metapolitics*. Translated by Jason Barker. London: Verso Press, 2005.
———. *Theoretical Writings*. Translated by Ray Brassier and Alberto Toscano. London: Continuum, 2006.
Bailyn, Bernard. *The Ideological Origins of the American Revolution, Enlarged Edition*. Cambridge, MA: Harvard University Press, 1992.
Baker, Jr., Houston A. *Workings of the Spirit: The Poetics of Afro-American Women's Writing*. Chicago: University of Chicago Press, 1991.
Bakhtin, Mikhail. *The Dialogic Imagination: Four Essays*. Edited by Michael Holquist. Translated by Caryl Emerson and Michael Holquist. Austin: University of Texas Press, 1982.
———. *Rabelais and His World*. Translated by Hélène Iswolsky. Bloomington: Indiana University Press, 1984.
Barker-Benfield, G. J. *The Culture of Sensibility: Sex and Society in Eighteenth-Century Britain*. Chicago: University of Chicago Press, 1992.
Barnard, Philip, and Stephen Shapiro. Introduction. *Ormond; or, The Secret Witness: With Related Texts*, edited by Philip Barnard and Stephen Shapiro, ix–lii. Indianapolis: Hackett Publishing Company, 2009.
Barnard, Philip, Mark L. Kamrath, and Stephen Shapiro, eds. *Revising Charles Brockden Brown: Culture, Politics, and Sexuality in the Early Republic*. Knoxville: University of Tennessee Press, 2004.
Barnes, Elizabeth. *States of Sympathy: Seduction and Democracy in the American Novel*. New York: Columbia University Press, 1997.
Baym, Nina. *Woman's Fiction: A Guide to Novels by and about Women in America, 1820–1870*. 2nd ed. Urbana: University of Illinois Press, 1993.
Beecher, Henry Ward. "Sermon by Rev. Henry Ward Beecher." In *Echoes of Harper's Ferry*, edited by James Redpath, 255–79. Boston: Thayer and Eldridge, 1860.
Beidler, Philip D. *First Books: The Printed Word and Cultural Formation in Early Alabama*. Tuscaloosa: University of Alabama Press, 1999.
Beiser, Frederick C. *The Sovereignty of Reason: The Defense of Rationality in the Early English Enlightenment*. Princeton, NJ: Princeton University Press, 1996.
Bell, Bernard W. *The Afro-American Novel and Its Tradition*. Amherst: University of Massachusetts Press, 1987.
Bellamy, Edward. *Equality*. Toronto: George N. Morang, 1897.

---. *Looking Backward 2000–1887*. Edited by Matthew Beaumont. New York: Oxford University Press, 2007.
Bellin, Joshua David. *The Demon of the Continent: Indians and the Shaping of American Literature*. Philadelphia: University of Pennsylvania Press, 2001.
---. *Medicine Bundle: Indian Sacred Performance and American Literature, 1824–1932*. Philadelphia: University of Pennsylvania Press, 2008.
---. "Red Routes: William Apess and Nativist Prophecy." *Literature in the Early American Republic: Annual Studies on Cooper and His Contemporaries* 2 (2010): 45–80.
Bellis, Peter J. *Writing Revolution: Aesthetics and Politics in Hawthorne, Whitman, and Thoreau*. Athens: University of Georgia Press, 2003.
Bennett, Paula. "Phillis Wheatley's Vocation and the Paradox of the 'Afric Muse.'" *PMLA* 113.1 (1998): 64–76.
Bercovitch, Sacvan. *The American Jeremiad, Anniversary Edition*. Madison: University of Wisconsin Press, 2012.
---. *The Puritan Origins of the American Self, with a New Preface*. New Haven, CT: Yale University Press, 2011.
---. *The Rites of Assent: Transformations in the Symbolic Construction of America*. New York: Routledge, 1993.
Bergland, Renée L. *The National Uncanny: Indian Ghosts and American Subjects*. Hanover: University Press of New England, 2000.
Berlant, Lauren. *The Female Complaint: The Unfinished Business of Sentimentality in American Culture*. Durham: Duke University Press, 2008.
---. "Intuitionists: History and the Affective Event." *American Literary History* 20.4 (Winter 2008): 845–60.
Bertelsen, Lone, and Andrew Murphie. "An Ethics of Everyday Infinities and Powers: Félix Guattari on Affect and the Refrain." In *The Affect Theory Reader*, edited by Melissa Gregg and Gregory J. Seigworth, 138–57. Durham: Duke University Press, 2010.
Bhabha, Homi K. *The Location of Culture*. New York: Routledge, 1994.
Bird, Robert Montgomery. *Nick of the Woods, or The Jibbenainosay: A Tale of Kentucky*. Edited by Curtis Dahl. New Haven, CT: College & University Press, 1967.
Blake, David Haven. "Whitman's Ecclesiastes: The 1860 'Leaves of Grass' Cluster." *Huntington Library Quarterly* 73.4 (December 2010): 613–27.
Blake, William. *The Complete Poetry and Prose of William Blake, Newly Revised Edition*. Edited by David V. Erdman. New York: Anchor, 1988.
Bloch, Ruth H. *Visionary Republic: Millennial Themes in American Thought, 1756–1800*. New York: Cambridge University Press, 1988.
Bonomi, Patricia U. *Under the Cope of Heaven: Religion, Society, and Politics in Colonial America, Updated Edition*. New York: Oxford University Press, 2003.
Boucher, Jonathan. *A View of the Causes and Consequences of the American Revolution; In Thirteen Discourses, Preached in North America Between the Years 1763 And 1775: With an Historical Preface. By Jonathan Boucher, A. M. and F. A. S. Vicar of Epsom in the County of Surrey*. Vol. 1. London, 1797.

Bouton, Terry. *Taming Democracy: "The People," the Founders, and the Troubled Ending of the American Revolution*. New York: Oxford University Press, 2007.

Brackenridge, Hugh Henry. "The Battle of Bunkers-Hill." In *Representative Plays by American Dramatists (1765–1819)*, edited by Montrose J. Moses, 233–76. New York: E. P. Dutton & Co., 1918.

Brennan, Teresa. *The Transmission of Affect*. Ithaca, NY: Cornell University Press, 2004.

Brockwell, Charles. "Every Idle Untruth as a Revelation." In *Religious Enthusiasm and the Great Awakening*, edited by David S. Lovejoy, 65–67. Englewood Cliffs, NJ: Prentice-Hall, 1969.

Brodhead, Richard H. "Prophets in America ca. 1830: Emerson, Nat Turner, Joseph Smith." *Journal of Mormon History* 29.1 (2003): 42–65.

Brooks, Joanna. *American Lazarus: Religion and the Rise of African-American and Native American Literatures*. New York: Oxford University Press, 2003.

———. "Our Phillis, Ourselves." *American Literature* 82.1 (2010): 1–28.

Brooks, Lisa. *The Common Pot: The Recovery of Native Space in the Northeast*. Minneapolis: University of Minnesota Press, 2008.

Brown, Charles Brockden. *Ormond; or, The Secret Witness: With Related Texts*. Edited by Philip Barnard and Stephen Shapiro. Indianapolis: Hackett Publishing Company, 2009.

———. *Wieland* and *Memoirs of Carwin the Biloquist*. Edited by Jay Fliegelman. New York: Penguin, 1991.

Brown, T. Allston. *A History of the New York Stage, From the First Performance in 1732 to 1901*. Vol. 1 of *A History of the New York Stage*. New York: Dodd, Mead, 1902.

Brown, William Wells. *The Black Man: His Antecedents, His Genius, and His Achievements*, Basic Afro-American Reprint Library. New York: Johnson Reprint Corporation, 1968.

Buck-Morss, Susan. *Hegel, Haiti, and Universal History*. Pittsburgh: University of Pittsburgh Press, 2009.

Bullock, Steven C. *Revolutionary Brotherhood: Freemasonry and the Transformation of the American Social Order, 1730–1840*. Chapel Hill: University of North Carolina Press, 1996.

Burgett, Bruce. *Sentimental Bodies: Sex, Gender, and Citizenship in the Early Republic*. Princeton, NJ: Princeton University Press, 1998.

Burke, Edmund. *A Letter from the Right Honourable Edmund Burke to a Noble Lord, On the Attacks Made Upon Him and His Pension, in the House of Lords, by the Duke of Bedford and the Earl of Lauderdale, Early in the Present Sessions of Parliament*. London: printed for J. Owen, 1796.

———. *Reflections on the Revolution in France*. Edited by Conor Cruise O'Brien. New York: Penguin, 2004.

———. *The Speech of Edmund Burke, Esq; On Moving His Resolutions for Conciliation with the Colonies, March 22, 1775*. London: printed for J. Dodsley, 1775.

———. "*To* Charles O'Hara—[17] *August 1775*." In *Selected Letters of Edmund Burke*, edited by Harvey C. Mansfield Jr., 232. Chicago: University of Chicago Press, 1984.

Calloway, Colin G. *The American Revolution in Indian Country: Crisis and Diversity in Native American Communities*. New York: Cambridge University Press, 1995.

———. *The Shawnees and the War for America*. New York: Penguin, 2007.

Cappon, Lester J., ed. *The Adams-Jefferson Letters: The Complete Correspondence Between Thomas Jefferson and Abigail and John Adams*. Vol. 2 (1812–1826). Chapel Hill: University of North Carolina Press, 1959.

Carlyle, Thomas. *The French Revolution: A History*. New York: Modern Library, 2002.

Carpenter, Francis B. *Six Months at the White House with Abraham Lincoln: The Story of a Picture*. New York: Hurd and Houghton, 1866.

Carr, Helen. *Inventing the American Primitive: Politics, Gender and the Representation of Native American Literary Traditions, 1789–1936*. New York: New York University Press, 1996.

Carretta, Vincent. Introduction. *Phillis Wheatley: Complete Writings*, edited by Vincent Carretta, xiii–xxxvii. New York: Penguin, 2001.

Casender, Don Pedro. *The Lost Virgin of the South: An Historical Novel, Founded on Facts, Connected with the Indian War in the South, in 1812 to '15*. 2nd ed. Courtland, AL: M. Smith, 1833.

Castiglia, Christopher. *Interior States: Institutional Consciousness and the Inner Life of Democracy in the Antebellum United States*. Durham: Duke University Press, 2008.

Cave, Albert A. *Prophets of the Great Spirit: Native American Revitalization Movements in Eastern North America*. Lincoln: University of Nebraska Press, 2006.

Cayton, Andrew R. L. "'Noble Actors' upon 'the Theatre of Honour': Power and Civility in the Treaty of Greenville." In *Contact Points: American Frontiers from the Mohawk Valley to the Mississippi, 1750–1830*, edited by Andrew R. L. Cayton and Fredrika J. Teute, 235–69. Chapel Hill: University of North Carolina Press, 1998.

Chapman, Mary, and Glenn Hendler, eds. *Sentimental Men: Masculinity and the Politics of Affect in American Culture*. Berkeley: University of California Press, 1999.

Chauncy, Charles. "Enthusiasm Described and Caution'd Against." In *The Great Awakening: Documents Illustrating the Crisis and Its Consequences*, edited by Alan Heimert and Perry Miller, 228–56. Indianapolis: Bobbs-Merrill Company, 1967.

———. "The Heat and Fervour of Their Passions." In *Religious Enthusiasm and the Great Awakening*, edited by David S. Lovejoy, 71–80. Englewood Cliffs, NJ: Prentice-Hall, 1969.

———. "Seasonable Thoughts on the State of Religion." In *The Great Awakening: Documents Illustrating the Crisis and Its Consequences*, edited by Alan Heimert and Perry Miller, 291–304. Indianapolis: Bobbs-Merrill Company, 1967.

Chireau, Yvonne P. *Black Magic: Religion and the African American Conjuring Tradition*. Berkeley: University of California Press, 2003.

Clark, J. C. D. *The Language of Liberty, 1660–1832: Political Discourse and Social Dynamics in the Anglo-American World*. New York: Cambridge University Press, 1994.

Clewis, Robert R. *The Kantian Sublime and the Revelation of Freedom*. New York: Cambridge University Press, 2009.
Coleridge, Samuel Taylor. *Lay Sermons*. Edited by R. J. White. Vol. 6 of *The Collected Works of Samuel Taylor Coleridge*. Princeton, NJ: Princeton University Press, 1972.
———. *The Literary Remains of Samuel Taylor Coleridge*. Vol. 2. Edited by Henry Nelson Coleridge. London: William Pickering, 1836.
Colton, George H. *Tecumseh; Or, the West Thirty Years Since: A Poem*. New-York: Wiley and Putnam, 1842.
Comay, Rebecca. *Mourning Sickness: Hegel and the French Revolution*. Stanford, CA: Stanford University Press, 2010.
Comment, Kristin M. "Charles Brockden Brown's *Ormond* and Lesbian Possibility in the Early Republic." *Early American Literature* 40.1 (2005): 57–78.
Connecticut Assembly. "Be It Enacted ... That If Any Minister ... Any Person Whosoever." In *Religious Enthusiasm and the Great Awakening*, edited by David S. Lovejoy, 68–71. Englewood Cliffs, NJ: Prentice-Hall, 1969.
Connor, George E. "The Awakening of Edward Bellamy: *Looking Backward* at Religious Influence." *Utopian Studies* 11.1 (2000): 38–50.
Cotton, John. "*Sixteene Questions of Serious and Necessary Consequence.*" In *The Antinomian Controversy, 1636–1638: A Documentary History*, edited by David D. Hall, 43–59. 2nd ed. Durham: Duke University Press, 1990.
"Coulter on Wall Street Protests." *Follow the Money with Eric Bolling. Fox Business Video* (4 Oct. 2011), http://video.foxbusiness.com/v/1198931921001/coulter-on-wall-street-protests/?#sp=show-clips. 1 Nov. 2011.
Coviello, Peter. *Intimacy in America: Dreams of Affiliation in Antebellum American Literature*. Minneapolis: University of Minnesota Press, 2005.
Cruickshank, Dan. *London's Sinful Secret: The Bawdy History and Very Public Passions of London's Georgian Age*. New York: St. Martin's Press, 2009.
Cushman, H. B. *History of the Choctaw, Chickasaw and Natchez Indians*. Norman: University of Oklahoma Press, 1999.
Davidson, Cathy N. *Revolution and the Word: The Rise of the Novel in America, Expanded Edition*. New York: Oxford University Press, 2004.
Davis, Curtis Carroll. "Virginia's Unknown Novelist: The Career of J. S. French, a Southern Colonel of Parts." *The Virginia Magazine of History and Biography* 60.4 (Oct. 1952): 551–81.
Davis, David Brion, ed. *The Fear of Conspiracy: Images of Un-American Subversion from the Revolution to the Present*. Ithaca, NY: Cornell University Press, 1971.
Davis, Lennard J. *Bending Over Backwards: Disability, Dismodernism, and Other Difficult Positions*. New York: New York University Press, 2002.
"Davis' Inaugural, February 18, 1861." In *The Alabama Confederate Reader*, edited by Malcolm C. McMillan, 57–62. Tuscaloosa: University of Alabama Press, 1992.
De Forest, John W. *Miss Ravenel's Conversion from Secession to Loyalty*. Edited by Gary Scharnhorst. New York: Penguin, 2000.

Delany, Martin R. *Blake; or, the Huts of America*. Edited by Floyd J. Miller. Boston: Beacon Press, 1970.

———. *A Documentary Reader*. Edited by Robert S. Levine. Chapel Hill: University of North Carolina Press, 2003.

Deleuze, Gilles, and Félix Guattari. *A Thousand Plateaus: Capitalism and Schizophrenia*. Translated by Brian Massumi. Minneapolis: University of Minnesota Press, 1987.

Deloria, Philip J. *Playing Indian*. New Haven, CT: Yale University Press, 1999.

Derrida, Jacques. *Acts of Religion*. Edited by Gil Anidjar. New York: Routledge, 2002.

———. *Deconstruction in a Nutshell: A Conversation with Jacques Derrida*. Edited by John D. Caputo. New York: Fordham University Press, 1996.

———. *The Gift of Death, Second Edition* and *Literature in Secret*. Translated by David Wills. Chicago: University of Chicago Press, 2008.

———. *Of Hospitality: Anne Dufourmantelle Invites Jacques Derrida to Respond*. Translated by Rachel Bowlby. Stanford, CA: Stanford University Press, 2000.

Derrida, Jacques, and Maurizio Ferraris. *A Taste for the Secret*. Edited by Giacomo Donis and David Webb. Translated by Giacomo Donis. Malden: Polity Press, 2001.

Detsi-Diamanti, Zoe. "Sarah Pogson's *The Female Enthusiast* (1807) and American Republican Virtue." *Polish Journal for American Studies* 8 (2014): 17–31.

"Dialogue on Civil Liberty, Delivered at a Public Exhibition in Nassau-Hall. Jan. 1776." *The Pennsylvania Magazine; or, American Monthly Museum* 2 (April 1776): 157–67.

Dickinson, Emily. *The Poems of Emily Dickinson: Reading Edition*. Edited by R. W. Franklin. Cambridge, MA: Belknap Press of Harvard University Press, 2005.

Dodd, Donald B., and Wynelle S. Dodd. *The Civil War in Winston County Alabama: "The Free State."* Jasper, AL: Northwest Alabama Publishing Co., 1979.

Donaldson, Laura E. "Making a Joyful Noise: William Apess and the Search for Postcolonial Method(ism)." *Interventions: International Journal of Postcolonial Studies* 7.2 (2005): 180–98.

Doolen, Andy. "'Be Cautious of the Word "Rebel"': Race, Revolution, and Transnational History in Martin Delany's *Blake; or, The Huts of America*." *American Literature* 81.1 (2009): 153–79.

Douglass, Frederick. *Autobiographies*. Edited by Henry Louis Gates, Jr. New York: Library of America, 1994.

———. *The Heroic Slave: A Cultural and Critical Edition*. Edited by Robert S. Levine, John Stauffer, and John R. McKivigan. New Haven, CT: Yale University Press, 2015.

———. *Selected Speeches and Writings*. Edited by Eric Foner and Yuval Taylor. Chicago: Chicago Review Press, 2000.

Dowd, Gregory Evans. *A Spirited Resistance: The North American Indian Struggle for Unity, 1745–1815*. Baltimore: Johns Hopkins University Press, 1992.

———. "Thinking and Believing: Nativism and Unity in the Age of Pontiac and Tecumseh." *American Indian Quarterly* 16.3 (Summer 1992): 309–37.
Doyle, Laura. *Freedom's Empire: Race and the Rise of the Novel in Atlantic Modernity, 1640–1940*. Durham: Duke University Press, 2008.
Drake, Benjamin. *Life of Tecumseh, and of His Brother the Prophet; with a Historical Sketch of the Shawanoe Indians*. Cincinnati: E. Morgan & Co., 1841.
Du Bois, W. E. B. *The Souls of Black Folk*. New York: Penguin, 1989.
Earle, William. *Obi; or, The History of Three-Fingered Jack*. Edited by Srinivas Aravamudan. Ontario: Broadview, 2005.
Edelstein, Tilden G. *Strange Enthusiasm: A Life of Thomas Wentworth Higginson*. New Haven, CT: Yale University Press, 1968.
Edmunds, R. David. *The Shawnee Prophet*. Lincoln: University of Nebraska Press, 1985.
———. *Tecumseh and the Quest for Indian Leadership*. Boston: Little, Brown and Co., 1984.
———. "Tecumseh, The Shawnee Prophet, and American History: A Reassessment." *Western Historical Quarterly* 14.3 (1983): 261–76.
Edwards, Jonathan. *The Great Awakening*. Edited by C. C. Goen. Vol. 4 of *The Works of Jonathan Edwards*. New Haven, CT: Yale University Press, 1972.
Ellison, Julie. *Cato's Tears and the Making of Anglo-American Emotion*. Chicago: University of Chicago Press, 1999.
Emerson, Ralph Waldo. *Selected Writings of Emerson*. Edited by Donald McQuade. New York: Modern Library, 1981.
Emmons, Richard. *The Fredoniad; or, Independence Preserved. An Epic Poem on the Late War of 1812*. Boston: W. Emmons, 1827.
———. *Tecumseh; or, The Battle of the Thames, a National Drama, in Five Acts*. New York: Elton & Harrison, 1836.
Epstein, Dena J. *Sinful Tunes and Spirituals: Black Folk Music to the Civil War*. Urbana: University of Illinois Press, 1977.
Erdman, David V. *Blake: Prophet against Empire*. Princeton, NJ: Princeton University Press, 1969.
Erkkila, Betsy. "Phillis Wheatley and the Black American Revolution." In *A Mixed Race: Ethnicity in Early America*, edited by Frank Shuffelton, 225–40. New York: Oxford University Press, 1993.
———. "'To Paris with my Love': Whitman among the French Revisited." *Revue Française d'Études Américaines* no. 108 (May 2006): 7–22.
———. "Whitman and the Homosexual Republic." In *Walt Whitman: The Centennial Essays*, edited by Ed Folsom, 153–71. Iowa City: University of Iowa Press, 1994.
———. *Whitman the Political Poet*. New York: Oxford University Press, 1989.
Everett, Edward, and Caleb Cushing. "Speeches at Faneuil Hall," 8 December 1859. In *The Tribunal: Responses to John Brown and the Harpers Ferry Raid*, edited by John Stauffer and Zoe Trodd, 178–83. Cambridge, MA: Belknap Press of Harvard University Press, 2012.

"The Examination of Mrs. Anne Hutchinson at the Court at Newton." In *The Antinomian Controversy, 1636–1638: A Documentary History*, edited by David D. Hall, 311–48. 2nd ed. Durham: Duke University Press, 1990.

Fessenden, Tracy. *Culture and Redemption: Religion, the Secular, and American Literature*. Princeton, NJ: Princeton University Press, 2007.

Fisher, Philip. *Hard Facts: Setting and Form in the American Novel*. New York: Oxford University Press, 1985.

Fliegelman, Jay. *Declaring Independence: Jefferson, Natural Language, & the Culture of Performance*. Stanford, CA: Stanford University Press, 1993.

Folsom, Ed. "'A spirit of my own seminal wet': Spermatoid Design in Walt Whitman's 1860 *Leaves of Grass*." *Huntington Library Quarterly* 73.4 (December 2010): 585–600.

Foner, Eric. *Tom Paine and Revolutionary America*. New York: Oxford University Press, 1976.

———. "Tom Paine's Republic: Radical Ideology and Social Change." In *The American Revolution: Explorations in the History of American Radicalism*, edited by Alfred F. Young, 187–232. Dekalb: Northern Illinois University Press, 1976.

Ford, Sarah. "Liberty Contained: Sarah Pogson's *The Young Carolinians; or, Americans in Algiers*." *Early American Literature* 41.1 (2006): 109–28.

Forde, Maarit, and Diana Paton. Introduction. *Obeah and Other Powers: The Politics of Caribbean Religion and Healing*, edited by Diana Paton and Maarit Forde, 1–42. Durham: Duke University Press, 2012.

Foucault, Michel. *The Politics of Truth*. Edited by Sylvère Lotringer. Translated by Lysa Hochroth and Catherine Porter. Los Angeles: Semiotext(e), 2007.

Frank, Jason. "'Besides Our Selves': An Essay on Enthusiastic Politics and Civil Subjectivity." *Public Culture* 17.3 (2005): 371–92.

———. *Constituent Moments: Enacting the People in Postrevolutionary America*. Durham: Duke University Press, 2010.

Franklin, John Hope. *The Militant South, 1800–1861*. Urbana: University of Illinois Press, 1956.

Franklin V, Benjamin. Introduction. *The Plays and Poems of Mercy Otis Warren*, edited by Benjamin Franklin V, vii–xxviii. Delmar: Scholars' Facsimiles & Reprints, 1980.

Freeman, Elizabeth. "Enthusiasm." Conference Paper. *MLA Convention*. Mark Hopkins Hotel, San Francisco, CA. 27–29 Dec. 2008.

French, James Strange. *Elkswatawa; or, The Prophet of the West. A Tale of the Frontier*. New York: Harper & Brothers, 1836.

Freud, Sigmund. *Writings on Art and Literature*. Stanford, CA: Stanford University Press, 1997.

Fritz, Christian G. *American Sovereigns: The People and America's Constitutional Tradition before the Civil War*. New York: Cambridge University Press, 2008.

Gallup-Diaz, Ignacio, Andrew Shankman, and Davis J. Silverman, eds. *Anglicizing America: Empire, Revolution, Republic*. Philadelphia: University of Pennsylvania Press, 2015.

Gatens, Moira. "Privacy and the Body: The Publicity of Affect." In *Privacies: Philosophical Evaluations*, edited by Beate Rössler, 113–32. Stanford, CA: Stanford University Press, 2004.

Gates, Jr., Henry Louis. *The Trials of Phillis Wheatley: America's First Black Poet and Her Encounters with the Founding Fathers*. New York: Basic Civitas Books, 2003.

Geggus, David P., ed. *The Impact of the Haitian Revolution in the Atlantic World*. Columbia: University of South Carolina Press, 2001.

Genovese, Eugene D. *From Rebellion to Revolution: Afro-American Slave Revolts in the Making of the Modern World*. Baton Rouge: Louisiana State University Press, 1979.

Genoways, Ted. *Walt Whitman and the Civil War: America's Poet During the Lost Years of 1860–1862*. Berkeley: University of California Press, 2009.

Giles, Paul. *The Global Remapping of American Literature*. Princeton, NJ: Princeton University Press, 2011.

Gilman, Arthur, ed. *Theatrum Majorum. The Cambridge of 1776*. Cambridge: Lockwood, Brooks, and Co., 1876.

Gilroy, Paul. *The Black Atlantic: Modernity and Double-Consciousness*. Cambridge, MA: Harvard University Press, 1993.

Goldsmith, Steven. *Blake's Agitation: Criticism and the Emotions*. Baltimore: Johns Hopkins University Press, 2013.

Gould, Philip. "Virtue, Ideology, and the American Revolution: The Legacy of the Republican Synthesis." *American Literary History* 5.3 (Autumn 1993): 564–77.

"Gouverneur Morris to [John] Penn (20 May 1774)." In *English Historical Documents: American Colonial Documents to 1776*, edited by Merrill Jensen, 1860–63. Vol. 9 of *English Historical Documents*. New York: Oxford University Press, 1955.

Griffin, Stephen M. "Constituent Power and Constitutional Change in American Constitutionalism." *The Paradox of Constitutionalism: Constituent Power and Constitutional Form*, edited by Martin Loughlin and Neil Walker, 49–66. New York: Oxford University Press, 2007.

Griffitts, Hannah. "Upon Reading a Book entituled Common Sense." In *American Poetry: The Seventeenth and Eighteenth Centuries*, edited by David S. Shields, 561–63. New York: Library of America, 2007.

Grossberg, Lawrence. "Affect's Future: Rediscovering the Virtual in the Actual." In *The Affect Theory Reader*, edited by Gregory J. Seigworth and Melissa Gregg, 309–38. Durham: Duke University Press, 2010.

Grünzweig, Walter. "'For America—For All the Earth': Walt Whitman as an International(ist) Poet." In *Breaking Bounds: Whitman and American Cultural Studies*, edited by Betsy Erkkila and Jay Grossman, 238–50. New York: Oxford University Press, 1996.

Guelzo, Allen C. "The Literature of the Colonial Revivals of Religion, 1735–1760." In *New Directions in American Religious History*, edited by Harry S. Stout and Darryl G. Hart, 141–72. Oxford: Oxford University Press, 1998.

Gustafson, Sandra M. "American Literature and the Public Sphere." *American Literary History* 20.3 (2008): 465–78.
———. *Eloquence is Power: Oratory & Performance in Early America*. Chapel Hill: University of North Carolina Press, 2000.
———. "The Genders of Nationalism: Patriotic Violence, Patriotic Sentiment in the Performances of Deborah Sampson Gannett." In *Possible Pasts: Becoming Colonial in Early America*, edited by Robert Blair St. George, 380–99. Ithaca, NY: Cornell University Press, 2000.
———. *Imagining Deliberative Democracy in the Early American Republic*. Chicago: University of Chicago Press, 2011.
———. "Nations of Israelites: Prophecy and Cultural Autonomy in the Writings of William Apess." *Religion & Literature* 26.1 (Spring 1994): 31–53.
Hall, David D., ed. *The Antinomian Controversy, 1636–1638: A Documentary History*. 2nd ed. Durham: Duke University Press, 1990.
Hampson, Rick. "War of 1812 bicentennial: USA shrugs as Canada goes all out." *USA TODAY* (15 June 2012), http://usatoday30.usatoday.com/news/nation/story/2012-06-14/war-of-1812-bicentennial/55603666/1. 22 December 2015.
Hancock, John. *An Oration; Delivered March 5, 1774, At the Request of the Inhabitants of the Town of Boston: To Commemorate the Bloody Tragedy of the Fifth of March, 1770. By the Honorable John Hancock, Esq; [Five Lines in Latin from Virgil]*. New Haven, CT: Thomas and Samuel Green, 1774.
Harding, Vincent. "Symptoms of Liberty and Blackhead Signposts: David Walker and Nat Turner." In *Nat Turner: A Slave Rebellion in History and Memory*, edited by Kenneth S. Greenberg, 79–102. New York: Oxford University Press, 2003.
Hatch, Nathan O. *The Sacred Cause of Liberty: Republican Thought and the Millennium in Revolutionary New England*. New Haven, CT: Yale University Press, 1977.
Hawes, Clement. *Mania and Literary Style: The Rhetoric of Enthusiasm from the Ranters to Christopher Smart*. New York: Cambridge University Press, 1996.
Hawthorne, Nathaniel. *The Scarlet Letter and Other Writings*. Edited by Leland S. Person. New York: W. W. Norton & Co., 2004.
———. *Tales and Sketches*. Edited by Roy Harvey Pearce. New York: Library of America, 1982.
Haynes, Carolyn. "'A Mark for Them All to . . . Hiss at': The Formation of Methodist and Pequot Identity in the Conversion Narrative of William Apess." *Early American Literature* 31.1 (1996): 25–44.
Heimert, Alan. *Religion and the American Mind: From the Great Awakening to the Revolution*. Cambridge, MA: Harvard University Press, 1966.
Heimert, Alan, and Perry Miller, eds. *The Great Awakening: Documents Illustrating the Crisis and Its Consequences*. Indianapolis: Bobbs-Merrill Company, 1967.
Hendler, Glenn. *Public Sentiments: Structures of Feeling in Nineteenth-Century American Literature*. Chapel Hill: University of North Carolina Press, 2001.
Herd, David. *Enthusiast!: Essays on Modern American Literature*. Manchester: Manchester University Press, 2007.

Heyd, Michael. *"Be Sober and Reasonable": The Critique of Enthusiasm in the Seventeenth and Early Eighteenth Centuries*. Leiden: E. J. Brill, 1995.

Hickman, Jared. "Globalization and the Gods, or the Political Theology of 'Race'." *Early American Literature* 45.1 (2010): 145–82.

Higginson, Thomas Wentworth. *Black Rebellion: A Selection from Travellers and Outlaws*. New York: Arno Press, 1969.

Hill, Christopher. *The World Turned Upside Down: Radical Ideas During the English Revolution*. New York: Penguin, 1991.

Hoerder, Dick. "Boston Leaders and Boston Crowds, 1765–1776." In *The American Revolution: Explorations in American Radicalism*, edited by Alfred F. Young, 233–71. Dekalb: Northern Illinois University Press, 1976.

Hoffer, Peter Charles. *Cry Liberty: The Great Stono River Slave Rebellion of 1739*. New York: Oxford University Press, 2010.

"From *House of Commons Sessional Papers*." In *Obi; or, The History of Three-Fingered Jack*, edited by Srinivas Aravamudan, 168–81. Ontario: Broadview, 2005.

Howard, James H. *Shawnee!: The Ceremonialism of a Native Indian Tribe and Its Cultural Background*. Athens: Ohio University Press, 1981.

Howe, Susan. *The Birth-mark: Unsettling the Wilderness in American Literary History*. Hanover: University Press of New England, 1993.

Hsu, Hsuan L. *Geography and the Production of Space in Nineteenth-Century American Literature*. New York: Cambridge University Press, 2010.

Hume, David. *Essays: Moral, Political, and Literary*. Edited by Eugene F. Miller. Indianapolis: Liberty Classics, 1987.

Hutchinson, George B. *The Ecstatic Whitman: Literary Shamanism & the Crisis of the Union*. Columbus: Ohio State University Press, 1986.

Imlay, Gilbert. *The Emigrants*. Edited by W. M. Verhoeven and Amanda Gilroy. New York: Penguin, 1998.

[Inglis, Charles]. *The True Interest of America Impartially Stated, in Certain Strictures on a Pamphlet Intitled Common Sense. By an American*. 2nd ed. Philadelphia: James Humphreys, Junr., 1776.

Irlam, Shaun. *Elations: The Poetics of Enthusiasm in Eighteenth-Century Britain*. Stanford, CA: Stanford University Press, 1999.

Isaac, Rhys. "Preachers and Patriots: Popular Culture and the Revolution in Virginia." In *The American Revolution: Explorations in the History of American Radicalism*, edited by Alfred F. Young, 125–56. Dekalb: Northern Illinois University Press, 1976.

———. *The Transformation of Virginia, 1740–1790*. Chapel Hill: University of North Carolina Press, 1982.

Jameson, Fredric. *Valences of the Dialectic*. London: Verso Press, 2009.

Jaudon, Toni Wall. "Obeah's Sensations: Rethinking Religion at the Transnational Turn." *American Literature* 84.4 (2012): 715–41.

Jefferson, Thomas. "From *Notes on the State of Virginia*." In *The Declaration of Independence*, edited by Garnet Kindervater, 79–82. London: Verso Press, 2007.

Johnson, Samuel. "Enthusiasm." *A Dictionary of the English Language: In Which the Words are Deduced from their Originals, and Illustrated in their Different Significations by Examples from the Best Writers. To Which are Prefixed, A History of the Language, and an English Grammar. By Samuel Johnson, A. M. In Two Volumes.* Vol. 1. 2nd ed. London: W. Strahan, 1755-56.

Jones, David. *A Journal of Two Visits Made to Some Nations of Indians on the West Side of the River Ohio, in the Years 1772 and 1773.* Burlington, NJ: Isaac Collins, 1774.

Jones, Esq., George. *Tecumseh and the Prophet of the West, An Original Historical Israel-Indian Tragedy, in Five Acts.* London: Longman, Brown, Green, & Longmans, 1844.

Juster, Susan. *Disorderly Women: Sexual Politics & Evangelicalism in Revolutionary New England.* Ithaca, NY: Cornell University Press, 1994.

Kammen, Michael. *A Season of Youth: The American Revolution and the Historical Imagination.* New York: Oxford University Press, 1980.

Kamrath, Mark L., and Stephen Shapiro, eds. *Revising Charles Brockden Brown: Culture, Politics, and Sexuality in the Early Republic.* Knoxville: University of Tennessee Press, 2004.

Kant, Immanuel. *The Conflict of the Faculties (Der Streit der Fakultäten).* Translated by Mary J. Gregor. New York: Abaris, 1979.

———. *Critique of the Power of Judgement.* Edited by Paul Guyer. Translated by Paul Guyer and Eric Matthews. New York: Cambridge University Press, 2000.

———. *Gesammelte Schriften.* Edited by the Royal Prussian (later German) Academy of Sciences. 29 vols. Berlin: Georg Reimer, later Walter de Gruyter & Co., 1900-.

———. *Observations on the Feeling of the Beautiful and the Sublime and Other Writings.* Edited by Patrick Frierson and Paul Guyer. New York: Cambridge University Press, 2011.

———. *Political Writings.* Edited by Hans Reiss. Translated by H. B. Nisbet. New York: Cambridge University Press, 1991.

Kaplan, Amy. *The Anarchy of Empire in the Making of U.S. Culture.* Cambridge, MA: Harvard University Press, 2002.

Karafilis, Maria. "Spaces of Democracy in Harriet Beecher Stowe's *Dred*." *Arizona Quarterly: A Journal of American Literature, Culture, and Theory* 55.3 (Autumn 1999): 23-49.

Kaufmann, Michael W. "The Religious, the Secular, and Literary Studies: Rethinking the Secularization Narrative in Histories of the Profession." *New Literary History* 38.4 (Autumn 2007): 607-28.

Keane, John. *Tom Paine: A Political Life.* Boston: Little, Brown and Company, 1995.

Kilgore, John Mac. "Nat Turner and the Work of Enthusiasm." *PMLA* 130.5 (2015): 1347-62.

Klein, Lawrence E. "Sociability, Solitude, and Enthusiasm." In *Enthusiasm and Enlightenment in Europe, 1650-1850,* edited by Lawrence E. Klein and Anthony J. La Vopa, 153-77. San Marino: Huntington Library, 1998.

Klein, Lawrence E., and Anthony J. La Vopa, eds. *Enthusiasm and Enlightenment in Europe, 1650–1850*. San Marino: Huntington Library, 1998.

Klinck, Carl F., ed. *Tecumseh: Fact and Fiction in Early Records*. Englewood Cliffs, NJ: Prentice-Hall, 1961.

Knox, Ronald A. *Enthusiasm: A Chapter in the History of Religion*. Notre Dame: University of Notre Dame Press, 1950.

Konkle, Maureen. *Writing Indian Nations: Native Intellectuals and the Politics of Historiography, 1827–1863*. Chapel Hill: University of North Carolina Press, 2004.

Kornblith, Gary J., and John M. Murrin. "The Making and Unmaking of an American Ruling Class." In *Beyond the American Revolution: Explorations in the History of American Radicalism*, edited by Alfred F. Young, 27–79. Dekalb: Northern Illinois University Press, 1993.

Kritzer, Amelia Howe. Introduction. In *Plays by Early American Women, 1775–1850*, edited by Amelia Howe Kritzer, 1–28. Ann Arbor: University of Michigan Press, 1995.

Lakomäki, Sami. *Gathering Together: The Shawnee People through Diaspora and Nationhood, 1600–1870*. New Haven, CT: Yale University Press, 2014.

Lang, Amy Schrager. *Prophetic Woman: Anne Hutchinson and the Problem of Dissent in the Literature of New England*. Berkeley: University of California Press, 1987.

Lanier, Sidney. *Florida: Its Scenery, Climate, and History. With an Account of Charleston, Savannah, Augusta, and Aiken, and a Chapter for Consumptives; Being a Complete Hand-Book and Guide*. Philadelphia: J. B. Lippincott & Co., 1875.

Larkin, Edward. "Nation and Empire in the Early US." *American Literary History* 22.3 (Fall 2010): 501–26.

———. *Thomas Paine and the Literature of Revolution*. New York: Cambridge University Press, 2005.

Layson, Hana. "Rape and Revolution: Feminism, Antijacobinism, and the Politics of Injured Innocence in Brockden Brown's *Ormond*." *Early American Studies: An Interdisciplinary Journal* 2.1 (Spring 2004): 160–91.

Leacock, John. "The Fall of British Tyranny; or, American Liberty." In *Representative Plays by American Dramatists (1765–1819)*, edited by Montrose J. Moses, 277–350. New York: E. P. Dutton & Co., 1918.

———. *John Leacock's "The First Book of the American Chronicles of the Times, 1774–1775."* Edited by Carla Mulford. Newark: University of Delaware Press, 1987.

Leaves of Grass Imprints: American and European Criticisms on "Leaves of Grass." Boston: Thayer and Eldridge, 1860.

Lepore, Jill. *New York Burning: Liberty, Slavery, and Conspiracy in Eighteenth-Century Manhattan*. New York: Vintage, 2005.

Letter, Joseph J. "Reincarnating Samuel Woodworth: Native American Prophets, the Nation, and the War of 1812." *Early American Literature* 43.3 (2008): 687–713.

"Letters from Northern Women." In *Echoes of Harper's Ferry*, edited by James Redpath, 413–26. Boston: Thayer and Eldridge, 1860.

Levin, Joanna, and Edward Whitley, eds. *Whitman among the Bohemians*. Iowa City: University of Iowa Press, 2014.
Levine, Lawrence W. *Black Culture and Black Consciousness: Afro-American Folk Thought from Slavery to Freedom, 30th Anniversary Edition*. New York: Oxford University Press, 2007.
Levine, Robert S. Introduction. *Dred: A Tale of the Great Dismal Swamp*. Edited by Robert S. Levine, ix–xxxii. Chapel Hill: University of North Carolina Press, 2006.
Lewis, I. M. *Ecstatic Religion: A Study of Shamanism and Spirit Possession*. 3rd ed. London: Routledge, 2003.
Lewis, Paul. "Attaining Masculinity: Charles Brockden Brown and Woman Warriors of the 1790s." *Early American Literature* 40.1 (2005): 37–55.
Leypoldt, Günter. *Cultural Authority in the Age of Whitman: A Transatlantic Perspective*. Edinburgh: Edinburgh University Press, 2009.
Lincoln, Abraham. *Speeches and Writings: 1859–1865*. Edited by Don E. Fehrenbacher. New York: Library of America, 1989.
Linebaugh, Peter. Introduction. In *Peter Linebaugh Presents Thomas Paine*, edited by Jessica Kimpell, vii–xxxvii. London: Verso Press, 2009.
Linebaugh, Peter, and Marcus Rediker. *The Many-Headed Hydra: Sailors, Slaves, Commoners, and the Hidden History of the Revolutionary Atlantic*. Boston: Beacon Press, 2000.
Lionnet, Françoise, and Shu-mei Shih, "Introduction: Thinking through the Minor, Transnationally." In *Minor Transnationalism*, edited by Françoise Lionnet and Shu-mei Shih, 1–23. Durham: Duke University Press, 2005.
Lippard, George. *The Quaker City; or, The Monks of Monk Hall*. Edited by David S. Reynolds. Amherst: University of Massachusetts Press, 1995.
Long, Lisa A. *Rehabilitating Bodies: Health, History, and the American Civil War*. Philadelphia: University of Pennsylvania Press, 2004.
Longmore, George. *Tecumthe, a Poetical Tale: In Three Cantos*. Edited by Mary Lu MacDonald. London, Ontario: Canadian Poetry Press, 1993.
Loughlin, Martin. "Constituent Power Subverted: From English Constitutional Argument to British Constitutional Practice." In *The Paradox of Constitutionalism: Constituent Power and Constitutional Form*, edited by Martin Loughlin and Neil Walker, 27–48. New York: Oxford University Press, 2007.
Loughlin, Martin, and Neil Walker. Introduction. *The Paradox of Constitutionalism: Constituent Power and Constitutional Form*, edited by Martin Loughlin and Neil Walker, 1–8. New York: Oxford University Press, 2007.
Lovejoy, David S. "'Desperate Enthusiasm': Early Signs of American Radicalism." In *The Origins of Anglo-American Radicalism*, edited by Margaret C. Jacob and James R. Jacob, 214–25. Atlantic Highlands, NJ: Humanities Press International, 1991.
———, ed. *Religious Enthusiasm and the Great Awakening*. Englewood Cliffs, NJ: Prentice-Hall, 1969.
———. *Religious Enthusiasm in the New World: Heresy to Revolution*. Cambridge, MA: Harvard University Press, 1985.

Lover of Peace. "Thoughts on Defensive War." *The Pennsylvania Magazine; or, American Monthly Museum* 1 (July 1775): 313–14.
Lukács, Georg. *The Theory of the Novel*. Translated by Anna Bostock. Cambridge: M.I.T. Press, 1971.
Lyotard, Jean-François. *The Differend: Phrases in Dispute*. Translated by Georges Van Den Abbeele. Minneapolis: University of Minnesota Press, 1988.
———. *Enthusiasm: The Kantian Critique of History*. Translated by Georges Van Den Abbeele. Stanford, CA: Stanford University Press, 2009.
Maier, Pauline. *From Resistance to Revolution: Colonial Radicals and the Development of American Opposition to Britain, 1765–1776*. New York: W. W. Norton & Co., 1991.
Marini, Stephen A. *Radical Sects of Revolutionary New England*. Cambridge, MA: Harvard University Press, 1982.
Marx, Karl. *Capital, Volume 1*. Translated by Ben Fowkes. New York: Penguin, 1990.
Maslan, Mark. *Whitman Possessed: Poetry, Sexuality, and Popular Authority*. Baltimore: Johns Hopkins University Press, 2001.
Massumi, Brian. *Parables for the Virtual: Movement, Affect, Sensation*. Durham: Duke University Press, 2002.
May, Henry F. *The Enlightenment in America*. New York: Oxford University Press, 1976.
McPherson, James M. *Battle Cry of Freedom: The Civil War Era*. New York: Oxford University Press, 1988.
McRuer, Robert. *Crip Theory: Cultural Signs of Queerness and Disability*. New York: New York University Press, 2006.
Mee, Jon. *Dangerous Enthusiasm: William Blake and the Culture of Radicalism in the 1790s*. Oxford: Clarendon Press, 1992.
———. *Romanticism, Enthusiasm, and Regulation: Poetics and the Policing of Culture in the Romantic Period*. New York: Oxford University Press, 2003.
Melville, Herman. *Battle-Pieces and Aspects of the War*. New York: Da Capo Press, 1995.
———. *Moby-Dick*. 2nd ed. Edited by Hershel Parker and Harrison Hayford. New York: W. W. Norton & Co., 2002.
———. *Pierre, Israel Potter, The Piazza Tales, The Confidence-Man, Billy Budd, Uncollected Prose*. Edited by G. Thomas Tanselle. New York: Library of America, 1984.
Merish, Lori. *Sentimental Materialism: Gender, Commodity Culture, and Nineteenth-Century American Literature*. Durham: Duke University Press, 2000.
Methodism Vindicated, From the Charge of Ignorance and Enthusiasm. Margate: W. Epps and J. Parson, 1795.
Middlekauff, Robert. *The Glorious Cause: The American Revolution, 1763–1789*. Revised and expanded ed. New York: Oxford University Press, 2005.
Mihm, Stephen. "'A Limb Which Shall Be Presentable in Polite Society': Prosthetic Technologies in the Nineteenth Century." In *Artificial Parts, Practical Lives: Modern Histories of Prosthetics*, edited by Katherine Ott, David

Serlin, and Stephen Mihm, 282–99. New York: New York University Press, 2002.

Miller, Perry. *Errand into the Wilderness*. Cambridge, MA: Belknap Press of Harvard University Press, 1956.

Mitchell, David T. "Narrative Prosthesis and the Materiality of Metaphor." In *Disability Studies: Enabling the Humanities*, edited by Sharon L. Snyder, Brenda Jo Brueggemann, and Rosemarie Garland-Thomson, 15–30. New York: Modern Language Association, 2002.

Mitchell, David T., and Sharon L. Snyder. *Narrative Prosthesis: Disability and the Dependencies of Discourse*. Ann Arbor: University of Michigan Press, 2000.

Mitchell, Silas Weir. "The Case of George Dedlow." In *To Live and Die: Collected Stories of the Civil War, 1861–1876*, edited by Kathleen Diffley, 209–22. Durham: Duke University Press, 2002.

Modern, John Lardas. *Secularism in Antebellum America: With Reference to Ghosts, Protestant Subcultures, Machines, and their Metaphors*. Chicago: University of Chicago Press, 2011.

"Monthly Intelligence: London, May 26. America." *The Pennsylvania Magazine; or, American Monthly Museum* 1 (July 1775): 333–38.

"Monthly Intelligence: New-England. His Excellency's Answer. New-York. Georgia. South-Carolina. North-Carolina. Virginia. Philadelphia. In Congress, March 6, 1776. Inventory of Stores, taken at Fort Montague, March 3, 1776. In Assembly." *The Pennsylvania Magazine; or, American Monthly Museum* 2 (April 1776): 194–200.

Moon, Michael. *Disseminating Whitman: Revision and Corporeality in Leaves of Grass*. Cambridge, MA: Harvard University Press, 1991.

———. "Solitude, Singularity, Seriality: Whitman vis-à-vis Fourier." *ELH* 73.2 (2006): 303–23.

More, Henry. *Enthusiasmus Triumphatus; or, A Brief Discourse of the Nature, Causes, Kinds, and Cure of Enthusiasm*. Los Angeles: The Augustan Reprint Society, 1966.

Morrish, Ivor. *Obeah, Christ and Rastaman: Jamaica and Its Religion*. Cambridge: James Clark, 1982.

Moseley, Benjamin. "*A Treatise on Sugar*." In *Obi; or, The History of Three-Fingered Jack*, edited by Srinivas Aravamudan, 160–68. Ontario: Broadview, 2005.

Mulford, Carla. Introduction. *John Leacock's "The First Book of the American Chronicles of the Times, 1774–1775,"* edited by Carla Mulford, 11–48. Newark: University of Delaware Press, 1987.

Murison, Justine S. *The Politics of Anxiety in Nineteenth-Century American Literature*. New York: Cambridge University Press, 2011.

Murrin, John M. "England and Colonial America: A Novel Theory of the American Revolution." In *Anglicizing America: Empire, Revolution, Republic*, edited by Ignacio Gallup-Diaz, Andrew Shankman, and Davis J. Silverman, 9–19. Philadelphia: University of Pennsylvania Press, 2015.

Nash, Gary B. "Social Change and the Growth of Prerevolutionary Urban Radicalism." *The American Revolution: Explorations in the History of American*

Radicalism, edited by Alfred F. Young, 3–36. Dekalb: Northern Illinois University Press, 1976.

———. *The Unknown American Revolution: The Unruly Birth of Democracy and the Struggle to Create America*. New York: Viking Penguin, 2005.

Negri, Antonio. *Insurgencies: Constituent Power and the Modern State*. Translated by Maurizia Boscagli. Minneapolis: University of Minnesota Press, 2009.

Nelson, Dana D. *Commons Democracy: Reading the Politics of Participation in the Early United States*. New York: Fordham University Press, 2016.

Norton, Charles Eliot. "To Mrs. Edward Twisleton," December 13, 1859. In *The Tribunal: Responses to John Brown and the Harpers Ferry Raid*, edited by John Stauffer and Zoe Trodd, 184–87. Cambridge, MA: Belknap Press of Harvard University Press, 2012.

Oates, Stephen B. *To Purge this Land with Blood: A Biography of John Brown*. 2nd ed. Amherst: University of Massachusetts Press, 1984.

O'Conor, Charles. "Speech." In *Echoes of Harper's Ferry*, edited by James Redpath, 281–99. Boston: Thayer and Eldridge, 1860.

Odell, Rev. Jonathan. "The Word of Congress." In *The Loyalist Poetry of the Revolution*, edited by Winthrop Sargent, 38–55. Boston: Milford House, 1972.

Oliver, Peter. "[F]rom '*The Origin & Progress of the American Rebellion*.'" In *The American Revolution: Writings from the War of Independence*, edited by John Rhodehamel, 44–52. New York: Library of America, 2001.

"On the Late Continental Fast." *The Pennsylvania Magazine; or, American Monthly Museum* (July 1775): 309–10.

O'Neale, Sondra. "A Slave's Subtle War: Phillis Wheatley's Use of Biblical Myth and Symbol." *Early American Literature* 21.2 (Fall 1986): 144–65.

O'Rourke, James. "The Revision of *Obi; or, Three-Finger'd Jack* and the Jacobin Repudiation of Sentimentality." *Nineteenth-Century Contexts* 28.4 (December 2006), 285–303.

Paine, Thomas. *Collected Writings*. Edited by Eric Foner. New York: Library of America, 1984.

———. *A Letter to George Washington, President of the United States of America*. London: printed for the booksellers, 1797.

Parker, Theodore. "Two Letters." In *Echoes of Harper's Ferry*, edited by James Redpath, 73–92. Boston: Thayer and Eldridge, 1860.

Pearce, Roy Harvey. "Whitman Justified: The Poet in 1860." In *Whitman: A Collection of Critical Essays*, edited by Roy Harvey Pearce, 37–59. Englewood Cliffs, NJ: Prentice-Hall, 1962.

Pease, Donald E. *The New American Exceptionalism*. Minneapolis: University of Minnesota Press, 2009.

Peters, Samuel. *General History of Connecticut*. Edited by Samuel Jarvis McCormick. New York: D. Appleton and Co., 1877.

Peyer, Bernd C. *The Tutor'd Mind: Indian Missionary-Writers in Antebellum America*. Amherst: University of Massachusetts Press, 1997.

Phillips, Wendell. "The Lesson of the Hour." In *Echoes of Harper's Ferry*, edited by James Redpath, 43–66. Boston: Thayer and Eldridge, 1860.

———. "The Puritan Principle." In *Echoes of Harper's Ferry*, edited by James Redpath, 105-18. Boston: Thayer and Eldridge, 1860.

Plato. *Ion*. Translated by Paul Woodruff. In *Plato: Complete Works*, edited by John M. Cooper, 937-49. Indianapolis: Hackett, 1997.

Pocock, J. G. A. "Enthusiasm: The Antiself of Enlightenment." In *Enthusiasm and Enlightenment in Europe, 1650-1850*, edited by Lawrence Klein and Anthony J. La Vopa, 7-28. San Marino: Huntington Library, 1998.

———. "Radical Criticisms of the Whig Order in the Age between Revolutions." In *The Origins of Anglo-American Radicalism*, edited by Margaret C. Jacob and James R. Jacob, 35-59. Atlantic Highlands, NJ: Humanities Press International, 1991.

Pogson, Sarah. "*The Female Enthusiast: A Tragedy in Five Acts*." In *Plays by Early American Women, 1775-1850*, edited by Amelia Howe Kritzer, 137-81. Ann Arbor: University of Michigan Press, 1995.

Post, Charles. *The American Road to Capitalism: Studies in Class-Structure, Economic Development, and Political Conflict, 1620-1877*. Leiden: Brill, 2011.

Price, Kenneth M. "Love, War, and Revision in Whitman's Blue Book." *Huntington Library Quarterly* 73.4 (December 2010): 679-92.

"The *Publisher*'s Preface." *The Pennsylvania Magazine; or, American Monthly Museum* 1 (Jan. 1775): 3-4.

Querno, Camillo. "The American Times.: A Satire in Three Parts." In *The Loyalist Poetry of the Revolution*, edited by Winthrop Sargent, 1-37. Boston: Milford House, 1972.

Raboteau, Albert J. *Slave Religion: The "Invisible Institution" in the Antebellum South*. New York: Oxford University Press, 1978.

Rancière, Jacques. *Dis-agreement: Politics and Philosophy*. Translated by Julie Rose. Minneapolis: University of Minnesota Press, 1999.

Reckson, Lindsay V. "A 'Reg'lar Jim Dandy': Archiving Ecstatic Performance in Stephen Crane." *Arizona Quarterly: A Journal of American Literature, Culture, and Theory* 68.1 (Spring 2012): 55-86.

Redpath, James, ed. "Dedication" and "Preface." In *Echoes of Harper's Ferry*, 3-9. Boston: Thayer and Eldridge, 1860.

Reed, Peter P. *Rogue Performances: Staging the Underclasses in Early American Theatre Culture*. New York: Palgrave Macmillan, 2009.

Reynolds, David S. "'Affection shall solve every one of the problems of freedom': Calamus Love and the Antebellum Political Crisis." *Huntington Library Quarterly* 73.4 (December 2010): 629-42.

———. *John Brown, Abolitionist: The Man Who Killed Slavery, Sparked the Civil War, and Seeded Civil Rights*. New York: Vintage, 2006.

Richards, Jeffrey H. *Theater Enough: American Culture and the Metaphor of the World Stage, 1607-1789*. Durham: Duke University Press, 1991.

Richards, Phillip M. "Phillis Wheatley, Americanization, the Sublime, and the Romance of America." *Style* 27.2 (Summer 1993): 194-221.

Richardson, Alan. "Romantic Voodoo: Obeah and British Culture, 1797-1807." In *Sacred Possessions: Vodou, Santería, Obeah, and the Caribbean*, edited by

Margarite Fernández Olmos and Lizabeth Paravisini-Gebert, 171–94. New Brunswick, NJ: Rutgers University Press, 1997.

Richardson, John. *The Canadian Brothers; or, The Prophecy Fulfilled: A Tale of the Late American War*. Edited by Donald Stephens. Montreal: McGill-Queen's University Press, 1992.

———. *Tecumseh; or, the Warrior of the West: A Poem, in Four Cantos*. London: printed for R. Glynn, 1828.

Richardson Jr., Robert D. *Emerson: The Mind on Fire*. Berkeley: University of California Press, 1995.

Rifkin, Mark. *Manifesting America: The Imperial Construction of U.S. National Space*. New York: Oxford University Press, 2009.

Roach, Joseph R. *Cities of the Dead: Circum-Atlantic Performance*. New York: Columbia University Press, 1996.

Robespierre, Maximilien. *Virtue and Terror*. Edited by Jean Ducange. Translated by John Howe. London: Verso Press, 2007.

Rosenberg, Jordana. *Critical Enthusiasm: Capital Accumulation and the Transformation of Religious Passion*. New York: Oxford University Press, 2011.

Rosswurm, Steven. "'As a Lyen out of His Den': Philadelphia's Popular Movement, 1776–80." In *The Origins of Anglo-American Radicalism*, edited by Margaret C. Jacob and James R. Jacob, 279–302. Atlantic Highlands, NJ: Humanities Press International, 1991.

Rucker, Walter C. *The River Flows On: Black Resistance, Culture, and Identity Formation in Early America*. Baton Rouge: Louisiana State University Press, 2006.

Rutkow, Ira M. *Bleeding Blue and Gray: Civil War Surgery and the Evolution of American Medicine*. New York: Random House, 2005.

Ruttenburg, Nancy. *Democratic Personality: Popular Voice and the Trial of American Authorship*. Stanford, CA: Stanford University Press, 1998.

Samuels, Shirley, ed. *The Culture of Sentiment: Race, Gender, and Sentimentality in Nineteenth-Century America*. New York: Oxford University Press, 1992.

Sarkela, Sandra J. "Freedom's Call: The Persuasive Power of Mercy Otis Warren's Dramatic Sketches, 1772–1775." *Early American Literature* 44.3 (2009): 541–68.

Sayre, Gordon M. *The Indian Chief as Tragic Hero: Native Resistance and the Literatures of America, from Moctezuma to Tecumseh*. Chapel Hill: University of North Carolina Press, 2005.

Scales, Laura Thiemann. "Narrative Revolutions in Nat Turner and Joseph Smith." *American Literary History* 24.2 (Summer 2012): 205–33.

Scarry, Elaine. *The Body in Pain: The Making and Unmaking of the World*. New York: Oxford University Press, 1985.

Scholnick, Robert J. "'How Dare a Sick Man or an Obedient Man Write Poems?': Whitman and the Dis-ease of the Perfect Body." In *Disability Studies: Enabling the Humanities*, edited by Sharon L. Snyder, Brenda Jo Brueggemann, and Rosemarie Garland-Thomson, 248–59. New York: Modern Language Association, 2002.

Schoolman, Martha. *Abolitionist Geographies*. Minneapolis: University of Minnesota Press, 2014.

———. "White Flight: Maroon Communities and the Geography of Antislavery in Higginson and Stowe." In *American Literary Geographies: Spatial Practice and Cultural Production, 1500–1900*, edited by Martin Brückner and Hsuan L. Hsu, 259–78. Newark: University of Delaware Press, 2007.

Scott, James C. *The Art of Not Being Governed: An Anarchist History of Upland Southeast Asia*. New Haven, CT: Yale University Press, 2009.

———. *Domination and the Arts of Resistance: Hidden Transcripts*. New Haven, CT: Yale University Press, 1990.

Sedgwick, Catharine Maria. *Hope Leslie; or, Early Times in the Massachusetts*. Edited by Mary Kelley. New Brunswick, NJ: Rutgers University Press, 1993.

Seigworth, Gregory J., and Melissa Gregg. "An Inventory of Shimmers." In *The Affect Theory Reader*, edited by Melissa Gregg and Gregory J. Seigworth, 1–25. Durham: Duke University Press, 2010.

Shaffer, Jason. "Making 'an Excellent Die': Death, Mourning, and Patriotism in the Propaganda Plays of the American Revolution." *Early American Literature* 41.1 (2006): 1–27.

———. *Performing Patriotism: National Identity in the Colonial and Revolutionary American Theater*. Philadelphia: University of Pennsylvania Press, 2007.

Shaftesbury, Anthony Ashley Cooper, Third Earl of. *Characteristics of Men, Manners, Opinions, Times*. Edited by Lawrence E. Klein. Cambridge: Cambridge University Press, 1999.

Shanks, Henry T. *The Secession Movement in Virginia, 1847–1861*. Richmond: Garrett and Massie, 1934.

Shields, John C. "Phillis Wheatley's Theoretics of the Imagination: An Untold Chapter in the History of Early American Literary Aesthetics." In *New Essays on Phillis Wheatley*, edited by John C. Shields and Eric D. Lamore, 337–70. Knoxville: University of Tennessee Press, 2011.

Shields, John C., and Eric D. Lamore, eds. *New Essays on Phillis Wheatley*. Knoxville: University of Tennessee Press, 2011.

Silverman, Kenneth. *A Cultural History of the American Revolution*. New York: Thomas Y. Crowell Company, 1976.

Simpson, David. "Destiny Made Manifest: The Styles of Whitman's Poetry." In *Nation and Narration*, edited by Homi K. Bhabha, 177–96. New York: Routledge, 1990.

Smith, Caleb. *The Oracle and the Curse: A Poetics of Justice from the Revolution to the Civil War*. Cambridge, MA: Harvard University Press, 2013.

Smith, Capt. J. F. D. "Verses Written in Captivity." In *The Loyalist Poetry of the Revolution*, edited by Winthrop Sargent, 107–8. Boston: Milford House, 1972.

Smith, Orianne. *Romantic Women Writers, Revolution, and Prophecy: Rebellious Daughters, 1786–1826*. New York: Cambridge University Press, 2013.

Smith, Theophus H. *Conjuring Culture: Biblical Formations of Black America*. New York: Oxford University Press, 1994.

Smith, William. *Historical Memoirs from 12 July 1776 to 25 July 1778 of William Smith*. Edited by William H. W. Sabine. New York: Colburn & Tegg, 1958.

Sollors, Werner. *Beyond Ethnicity: Consent and Descent in American Culture*. New York: Oxford University Press, 1986.

Sowder, Michael. *Whitman's Ecstatic Union: Conversion and Ideology in Leaves of Grass*. New York: Routledge, 2005.

Stacy, Jason. Introduction. *Leaves of Grass, 1860: The 150th Anniversary Facsimile Edition*. Edited by Jason Stacy. Iowa City: University of Iowa Press, 2009.

Staël-Holstein, Anne Louise Germaine de. *Germany*. Vol. 2. New York: Derby & Jackson, 1859.

Stampp, Kenneth M. *And the War Came: The North and the Secession Crisis, 1860–1861*. Baton Rouge: Louisiana State University Press, 1970.

Stansbury, Joseph. "Epigram." *The Loyal Verses of Joseph Stansbury and Doctor Jonathan Odell; Relating to the American Revolution*, edited by Winthrop Sargent, 6. Albany: J. Munsell, 1860.

Stauffer, Donald Barlow. "Opera and Opera Singers." In *Walt Whitman: An Encyclopedia*, edited by J. R. LeMaster and Donald D. Kummings, 484–86. New York: Routledge, 1998.

Stauffer, John. Foreword. *American Protest Literature*, edited by Zoe Trodd, xi–xviii. Cambridge, MA: Belknap Press of Harvard University Press, 2008.

Stern, Julia A. *The Plight of Feeling: Sympathy and Dissent in the Early American Novel*. Chicago: University of Chicago Press, 1997.

Stiles, Isaac. "A Looking-Glass for Changelings." In *The Great Awakening: Documents Illustrating the Crisis and Its Consequences*, edited by Alan Heimert and Perry Miller, 305–22. Indianapolis: Bobbs-Merrill Company, 1967.

Stowe, Harriet Beecher. *Dred: A Tale of the Great Dismal Swamp*. Edited by Robert S. Levine. Chapel Hill: University of North Carolina Press, 2006.

———. *A Key to Uncle Tom's Cabin; Presenting the Original Facts and Documents upon Which the Story is Founded, Together with Corroborative Statements Verifying the Truth of the Work*. Boston: John P. Jewett and Co., 1854.

———. *Uncle Tom's Cabin*. 2nd ed. Edited by Elizabeth Ammons. New York: W. W. Norton & Co., 2010.

Stuart, Nancy Rubin. *The Muse of the Revolution: The Secret Pen of Mercy Otis Warren and the Founding of a Nation*. Boston: Beacon Press, 2008.

Sugden, John. "Early Pan-Indianism; Tecumseh's Tour of the Indian Country, 1811–1812." *American Indian Quarterly* 10.4 (Autumn 1986): 273–304.

———. *Tecumseh: A Life*. New York: Henry Holt and Co., 1997.

Sundquist, Eric J. *To Wake the Nations: Race in the Making of American Literature*. Cambridge, MA: Belknap Press of Harvard University Press, 1993.

Tamarkin, Elisa. *Anglophilia: Deference, Devotion, and Antebellum America*. Chicago: University of Chicago Press, 2007.

Tanner, John. *The Falcon: A Narrative of the Captivity and Adventures of John Tanner*. New York: Penguin, 2000.

Taves, Ann. *Fits, Trances, & Visions: Experiencing Religion and Explaining Experience from Wesley to James*. Princeton, NJ: Princeton University Press, 1999.

Taylor, Alan. *American Colonies: The Settling of North America*. New York: Penguin, 2001.

———. *The Civil War of 1812: American Citizens, British Subjects, Irish Rebels, & Indian Allies*. New York: Vintage, 2011.

Taylor, Charles. *A Secular Age*. Cambridge, MA: Belknap Press of Harvard University Press, 2007.

Tennenhouse, Leonard. *The Importance of Feeling English: American Literature and the British Diaspora, 1750–1850*. Princeton, NJ: Princeton University Press, 2007.

"The Testimony of Harvard College against George Whitefield." In *The Great Awakening: Documents Illustrating the Crisis and Its Consequences*, edited by Alan Heimert and Perry Miller, 340–53. Indianapolis: Bobbs-Merrill Company, 1967.

Thomas, M. Wynn. " 'Till I hit upon a name': 'Calamus' and the Language of Love." *Huntington Library Quarterly* 73.4 (December 2010): 643–57.

———. *Transatlantic Connections: Whitman U.S., Whitman U.K.* Iowa City: University of Iowa Press, 2005.

Thoreau, Henry David. "A Plea for Capt. John Brown." In *Echoes of Harper's Ferry*, edited by James Redpath, 17–42. Boston: Thayer and Eldridge, 1860.

Tichi, Cecelia. "Novels of Civic Protest." In *The Cambridge History of the American Novel*, edited by Leonard Cassuto, Clare Virginia Eby, and Benjamin Reiss, 393–408. New York: Cambridge University Press, 2011.

Tiro, Karim M. "Denominated 'SAVAGE': Methodism, Writing, and Identity in the Works of William Apess, a Pequot." *American Quarterly* 48.4 (1996): 653–79.

"To the Publisher of the Pennsylvania Magazine." *The Pennsylvania Magazine; or, American Monthly Museum* 1 (Jan. 1775): 9–12.

Tomkins, Silvan. *Shame and Its Sisters: A Silvan Tomkins Reader*, edited by Eve Kosofsky Sedgwick and Adam Frank. Durham: Duke University Press, 1995.

Toscano, Alberto. *Fanaticism: On the Uses of an Idea*. London: Verso Press, 2010.

Tragle, Henry Irving, ed. *The Southampton Slave Revolt of 1831: A Compilation of Source Material*. New York: Vintage Books, 1973.

Traubel, Horace. *With Walt Whitman in Camden*. Vol. 1. Boston: Small, Maynard & Co., 1906.

———. *With Walt Whitman in Camden*. Vol. 5. Edited by Gertrude Traubel. Carbondale: Southern Illinois University Press, 1964.

———. *With Walt Whitman in Camden*. Vol. 6. Edited by Gertrude Traubel and William White. Carbondale: Southern Illinois University Press, 1982.

Trumbull, John. *The Satiric Poems of John Trumbull*. Edited by Edwin T. Bowden. Austin: University of Texas Press, 1962.

Tucker, Susie I. *Enthusiasm: A Study in Semantic Change*. New York: Cambridge University Press, 1972.

Turner, Nat. *The Confessions of Nat Turner and Related Documents*. Edited by Kenneth S. Greenberg. Boston: Bedford/St. Martin's, 1996.

Twomey, Richard J. "Jacobins and Jeffersonians: Anglo-American Radical Ideology, 1790–1810." In *The Origins of Anglo-American Radicalism*, edited by

Margaret C. Jacob and James R. Jacob, 313–28. Atlantic Highlands, NJ: Humanities Press International, 1991.

Voltaire. *Oeuvres complètes de Voltaire.* 143 volumes. Geneva, Banbury, and Oxford, 1968–.

———. *Philosophical Dictionary.* Edited and translated by Theodore Besterman. New York: Penguin, 2004.

———. *The Works of Voltaire: A Contemporary Version.* 22 volumes. Translated by William F. Fleming. New York: St. Hubert Guild, 1901.

Wald, Priscilla. *Constituting Americans: Cultural Anxiety and Narrative Form.* Durham: Duke University Press, 1995.

Waldstreicher, David. "The Wheatleyan Moment." *Early American Studies: An Interdisciplinary Journal* 9.3 (Fall 2011): 522–51.

Walker, Corey D. B. *A Noble Fight: African American Freemasonry and the Struggle for Democracy in America.* Urbana: University of Illinois Press, 2008.

Warner, Michael. "Civil War Religion and Whitman's *Drum-Taps.*" In *Walt Whitman, Where the Future Becomes Present*, edited by David Haven Blake and Michael Robertson, 81–90. Iowa City: University of Iowa Press, 2008.

———. *Publics and Counterpublics.* New York: Zone, 2002.

Warren, Joseph. *An Oration Delivered March 5th, 1772. At the Request of the Inhabitants of the Town of Boston; to Commemorate the Bloody Tragedy of the Fifth of March, 1770.* In *The American Revolution: Writings from the Pamphlet Debate: Volume 1, 1764–1772*, edited by Gordon S. Wood, 743–57. New York: Library of America, 2015.

Warren, Mercy Otis. *Observations on the New Constitution, and on the Foederal and State Conventions. By a Columbian Patriot.* [New York] Boston: Thomas Greenleaf, 1788.

———. *The Plays and Poems of Mercy Otis Warren.* Edited by Benjamin Franklin V. Delmar: Scholars' Facsimiles & Reprints, 1980.

Warren, Stephen. *Worlds the Shawnees Made: Migration and Violence in Early America.* Chapel Hill: University of North Carolina Press, 2014.

Warrior, Robert Allen. *Tribal Secrets: Recovering American Indian Intellectual Traditions.* Minneapolis: University of Minnesota Press, 1995.

Washington, George, and Thomas Mifflin. "Speeches in the Continental Congress." In *The American Revolution: Writings from the War of Independence*, edited by John Rhodehamel, 793–95. New York: Library of America, 2001.

Waterman, Bryan. *Republic of Intellect: The Friendly Club of New York City and the Making of American Literature.* Baltimore: Johns Hopkins University Press, 2007.

Weales, Gerald. "*The Adulateur* and How It Grew." *The Library Chronicle* 43.2 (Winter 1979): 103–33.

Weaver, Jace. *That the People Might Live: Native American Literatures and Native American Community.* New York: Oxford University Press, 1997.

Webster, Noah. *An American Dictionary of the English Language.* Vol. 1. New York: S. Converse, 1828.

Wheatley, Henry. *London, Past and Present: Its History, Associations, and Traditions.* Vol. 4. London: John Murray, 1891.

Wheatley, Phillis. *Phillis Wheatley: Complete Writings*. Edited by Vincent Carretta. New York: Penguin, 2001.
Wheelwright, John. "A Fast-Day Sermon." In *The Antinomian Controversy, 1636–1638: A Documentary History*, edited by David D. Hall, 152–72. 2nd ed. Durham: Duke University Press, 1990.
Whitaker, Nathaniel. *A Funeral Sermon, On the Death of the Reverend George Whitefield, Who died suddenly at Newbury-Port, in Massachusetts-Bay, On Sabbath Morning, about Six o'Clock, September 30, 1770, Preached in Salem, On Wednesday the 17th of October following*. Salem: Samuel Hall, 1770.
White, Richard. *The Middle Ground: Indians, Empires, and Republics in the Great Lakes Region, 1650–1815*. New York: Cambridge University Press, 1991.
Whitman, Walt. *The Collected Writings of Walt Whitman*. Edited by Gay Wilson Allen and Sculley Bradley. New York: New York University Press, 1961–84.
———. *Complete Prose Works*. Philadelphia: David McKay, 1892.
———. *Drum-Taps*. New York: 1865.
———. "The Law is grand." Berg Coll+Whitman, Walt. Holograph literary fragments (3 vols.) Volume 1 (no. 8). The Henry W. and Albert A. Berg Collection of English and American Literature, The New York Public Library, Astor, Lenox and Tilden Foundations.
———. *Leaves of Grass, 1860*. The 150th Anniversary Facsimile Edition. Edited by Jason Stacy. Iowa City: University of Iowa Press, 2009.
———. *Leaves of Grass* [1871]. Washington D. C.: 1871.
———. *Leaves of Grass and Other Writings*. Edited by Michael Moon. New York: W. W. Norton & Co., 2002.
———. *Notebooks and Unpublished Prose Manuscripts*. 6 vols., edited by Edward F. Grier. New York: New York University Press, 1984.
———. "Resurgemus." *New York Daily Tribune* 21 June 1850: 3.
———. *Walt Whitman's Civil War*. Edited by Walter Lowenfels. New York: Da Capo Press, 1989.
Whittier, John G., and William Lloyd Garrison. "Poem on John Brown, by John G. Whittier; and his Controversy with William Lloyd Garrison thereon." In *Echoes of Harper's Ferry*, edited by James Redpath, 303–15. Boston: 1860.
Willard, Carla. "Wheatley's Turn of Praise: Heroic Entrapment and the Paradox of Revolution." *American Literature* 67.2 (June 1995): 233–56.
Williams, Joseph J. *Voodoos and Obeahs: Phases of West India Witchcraft*. New York: AMS Press, 1970.
Willis, Patricia C. "Phillis Wheatley, George Whitefield, and the Countess of Huntingdon in the Beinecke Library." *The Yale University Library Gazette* 80.3/4 (April 2006): 161–76.
Wilson, James. *The Earth Shall Weep: A History of Native America*. New York: Grove Press, 1998.
Winthrop, John. "A Short Story of the Rise, reign, and ruine of the Antinomians, Familists & Libertines." In *The Antinomian Controversy, 1636–1638: A*

Documentary History, edited by David D. Hall, 199–310. Durham: Duke University Press, 1990.

Wisecup, Kelly, and Toni Wall Jaudon. "On Knowing and Not Knowing About Obeah." *Atlantic Studies* 12.2 (2015): 129–43.

Wish, Harvey. "The Slave Insurrection Panic of 1856." *The Journal of Southern History* 5.2 (1939): 206–22.

Womack, Craig S. *Red on Red: Native American Literary Separatism*. Minneapolis: University of Minnesota Press, 1999.

"'The Wonderful Wandering Spirit.'" In *The Great Awakening: Documents Illustrating the Crisis and Its Consequences*, edited by Alan Heimert and Perry Miller, 147–51. Indianapolis: Bobbs-Merrill Company, 1967.

Wood, Gordon S. "Disturbing the Peace." *The New York Review of Books* 42.10 (8 June 1995), http://www.nybooks.com.proxy.lib.fsu.edu/articles/1995/06/08/disturbing-the-peace/ (24 December 2015).

———. *Empire of Liberty: A History of the Early Republic, 1789–1815*. New York: Oxford University Press, 2009.

———. *The Radicalism of the American Revolution*. New York: Alfred A. Knopf, 1992.

———. "Religion and the American Revolution." In *New Directions in American Religious History*, edited by Harry S. Stout and Darryl G. Hart, 173–205. New York: Oxford University Press, 1998.

Woodworth, Samuel. *The Champions of Freedom, or The Mysterious Chief, A Romance of the Nineteenth Century, Founded on the Events of the War, Between the United States and Great Britain, Which Terminated in March, 1815*. New-York: Charles N. Baldwin, 1816.

Young, Alfred F. "English Plebeian Culture and Eighteenth-Century American Radicalism." In *The Origins of Anglo-American Radicalism*, edited by Margaret C. Jacob and James R. Jacob, 185–212. Atlantic Highlands, NJ: Humanities Press International, 1991.

———. Introduction. *Beyond the American Revolution: Explorations in the History of American Radicalism*, edited by Alfred F. Young, 3–24. Dekalb: Northern Illinois University Press, 1993.

———. *Liberty Tree: Ordinary People and the American Revolution*. New York: New York University Press, 2006.

Yuan, David D. "Disfigurement and Reconstruction in Oliver Wendell Holmes's 'The Human Wheel, Its Spokes and Felloes.'" In *The Body and Physical Difference: Discourses of Disability*, edited by David T. Mitchell and Sharon L. Snyder, 71–88. Ann Arbor: University of Michigan Press, 1997.

Zupančič, Alenka. "Enthusiasm, Anxiety and the Event." *Parallax* 11.4 (2005): 31–45.

Index

Able-bodiedness, 196
Abolition, 22, 24, 33
Abolitionism, 26, 146
Abolitionists, 14, 17, 175
Adams, John, 6, 73, 78, 85, 96
Adams, Samuel, Jr., 73, 74, 78
Addison, Joseph, 74–75, 86
Adulateur, The (Warren), 68, 74–80, 81, 82, 224 (n.54)
Affect, 19, 20, 24
African and Afro-Protestant revival, 27
African colonization, 146, 154, 157
African religions, 16, 138
Africans: America, relationship with, 92; hopes, redeeming of, 94; stereotypes of, 149; West African slaves, 131, 135–36
"After All, Not to Create Only" (Whitman), 210–211
Age of Enthusiasm, 5
Aitken, Robert, 81
Albion's angel, 8–9
Alboni, Marietta, 189–90
Alcott, Amos Bronson, 38–39
Alcott, Louisa May, 174–75, 197–98
America a Prophecy (Blake), 7–11, 10
American colonies, development of, 66
American Dictionary of the English Language (1828), 16
American dissent, features of, 75
American enthusiasm, 11, 50
American exceptionalism, 11, 65–66
American freedom, 23–24, 92
American independence, 67
American Indians. *See* Native Americans

American liberalism, 65
American literature, post–Civil War, 11
American literature, pre–Civil War, 7
American materialism, 201
American protest literature, 67
American Revolution: antinomianism and, 71, 78; causes of, 66–67; Civil War linked to, 29–30, 195–96; colonial resistance leading up to, 26; conservative/moderate nature of, 65–67; constituent memory of, 44; critique of, 94–95; Oliver Cromwell as inspiration for, 44–45; English Revolution, return of, 12; enthusiasm, language of, 93; enthusiastic roots during, 65; fasting during, 83–84; fictional references to, 115, 116; French Revolution and, 3–4, 6, 7, 49; ideals, compromise of, 94–97; incomplete, 97, 160; literature during, 61, 68; narratives of, 66–67; Native Americans and, 26–27, 99, 100, 102, 129; perception, toned down of, 6; poetry, 26; political enthusiasm of, 99; prelude to, 57; rites of dissent role in, 66–67; second revolution, threat of, 6; slave struggle as continuation of, 23–24; as species of enthusiasm, 68; as strike, 201; transformative effects of, 39
American Revolution, Second, 178
American self, 65, 67
Anabaptist movement (Münster), 4, 35
Anabaptists, German, 35, 52
Anderson, Robert, 135
Anglicization thesis, 65, 66, 67, 223 (n.6)

Anglo-American civil war. *See* American Revolution; War of 1812
Anti-American activity, 13
Antichrist, 84
Antienthusiasm, 35
Antinomian Crisis, 1636–1638, 5, 39, 50–51
Antinomianism, 25–26, 63, 71, 78
Antinomian revolt, 12, 35
Antislavery novels, 164
Apess, William, 27, 102, 122–29
"Apostroph" (Whitman), 181
Arendt, Hannah 3, 213 (n.9)
Artist complex, 36
Assembly of Churches, 51–52
Atlantic revolution, 8
Attucks, Crispus, 90
Authority, constituent foundation of, 48–49
Autographs for Freedom, 155

Badiou, Alain, 20–21
Bakhtin, Mikhail, 144–45, 163
Barnard, Philip, 61
Bastille, attack on, 49, 50
Bastille Day, 139
Battle of Bunkers-Hill, The (Brackenridge), 69
Baxter, Sylvester, 207
Beecher, Henry Ward, 179
Beidler, Philip, 230 (n.92)
Beiser, Frederick, 15
Bellamy, Edward, 203–8, 211
Bellin, Joshua David, 122
Bercovitch, Sacvan, 3, 52, 65–66, 67
Bergland, Renée, 117–18
Bible, 152, 153
Biblical constitutionalism, 39
Black American Revolution, missing, 96–97, 160, 163, 164
Black counterhistory, 23–24, 92
Black Culture and Black Consciousness (Levine), 136
Black emancipation, 22–23, 163–64
Black freemasonry, 131, 132, 137, 156–57

Black history, modern, 145
Black inactivity, convulsive crisis of, 164
Black internationalism, 156
Black liberation movement, transnational, 177
Black magic, 136, 137, 160
Black music, 164
Black revivalism, 27, 131, 135, 137
Blacks: dissent, 97; emancipation for, 143; enthusiasms, 87–94, 134, 136–37, 138–39, 142, 144, 145–46, 147–48, 149, 152, 153, 154–55, 156, 158, 161, 163–64; resistance by, 130, 131, 143–44 (*see also* slave revolts); rites of dissent among, 88; as soldiers, 198; as "terror" agents, 14
Blake (Delany), 27, 134, 146, 155–64
Blake, William: dangerous enthusiasm, resurrection of, 18; enthusiasm described by, 19–20; as enthusiasm poster boy, 7; redeemed captives, historic incarnation of, 23; works by, 7–11, *10*
Bloch, Ruth, 70
Blockade of Boston, The, 71
Böhme, Jacob, 131
Boone, Daniel, 102
Boston Massacre, 1770, 74, 77, 87, 90
Boucher, Jonathan, 70–71, 94–95
Boukman, Dutty, 139
Brackenridge, Hugh Henry, 69
Brainerd, David, 128
Brennan, Teresa, 19
British authorities, common struggle against, 71
British literature, enthusiasm as theme in, 7
Brockwell, Charles, 55–56
Brooklyn, Battle of, 195
Brooks, Joanna, 13
Brown, Charles Brockden, 26, 39, 60–64, 222 (n.170)
Brown, John: abolitionist views on, 169; commentaries on, 2, 150, 165,

270   Index

175–76, 178–79; Confederate views on, 177; enthusiasm of, 171, 182; Harper's Ferry, raid on, 27, 165, 167, 175; poetry, 194; songs, 192; Nat Turner, story revived by, 131; Walt Whitman, compared to, 180
Brown, William Wells, 161–62
Buchanan, James, 169, 170
Buck-Morss, Susan, 12
Burke, Edmund: American and French Revolutions compared by, 3–4; constitution and government synthesized by, 49; enthusiasm and fanaticism relationship analyzed by, 14; events preceding, 52; French Revolution critiqued by, 47–48; predecessors of, 34–35; Richard Price, criticized by, 113; Voltaire criticized by, 38; George Washington, views on, 70
Burning fragment metaphor, 179
Burns, Anthony, 131

Cadet Revolution (November Uprising), 130
Canada, 12, 98
Capitalism, 65, 202
Captives, redeemed, 8–9, 23
Caribbean emancipations, 12
Caribbean slavery, end of, 22
Carlyle, Thomas, 1
Carr, Helen, 99–100
"Case of George Dedlow, The" (Mitchell), 175
Catholic Spain, 54, 55
Cato, A Tragedy (Addison), 74–75, 76, 86
Cato the Younger, 75
Caucasian War, 130
"Centenarian's Story, The" (Whitman), 195–96
Champions of Freedom, The (Woodworth), 26–27, 102, 114–18, 121
Charlotte Temple, 58

Chauncy, Charles, 56
Children of Israel, black identification with, 158
Chireau, Yvonne, 137
Christ, 51, 155
Christianity: African and black practice of, 137–38; Native American converts to, 122, 123–24, 126–27, 128; Protestant Evangelical, 33–34; religions other than, 133; slave insurrections and, 158
Christian sects, 105–6
Christian virtues, 91
Church, antinomian campaign against, 35
Civil liberties, 17, 33, 84, 86–87, 91
Civil War: abolitionist views on, 169–70; aftermath and legacy of, 199–211; American Revolution linked to, 29–30, 195–96; enthusiasm and, 176; essays on, 130; events, other, interpretation in light of, 12; hospitality during, 198; literary history of, 26; literature on, 27–30; narratives of, 172–73, 175; poetry, 200; revolutionary tradition, extension of, 165; wounded soldiers in, 174–75, 198–99
Class conflict, denial of, 11
Class distinctions, 71, 201–2
Classical-deliberative rhetoric, 67
Classical enthusiasm, 141
Cold War, 11
Coleridge, Samuel Taylor, 32, 33
Colonialism, 26
Colored Patriots of the American Revolution, The (Nell), 146
Common Sense (Paine), 84, 85–86
Communist movements, 202
Concord, Battle of, 82
Confederacy, 172–73, 174; political cartoons, 176, 176–77, 180
Confederate empire, 28
Confidence, 16
Congress Sunday, 83

Index 271

Conjure religion: Christianity and, 137; development of, 138; in fiction, 149, 158, 159, 160, 161; Moses and, 158; overview of, 132–36; revival democracy drawing from, 148; Romanticism, role in, 139–40; slave rebellion fomenting, role in, 27, 131
Connecticut Stamp Act protest, 1765, 72
Conservative enthusiasm, 17
Constituent memory, 50
Constituent Moments (Frank), 13
Constituent power: agent of, 46; Christ as, 51; definition and defense of, 42–43; enthusiasm and event in relationship to, 25; Kantian attack on, 138; literary treatment of, 43–45, 56–57; of Native Americans, 102, 106; and paradox of constitutionalism, 40–50; political theory of, 22; against state and church, 71; theological vision of, 25–26; theory of, 65; of women, 39, 57, 58–64
Constituent tyranny, 49
Constituted power, extralegal confrontation with, 44
Constituting Americans (Wald), 143
Constitution, 1787, 94, 95
Constitution, relationship to government, 49
Constitutional Convention of 1787, 43
Constitutionalism, paradox of, 41–42, 47, 49
Constitutions, revolutions bringing about, 45–46
Contest of Faculties, The (Kant), 20, 40–42
Continental Army, chaplains in, 70
Convulsive address, 25
Convulsive affect, 25
Convulsive crisis, 25
Convulsiveness (term), 27–28
Coquette, The, 58
Corday, Charlotte, 58–59, 61
Cotton, John, 51, 52

Coulter, Ann, 2–3
"Counterpublic," enthusiasm as, 13
Covenant theology, 50
Creeks, 119, 120, 121
Creole slave rebellion, 1841, 23–24
Critique of the Power of Judgment (Kant), 46–47
Cromwell, Oliver: Anglo-American Puritan heritage, role in, 34; as enthusiasm supporter, 31; as fanatic, 37–38; literary treatment of, 43, 44–45; Thomas Müntzer, comparison to, 35; republic, despotic, attempt to establish, 46; Shawnee Prophet compared to, 114; on society fluidness, 32; as symbol *versus* historical person, 217 (n.21); George Washington, compared to, 69, 72
"Crowd psychology," 19
Cuba, 155, 156
Cudjoe (Maroon leader), 131
"Curse," 13

Dale, Samuel, 108
Davidson, Cathy, 58
Davis, Jefferson, 172–73
Davis, Rebecca Harding, 203
Declaration of Independence: in fiction, 153; Native American grievances, statement of compared to, 108; in published form, 80, 85; revolutionary conditions set forth in, 43; satires on, 96
De Forest, John W., 200
Delany, Martin, 12, 27, 134, 146, 155–64
Deleuze, Gilles, 19
Democracy: to come, 30; defense of, 44; enthusiasm for, 49; intervention for, 28; literary treatment of, 58; performative, 73; progressive, 201; serving, 29; vision of, 48, 73
Democratic dissent, 68
Democratic ideals, counterrevolution against, 94
Democratic political struggle, 13–14

Democratic possibility, ideals of, 13
Democratic-Republican Societies, 95
Democratic Vistas (Whitman), 196–97
Derrida, Jacques, 143, 182–83
Dial, The (Alcott), 38–39
Dickinson, Emily, 63–64, 172
Dickinson, John, 73
Dionysian rites, 48
Disability as metaphor, 171–72, 174–75, 186
Dismal Swamp: in *Blake* (Delany), 155–56, 159, 160; in *Dred* (Stowe), 146, 147, 150, 151, 152–53
Dismemberment: fomenting of civil, 175–76, 179; as metaphor, 182, 183, 185–86, 187, 194; politics of, 27, 170, 171, 173, 174–75, 199–200; Union produced through, 196–97
Disobedience, doctrine of, 124
Dissent: enthusiasm connected to, 1, 39; event uniting aspirations and particularities of, 22; features of, 75; historic approaches to early modern and Anglo-American, 6; by mobs, 87; performance of, 73; right to, 39, 211; rites of, 66–67, 78–79, 88, 97, 105, 109, 208
"Dithyrambus, Dithyramb" (Whitman), 30
Divine authority, illegitimate claim to, 16
Divine enthusiasm, 78
Domestic rationalism, 39
Douglass, Frederick, 22, 23–24, 146, 155, 175
Doyle, Laura, 134
Drake, Benjamin, 107, 109–10, 114
Dred (Stowe): as antislavery novel, 134; *Blake* (Delany) compared to, 163–64; as novel of enthusiasm, 27, 144, 146; overview of, 147–55; Nat Turner, as inspiration for, 140–41, 142
Drum-Taps (Whitman), 29, 166, 181, 195, 196
Du Bois, W. E. B., 135

Earle, William, 140
Echoes of Harper's Ferry (Redpath), 165, 177–78, 182
Edwards, Jonathan, 32–33, 65
Egalitarian principle, 21
"Eighteen Sixty-One" (Whitman), 196
Elect, community of, 51
"Elegiac Poem" (Wheatley), 68, 87–88
Eleutheromania, 1, 30
Elkswatawa (French), 26–27, 102, 110–14, 121
Emancipation: Caribbean, 12; enthusiastic creed of, 200; ideals, enthusiasm linked to, 17; politics of, 1; universal nature of, 22
Emancipation Proclamation, 198
Embodied voice, 13
Emerson, Ralph Waldo: American identity narrative, participation in, 65; John Brown, commentary on, 166; Oliver Cromwell, views on, 45; on enthusiasm, 31–32, 33–34, 38; satires of, 34
Emigrants, The (Imlay), 7
Emotion (defined), 19
Empire of Liberty, 6
English Civil War: American Revolution comparison to, 71, 72; Anabaptist rebellion, comparison to, 35; analysis of, 5; French Revolution compared to, 4; legacy of, 2; women as prophets in, 53
English enthusiasm, 26
Englishness, 66, 72
English Revolution, 2, 12
Enlightened absolutism, 49
Enlightenment: critique of, 5; defined, 40; emergence of, 15; enemy of, 36; enthusiasm and, 33, 139; historical sign of, 41; language of, 56; motto of, 31; Revolutionary, 70; without revolution, 179

Enthusiasm: absence from historical narrative, 6; American colonial history of, 39; analysis of, 18–19; as anti-American activity, 13; categories of, 15–17; classical, 141; critique of, 15, 55–57; cultures of, 73; defined, 1, 2, 16, 17–18, 20, 31, 36–37, 41, 46, 113, 138, 180–81; deflation of, 163; English, 26; and enlightenment, 33, 139; global remapping of, 11; historic roots *versus* modern phenomenon, 18–19; inciting, 164; language of, 5, 70–71, 93, 101, 137; in literature, 7, 27, 145–46, 147–48, 149, 150–51, 152, 153, 170; meaning, shift in, 6, 30, 35–36, 39; metaphors for, 8; motto of, 31; narrative lacking for, 199; policing/channeling, 79; political-theological tradition of, 50; post–Civil War, 199–201, 203–7, 209–10, 211; regulation of, 35; restraint on, 198; scholarship, writings, on, 213 (n.2), 217 (n.14); spirit of, 117; studies of, 2; terminal for, 30; theory and genealogy of, 31–39; true *versus* false, 47, 79, 115

Enthusiasm Described and Caution'd Against (Chauncy), 56

Enthusiasm display'd: or, the Moor Fields congregation (print), 89, 89–90

Enthusiasm of love, 15–16

Enthusiasm of thought (term), 53

Enthusiasmus Triumphatus (More), 34–35

Enthusiastic politics, 11, 13, 25, 67, 102

Enthusiastic speech, 13

Enthusiastic tradition, events attached to, 26

Enthusiasts, revelations of, 52

Equality (Bellamy), 205–6

Equality, maxim of, 28

Equality advocates, perceived threat of, 14

Erkkila, Betsy, 168–69

Essays, political resistance as aim of, 83

"Essay on the Maladies of the Head" (Kant), 32

Ethics, constituent power entrusted to, 42

Ethos of enthusiasm, political, 25

Eulogy on King Philip (Apess), 128, 129

"Europe, The 72d and 73d Years of These States" (Whitman), 188, 191–93

European liberation movements, 12

Evangelical tradition, 13

Event (defined), 20–22

Event narrative, 24–25

Faction (defined), 71

Fallen Timbers, Battle of, 1794, 103, 115, 117, 118

Fall of British Tyranny, The (Leacock), 69

False enthusiasm, 47, 79, 115

False revelations, combating, 52

Family as social and political affiliation, 58

Fanaticism: enthusiasm relationship to, 14, 17, 36–38, 46, 57; language of, 45

Fanaticism (Toscano), 13

Fast days, 50, 51, 83

Federalism, 63

Federal Republic (term), 95, 96

Female chastity, 58

Female Enthusiast, The (Pogson), 26, 39, 58–60

Ferdinand VII (King of Spain), 119

First Book of the American Chronicles of the Times, The (Leacock), 72

Foner, Eric, 85

Fort Mims Massacre, 119, 120

Fort Sumter, 196

Fort Wayne, Treaty of, 1809, 98–99, 118

Foucault, Michel, 40, 41

"France, the 18th Year of These States" (Whitman), 188, 189, 190, 191

France, U.S. foreign policy with, 96

Franco-American Alliance, 1778, 94
Francophobia, 4
Franco-Prussian War, 182
Frank, Jason, 13, 66, 67
Freedom, idea of, 47
Freedom's Empire (Doyle), 134
Free enterprise, 66
Freeman, Elizabeth, 18
French, James Strange, 26–27, 102, 110–14, 121
French Revolution: American Revolution and, 3–4, 6, 7, 49; analysis of, 20; critiques and debates on, 3–5, 47–50, 56; enthusiasms, 139; Immanuel Kant, stance on, 45, 47; legacy of, 2; literary treatment of, 58–60; moral cause, 40–41; Occupy Wall Street protests compared to, 2–3; poetry, 189; references to, 95; slave insurrection as extension of, 12; spiritual enthusiasm of, 138; as strike, 201; wars, 96
Freud, Sigmund, 142–43
Friendly Club, 63
Fritz, Christian, 43
Fugitive Slave Act, 131, 179
Funeral Sermon (Whitaker), 91

Genre, enthusiast use of, 24
German Peasants' War, 1524–1525, 35
Ghent, Treaty of, 120
Giles, Paul, 11
Gilroy, Paul, 145, 232 (n.46)
Global Remapping of American Literature, The (Giles), 11
God, 34, 161
Goldsmith, Steven, 18, 19
Gordon Riots, 3, 7
Government, constitution, relationship to, 49
Government, legalistic character of, 50
Grace, covenant of, 51
Great Awakening, First (1740s), 5, 39, 54, 55, 72
Great Awakening, Second, 33, 106, 107
Great Britain: crisis with, publications, impact on, 81; economic alliance with, 94; Revolution-era France compared to, 3–4; U.S. foreign policy with, 96; war against Spain, 54
Greece, ancient, 48
Greenville, Indiana, 104
Greenville, Treaty of, 1795, 98–99, 103, 111
Gregg, Melissa, 19
Griffitts, Hannah, 85–86
Guattari, Félix, 19
Gustafson, Sandra, 67, 77

Haitian Revolution, 139, 153, 155
Hamlet, 75
Hancock, John, 77–78, 90
Harper's Ferry, raid on, 27, 130, 165, 167, 175–76, 177, 178
Harrison, William Henry, 109
Hawes, Clement, 2
Hawthorne, Nathaniel: American identity narrative, participation in, 65; enthusiasm interpreted by, 39, 53; works by, 43–45, 52–54, 56–57, 141–42, 220 (n.122)
Hegel, G. W. F., 138
Henry, Patrick, 77
Heroic Slave, The (Douglass), 23–24, 155
Hickman, Jared, 138
"Hidden transcript" (concept), 143–44, 158–59
Higginson, Thomas Wentworth, 130–32, 139, 165, 231 (n.2)
Historical events, 20–22
Holland, Edwin Clifford, 139
Homosexuality, 180
Hospitality, practice of, 182–83, 187
Hospital Sketches (Alcott), 174–75, 197–98
Howe, Susan, 63
Human liberty, 22

Human race, continual improvement of, 20, 40
Hume, David, 17
Hurston, Zora Neale, 158
Hutchinson, Anne, 25, 50–51, 52–53, 56, 63

Ideal, enthusiasm directed toward, 41
Ideological alternatives, historical amnesia concerning, 6
Imagination, heat of, 16, 17
Imlay, Gilbert, 7
Impassivity (defined), 31
Importance of Feeling English, The (Tennenhouse), 66
Increase of the Kingdom of Christ, The (Apess), 127
Indian Biography (Thatcher), 106
Indian Nullification of the Unconstitutional Laws of Massachusetts Relative to the Marshpee Tribe (Apess), 128
Indigenous cultures, 26
Indigenous peoples, renegade, 4, 5
Indigenous resistance, 27, 130
Insurgencies: Constituent Power and the Modern State (Negri), 42
International destiny, 195
International revolt, 12
Ion (Plato), 219 (n.92)
Irvington, Washington, 115
Isaac, Rhys, 72

Jackson, Andrew, 119
Jacobinism, 63
Jacobin purges, 59, 61
Jameson, Fredric, 20
Jaudon, Toni Wall, 133
Jay Treaty, 94, 96
Jefferson, Thomas, 6, 97, 107, 108
Jeffersonianism, 63
"John Brown's Body" (song), 192
Johnson, Samuel, 16
Jones, David, 106
Julius Caesar, 75
Jungle, The (Sinclair), 203

Kant, Immanuel: Henry Ward Beecher, compared to, 179; constitution and government synthesized by, 49; enthusiasm discussion preoccupying, 58; enthusiasm theory of, 22, 32, 39, 45–47, 57, 59; essays and lecture transcripts on, 40; on French Revolution, 20, 40–41; works by, 40–42, 45, 46–47
Key to Uncle Tom's Cabin, A (Stowe), 148

Language of enthusiasm, 18, 25–26
Lanier, Sidney, 164
Larkin, Edward, 225 (n.86)
Leacock, John, 69, 72
Leaves of Grass (Whitman), 27, 165, 167, 169, 180, 181, 183–88, 191, 193, 196, 208
"Lesson of the Hour, The" (Phillips), 178
Letter . . . to a Noble Lord (Burke), 3–4
Letter to Washington (Paine), 96
Levine, Lawrence, 136
Lexington, Battle of, 82
Liberal-secular thought, 15
Liberation, dramatic depiction of, 80
Liberation movements, 2, 154, 177
Liberian colonization, 146
Liberty: in balance, 75; cry for, 97; love of, 12, 68, 82, 129; narrative of, 134; politics of, 113; sacrificing for, 194–95; test of, 64
"Liberty Song" (Dickinson), 73
"Liberty Tree" (song poem) (Paine), 84–85
Life in the Iron Mills (Davis), 203
Life of Tecumseh (Drake), 107
Lincoln, Abraham: John Brown, connection to, 177; John Brown, criticized by, 2, 165; on Confederacy, 172; dismemberment metaphor used by, 173–74; Emancipation Proclamation, 198; Recon-

struction, 199; slavery views and policies of, 165, 175
Lippard, George, 7
Literary culture of enthusiasm, 7
Literary realism, 200
Literature, affect in, 18
Literatures of enthusiasm, 1, 25
Little Turtle (Miami chief), 117
Logos of enthusiasm, political, 25
Long, Lisa, 174
Looking Backward (Bellamy), 203–5, 206–8
Lord Dunmore's War, 102
Lost Virgin of the South, The ("Don Pedro Casender"), 26–27, 102, 118–22, 126
Loyalists, 69–71
Ludlow, Edmund, 38
Lukács, Georg, 144
Lyotard, Jean-François, 20

Mahomet, 38
Manifest destiny, 6, 122, 169, 195
Mansong, Jack (Three-Fingered Jack), 136, 140, 142, 144, 159
Marat, Jean-Paul, 58, 59, 60, 61
Marginalized communities, 13
Maroon insurrections, 130, 131
Mashpee tribe, 128, 129
Masses, catering to, 54
Massumi, Brian, 19
May, Henry, 70
McRuer, Robert, 170
Mee, John, 35
Melville, Herman, 7, 61, 142, 166, 200
Memoranda during the War (Whitman), 27
Mental uplift, modality of, 16
Mercantilism, 63
Metaphysics of Morals, The (Kant), 45
Metapolitics (Badiou), 21
M'Fingal (Trumbull), 69–70
Miami Indians, 115, 116, 117, 118
Middle class, 12, 65–66, 202
Mifflin, Thomas, 70

Millennialism, language of, 85
Millennialism, Puritan, 76
Millennial sects, 35
Millennial spirit of revivalism, 127
Miss Ravenel's Conversion from Secession to Loyalty (De Forest), 200
Mitchell, David, 171
Mitchell, Silas Weir, 175
Mobs, 6, 87, 89
Moby-Dick, 61, 142
Modern, John Lardas, 13
Montgomery, Robert, 100
"Monthly Intelligence" (magazine section), 85, 94
Moon, Michael, 167, 168, 236 (n.20)
Moral/cultural values, 16
Moral enthusiasm, 39
Morality, conventional, 35
Moral principle, 33
Moral progress, 41
More, Henry, 34–35, 56
Moseley, Benjamin, 136
Moses, 158
Multidenominationalism, 66
Münster Rebellion, 1534–1535, 35, 52, 56
Müntzer, Thomas, 35
Murison, Justine, 148
"My Kinsman, Major Molineux" (Hawthorne), 56–57

"Narrative prosthesis" (term), 171, 174
Nash, Gary, 66, 73
National affiliations, 11–12
Nationalist phase of American literature, 11
National Uncanny, The (Bergland), 117
Nation-state, 11, 12
Native American confederacy: controversy surrounding, understanding, 102; death of, 110; in fiction, 111, 114, 119; leadership, 107; movement for, 26–27; Northwestern confederation, 98–99, 102–3; war of independence, 118

Index 277

Native American dispossession, 26, 125–26
Native American nations, 98
Native American politics, 100–101, 113–14, 121, 122
Native American Revolution, 12, 100, 101, 129
Native Americans: American Revolution impact on, 99; constituent power, 102, 106; displacement of, 118, 122; enthusiasm of, 6, 18, 100, 104, 105–6, 109–10, 113, 118, 120, 121, 122–29; military action against, 96; of Northwest Territory, 103; religion among, 122, 123–24, 126–27, 128; rites of dissent, 109; self-determination and tribal sovereignty, struggle for, 101; subordination and dispossession of, 99–100; as "terror" agents, 14; "virtues of the Indian," 99–100; white threat against, 108
Native religions, 16
Natural right, 41
Natural rights philosophy, 33–34
"Nature" (Emerson), 33
Nazi Germany, 2–3
Negri, Antonio, 3, 42–43, 213 (n.9)
Negro Plot of 1741, 88
Nell, William Cooper, 146
Nick of the Woods (Montgomery), 100
Nonconformists, 5
Northwestern confederation of United Indian Nations, 98–99, 102–3
Northwest Territory, Native Americans of, 103
Notes on the State of Virginia (Jefferson), 97
November Uprising (Cadet Revolution), 130

Obeah, 131, 133, 135, 136, 138, 139–40, 148, 159
"Obeah's Sensations" (Jaudon), 133
Obi (Earle), 140

Observations on the Feeling of the Beautiful and Sublime (Kant), 46
Observations on the New Constitution (Warren), 95
Occupy Wall Street protests, 2–3
Oliver, Peter, 70
"On the Late Continental Fast" (Paine), 84
Oracle of Delphi, 36
Oratory, 13
Ormond (Brown), 26, 39, 60–64
"O Star of France" (Whitman), 182, 194, 203
Other, Native Americans as, 100
Otis, James, Jr., 73, 74

Pacifism, 84, 115
Paine, Thomas: American identity narrative, participation in, 65; American Revolutionary literature by, 26; constituent power theory of, 48–49; enthusiasm form adopted by, 39, 86, 95; on French Revolution, 47, 49–50; national and transnational affiliations, attempts to establish, 12; as outsider, 68; as *Pennsylvania Magazine* editor and contributor, 68, 81–82, 84–85; in post-Revolutionary era, 94, 95, 96; Phillis Wheatley, compared to, 88; works by, 48–50, 84, 85–86
Pan-Indian movement, 99, 107
Pan-Indian nationalism, 128
Paris Commune, 1871, 182
Parker, Theodore, 178
Passion, violence of, 16
Passions, enthusiasm as disorder of, 34
Pathos of enthusiasm, political, 25
Patriotic dead, invoking, 77, 90
Patriotic enthusiasm, 15–16
Patriots, defeat of, 79
Pearce, Roy Harvey, 168, 236 (n.20)
Pease, Donald, 11
Pennsylvania Magazine, 68, 80–87, 94

Periodical culture, eighteenth-century, 81
Peter, Hugh, 4, 90
Philip, King, 112, 123, 128, 129
Phillips, Wendell, 178
Philosophical Dictionary (Voltaire), 36
Pierre (Melville), 7
Plácido, 155, 161–62
"Playing Indian" (term), 100
Pocock, J. G. A., 35
Poems, Dramatic and Miscellaneous (Warren), 96
Poems on Various Subjects, Religious and Moral (Wheatley), 91–92, 97
Poetic enthusiasm, 15–16
Poetry, political resistance as aim of, 83
Pogson, Sarah, 26, 39, 58–60
Political affect, 19
Political bodies, lived experience, rituals and expressions of, 20
Political dissent, alienating unwonted, 16–17
Political enthusiasm: adoption of, 67; criticism of, 34; defined, 17, 72–73; elision of U.S., 2, 19; indigenous resistance as, 27; in margins of American literary history, 63; in post-Revolutionary era, 94, 95; post-Revolutionary suppression of, 68; private, 170; religious enthusiasm transformation into, 73; slavery opposition and, 88; studying, 1; tyranny, resistance to addressed by, 18
Political enthusiasts, 5–6
Political events, enthusiastic ideals relationship to, 17
Political freedoms, 137
Political justice, actions for, 1
Political resistance, essays and poetry in service of, 83
Political revolution, 33
Political speeches, religious elements in, 77–78
Political theory, 13–14

Politics, 21, 42, 48
Politics of enthusiasm: American literature connection to, 22–24; in black history, 132; conjure and, 132–34; defined, 198; post–Civil War, 199–200; "proper" sentiment and sensibility limits exceeded by, 26
Politics of Truth, The (Foucault), 40
Polk, President, 169
Pontiac, 112
Popular movements, 67
Popular sovereignty, 43
Post-Protestant secularism (term), 15
Poverty, strike against, 201
Present, relationship to thought, 40
Price, Richard, 4, 48, 113
Progressive Movement, 203
Prophecy (term), 180
Prophetic-biblical rhetoric, 67
Prophetic enthusiasm, indigenous cultures of, 26
Prophetstown, Indiana, 99, 104, 109, 111
Proslavery literature, 34
Prospero, 114, 122
Prosser, Gabriel, 130, 139, 146
Protest, enthusiasm as style of, 13
Protestant Evangelical Christianity, 33–34
Protestantism: Africanized forms of, 138; Anglo-American, 33; enthusiasm role vis-à-vis, 15; radical, religious sects associated with, 35; as unmarked category, 15
Protestant rebellions (Münster), 5
Protest literature, 67
Psycho-physiological excess, 16
Public assembly, 13
Puritan enthusiasm, language against, 69
Puritanism: American self, influence on, 65, 67; anti-enthusiasm element in, 5; cartoon depiction of, 177; defined, 50; enthusiasm in opposition to, 32; heritage, revamping of, 34; millennialism in, 76; in politics, 4

Index 279

Puritan Origins of the American Self, The (Bercovitch), 65
Puritan orthodoxy, 5
Puritan Revolution, 83
Puritan ruling class, 39
Puritan thesis, 65

Quaker City, The (Lippard), 7
Quakers: criticism of, 35, 63, 84, 115; Native Americans, relations with, 122; nativist prophets amenable to, 105; Prosser revolt meant to spare, 139
Queer sexuality, 170
Queer womanhood, 63
Questions on the Encyclopedia (Voltaire), 36–37

Rabelais and His World (Bakhtin), 145
Raboteau, Albert, 137–38, 233 (n.56)
Race as category, 138
Rancière, Jacques, 211
Reason, enthusiasm combined with, 37
Rebellion, enthusiasm relationship to, 17–18
Reconstruction, 199
Redpath, James, 165, 167, 177–78, 182
Reflections on the Revolution in France (Burke), 4, 47–48
Rehabilitating Bodies (Long), 174
Reign of Terror, 139
Religion: and enthusiasm, 13; as philosophical and scientific inquiry object, 15; and politics, 48; rituals of, 137
Religious communal practices, Revolutionary era, 83–84
Religious elements, political speeches incorporating, 77–78
Religious encounter in poetry, 90
Religious enthusiasm: essence of, 16; in fiction, 153; as genre of discourse, 15–16; Native American and revival enthusiasms compared, 113; political enthusiasm, transformation into, 73; political implications of, 91; Puritan ruling class, opposition as manifested by, 39
Religious enthusiasts, 5–6, 34
Religious liberty, 33, 84
Religious pluralism, 54
Religious revolutions, 33
Religious sects, 35
Religious-secular continuum, 14–15
Religious-secular ideology, 15
"Renewed Attempt to Answer the Question: 'Is the Human Race Continually Improving?', A" (Kant), 45–46
Republic, early, 94, 95
Republic, formation of, 26
Republican political theory, 15
Resistant Native, tropes of, 100
Responsive spectatorship, 41
Resurrection (defined), 21
Revival democracy, 67, 148
Revival enthusiasms, 33, 89, 113
Revivalism: African Christian influence on, 137; black, 27, 131, 135, 137; in black insurrection, 27, 131; in fiction, 151; millennial spirit of, 127; politicized, 151
Revivalist (defined), 67
Revivalists, social order promoted by, 54
Revival of revolt as literary theme, 8, 9
Revolt of revival as literary theme, 8
Revolution: defined, 40, 41; Enlightenment without, 179; fomenting, 177–78; right to *versus* outcomes, constitutional effects and moral idea of, 41–42; stirring life of, 64; as strike, 201
Revolutionary Church Militant, 84
Revolutionary Enlightenment, 70
Revolutionary War. *See* American Revolution
Richards, Jeffrey, 75–76
Richardson, Alan, 139–40

Rifkin, Mark, 101
Rights of Man (Paine), 48–50
Rites of Assent (Bercovitch), 65
Robespierre, 217 (n.21)
Romantic era, 7, 57
Romanticism, British, 33
Romanticism, Enthusiasm, and Regulation (Mee), 35
Romantic novel, 144
Rosenberg, Jordana, 11
Rousseau, 48
Rucker, Walter, 136
Russian Revolution, 2–3

Sanborn, Frank, 167
Scarlet Letter, The (Hawthorne), 52–54, 141–42
Scholnick, Robert, 196, 240 (n.146)
Scott, James, 143, 233 (n.78)
Script analysis, 25
"Secret" (concept), 143
Sect (defined), 71
Sectional crisis, 26, 170
Secularization, 15
Seigworth, Gregory, 19
Self, absorption and loss of, 33
Selfhood, 33, 39
Seminoles, 118–19, 121–22
Sense, delusion of, 47
Sensibility, discourse of, 35
Sentiment, 39, 58
Sentimentalism, 12; scholarly views of, 221 (n.156)
Sentimentality, enthusiasm relationship to, 12–13, 57
Sequel to Drum-Taps (Whitman), 208
Sermonic oratory, 67
Shakers, 33, 106–7
Shapiro, Stephen, 61
Shawnee Prophet. *See* Tenskwatawa (Shawnee Prophet)
Shawnees, 102–3, 111, 128
Shields, John, 226 (n.123)
Simpson, David, 196, 240 (n.146)
Sinclair, Upton, 203

Slave culture, 137, 139
Slave emancipation: abolitionist promotion of, 14; American Revolution and, 24; Unionism and, 198
Slave revolts: essays on, 130–32; as extension of other revolutions, 12; in fiction, 27, 148, 151, 155, 158–64; global liberation movements, association with, 154; pre-American Revolution, 54; race and rebellion rituals and, 136–37; Revolutionary advocacy of, 73
Slave rights, 138
Slavery: American Revolution and, 88; black enthusiasm under, 136; blacks as resisters of, 14; Civil War and, 28, 174, 175; conditions of, 92, 143; end sought to, 88; literary history of, 26; poetry addressing, 92, 93–94; resistance to, 144, 146–47, 158; as threat to Union, 172; trajectory of women's release from, 9; as unsolved problem, 30
Slaves, renegade, 4, 5, 6, 17
Slave-trade abolition, 33
Smith, Caleb, 13, 148
Smith, Theophus, 132
Smith, William, 85
Smyth, J. F. D., 69
Snider, Christopher, 87
Social change, 67
Socialist movements, 202
Social order, promotion of, 54
Social protest, 26
Some Thoughts Concerning the Present Revival of Religion in New England (Edwards), 32–33
"Song of the Exposition" (*originally* "After All, Not to Create Only") (Whitman), 210–11
"Songs of Insurrection" (Whitman), 27, 182, 188–95, 208, 210, 211
Son of the Forest, A (Apess), 102, 123–27, 128

Index 281

Sons of Liberty, 73–74
South, secession of, 169, 175
Spain, 54, 55
"Spirit Whose Work is Done" (Whitman), 208
Staël, Germaine de, 17
State, power of, 21, 22
State authority, absolute nature of, 42
States, address to, 28
Statesman's Manual, The (Coleridge), 32
Status quo, enthusiasm relationship to, 15–16
Stauffer, John, 67
Stiles, Isaac, 55, 56
"Still Though the One I Sing" (Whitman), 188, 209–10, 211
Stono Rebellion, South Carolina, 1739, 54, 137
Stowe, Harriet Beecher: cartoon depiction of, 177; enthusiasm as seen by, 142; national and transnational affiliations, attempts to establish, 12; works by, 27, 134, 140–41, 146–55
Sundquist, Eric, 134
Superstition, 17

Tacky's Rebellion, 1760, 135–36, 159
Tanner, John, 104
Taylor, Charles, 38
Technological industry, 201
Tecumseh (Shawnee leader): defeat of, 110; enthusiasm, performance of, 107–8, 110; father, killing of, 102; in fiction, 111, 112, 119; indigenous protest mobilized by, 26, 117; pan-Indian movement associated with, 99; Prophet's message spread by, 105, 107–8
Tennenhouse, Leonard, 66
Tenskwatawa (Shawnee Prophet): controversy surrounding, understanding, 102; in fiction, 110–14, 116, 119–20; indigenous protest mobilized by, 26; Native American leaders, other compared to, 129; as pan-Indian movement leader, 99, 107; as political foe, 107, 109, 112; religious enthusiasm of, 107; revitalization movement, 104–6, 111–12; sacred slabs of, 228 (n.35); as ultimate other, 100; vision of, 103–4
Terrorism, 13–14
Thatcher, B. B., 106
Thayer, William, 167, 180
"Theatre of action," 75, 76, 80
Theophilus Misodaemon (pseudonym), 55
Thoreau, Henry David, 178
Thought, relationship to present, 40
"Thoughts on Defensive War" (Paine), 84
Three-Fingered Jack (Jack Mansong), 136, 140, 142, 144, 159
Tippecanoe, Battle of, 109–10, 112–13, 114, 116, 118
"To a Certain Cantatrice" (Whitman), 188, 189–90, 191
"To a Foil'd European Revolutionaire" (Whitman), 188, 193–95
"To His Excellency General Washington" (Wheatley), 68, 87
Tomkins, Silvan, 24
Toscano, Alberto, 13, 14
Toussaint L'Ouverture, 140, 153
Townshend Acts, 73
Tradition, constituent foundation of, 48–49
Tragic play as metaphor, 36
Tramp and Strike Question, 201–2
Transcendentalism, 33, 34, 38
Transmission of Affect, The (Brennan), 19
Transnational affiliations, 11–12
Transnationalism, 11–12
Transnationalist phase of American literature, 11
Traubel, Horace, 207
Travellers and Outlaws (Higginson), 130–32

Trodd, Zoe, 67
Trumbull, John, 69–70
Truth, expanding, building on and revising, 21
Truth procedure (defined), 21
Tucker, Susie, 8, 35
Turner, Nat: cultural criticism of, 138; essays on, 130, 131; fictional characters inspired by, 140–41, 149; fictional references to, 154, 159, 160; rebellion, 110, 155; as slave enthusiast, 138, 141, 142; tales of, 146
Tyranny, resistance to, 18

"Uncanny, The" (Freud), 142–43
Uncle Tom's Cabin (Stowe), 146–47, 154
Union, Civil War and fate of, 28
Union, political dismemberment of, 27
Unionism, vision of analyzed, 28–29
U.S. expansionism, 14, 98–99, 109
U.S. history, understanding, 29
U.S. imperialism, 12, 26, 113, 118, 120–22
U.S. origins, 11
U.S. policy, critique of, 101
"Universal history," 12
"Uprising" (term), 148
"Utilitarian View of the Monitor's Fight, A" (Melville), 200

Vain belief, 16
Vesey, Denmark: essays on, 130, 131; fictional references to, 149, 153, 159; Haitian influence on, 139; plot, 155; reports of, 146
View of the Causes and Consequences of the American Revolution, A (Boucher), 94–95
"Visit to the Opera, A" (Whitman), 190
Voltaire, 36–39, 45, 56, 58
Vodou, 132, 135, 139.

Wabash, Battle of, 1791, 96, 103
Wald, Priscilla, 143

"Walt Whitman's Caution" (poem), 188–89
"Walt Whitman's Caution" (*later named* "To the States") (Whitman), 188–89, 190
War, arguments for necessity of, 146
Warner, Michael, 13, 240 (n.145)
War of 1812: historic repression of, 98; language of enthusiasm in, 101; literature of, 26–27, 102, 110–22; as Native American Revolution, 12, 26–27, 99; Native Americans as participants in, 124–26
Warren, James, 73
Warren, Joseph, 77
Warren, Mercy Otis: American Revolutionary literature by, 26, 68, 81, 82; commentaries on writings of, 86; enthusiasm performance in, 73–80; as political enthusiasm voice, 95–96; in post-Revolutionary era, 94, 95–96; Phillis Wheatley, compared to, 88
Washington, George: John Brown, compared to, 178; Constitution, attitude concerning, 95; death of, 68; fictional references to, 116, 117; Native American commentary on, 103; Thomas Paine, attitude toward, 96; poetry addressed to, 68, 87, 88, 92–94; poetry dedicated to, 96; political enthusiasm, alleged of, 69, 71, 72; in post-Revolutionary era, 94–95; role model, 75; specter of, 195; spirit of, 117, 118; "theatre of action" reference made by, 76; threats against, 6; Denmark Vesey, compared to, 153; Phillis Wheatley, attitude toward, 97; writings about, 69, 71
Waterman, Bryan, 222 (n.178)
Wayne, Anthony, 103
Webster, Noah, 16, 17
Webster's Dictionary, 138
West African secret societies, 132

Index   283

West African slaves, 131, 135–36
West India Emancipation, 1834, 23–24
West Indies, war for control of, 54
Wheatley, Phillis: American Revolutionary literature by, 26; enthusiasm in, 68, 87–94, 95, 97; national and transnational affiliations, attempts to establish, 12; in post-Revolutionary era, 95, 96–97
Wheelwright, John, 50, 51
Whiskey Rebellion, 1791–1794, 95, 96
Whitaker, Nathaniel, 91
Whitefield, George: controversy surrounding, 88–90; Jonathan Edwards, commentary on, 32–33; parodies of, 89, 89–90; poetry in honor of, 68, 87–88, 90–92
Whitfield, James M., 162
Whitman, Walt: Edward Bellamy, critique of, 207–8; as Civil War nurse, 171, 197, 198; Civil War writings of, 27–30, 195–97; as enthusiasm advocate, 2, 165–66, 170, 179, 181–82, 197, 198, 203, 209–10; homosexuality, 180; poetic works by, 165; political views, 167, 168–69; politics of dismemberment, 170, 188–95; post–Civil War writings of, 200–203, 208–11
Willard, Carla, 92
"Winds of Will" (term), 64
Winthrop, John, 51, 52, 56
Wish, Harvey, 146
Women: constituent power of, 39, 57, 58–64; enthusiasm of, 58–64; literature, 63; political power, 25–26, 51–52; politicized, 5; as prophets, 53, 57; as religious sect founders, 53; social power, 25–26; as soldiers, 61–62
"Wonderful Wandering Spirit" (term), 55, 57, 88
Wood, Gordon, 3, 68, 99, 106, 213 (n.9)
Woodworth, Samuel, 26–27, 102, 114–18, 121
Woolfolk, Ben, 131
Works, covenant of, 51
"Worship of the North" (political cartoon), 176, 176–77, 180
Wreaths of desire as literary theme, 9–11, 10

"Year of Meteors" (Whitman), 165–67, 181, 195